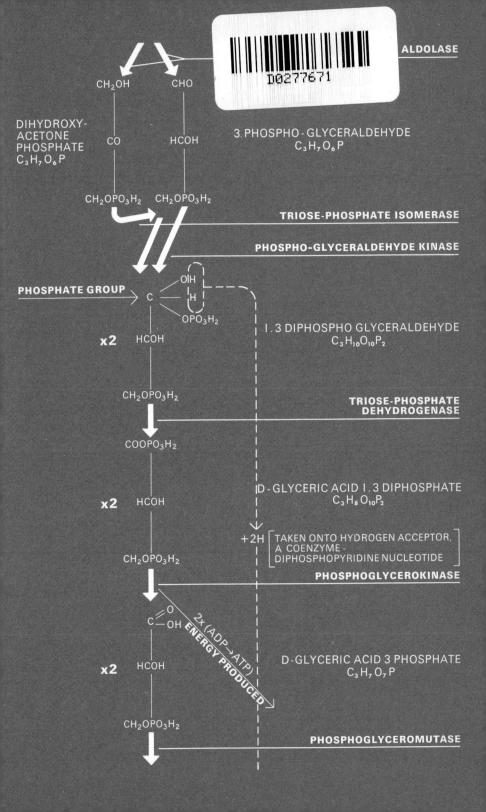

VENDANGE

A Study of Wine and Other Drinks

Andrew Durkan, M.H.C.I., M.C.F.A.

*Lecturer, School of Hotel Keeping and Catering,
Ealing Technical College*

EDWARD ARNOLD

First published 1971
by Edward Arnold (Publishers) Ltd.,
41 Maddox Street,
London, W1R 0AN

ISBN 0 7131 1662 5

Printed in Great Britain by R. & R. Clark Ltd., Edinburgh

CONTENTS

PREFACE

Vendange—the gathering or harvesting of the grapes, is I feel a appropriate title for this book, when freely translated to mean the gathering of knowledge about wines.

The book has been written for the 'student' of wine, whether in his home, his shop, his restaurant or hotel. Primarily though, it is intended for those students taking Courses in Hotel and Catering Management, for such examinations as: The Ordinary and Higher National Diplomas in Hotelkeeping and Catering, The Professional Membership Examinations of the Hotel and Catering Institute, The Diploma and Certificate Courses of the Wine and Spirit Association, The Diploma and Certificate Courses of the National Trade Development Association and the City and Guilds 453 Alcoholic Beverage Certificate.

The material for the book was obtained through many years association with the family Bar business in the West of Ireland; through working in Dijon the heart of the Burgundy country; through many trips abroad to the vineyards; through numerous visits to breweries, distilleries and liqueur elaborations; through study and reading, and through discussion with the many fine people one encounters in the wine and spirit business.

Although I cannot honestly say I have tasted every drink mentioned in this book, I have tried valiantly to be knowledgeable. The best way to know about a drink is to drink it, and my own *vendage* was most pleasurable.

A book so wide in its scope must of necessity have some limitations. Perhaps I have given some drinks more attention than others. This is not because of personal preference but because the drinks and their production needed more descriptive detail. I could have included a chapter on the licensing laws but there is speculation that these may very well be changed. Maybe a special chapter on buying and storing wine would have been useful but some of this information is to be found in different Chapters in the book.

I have persistently endeavoured to be accurate, sending scripts to experts for opinions and correction, and there have been times when the experts have disagreed with each other. However, I hasten to add that blame for any inaccuraces found in this book can only in fairness, be laid on my own shoulders.

Finally I hope the book will induce thought, study and discussion and that it will be worthy of all three.

A. D.
1971.

MAPS AND DIAGRAMS

LIST OF PLATES

Those photographs which were not taken by the author are acknowledged below.

Between pages 54 and 55

1 The vine in winter straddling the offices of a Sherry shipper in
  Jerez de la Frontera
2 A landscape of vines at Bolzano, Northern Italy
3 The Pergola system of training the vines at Merano, South Tyrol
4 Terraces of Port wine vines above the River Douro
5 Close-up of the terraces and the schistose soil predominant in the
  Douro district
6 The Riesling vine being supported by high poles in the Moselle
  vineyards
7 Treating the vine with insecticides in the Côtes-du-Rhône

Food from France

8 Grapes in the early stage of development being trained along wire
  strands in Cognac

Between pages 118 and 119

9 A tonelero at work on a sherry cask (butt)
10 Sauternes grapes in their later stage of ripeness. This is known as
   pourriture noble (noble rot)   *Food from France*
11 Wine press lying idle awaiting the *vendagne*
12 Gathering Madeira grapes grown over high trellises

Madeira Wine Bureau

Vendange

ACKNOWLEDGEMENTS

Many people helped in a variety of ways whilst I was writing this book. Without their collaboration this volume would not have been possible. I would particularly like to thank the following persons and firms.

John Scurr who has unfortunately died since the book has gone to print, Neill Fraser Petch, Charles Oliver Hall, Armand Borisewitz, Lord Kinross, Felix Vigne, The E. D. O'Brien Organisation, Frank Carney, Luke Bayard, Lord Murray of Newhaven, Clive Williams M.W., Comtesse Emmanuel de Maigret of Möet & Chandon, Épernay; Patrick Forbes Managing Director, Möet & Chandon, London; the firm of Ruinart at Rheims, the Comité Interprofessionel du Vin de Champagne, John Doxat and the House of Booths', Gabriel González Gilbey and Manuel Ma González Gordon of González Byass, Jerez de la Frontera; G. W. Hawkings-Byass, Managing Director, González Byass, London; James Taylor Sinclair of González Byass, Oporto; Irish Whiskey Distillers Association in Dublin, Messrs. Hennessy in Cognac, George J. Bull, Gilbey Twiss Ltd; the firm of Pernod in Paris, Cruse Père et Fils in Bordeaux, Michael Hasslacher and the firm of Deinhard, London and Coblenz; Patriarche Père et Fils, Beaune; Dr. Walter von Walther and Dr. Springer of the Camera di Commercio, Industria E Agricoltura, Bolzano-Bozen, Italy Cusinier of Paris, Wally Kahn & Michael Broadbent M.W.

Finally, I would like to record my gratitude to colleagues at Ealing and to my publisher.

ANDREW DURKAN

London, 1971

ᘓ 1 ᘒ

THE HISTORICAL
BACKGROUND TO DRINK

WHETHER drink is the curse of the working man, or *vice versa* as some would have it, is a question that seems to have been posed only in modern times, for the ancestors of all our yesterdays were content and grateful enough to recognise fermented liquor as a blessing that provided one of the rare solaces in their uncomfortable and savage world. The world is now much more comfortable and less immediately savage but, as the benefit of solaces may raise moral objections, it is perhaps best just to remember that those who enjoy wines and other alcoholic drinks to-day are the inheritors and successors of countless generations who, throughout the world, also found pleasure in them. It is a moot point whether the consequences would have been so dire if Adam and Eve had succumbed to the temptation of the grape instead of the apple. The opportunity must have been there, for the grape-vine is as old as History itself.

The earliest evidence is found in the fossils of some sixty million years ago, though it is improbable that this grape could have been used for making wine. Coming somewhat nearer to our own times, a vine is found in the relics of the quaternary period of the Upper Palaeolithic Age, about 100000 years ago; it was a vine whose fruit was capable of producing wine and is probably the original source of the many species of vines and varieties of wine which successive civilisations have developed all over the world.

Fable, however, must be relied upon to give a clue to the discovery of wine. A lady of King Jamshid's court in Persia is reported to have been

1

so driven to desperation by the loss of royal favour that she decided to end her life by draining the juice of some eating grapes which had gone bad in a storage jar. She succumbed to the fermented juices, slept and awoke to find that the stresses and strains which had made life intolerable had dispersed. She returned to the source of her relief and presumably her conduct became so remarkable that she was noticed again by King Jamshid who, with his court, forthwith enjoyed and made full use of this new drink.

The first chapters of Genesis tell stories of the creation and earliest history of mankind. When Noah made the revolutionary change from a nomadic to a settled life, it was perhaps significant that this first husbandman 'planted a vine yard: and he drank of the wine, and was drunken'. Reference to wine and its characteristics is found throughout both Old and New Testaments.

It is certain, however, that viticulture and wine drinking had started by 4000 B.C. The first developments were in the Middle or Near East—around the Caspian Sea and in Mesopotamia—about 6000–4000 B.C., in Asia Minor and Phoenicia about 3000 B.C. Texts from the tombs of the 5th, 6th and 7th dynasties of Egypt prove conclusively that wine was in general use throughout Egypt in 2750–2500 B.C. The tide continued to flow westwards.

Wine making and drinking in Europe accompanied the spread of Greek civilisation, first in the Aegean and then on the mainland about the 16th century B.C. But the foundations of viticulture throughout Western Europe owed their origin and strength to the ever-widening influence of the Roman Empire after the decline of Greece, starting in Italy, Sicily and North Africa about 1000 B.C. By the 1st century, the wine industry had taken root so firmly and grown so rapidly that wine was being exported to other countries in the Western Mediterranean and to Spain and Gaul, the last two of which developed their own vineyards over the next few centuries to such an extent that they surpassed their Roman tutors. The foundations of French, German and Spanish wine production were, however, well and truly laid by the Romans.

They also brought the grape vine to Britain but for climatic reasons cultivation was not widespread. There were certainly vineyards in Anglo-Saxon times but it was probably the Normans who stimulated the planting of vines in England, a development which was extended by the Church. There are said to have been about forty vineyards at the time of the Domesday Book and about another hundred were planted by the time of the dissolution of the monasteries in the first half of the 16th century. There are vineyards today which produce some interesting wines but the British have had to rely for their needs almost entirely on imports. The danger in warmer climates of contaminated drinking water supplies was undoubtedly a stimulus to wine drinking by the general population in other countries but the use of wines in England was confined for a long time to the wealthier classes; English literature bears ample testimony to this. One hundred years ago, the consumption of imported wine in Great Britain had reached about 6½ million gallons a year.

Exploration, conquest and settlement each led in its turn to the introduction of the vine wherever climatic conditions made it possible—Mexico, the Argentine, the Cape of Good Hope and California developed vineyards in the 16th and 17th centuries; Australia and New Zealand followed at the beginning of the 19th century. And so the story goes to the point where vine growing and wine drinking are universal.

It would be a mistake to assume that wines are the only drinks that have a long history behind them or that they are the most important. The encyclopaedias list under what they prosaically and unromantically classify as 'alcoholic beverages' a host of other drinks.

There are the beers, produced by the fermentation of different grains, or beer-like drinks such as mead, made from honey and grain. Such drinks spread most rapidly in the countries where soil and climate were not really suitable for viticulture. Brewing probably started in Babylon and beer from malted barley was certainly available about 6000 B.C., coming to Egypt in about 2000 B.C. It spread, like viticulture, with the rising tides of Greek and Roman cultures. Brewing in Britain was introduced by the Romans and was well established in Anglo-Saxon times; its importance in this country is indicated by the estimate that over four-fifths of the alcohol consumed in the United Kingdom is drunk as beer.

Beer-like drinks were also a feature of life in the Far East at an early date, the basic grain being rice. They featured in China in the second millennium B.C. and are common today in drinks such as *saké* of Japan or *suk* in Korea.

Finally, there are the distilled drinks such as whisky, brandy, rum, gin and vodka, many of which are of great significance in Britain. Distillation is reported to have been known in the East long before it was introduced in the West. Brandy is recorded in Italy in the 13th century and was wide-spread in Europe by the middle of the 17th century. The production of rum from the distillation of molasses from the West Indies dates from about the same time. Whisky distillation was a feature of Scottish life from the 15th century but as a commercial product it dates from as late as 1823 when whisky was first successfully earmarked as a source of taxation and when small private stills were prohibited. Irish whiskey was on the English market well before Scotch whisky, but it was the introduction of judicious blending of *patent* and *pot still* whiskies in the 1850's that led to Scotch dominating the position in British and world markets.

Enough has been written to indicate that the consumption of drinks containing alcohol is wide-spread and has a venerable and honourable history. Feasting, often religious in origin, has been a feature of all the great civilisations dating from at least 6000 B.C. and it is more than probable that alcohol, in some form or other, played an important part in these celebrations.

In Britain, however, one of the most remarkable gastronomic developments in recent years has been the growth in the use of wines and other drinks not only in feasts, banquets, public dinners and the like but in the home. Take, for example, the increases in the imports of wine and brandy shown here:

	Wines (in 000s gallons)	Brandy (in 000s proof gallons)
1956	14 363	789
1957	16 142	827
1958	15 360	853
1966	30 122	1409
1967	34 166	1634
1968	39 716	1863

The causes of this change in habits are numerous, but four seem to be fundamental. Firstly, there is a growing appreciation of the pleasure and satisfaction to be derived by the judicious choice of wines and other drinks not only for feasts but also as an accompaniment to more modest meals at home. In these days as the speed of everyday life accelerates at an alarming rate and as the complexities of the day's work get greater, the relaxation afforded by good food and drink in the privacy of one's home or the company of one's friends assumes an increasing importance. Secondly, the change in economic and social patterns following the gradual growth in this country's wealth has resulted in a widened distribution of spending power and has made it possible for increased numbers of people to enjoy the wines and other drinks that are available. Thirdly, the growing custom, especially among younger people, of spending holidays on the Continent has introduced hundreds of thousands to the subtlety and satisfaction to be found in the selection and choice of wines. Fourthly, there is a new trend in drinking out which is rapidly gaining in popularity. Instead of the customary evening or weekend pubbing people are now turning to the very comfortable, atmospheric wine lodges which are sprouting up all over the larger cities. Also recently a great many self-service establishments have begun to stock wine and other drinks on their shelves at prices to attract the housewife. Britain is relatively affluent and ours is a society in which people still have a modicum of decision on how their earnings can be spent. The use and appreciation of wines and other drinks have become an outlet for the personal choice of more and more people.

Nowadays it is probable that a display of too much connoisseurship about alcoholic drinks may give one a reputation as a social bore, but ignorance of the subject may easily lead to other social blunders and, more importantly, to sufferance of impositions over price and quality. Most of us will want to have a sound general knowledge of wines and other drinks so that we can make reasonable choices in our purchases, know how best to appreciate and serve the drinks and join in intelligent, if not recondite, conversation. The aim of this book is to impart this knowledge, and also to assist caterers and hotel-keepers, and those training as such, to have the expert competence which will gain them the trust and continued patronage of their customers. Discussion between wine merchant and cellar-mansioned lord has been going on for years to the added reputation of the merchant and the bland satisfaction of the lord. Similar reciprocity ought to be encouraged, and may well be necessary for self-protection, between Boniface and Barleycorn whether they meet in bars, butteries or best restaurants.

⌘ 2 ⌘

INTRODUCTION TO WINE

R URAL worthies may comfort themselves, or frighten their visitors, with home-made drinks made from the produce of their kitchen gardens and which they flatter with the appellation 'wine'. Soft-drink manufacturers may pirate the same name for the purpose of market exaggeration. But we cannot allow the use of the name 'wine' to any concoction, however pleasant or potent, other than *fermented grape juice*. Indeed the use of the name must be limited further for the reason that, of the numerous varieties of grape-bearing vines, only those of the genus *Vitis* produce palatable wine and, of this genus, only the species *Vitis vinifera* produces very good or great wine.

Appreciation of wine must therefore be based upon some knowledge of where the *Vitis vinifera* vines are grown and then upon an understanding of the application of the process of fermentation to the fruits of those vines.

THE VINE

Fortunately, the *Vitis* genus of vine grows naturally in nearly all the world's temperate regions, although the natural homeland of the *vinifera* species is limited to the European Mediterranean zone. The plant itself can proliferate into numerous varieties within its species, it will readily accept grafting from other species and it is susceptible to hybridisation. Calamities such as the *Phylloxera vastatrix* plague on the European vines were overcome by the grafting of the native vine on to the American root stock. Experiments by viticulturists have improved species or transferred species to other areas. The Romans in particular introduced the Mediterranean species to central and northern France and to Germany.

For these reasons it would need a botanist, aided by an historian, to trace the various factors which have led to the cultivation of vines as they are now grown. All we need say here is that in most of the important wine-producing areas of the world the favourite vine is likely to be an artificially improved plant or an introduced plant rather than a natural growth of the area. In appropriate chapters later in this book, the principal species of vine or vines used in particular countries and areas are indicated.

Of course, the vine cannot usefully be cultivated without a proper environment of climate, soil and expertise.

CLIMATE

The vine will grow most rewardingly in the latitudes between 28 and 50 degrees, north and south, and it is at the northerly limits of these latitudes that the great wines such as Champagne, Bordeaux and Burgundy, the Rhine and Moselle wines and the famous Hungarian Tokay are produced. Climate or local weather influences these and all other wines. When the weather is favourable, excellent wines, of their type, are produced, but too much or too little of any of the usual elements will cause a disappointing or even a disagreeable wine to result. While the vinegrower can generally make up for soil deficiency by replacing that which has been extracted by the vine during the year, can combat vine pests and diseases and can ensure the strength and health of the vine by judicious pruning and training, he can do practically nothing about the weather, although experimentation in this direction is now being carried out.

Ideally, winter in the vineyards needs to be short, cold but not severely so, and with a good supply of rain. Spring should be mild, even warm, with those beneficial April showers. Summers ought to be long and hot with a nice balance of rain, preferably in mild showers, with plenty of morning and evening dew. Although a good deal of sunshine is required, a good daily average is very much better than short scorching bursts. The crucial months of September and October are best benefited by an Indian summer with a little rain. It is the rains of winter and spring that mature the vine, the heat of early summer that gives health to the grape and the strong sun of late summer that develops the sugar in the grape and minimises the acidity within the grape. Too much sun, as in tropical climates, produces dull, lazy, flat wines. Insufficient sun on the other hand produces sharp, sour wines. It is, as we have said before, the balance that counts. The ideal balance is estimated to be 1300 hours of sunshine plus 178 mm rainfall per year.

There are, unfortunately, serious climatic hazards which affect the vineyards. The worst are the late frosts which play havoc with the vine in bud or flower. Hail storms or strong winds can devastate whole vineyards, their ferocity snapping away whole bunches of fruit from the vines. Heavy rain in late August or in September, when the grapes are reaching full ripeness, will swell the grapes, causing their skins to become fragile, perhaps even to burst open, bringing ruin to the crop.

In warmer regions, vine roots need all the moisture they can get so the plants are spaced widely and the grapes are kept close to the ground in order to benefit from reflected heat during the day and accumulated heat during the night. In the colder districts, because of the frost hazard, the vines are trained in such a way that the grape bunches are kept well above ground level and the rows of vines are spaced to gain maximum benefit from the sunshine.

SOIL

It is generally acknowledged that grapes grown on the poorest soil, often in places very difficult to till, will produce better wine than those grown in richer soil, although the latter will produce grapes more abundantly. Mountain slopes, especially when the vineyards are positioned to take advantage of the sun, and lakeside and riverside lands, which benefit from the sunshine reflected from the water, seem to be the favoured vineyard settings. The most satisfactory soils are those composed of chalk on limestone, pebbles, slate, gravel and schist (a crumbly form of granite). All these soils contain those traces of minerals which are largely responsible, in their various ways, for the variety in the taste and bouquet characteristics of the wines we drink. They allow air and moisture to penetrate easily to the vine roots but also afford good drainage; important because the roots will not tolerate soaking in water. Flooding of the roots can kill a vine.

These soils also have the ability to store heat which reduces the coolness of the night air; and during the day they reflect sunrays on to the vine in grape. Of the famous European wine regions, Bordeaux, which is basically land reclaimed from the sea, has all the above soils in close proximity; Champagne, Cognac, parts of Burgundy and the best Sherry district have limestone or chalk; the German vineyards have much slate and the Port wine region has schist.

THE GRAPE

It is early in June that the vine starts to flower in the northern hemisphere, although the blossom is not easily noticeable because it is green in colour. The flowers have a scent of their own, and some optimists put their confidence in the aroma of the vine in flower as an aphrodisiac —perhaps a wish to prolong spring fever! Soon fertilised by pollination, the flower takes about a hundred days to ripen. At first, the embryo grapes look like green blobs on a multitude of fingers, and at this stage it is wise for some pruning to be carried out to relieve those vines that promise to be overproductive.

As the green blobs grow into grapes, their bullet-hard texture gets softer. As they increase in size they become lighter in colour and their content of malic acid progressively decreases. By the time the grapes are ripe, their skins have become more transparent and yeast cells settle to form the characteristic bloom on the skins, ready to raid the sugar within. Meanwhile, tannic acid, usually known as tannin, is developing mainly in the stalks and pips. During the final month of ripening the delicate fruit needs a lot of sunshine and a little rain. Too much rain will swell the grapes, which will then produce a watery wine; too much humidity will encourage such diseases as Grey Rot.

The diagram opposite shows the grape made up of: its stalk, providing tannin; a few pips, providing tannin and acids; its skin, providing tannin, acids and pigment; its main pulp, three-quarters of which in weight is water and the remainder sugar, some mineral substances between the skin and the pulp, and, on the outside of the skin, bloom which is yeast and other micro-organisms. The stalk and pips make up about 7 per cent. of the weight of the grape, the skin about 10 per cent., the mineral substances about 2 per cent., and the pulp about 81 per cent. In weight the bloom is negligible.

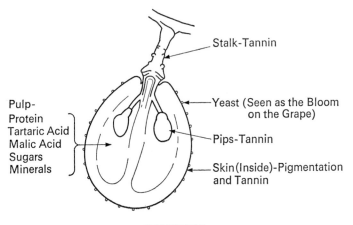

Stalk-Tannin

Pulp-
Protein
Tartaric Acid
Malic Acid
Sugars
Minerals

Yeast (Seen as the Bloom on the Grape)

Pips-Tannin

Skin (Inside)-Pigmentation and Tannin

EXPERTISE

Given a compatible soil, satisfactory variations of weather and a situation that takes advantage of direct or reflected rays of the sun, the vines will still need diligent and expert husbandry following an annual cycle of work in the vineyards.

After the previous vintage, the vineyards are given a good tidying. The old unproductive vines are uprooted, and the stakes, trellises and wire-training strands are strengthened or replaced. Some ploughing will aerate the soil, some of which will be banked around the vine roots while ensuring that the grafting point is still above the soil. This banking offers protection against winter frosts. In winter and early spring, the soil is fertilised and the vine shoots are untied from the wire strands in order to ease the removal of any insects in the tying hooks and to facilitate pruning. Pruning the vines is the next stage, an essential and important operation to curtail surplus vegetative growth. This intervention by man in the natural process induces the plant to produce a greater yield of fruit. A proper balance must leave enough vegetative growth to maintain the life of the vines.

The vines are trained according to one or other of three classical methods, or by variations of these methods—the *Cordon*, the *Gobelet* and the *Espalier*. Variations such as the Pergola method have developed from these.

The *Cordon* system of which the Dr. Guyot method is a prime example uses a permanent stump of vine. From this permanent stump, the Dr. Guyot method cultivates one horizontal and two vertical shoots. At the end of each season the horizontal shoot, which produced the crop, is cut away and one of the vertical shoots is bent over to replace it as the next year's fruit-yielding shoot. The remaining vertical shoot is pruned so that it will eventually produce two vertical replacement shoots. This system curtails the growth of vegetation where it is not wanted and encourages a maximum yield of fruit. Normally, the vines are trained under this system along supports such as wire strands. There is also a double Dr. Guyot system having two horizontal fruiting shoots and necessarily three vertical shoots. This system although it increases quantity is inclined to reduce quality.

The *Gobelet* method cultivates the vine in one vertical trunk with branches rising and spreading from it to form the shape of a goblet. Hence the name. The vines pruned by this method are normally self-supporting.

The *Espalier* method grows the vine as a fan based on vertical shoots rising upwards from two horizontal arms. The shoots are usually trained on trellises or on wire supports.

In spring, new vines are planted to replace those uprooted after the vintage; weeds are kept down and the soil is ploughed again. This second aeration of the soil is essential for growing grapes for the best quality wines. Vegetative growth is again restrained by pruning some of the buds and by removing any suckers below the grafting point. In May, especially, frost has to be guarded against, and this is done either by direct heat from fires emitting flames or smoke or by spraying the vines with water mist.

In summer, the vines are tied to their supports, and the ground is weeded again. Fungal pests and diseases are attacked with sprayed insecticides, the application of which gives a side-line benefit in that the human temptation to go 'scrumping' is defeated. They say in Spain, 'Young girls and grapes are difficult to guard', but we may suppose that now, with the spraying of the grapes, the former present the greater problem. The ends of the shoots are now trimmed of unwanted foliage and, in the more northerly areas, leaves are pruned to increase the sun's penetration to the grapes. Many of these processes are frequently repeated during the vinegrowing season.

In early autumn, the vinegrower prepares his pressing house, vats, casks and cellars ready for the vintage. Hygiene is his main concern, and everything has to be scoured and disinfected. One of the most

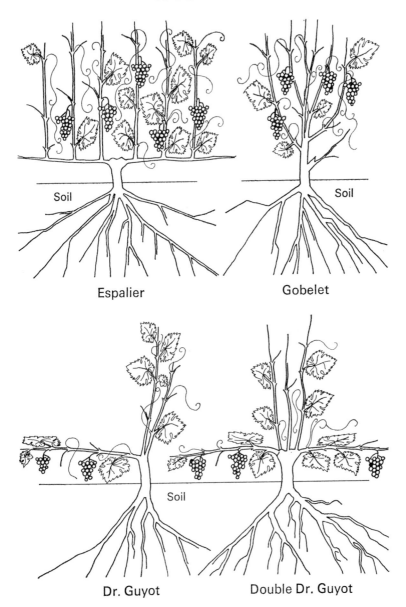

Espalier

Gobelet

Dr. Guyot

Double Dr. Guyot

Pruning Systems

satisfactory ways of cleaning is by the use of high-pressured sprays of water with detergent, and then the equipment is disinfected, usually with sulphur dioxide solution. A final rinsing with water washes away all remnants of detergent and disinfectant, for any foreign smells in the vicinity of the pressing house or cellar will quickly contaminate the grapes or the wine. And so to the harvest, but before leaving the labours of the vineyard, some appreciation is necessary of the diseases and ailments to which the vine is susceptible for these are a regular worry to the cultivator and, consequently, expensive research is aimed at their destruction.

Phylloxera vastatrix has been as devastating to the vine in Europe as were the plagues to mankind during mediaeval times. Caused by a vine louse native to North America, especially east of the Rocky Mountains, the disease devastated the European vineyards in the latter half of the 19th century, and no other disease has caused such ruin to the vineyards of the world. Carried over to Europe, possibly with table grapes, but more likely with plants imported for experimental use in research for a cure for *oidium*, the horrid louse was first noticed in Europe by Professor Woodward in the vinery at Kew Gardens in 1863. About the same time, it attacked some vineyards in Provence in France. From then on for the next thirty years or so the louse ravaged almost all the world's vineyards. It appeared in Austria and Hungary in 1868, Bordeaux in 1869, Beaujolais and the Rhône Valley in 1870, Switzerland in 1872, Germany in 1874, Spain, Portugal and Madeira in 1876, Burgundy in 1878, Italy in 1879, South Africa in 1886, Algiers in 1887 and Champagne and California in 1890.

Phylloxera is an Aphid, rather more than a millimetre long, yellow-green to yellowish-brown in colour, with red eyes. When the insect attacks, the vine becomes stunted and produces fewer leaves. Then the leaves become discoloured and galls are sometimes found under the leaves. The main attack is against the roots of the vine which first exhibit small knotty tumours or swellings of a yellowish colour and then decay, as the tumours darken, to rot under a dead vine.

Many millions of pounds were spent in trying to combat the disease, which had rendered all the vineyards, with just a few exceptions, useless. Many more millions were lost by the many engaged in the wine industry, and also to governmental revenues. It was estimated that France alone was losing £50,000,000 a year and, perhaps adding insult to injury, Scotland found an outlet on the Continent for whisky as a substitute for the brandy which could no longer be distilled while there was no wine. Many attempts on cures were made without success. A mite which could overcome the louse was imported from America but its depredations could not keep up with the louse's fertility. Then the vineyards were flooded, or the vine roots were injected, with a solution of carbon disulphide—but to little avail.

The vinegrowers were in despair. Suddenly it was noticed that it was the *Vitis vinifera* vines which had succumbed, but that other species of the *Vitis* vines in America were immune to the disease. Some of these were brought to Europe and they did indeed withstand the disease. However, the wines produced from the grapes of these imported vines had a pronounced foxy taste, which was not at all palatable to the European. So it was decided to try to graft the native vine on to the American rootstock. Eventually, a suitable rootstock (*Porte-Greffe*, i.e. 'Carry graft') compatible with the European soils was discovered, and of the American varieties available the *Vitis labrusca*, the *Vitis riparia* and the *Vitis rupestris* proved the most harmonious. After initial disappointments when the grafting would not take, success was attained when grafting-stations were established with hot houses and nurseries ensuring that the stock and root reached early unison, and grew strong and sturdy before being taken to be planted in the vineyards. Even then, it would take these vines some five or six years before they could produce grapes good enough for making wine. These grafted vines will have a life of some thirty to thirty-five years; a shorter life than that of the pre-*Phylloxera* vines, but the important thing is that the grapes they produce can make wines which maintain all the qualities and characteristics of the historic wines. It is rewarding that each variety has retained its own particular traits; the imported roots have not in any way influenced quality or type of wine.

Phylloxera is still prevalent in the soil and, without the American rootstock, the native vines would die within three years. Vines may still be seen with a knotted and deformed appearance, showing that grafting has not totally overcome the pest. A *Phylloxera* louse probably does not get much maternal care, for his mother must be quite busy producing an estimated 25 million lice a year. No wonder the louse is delinquent and no wonder that much research is still needed and still being done.

Mildew is a fungus which can wither the leaves and berries of a vine, particularly in wet sunless summers. It can be cured by a mixture of copper sulphate, quicklime and water, commonly known as 'Bordeaux mixture'. A particularly troublesome variety of mildew is *oidium*.

Oidium attacks vineleaves and grapes with a greyish powder. It stunts growth and it shrinks and bursts the grapes. Areas where the climate is hot and humid are most susceptible to this disease, which is combated by spraying the vines with sulphur.

Grey Rot. In most wine areas grey rot is abhorred as it alters the quality of the grape juice and affects the colour cells in the skins. It is prevalent in damp autumns, and the only real cure is an improvement in the weather. In certain areas, like Sauternes where the climate is suitable, grey rot is accepted as beneficial and it is known there as *Botrytis cinerea or Pourriture noble*, a paradoxical name meaning 'Noble Rot'.

Cochylis is the result of the activities of a night-flying moth, which lays its eggs in vines. The caterpillars from these eggs eat the blossoms and, later, the bunches of grapes. They are difficult to get at by spraying because of the protection afforded by their own silky web, but they can be controlled by the use of lead arsenate or other insecticides. The *Cochylis* moth likes fairly warm humid weather.

Rougeot is a fungus which causes sores to appear on vine leaves, which eventually die and fall off. Spraying with a copper solution is a remedy. *Rougeot* is not a regular hazard to the vines, and sometimes disappears from a vineyard for years.

Chlorose is the yellowing of the vine leaves, leaving them unable to nourish the grape. Its presence suggests that the particular type of vine is unsuitable for the particular soil. An attempted cure is the replacement of the plant by an appropriate species of vine or by the corrective use of appropriate fertilisers.

Browning usually occurs when careless pruning, aimed at increasing production, takes place. The vine leaves show brown stains and eventually fall off. Constant overproducing will soon weaken the vine.

Coulure can have a disastrous effect if bad weather occurs at the crucial stage, for the blossoms will fall off and the berries will become stunted and will not develop. Too much rain and soil deficiency is the principal cause, and careful fertilising is necessary to counteract the deficiency.

THE VINTAGE

Having diligently tended his vines through the year and done what he could against frost and pestilences, the wine-grower in early autumn can harvest his grapes. The grapes are cut in their bunches by secateurs or special sickles and any diseased or damaged grapes are cast aside. The sound grapes are taken as quickly as possible to the pressing houses, where they are weighed. Quick transport minimises oxidization. The start of the vintage or picking of the grapes is determined usually for the whole district on a fixed day, when the grapes have reached peak maturity and condition.

In a few regions, particularly Sauternes and Monbazillac in France, the Rhine and Moselle areas in Germany and the Tokay area of Hungary, some grapes may be left on the vines after the general vintage is over and long after they have ripened. These areas grow white thick-skinned grapes, and the weather is usually a pleasant combination of moisture and heat in late summer and early autumn. The moisture causes the fungus *Botrytis cinerea* to settle on the grapes, while the heat evaporates some of the water from the pulp of the grapes and also keeps the fungus in check. The grapeskins become thinner and the fungus causes minute cracks to form through which the water evaporates in the hot air. The grapes begin to wither, but their skins remain sufficiently tough to prevent their disintegration. They now appear shrivelled like raisins and their sugar content has been enriched to the extent of forming about 40 per cent. of the weight, compared with the ripe grape's maximum of 20 per cent. The acid content has been reduced and the glycerine content strengthened. The grapes are individually gathered with the aid of long scissors and the vineyard is gone over repeatedly to gather only the over-ripe fruit. This method yields a comparatively small amount of wine, but how luscious and liqueur-like are these almost oily-smooth tasting wines. Naturally they are expensive. The *Botrytis* Fungus, so disliked elsewhere as 'grey rot', is known in France as *Pourriture noble* and as *Edelfaule* in Germany. As a blessing, it is only natural to the places mentioned above and it is never found in very hot climates.

THE MANUFACTURE OF WINE

When the grapes are gathered to the pressing houses, the manufacture of the wine can begin, and indeed should begin without delay or too much air will get to the grapes in the presses. The process, however, is not one of simply squashing the grapes and collecting the juices. It is all important to apply the method found appropriate, whether by tradition or research, to the type of grape and the kind of wine to be produced. As already described, the grape has a number of ingredients besides the sugar and water of the pulp. As the grapes are pressed releasing *must* (unfermented grape juice) it is necessary to arrange that these ingredients are extracted or reinforced according to the end product desired. Besides the natural ingredients, the grapes have been sprayed with sulphur or its compounds, which have also been used to scour the presses. The sulphur takes an important part in the manufacture of wines as it will kill wild yeasts and harmful bacteria. It will also slow down fermentation or, if there is enough of it present, will bring fermentation to a halt. Sulphur dioxide, in a gaseous or liquid form or as a tabloid—in the form of potassium metabisulphide—is usually added to the grape juice to keep the wine sound or to prevent a second fermentation for natural sweet unfortified wines. The amount of sulphur must be precisely calculated and, in fact, the amount that may be used is strictly controlled by law. Some bottles of wine, when opened, give off a distinctive aroma of sulphur, which will soon disperse if the bottle is opened a little time before the contents are to be consumed.

Red Wine. Red wines are made from black grapes. Before pressing, it must be decided how much of the stalks, which are rich in tannin, should be removed. This decision will depend both on the condition of the grapes, whether they are fully ripe or less so, and on the type of wine to be produced, whether it is to be a quick maturing wine or to be allowed to run its natural course. Any destalking necessary is done with a special machine called an *égrappoir*, which has generally superseded the old method of rubbing the grapes through a metal mesh. The grapes are then crushed, which frees the pulp from the pips, skins and remaining stalks; and then the whole lot is macerated together in vats. The vats vary in size, those in hot climates being smaller and spaced well apart. The conico-cylindrical shaped vat is now favoured as it allows air to circulate freely. Wood is the best material for the vats although many are of cement, metal or modern synthetic materials. The vats are not filled to the top with the fluid *must* because the level rises by about one-fifth due to the agitation of fermentation.

White Wine—Black Grapes. Some black grapes can be used for making white wine—*Blanc de Noir*. These grapes are given a quick light pressing and the juice or *must* is immediately run off into the container, which may be a tank, a vat or a cask. The speed is essential, for any prolongation of the pressing would enable the antholyanine pigmentation contained in the skins to impart a dark colouring to the wine.

White Wine—White Grapes. Most white wine is made from white grapes, and this wine has the generic name of *Blanc de Blanc*. The stalks are not removed before pressing, but the *must* is quickly extracted from the crop leaving behind the pips, skins and stalks, and drained into the fermenting vat. Unlike the process for red wine, there is no maceration whatever.

Rosé Wines—Black Grapes. During the pressing of black grapes to make rosé wine, the skins are allowed to macerate with the *must* until the required degree of colouring has been extracted from them. At this point, the *must* is freed into another cask, where it continues to ferment while the skins have been left behind. After the pressing, a slight exaggeration of tincture is no cause for alarm as the yeast cells will absorb this during fermentation. Indeed, a slightly deeper colour than rosé is planned to allow for this yeast action. Rosé wine can also be made by blending red and white wine together until the desired hue has been achieved.

Pressing. There are many ways of pressing grapes and almost as many variations of the methods as there are wine regions. All methods are a progression from the old Egyptian method of squeezing the grapes in a large sheet knotted to form a tourniquet to apply the pressure. But the popular image of the pressing is undoubtedly the treading of the grapes, a method that is still extensively used but which is going out of fashion. The Bacchanalian scene of the stamping men and the singing women will remain in tradition although even in the Port, Sherry and Madeira districts, where the method was once universal, changes have taken place. Shortage of labour and the cost of paying for such long hours of labour are the reasons for the change, rather than any question of hygiene. There has never been any real hygienic risks from the treading because of the tremendous sterilising quality of alcohol.

Where the grapes are still trodden, they are placed in wooden or stone troughs, the men get in and tread the grapes. The juice runs from the troughs and is collected as *must* in casks or vats for fermentation. In the Sherry district, the treaders wear special studded boots called *Zapatos de Pisar*. The grape skins form a mat within a mesh of angled nails, and this prevents any crushing of the pips and stalks and thus stops the release of too much tannin into the *must*. When the treading is finished, the mash of pulp left in the troughs is usually taken to an hydraulic press which squeezes out any remaining juice from which secondary wines will be made.

There are three other principal methods of pressing. In the first, the grapes are put into a slatted wooden vat with a plate on top worked by an *hydraulic press*. As the plate is forced down the juice is squeezed from the fruit, and the *must* collected beneath the slats. The second method makes use of a *pneumatic press* of German origin. A deflated plastic or synthetic rubber bag is put into a cylinder into which the grapes are piled. The bag is then inflated and its pressure crushes the grapes. The *must* flows through a trough into a cask or vat. This method does not crush the pips or the stalks, so the tannin is not released.

In the third method, the grapes are placed in a *horizontal cylindrical press*; at each end of the cylinder there is a plate which is linked by chains to the other plate. The cylindrical drum is rotated while the chains are shortened, drawing the plates towards each other and crushing the grapes. The juice gushes through slits in the revolving drum while the chains keep the pulp in a loose mass. Another but less used method, is centrifugal pressing, which works on the same principle as does a spin dryer for clothes.

Fermentation. (This subject is dealt with in greater detail in Chapter 45.) The presence of yeast is essential to the fermentation of grape juice. Yeasts are microscopically small unicellular living organisms which settle, as bloom, on the skins of grapes—thousands of them on each grape. The yeast, *Saccharomyces ellipsoideus,* has the ability on contact to convert the natural sugar in the *must* into ethyl alcohol and carbon dioxide, roughly in equal parts.

During the pressing of white wines enough yeasts are washed into the *must* to initiate fermentation, but only enough to continue the process slowly. With black grapes more yeasts are provided in the *must,* by the repeated immersion by the cellar workers of the skins into the *must,* and the fermenting process is quicker. In some cold regions, fermentation may be slow and sluggish at the start. Consequently, some artificial heat is applied in the fermentation houses to a proportion of the *must.* Fermentation itself releases heat so care has to be taken, especially in the warmer climates, that the temperature of the *must* does not get too high, 15° to 18° Centigrade being the ideal. If, because of high temperature, the *must* ferments too quickly, a quick-maturing wine of inferior quality and shorter life-span will result. To prevent overheating, metal coils, known as attemperators, through which cold water runs, are inserted into the *must* to cool it down and to allow the yeasts to continue their work fully and naturally.

Sometimes the vineyard proprietor will give the wine yeast a flying start by introducing a mild dosage of sulphur dioxide to the *must.* Sulphur dioxide can kill off wild yeasts but fortunately wine yeasts have a degree of tolerance better than other organisms to this compound. He may, on the other hand, add a special yeast culture specific to the region he lives in and which is often developed and propagated in an oenological laboratory.

Red wines are generally fermented in vats in order to obtain the maximum amount of pigmentation from the grape skins, and it will usually take about six days for the best colouring to be obtained. During this time, the alcohol being produced by the fermentation will be extracting the colouring matter or pigmentation from the grapes until a balance is reached. After this balance has been reached, care must be taken to prevent a reversal of the colouring process. Leaving the skins in contact with the *must* for prolonged periods will not produce a richer hue for the wine. To keep the period as short as possible and to obtain maximum colouring, the skins must be kept submerged in the *must*.

For making rosé wine, the fermenting juice must be drawn off from the skins before it extracts too deep a pigmentation. The *must* is allowed to finish its fermenting in another vat, or else fermentation is stopped by the introduction of sulphur dioxide.

White wines, also, are often vinified in vats, but the best results are obtained by allowing the *must* to ferment in small casks, provided that a cool temperature can be maintained. The casks are only one-half or three-quarters filled to allow for oxygenation and expansion. Half-way through the fermentation the casks are filled completely, and so left until the end of the process. In some regions, white wines are now being fermented under pressure in a closed tank. The carbon dioxide is allowed only very gradually to escape. This system, it is claimed, will improve the bouquet of the wine.

In fermentation, the presence of oxygen (in the air) will stop the production of alcohol but, as soon as fermentation starts, the carbon dioxide as it is produced will bubble to the top as a frothing mass, similar in appearance to a boiling pot. The bubbles evaporate into the air and are then replaced by others, so that the froth forms on the surface a continuous shield against the penetration of oxygen from the air, which of course is not wanted. As carbon dioxide is heavier than air, it forms its own layer over the fermenting *must*. An exception is that minute quantities of oxygen are allowed to reach fermenting or maturing Sherry wine.

Fermentation stops when all the sugar in the *must* is converted or when, as in the case of sweet wines, the sugar content is so high that total conversion is not possible. Otherwise the fermentation may be stopped artificially by the addition of sulphur or alcohol. For some fortified wines it is stopped by the addition of grape spirit. However the fermentation is stopped, the stoppage is marked by the ending of the seething of the bubbles. The *must* has become wine, although the wine continues with a quiescent fermentation until it completes itself between six and twenty-five days later.

Many wines go through a further slow fermentation in cask, but this anaerobic fermentation has nothing to do with the conversion of sugar or the production of alcohol. It is simply a matter of bacteria attacking the malic acid in the wine and converting it into lactic acid and carbon dioxide. Glass weights are usually inserted above the bung holes so as to allow the carbon dioxide to escape, and to prevent air from entering. These are usually added soon after the wine has been transferred to cask.

Racking. When the beautiful agitation of the fermentation is finished, the young wine is full of countless unstable particles known as *lees*. In order to become bright, the wine has to be separated from these *lees* and this is done by *racking*. When the *lees* have settled, a tap is inserted into the cask just above the level of the *lees*. The wine pours out into huge jugs which are taken by the cellar workers and emptied into fresh clean casks. *Racking* usually takes place before the end of spring, preferably after a cold spell in fine and calm weather. If the wine is white and light and is destined for early bottling, it gets about four *rackings* before the end of March. Rosé and young light red wines for early drinking and with no particular staying power will get much the same treatment. Finer white wines and sweeter white wines are left much longer in cask to enable the bouquet to develop; and the substantial and quality red wines are also left for much longer, perhaps for three years or more. As wine is alive, it continues in the *racked* casks to throw down a deposit, so that in its second year it is tapped and *racked* three times, and then twice yearly in succeeding years. Although *racking* leaves the wine clear, it will not make it perfectedly so or brilliantly bright, and other clarifying methods are used to accomplish this.

Fining. This clarification and purification process relies on the principal of attraction between the substance to be removed and the fining agent. The *fining process* is carried out by putting into the wine various substances such as the whites of eggs, oxblood, gelatine, isinglass (bladder of the sturgeon) or milk. The agent, whichever one is used, comes in contact with the substance to be removed from the wine and forms a coagulated mesh, which traps the particles still in suspension and drags them to the bottom of the cask. Other *fining agents* such as Bentonite Clay from Wyoming (U.S.A.) and Lebrija Earth from Spain work as simple colloids. Wines which have an excess of metallic salts are cleared with blue fining (potassium ferrocyanide), otherwise these salts when exposed to the air tend to oxidize the wine, which would then have a cloudy appearance and a bitter taste. Traces of metal in the wine can be the result of fungicide spraying of the vines or the use of metal machinery in the earlier stages of the making of the wine. The blue fining will collect these traces into solids which can then be removed by *filtering*.

Filtering. Filtering, as the name implies, is sifting the wine through a porous surface, which looks like a pad of blotting-paper but which is probably made from asbestos or cellulose or a combination of the two. Sometimes wine centrifuges, based on the principle of the cream separator, are used for the *filtering*. Sterilisation filters have filter sheets with microscopic pores and they are used for wines which have a yeast contamination which, if left, would induce a secondary fermentation. These filters are now used instead of pasteurisation, which certainly sterilised the wine but the heating involved tended to change its character. As opposed to fining, filtration is purely a clarifying process simply to remove the deposits which cause cloudiness. Pasteurisation is continually being experimented with and one day this method may come back into vogue.

The wine is now ready for sale, whether in cask or bottle, or nowadays in special refrigerated containers. As a general rule, wine is bottled in the country where it will be consumed, but much of the finer wines and indeed some of the lesser wines are bottled in the country of origin.

Bottles and Bottling. Sometimes wine is sold to-day, perhaps unfortunately, in containers made of plastic or tin. But since goatskins were commercially discarded, the traditional containers for retailing wine have been glass bottles and there is no doubt that this is the best method known at present. Apart from its complete freedom from affecting the wine, glass can readily be made into attractively shaped bottles, and often by their very shape bottles proclaim the source of their contents.

White wines and some rosé wines are generally sold in clear-glass bottles, although some will be bottled in light-green or brown glass. The bottles for red wines and champagne are usually dark which minimises the chance of the sun or other strong light discolouring the wine. Most bottles for all wines have a *punt* or well at the bottom, the advantage of this is that the bottle is strengthened and the well will act as a stabiliser when pouring wine that has a sediment. The degree of sweetness in a white wine can easily be gauged in a clear-glass bottle, because *normally* the more deep or golden the wine looks, the sweeter the wine, providing of course that the wine has not been affected by an excess of air—maderization.

It is exceptional for wines to be bottled in old bottles because of the risk of contaminating the wine, and even the new bottles are often rinsed out with some of the actual wine to be bottled. If old bottles are used, they are certainly sterilised or washed with a sulphur solution. In modern premises the wine is led by tube from cask or vat to the automatic bottling plant, each unit can fill bottles at the rate of several thousands an hour. The bottling especially for the finer wines, is nearly always carried out in March, April or September when the weather is cool and the atmosphere comparatively germ free. If the weather is stormy or there is thunder about, it is wise to pause in the bottling process or else the wine may be affected.

Corks. As is so often the case these days, plastic and polythene are taking a place as a material with which to make bottle stoppers for wine. But they are not as satisfactory as the time-honoured cork, because the stoppers from these materials tend to warp and to impart a peculiar oxidised flavour to the wine. Cork is produced from cork oak, *Quercus suber*, and the best comes from Spain and Portugal, where the bark of each tree is harvested about every twelve years. The older the tree the finer the bark for making bottle corks. After harvesting the bark the cork is cut and shaped to fit the appropriate bottles.

At the bottling depots the new corks are washed and then steeped for a few hours first in warm water and then in the wine it is to bottle. The steeping must never be in boiling water, because this would make the dried-out cork hard instead of supple. The smooth end of the cork, that is the end without striations, should ideally lead the way into the bottle thus becoming the nearer end to the wine. This prevents the wine's seeping through the cork to cause 'weeping' or a loss of wine. Practically all corking of bottles is now done by machinery; as always, the bottling area must be kept clean and sterile because germs seem to like wine almost as keenly as do Oxford dons.

Wine in Bottle. After years of maturing in bottle, some wines emerge as 'thoroughbreds' while others of the same label may have faded into mediocrity. Much depends on where the bottle has been stored, which emphasises the importance of the position, temperature and other conditions of the cellar. For instance, wines mature faster near the sea or mountains, and cellars anywhere with an average temperature between 10 and 13 degrees centigrade give the most satisfactory results. It is sometimes thought that the chief contribution to the maturing of wine in bottle is the fact that the cork lets into the bottle minute quantities of air through its pores. But this cannot be entirely true because capsuled corks completely exclude air. What happens is that the wine will have retained some oxidation from the air which it absorbed while it was stored in cask or vat after fermentation. This oxygen together with that in the small pocket of air underneath the cork takes hydrogen from very small quantities of the ethyl alcohol to produce acetaldehyde. From this, small traces of acetic acid are formed, and the interaction of the acids and alcohols produces the esters which impart to the matured wine its aroma and bouquet as well as its flavour and smoothness. It is a combination of the two facts that air can infiltrate to the wine through the pores of the wooden casks and that the air is cut off from the wine in the sealed bottles, that is all important for wine development.

Long storage in bottle does not in itself mean the maturing of a fine wine. The conditions of storage and, even more, the quantity of the particular substances in the wine will dictate when a wine will reach maturity. The tannin and acid content will regulate the moment when a wine reaches its peak. That is the time to drink it most agreeably, and recognition of the time can only come with experience of appreciating and drinking, and frequent indulgence at that. Wine left bottled after it has reached its peak will gradually lose its qualities and may even maderize eventually.

As wines grow older, whether in cask or bottle, they usually change in colour. The colour of red wines lightens from purple-red to garnet-red after which brown tinges begin to show. Eventually after a good many years the colour will turn to *pelure d'oignon*—the colour of onion skins. White wines of course are not the colour of whitewash, but they have green-yellow or golden tinges. As they age the colours become intensified. If the intensification goes too far, the excess colour can be removed with charcoal fining, but this would tend to mar the wine, and of course would only be tried when the wine is in cask.

Binning. While wine is maturing, the bottles are laid horizontally so that the wine is in constant contact with the cork. The small pocket of air between the cork and the wine must be shifted, by a quick shake, to become an air-bubble at the top side of the horizontal bottle. This ensures that the cork will remain swollen in the bottle-neck.

THE MAKE-UP OF WINE

From following in some detail the processes involved in the making of wine, it is now possible to indicate what ingredients there are in the final beverage. Of course, water makes up most of the bulk and holds all the other ingredients in solution. The other ingredients include alcohol, several acids, glycerine, salts and minerals, glucose, laevulose, sulphur dioxide, tannin and certain aldelydes, esters and vitamins.

Most of the alcohol is ethyl alcohol (ethanol), and the volume of this will be between 8 and 16 per cent. of the whole, depending on the wine. There is also a minute quantity of methylalcohol present together with varying but small proportions of the higher alcohols. It is the ethyl alcohol and glycerine that cause *tears* or *legs* to form in a wine glass as the wine is being drunk.

The principal acids present in wine, apart from tannin, are tartaric, citric and malic acids, which come from the grape, and lactic acid which is produced during the malolactic fermentation. Acidity helps to preserve wine and it also imparts the tartness in the taste of wine.

Glycerine imparts smoothness and sweetness to wine, and its useful presence comes as a by-product from sugar during fermentation. Sugar in a grape can make up as much as a quarter of the weight of the grape. This sugar is glucose, made up of equal quantities of dextrose and D-Fructose. In a bad year especially in the more northerly climates as in Burgundy and Germany, the sugar content is low. Sugaring of the wine is then permitted. This dosing is called *chaptalisation* in France, a name commemorating a Dr. Chaptal who originated the idea, but in Germany it is called *Verbesserung* (improvement). The sugar used is cane sugar and it is usually added, when at all, to the *must* and not to *the* wine. The sugaring is strictly controlled. Its purpose is to bring the alcoholic content of the wine to the level in a wine of a good year. These sugared wines are not so fine as the normal wines and may even be coarse. Practically all the sugar goes during fermentation, but small quantities of glycerine, glucose and laevulose survive to go through to the final wine, and to add sweetness to it.

The salts and minerals remaining in the finished wine have come all the way through from the soil in which the grapes were grown, and they have a noticeable bearing on the taste of the wine. Tannin, originating in the pips, skins and stalks of the grapes or in smaller quantities from the wood of the casks, is an important ingredient for it gives the wine lasting power and adds flavour and body. Red wines, especially clarets, are rich in tannin which gives the wines their dry after-taste and the coating sensation on ones teeth. When a wine is deficient in tannin, some may be added in powder form. Tannin also has binding properties which are best illustrated by the crust which forms on the side of red wines in bottle as they advance in age.

Finally, the wine will contain sulphur dioxide in varying quantities which was added during the manufacturing and which will keep the wine healthy. There will also be aldehydes and esters formed by the interaction of acids and alcohol which will impart much of the bouquet to the wine. The bottled wine will also include traces of nitrogenous material and some of the vitamins, particularly vitamin A.

Some Wine Ailments. It will have been noticed that in the manufacture of wine repeated efforts are made to control the amounts of the minor ingredients which will eventually become part of the final product, either by reducing the amounts by such processes as *fining* and *filtering*, or by deliberately adding careful amounts of ingredients such as sulphur and tannin. According to the type of wine, so a balance of ingredients will be effected. It is not easy to judge this balance exactly, and in the end some wines may suffer from an excess or a shortage of one or other of the ingredients. It is as well to know the causes and the cures for these ailments.

Too much acidity may develop because over exposure to the air will have encouraged the vinegar microbe. An addition of alcohol should put this right. A drastic change in temperature may cause *cloudiness*, or this may result from an unwanted continuation of fermentation or from excess protein or bacterial actions. Fining will get rid of the cloudiness. Sometimes, *oiliness* will disappear of its own accord, otherwise the wine should be aired by pouring it out of, and then back into, the same cask, after which it should be filtered. Tartaric acid is soluble in water but not in alcohol, so an *excess of tartrate* may be precipitated in very cold temperatures as *crystals*. The *crystals*—potassium hydrogen tartrate—are harmless and they will fall to the bottom of the cask. If they appear in bottle, the remedy is to stand the bottle upright for some time before service. The *crystals* will fall to the bottom, leaving clear wine for drinking. *Excess sulphur* may be present in a wine, particularly if the wine has been bottled from the bottom of the cask. Most wines have been sulphured at some stage, and for most wines it is desirable to open the bottle some time before service to allow any sulphur fumes to escape into the atmosphere.

Some ailments can only develop when the wine is in bottle, such as the leakage known as *weeping*. This seeping of wine from the cork can be caused by a loose cork or a faulty cork, possibly one that is too striated, or a continuation of fermentation may push the cork loose. The wine in any bottle that is suffering in this way should be tested at once, and if it is still sound should be utilised immediately. A faulty cork may also cause the wine to be '*corked*'. A cork when extracted from a wine bottle should smell of wine, not of cork. The experience of tasting a truly *corked* wine comes very seldom, perhaps once or twice in a lifetime. The aroma will be musty and rancid; so will the taste. *Corked* wine drinks like it smells—horrible! Sometimes a wine will suffer from *bottle sickness*, just as some of us suffer air sickness on our first flight, but this will wear off quite naturally if the bottle is kept for a few months before being opened.

Of course wines may become faulty, or even go bad, if the equipment with which it came in contact during manufacture had not been properly cared for and sterilised. Wines may also be ruined if they are wrongly stored, say in an ill-kept cellar at an incorrect temperature, or, worse still, stored next to something with a strong odour, such as vinegar or petrol.

A popular accusation levelled against some wines is that the particular wine '*doesn't travel*'. The accusation is usually unfair, because practically all wines can now travel safely, sleeping in refrigerated tanks and reawakened on arrival in the cellar. When a wine has not travelled well it may be because it is either too young or too old when shipped, or because a correct balance was not aimed at initially, so that it becomes flat, has too much acidity or too little alcohol or as a result of the conditions it suffered on its journey. The temperatures may have varied between extremes, or the cargoes may have been badly handled. It is certainly most essential to give wine an acclimatising period in the importing country before it is put on sale.

Styles of Wine. The species of vine and type of grape, the climate, the soil and the methods of cultivating the vine and manufacturing the wine will all have had their effect on the type of wine produced. The most common are the table wines with an alcoholic strength between 8 and 16 per cent., but more usually between 10 and 13 per cent. Table wines include white, rosé and red wines.

White wines are made from black or white grapes, the juice of which is run off from the pressing into another cask or vat, where they will ferment without the skins, pips and stalks, left in the press. If the grapes have a low sugar content, which is all converted during fermentation, the wine will be dry. On the other hand, if the grapes have such a high sugar content that the yeasts are not capable of converting all of it during fermentation, the wine will be sweet. As already described, some grapes such as those gathered late in Sauternes are deliberately grown to produce a high percentage of sugar in the grapes, which remains to sweeten the wine. There are other methods of making sweet wine, mainly by stopping the process of fermentation before the yeast has converted all the sugar. This can be done by the introduction into the fermentation at the appropriate time of a calculated amount either of sulphur dioxide or grape spirit.

Rosé wines are classically made by leaving the grape skins immersed with the *must* during fermentation until the required degree of colouring has been obtained. The *must* is then run off to a separate container to finish fermenting without the presence of the skins.

Red wines are made from black grapes which are crushed, and the whole mass, juice, skins, stalks and pips, are kept together to ferment, during which time colour is extracted from the skins.

Fortified wines are wines with strength added by the addition of grape spirit. Examples of these are the wines Port, Sherry, Madeira, Málaga and Marsala. The alcohol may be added during fermentation so that some of the grape sugar remains unfermented, or at the end of the natural fermentation simply to increase the potency of the wine.

Mistelle wines are produced by adding alcohol to the unfermented grape juice, and they are used to sweeten some wines, including vermouths. The basis of vermouths is usually light dry wine flavoured with Alpine herbs and spices, orange peel etc., which are infused with the wine for some days together with some mistelle and grape spirit. Italian vermouths usually have a bigger proportion of mistelle than do the drier French vermouths. Some wines are made in Britain. They are mainly Port and Sherry types and they are generally made from imported concentrates of grape juice from the natural wine countries. The juice is fermented in England by specially cultured yeast, and the wine is matured in oak casks and later fortified. There are of course some natural table wines made in England from home-grown grapes. These may not be the best of wines, but are usually good value for the price charged and are much better to drink than the wine made by adding water to an extract of dried wine, as if it were instant coffee. British wines account for one bottle in four sold in Britain.

Pétillant or Spritzig Wines are slightly effervescent, but naturally so. They leave a prickling sensation on the palate due, in some regions, to the wine being bottled early or having been fermented in pressure tanks.

Perlwein is native to Germany and is semi-sparkling. It is made in pressure tanks and bottled under pressure.

Crémant Wine, or creaming wine, has a greater amount of effervescence than pétillant wine but less so than sparkling wines. Crémant wines are made from any growth of grapes in the Côte des Blancs region of Champagne, but it is more specifically associated with the village of Cramant. It may be found in France under the attractive name of *Crémant Cramant*.

Sparkling Wines are known as *Vins Mousseux*, a name which is applied to all sparkling wines other than Champagne although Champagne, if it needs a full title, is correctly called *Champagne Mousseux*. There are three methods of making sparkling wine, the Champagne method (*Méthode Champenoise*), the closed tank method (*Cuve Close*) and the *impregnation method*.

In the Champagne method, the different wines, after fermentation, are blended; then yeast and sugar are added to create a secondary fermentation which takes place in the bottle. The carbon dioxide remains trapped beneath the cork on top of the bottle and is chemically bonded to the wine. This is the reason why the effervescence is retained in the glass after the wine is poured for a longer time than from wines made by the other methods. In the *Méthode Cuve Close*, the wine is put into vitreous-coated pressure tanks, where sugar and yeast culture are added to cause a secondary fermentation, which can last for about three weeks. The wine is then cooled to precipitate the dead yeast etc. and run off under pressure into another tank leaving the débris behind. The wine is then filtered and bottled through special pressure filters. The *impregnation* is the least desirable method of all, as it results in a wine that goes grey and loses its effervescence quickly in the glass. The wine is put into pressurised tanks and carbon dioxide is injected through the wine, which is then bottled under pressure. The method may be varied by bottling the wine first and then injecting the carbon dioxide into each individual bottle.

Vintage Wines are those made in one particular year from a pressing of that year's grapes, when conditions have been favourable for the production of a wine of excellence. When a wine is sold as of vintage quality, the year in which it was made will be stated on the label on the bottle.

Non-vintage Wines are blended from wines made from the grapes of more than one year's pressing, and it is likely that the blend will include a proportion of a wine from an excellent year. They are much less expensive than vintage wines, but they can be very good value. A good guide to their quality can be the reputation of the shipper or the wine-merchant.

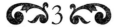

THE WINES OF FRANCE

DESPITE the outstanding reputations of St. Joan, the Sun King, Napoleon, the Academy Immortals and even General de Gaulle, the most world-famous characteristic of France is its wines. Many place names in France are better known as a wine,

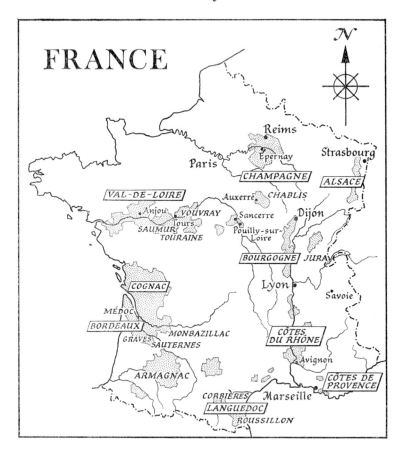

whether they represent a province like Champagne or an individual château.

The Romans are credited with laying the foundations of Western civilisation, and one of the foundation stones was the teaching of improved methods of viniculture to the Gauls. Perhaps this gift led to the eventual recognition of France as the centre or inspiration of Western civilisation. Certainly, since those days, wine has remained the habitual drink in France; wine leads to conversation, conversation to argument and argument to glimpses of truth. *In vino veritas.*

Of more mundane importance has been the agricultural, commercial and industrial effect of the cultivation of the grape. All French economic statistics will show high percentage figures deriving from the grape, whether relating to consumption or production, exports or imports, hectarage or volume. They will also reflect the many supporting occupations from the making of casks, corks, bottles, crates, machinery and tools for cultivation, storage and transport to the numerous army of salesmen and other middlemen. But the great wealth from the vineyards has emanated from the severe discipline imposed by the French *vignerons* themselves and stimulated by governmental or quasi-governmental wine regulations.

There is a ladder of quality in French wines, the bottom rung of which represents the very ordinary wines for everyday drinking. This is indicated on wine labels as V.C.C., an abbreviation of *vins ordinaires de consommation courante*. These wines are sometimes described as *vin supérieur* or *vin choisi*, but this does not indicate a better quality for they really are no more than blends of ordinary swilling wine. A step up the ladder from these are the *vins de marque*, which suggest blends of better wines. Like the V.C.C. wines they adhere to the regulations relating to blended wines and they must show on the label an alcoholic strength of at least 9·5° G.L.

On the next rung up are the *vins du pays*, and these wines have to be linked with a geographical source not larger than the department from which they come. They must have an alcoholic strength of not less than 8·5° G.L. although this degree of strength is reviewed each year. Next come *vins à appellation d'origine simple* (A.O.S. for short). These are simple wines of origin, similar to the *vins du pays* but with the added restriction that they must be produced from authorised vines and not from hybrids. Another step up come the *vins délimités de qualité supérieure* or V.D.Q.S., which are wines produced from approved vines cultivated according to a specific code. The grapes must be grown within delimited vineyards and areas and they must produce a wine with a minimum alcoholic content. The wines are tasted by a panel before the certificate is granted.

On the top rung of the ladder are the *vins à appellation d'origine contrôlée* or A.O.C., which are subject to the strictest control under French law and to control by the *Institut National Des Appellations d'Origine des Vins et Eaux-de-Vie*. The regulations of the *Institut* control the physical area of production, the approved classical vine species, the methods of cultivating the vine, the maximum yield of grapes per hectare, the minimum and potential alcoholic content and the method of wine making. In some regions the wines are required to undergo a tasting test. Similar controls also apply to the superior wine spirits that have been granted the A.O.C. designation. The strictness of the appellation control is illustrated by the fact that about 15 per cent. only of France's total wines qualify for this top designation.

Vineyard proprietors entitled to use A.O.C. are naturally very happy to indicate the fact on the labels on their wine bottles, and will often also show their pride by giving on the label the name of the vineyard, although this further delineation may sometimes be omitted in a poor year. If the wine is bottled on the vineyard estate, the fact is indicated on the label by the legend *Mis en Bouteille au Château* or *Mise du Château*. In Burgundy, *Domaine* would be substituted for *Château*. The following terms may also be shown on a label—*Mis en Bouteille à la Propriété*, meaning that the wine has been bottled by the grower or the proprietor though not necessarily on the vineyard of origin; and *Mis en Bouteille dans la Région de Production*, which signifies that the wine has been bottled within the region of its production. All these titles are extra guarantees of the authenticity of the wine.

ᏩᏩ4ᏩᏩ

BORDEAUX

I N 1152, Eleanor of Aquitaine married Henry Plantagenet, Duke of Anjou, who two years later became King of England as Henry II. The great wine districts of Bordeaux thus became part of the territories attached to the English Crown, for Gascony had been part of Eleanor's dowry. Bordeaux remained English for the next 300 years until the first Earl of Shrewsbury, John Talbot, was defeated at the battle of Castillon. It is therefore not surprising that considerable trade grew up between the excellent port of Bordeaux and England. The wine merchants of Bordeaux were granted favourable concessions. Who on the English throne could have denied them these concessions? For in the good old feudal fighting days many of the vineyards came into the ownership of gallant greedy knights whose family names can still be traced in many châteaux, including the famous Château Talbot, which the unlucky first Earl lost with his battle. Other English and Irish

BORDEAUX

RED WINES

WHITE WINES

RED & WHITE WINES

names, probably introduced by armour-clad marauders who chose the right side, can to this day be traced in the names of châteaux such as Boyd, Brown, Kirwan, Palmer and Haut-Brion, the last pleasantly refashioned from O'Brien.

The marriage of Henry and Eleanor was to lead to much friction between England and France, but perhaps it was worth it for the English have enjoyed the wines of Bordeaux ever since. The earliest shipments of red Bordeaux wines were known as Gascon wines. Later they were described as *clairet* or *clairette*, meaning clear light or bright, as they were much lighter in colour and body than they are today. A similar wine is still being made in the Premières Côtes de Bordeaux. The English called all Bordeaux red wines, claret, which seems to be a simple anglicisation of the French, although some claim that it derives from the Earl of Clare, a liege of Henry II, who presumably enjoyed his wine. The name is now generic for all red wines produced from grapes grown within the department of the Gironde. Bordeaux remains a very English-like town with many Anglo-Saxon names over the shops.

There are about 13 000 square kilometres of vineyards in Bordeaux, divided among some 60 000 vineyard owners. Between 350 and 450 million litres of wine are produced annually, just a little more white than red. No other wine region produces such an abundance of quality wine, and, in fact, over one third of all the *Appellation Contrôlée* wines in France come from Bordeaux. Bordeaux itself produces 2 600 000 hectolitres of A.O.C. wines.

Bordeaux is a town and port and the vineyards are situated in the department of the Gironde made up of the valleys of the river Gironde; its main tributary the Dordogne and the hills to the north of, and the land in between, the two rivers. On the south or west bank of the Gironde from the Atlantic almost to Bordeaux lies the famous district of the Médoc wines, and south of this stretch the Graves vineyards from Bordeaux to Cérons, the centre of Les Petites Graves vineyards. Continuing south on the same side of the river are the Sauternes vineyards. On the other bank of the Gironde, opposite Haut-Médoc (the southern part of the Médoc district), lies the Côtes de Blaye merging into the Côtes de Bourg at the confluence of the Gironde with the Dordogne. Higher up on this side of the Dordogne are the vineyards of Fronsac, Pomerol and St.-Émilion. Between the two rivers is land mainly occupied by the vineyards of Entre-Deux-Mers. The names given in this brief description of the Gironde district—i.e. the lands within the *Limité de l'appellation Bordeaux*—represent the larger hectarage of the particular vineyards, but there are other smaller areas which have given their names to wines of world renown, as well as many vineyards which produce reasonable wines without the distinctive names known in all the best cellars.

For there are hundreds of 'brands' of Bordeaux wine, and we must limit ourselves to a few comments on the wines from the following principal wine regions:

Red wines	Red and white wines	White wines
Médoc	Graves	Sauternes
St-Émilion	Bourg	Cérons
Pomerol	Blaye	Ste-Croix-du-Mont
Fronsac	1ères Côtes de Bordeaux	et Loupiac
	Entre-Deux-Mers	St-Macaire

Before commenting on these regions, something must be said about the climate, soil, type of grape and method of production.

Climate. Bordeaux has a reasonably mild climate with a winter average temperature of 4·5° C. Like most wine districts, however, it has its climatic hazards of snow, frost and hail. One has only to think of the year 1956 when enormous damage to the crop was caused by frost and the vines yielded about half the usual product. 1957 was hardly any better and more recently, in 1968, an overabundance of rain and lack of sunshine reduced not the quantity but the quality of the grapes which produced an acid harsh wine. On the whole the climate is not too unlike that of England, except that Bordeaux usually benefits from much finer late summers, which are of course essential for the proper ripening of the grapes.

Soil. The soil in the Gironde changes from *commune* to *commune*, often indeed from vineyard to vineyard, but almost everywhere it is of very poor quality for any husbandry other than the growing of the vine. It is mainly made up, in various combinations of gravel (*graves*), pebbles, limestone, clay and sand. These may be arranged in three broad categories. First the *graves* or gravel or quarty pebbles with sand or clay subsoils found in the Médoc and Graves vineyards; second, the clay soil with limestone or broken stones underneath, found on the hillsides; and third, the lands formed from alluvial deposits at the mouth of the River Gironde and along the valleys.

Grapes. In the vineyards of Bordeaux, the vines are mostly trained low to the ground, around one metre in height, in order to extract maximum sustenance from the earth. For red wines, the grape varieties are Cabernet Sauvignon, Cabernet Franc, Merlot, Malbec and Petit-Verdot. For white wines, the varieties are Sémillon, Sauvignon, Muscadelle and Merlot Blanc. Careful control ensures that all *appellation controlée* wines from Bordeaux are made from these varieties only. But it is exceptional to drink a wine made solely from one of these.

For example, many of the finest red wines are made from a blend made up of 80 per cent. Cabernet Sauvignon and 20 per cent. Merlot.

Production. The vintage usually starts in the last two weeks of September, although for the sweet white wines it may start later. The making of these sweet wines will be dealt with when we come to discuss the wines of Sauternes. The making of the other white wines is simply the extracting of the *must* from the grapes by pressing. The *must* alone is then put into clean casks where it ferments into wine. This wine is then matured in oak casks and, after racking and fining, is bottled after about nine to twelve months.

Clarets are a different problem for they take a long time to reach maturity and can then keep in prime condition for many years, sometimes for more than half a century. The pace of life today demands more immediate results and some of the Bordeaux proprietors, through new methods of vinification, have produced a wine that can be drunk at a much younger age. It is mainly the tannin content in wine which gives it longevity. The more tannin the longer the wine takes to mature, and the longer it will live. As already explained, the tannin comes from the stalks, pips and skins of the grapes. Obviously then, if you reduce the tannin content, you get a wine that matures more speedily without necessarily altering its quality. In order to bring about this quicker maturing, the grapes are put into a destalking machine called an *égrappoir-fouloir*. This machine separates the stalks from the grapes and also crushes the grapes. Without the stalks, the *must* obtained from the crushed grapes is transferred to fermentation vats, which are usually made of cement and specially lined, or of stainless steel. These tanks also obviate the tannin which could be imparted from the oak of the formerly used casks. After fermenting for about twelve days the wine is removed from the mass or débris into clean oak casks, a saving of about ten days in the fermenting process. The wine at this stage is known as *vin de cuvée* and it is stood above ground with glass stoppers in the bungs to prevent the entry of air and harmful bacteria. The casks are topped up occasionally to make up for loss by evaporation. Later the wine is transferred to casks below ground where the temperature is much cooler, generally about 13° C. The casks are racked from time to time and the wine is *fined* once or twice before it is bottled. Bottling takes place at about eighteen to twenty-four months after the vintage. The wine can now be drunk much sooner than before, perhaps after three or four years.

A more recent experiment is the *macération carbonique* system—which produces a wine which may be consumed virtually within months of having been made. To achieve this, whole grapes including stalks are put into large sealed vats and a slow fermentation begins *within* the grapes. At this stage no pressing whatsoever takes place until about the fourth day when the juice is removed from the skins and stalks to complete its fermentation in fresh vats. The end result is a light, fresh and fruity wine, delicate in colour. If a more robust and deeper-hued wine is required some grape *juice* is left in contact with the stalks and skins during the first four days of fermentation. This latter wine, more definite in character, is best suited to cold northern climates whereas the former is more favoured in hotter countries. Consequently the method used will depend on the destination of the wine.

There are, of course, the famous Châteaux which will not forsake the traditional method of slow fermentation in the manner prescribed by the early Castellans. Some have made experiments, but soon reverted to the methods of slow maturing that gained them, and will preserve for them, their exhalted reputations. There will always be a market for fine clarets, despite their very high prices, and it is to be hoped that there will always be sellers and buyers with the patience to get the best from the wine. It is the Bordeaux wines with the less-renowned names that will benefit most from the new methods of vinification by earlier marketing at prices which will be competitive to withstand the challenge for the table-wine market from Spain, Portugal and some Eastern European countries. The new methods also benefit us all in that a good and palatable claret will be available at reasonable prices without the bother of long cellarage. Both the connoisseur and the plain drinker gets full benefit from the growers and merchants of Bordeaux.

Classification. To mark the International Exhibition held in Paris in 1855 and at the suggestion, it is supposed, of Napoleon III, the Bordeaux Chamber of Commerce authorised the Society of Winebrokers to make a classification of Bordeaux wines. Sixty-one wines from the Médoc and one from Graves, all red, were considered good enough for inclusion in the classification and they were divided into the following *crus* or growths—*first growth*, four wines; *second growth*, sixteen wines; *third growth*, fourteen wines; *fourth growth*, eleven wines; *fifth growth*, seventeen wines. The principle adopted for the classification was that the best wines had fetched the highest prices; accordingly, the different growths were classified on the average price obtained for them over a number of years. In 1932, the rest of the Médoc wines were divided, in descending order of merit, as *crus exceptionnels, crus bourgeois, crus artisans* and *crus paysans*—perhaps a cruel and class-conscious selection of names. Sauternes wines were also classified in 1855 and other wines from other areas of Bordeaux have since been similarly dealt with, as we shall see.

Bordeaux

The Médoc is an area of flat land lying on the left bank of the Gironde and north-west of Bordeaux. The southern half of the area—Haut Médoc—produces the greatest concentration of the finest red wines in Bordeaux, perhaps in the world. The area is divided into *communes*, or parishes, the most important of which are Pauillac, Margaux, St-Estèphe, St-Julien and Cantenac. The four most famous wines from the Médoc are Château Latour, Château Lafite-Rothschild, Château Mouton Rothschild from the *commune* of Pauillac, and Château Margaux from the *commune* of Margaux. Although a small amount of dry or medium-dry white wines is made in the Médoc, they may not be classified as Médoc wine; they are sold as Bordeaux Supérieur or Bordeaux Blanc. All Médoc wines then, as far as sales-promotion is concerned, are red wines. The classification of 1855 still stands good, although changes of proprietorship and husbandry and fluctuations of fortune have reduced the accuracy of the classification, probably by nearly one-third. The basis for a revised classification was laid down in 1959, an outstanding wine year, but it is doubtful whether the revision will be carried out although the French government is now giving serious consideration to the matter. The classification of 1855 was as follows:

FIRST GROWTHS
Château Lafite-Rothschild *Pauillac*
Château Latour *Pauillac*
Château Margaux *Margaux*
Château Haut-Brion *Pessac, Graves*

SECOND GROWTHS
Château Mouton-Rothschild *Pauillac*
Château Rausan-Ségla *Margaux*
Château Rauzan-Gassies *Margaux*
Château Léoville-Lascases *Saint-Julien*
Château Léoville-Poyferré *Saint-Julien*
Château Léoville-Barton *Saint-Julien*
Château Durfort-Vivens *Margaux*
Château Lascombes *Margaux*
Château Gruaud-Larose *Saint-Julien*
Château Brane-Cantenac *Cantenac*
Château Pichon-Longueville-Baron-de-Pichon *Pauillac*
Château Pichon-Longueville-Comtesse-de-Lalande *Pauillac*
Château Ducru-Beaucaillou *Saint-Julien*
Château Cos-d'Estournel *Saint-Estèphe*

Château Montrose *Saint-Estèphe*

THIRD GROWTHS
Château Kirwan *Cantenac*
Château d'Issan *Cantenac*
Château Lagrange *Saint-Julien*
Château Langoa Barton *Saint-Julien*
Château Giscours *Labarde*
Château Malescot-Saint-Exupéry *Margaux*
Château Cantenac-Brown *Cantenac*
Château Palmer *Cantenac*
Château La Lagune *Ludon*
Château Desmirail *Margaux*
Château Calon-Ségur *Saint-Estèphe*
Château Ferrière *Margaux*
Château Marquis d'Alesme-Becker *Margaux*
Château Boyd-Cantenac *Cantenac*

FOURTH GROWTHS
Château Saint-Pierre Bontemps *Saint-Julien*
Chateau Saint-Pierre Sevaistre, *Saint-Julien*
Château Branaire-Ducru *Saint-Julien*
Château Talbot *Saint-Julien*

Château Duhart-Milon *Pauillac*
Château Pouget *Cantenac*
Château La Tour-Carnet *Saint-Laurent*
Château Rochet *Saint-Estèphe*
Château Beychevelle *Saint-Julien*
Château Le Prieuré *Cantenac*
Château Marquis-de-Terme *Margaux*

FIFTH GROWTHS
Château Pontet-Canet *Pauillac*
Château Batailley *Pauillac*
Château Grand-Puy-Lacoste *Pauillac*
Château Grand-Puy-Ducasse *Pauillac*

Château Lynch-Bages *Pauillac*
Château Lynch-Moussas *Pauillac*
Château Dauzac *Labarde*
Château Mouton-d'Armailhacq *Pauillac*
Château du Tertre *Arsac*
Château Haut-Bages-Libéral *Pauillac*
Château Pédesclaux *Pauillac*
Château Belgrave *Saint-Laurent*
Château Camensac *Saint-Laurent*
Château Cos-Labory *Saint-Estèphe*
Château Clerc-Milon-Mondon *Pauillac*
Château Croizet-Bages *Pauillac*
Château Cantemerle *Macau*

In the Médoc there are 6500 hectares (13 000 acres) of land under the vine, producing an annual average of 250 000 hectolitres (5 000 000 gallons) of wine. The maximum planting of vines allowed is 6 500 vines per hectare, each hectare producing on average 35 hectolitres of wine per year or 350 gallons per acre.

The Médoc wines get more graceful as they grow old, and even the least good of them improve with age. They usually have an alcoholic strength of 10° or 11° G.L. They have an all-round fineness and finesse, and a good bouquet, which also improves with age.

St-Émilion. The hilly countryside of St-Émilion is much more picturesque than the neat and tidy flatlands of the Médoc. Its wines are more robust and powerful with an alcoholic strength from 12° to 14° G.L. Given time, they reach perfection in balance. Certainly, the greatest of them—Château Ausone and Château Cheval Blanc—can compare with any of the great wines of the Médoc. Château Ausone takes its name from the poet Ausonius, who owned a vineyard there in the 4th century and, of course, frequently sang about the merits of the wine. It is said that Château Ausone would have been included in the 1855 classification as a first growth but for its limited production at the time, 15 tonneaux. It now produces 25 tonneaux per average year. St-Émilion wines have a brilliant yet deep colour and in body have a definite affinity to the best Burgundies.

The Official Classification of the Wines of St-Emilion (October 1954)

FIRST GREAT GROWTHS

Group. 'A' { Château Ausone and Château Cheval-Blanc

Group. 'B'
{
Château Beauséjour (Dufau)
Château Beauséjour (Fagouet)
Château Belair
Château Canon
Château Figeac
Clos Fourtet
Château La Gaffelière-Naudes
Château Magdelaine
Château Pavie
Château Trottevieille
This was followed by a further
list of sixty 'Great Growths'
}

Pomerol lies to the west of St-Émilion, a little to the north of the north bank of the River Dordogne, the main tributary of the Gironde. The light-sloping hills of Pomerol produce wines which have many of the characteristics of the wines of St-Émilion, but they are more rounded and smooth or velvety to the taste. Their appeal, like those of St-Émilion, is that they are nice medium wines somewhere between the Médoc and Burgundy wines in taste. Pomerol wines age well and usually have an alcoholic strength of 12° or 13° G.L. There is no official classification of Pomerol wines, but the finest growths are as follows:

Château Pétrus—*Cru Exceptionnel*

Other Principal Growths
{
Château La Conseillante
Château Gazin
Château Lafleur
Château Lafleur-Pétrus
Château Petit-Village
Château Trotanoy
Château Vieux-Château-Certan
Château Certan de May
Château L'Évangile
Château Nénin
Château Beauregard
Château Certan-Giraud
Clos de l'Église-Clinet
Château Lagrange
Château La Pointe
Château Latour-Pomerol
Château La Croix
Château La Croix-de-Gay
Domaine du Clos l'Église
Château Feytit-Clinet
Château Gombaude-Guillot
Château Mazeyres
Château Rouget
Château de Sales
}

It is generally agreed that Pomerol wines have a distinct taste of truffles.

Graves. The name Graves comes from the gravelly type of soil predominant in this area south and west of Bordeaux. To many people Graves is synonymous with a dry to medium-dry white wine, and indeed Graves is justly famous for such wines. Nevertheless, some of the most well-known and finest Bordeaux red wines, such as Château Haut-Brion, are also produced in this area. About three times as much white wine is made as red wine but, although the white wines can be very good, they are never great as are some of the red. When it comes to quality, there are twice as many thoroughbred reds as whites. Red Graves wines are big and robust; they may lack, after maturing, the mellowness of the Médoc wines and are slightly thinner on the palate but they show the finesse of good breeding with a distinctive bouquet and a clean crisp taste. Properly matured, they can last fifty years or more.

These wines must not be confused with the lesser *Graves-de-Vayres*, which come from an area just south-west of Libourne on the left bank of the Dordogne. Here again the red wines are better than the white. Some of the former can be quite good but the latter are very sweet and low in alcohol. Much of this finds its way to Germany.

To return to the Graves area on the left bank of the Garonne, from Bordeaux to Langon but skirting the areas producing Cérons, Barsac and Sauternes wines, is the gentle countryside with its low hills and pretty little rivers. It is mainly in the north of the area, near to Bordeaux itself, that most of the red wines are made and, indeed, have been made since Roman times. Red Graves have a fine authority and there are many who consider them the finest of all clarets. The classification of the principal red and white wines of the Graves is as follows:

	Red ●	White ■
PESSAC:		
Haut-Brion (classé 1er cru en 1855)	●	
Pape Clément	●	
TALENCE:		
La Mission Haut-Brion	●	
La Tour Haut-Brion	●	
Laville Haut-Brion		■
VILLENAVE D'ORNON:		
Couhins		■
LÉOGNAN:		
Haut-Bailly	●	
Carbonnieux	●	■
Domaine de Chevalier	●	■
Fieuzal	●	
Malartic-Lagravière	●	■
Olivier	●	■

Bordeaux

MARTILLAC:
Smith-Haut-Lafitte   ●
Latour-Martillac   ●   ▓

CADAUJAC:
Bouscaut   ●   ▓

Bourg. On the right bank of the Gironde, opposite the Médoc, is the Côtes de Bourg, a hilly terrain sometimes known as the Switzerland of the Gironde. The area produces both red and white wines, which may be sold under the names Bourg, Côtes de Bourg or Bourgeais. The red wines are better than the white wines, and although they are not as good as the wines from St-Émilion, they are somewhat similar to them in character.

Some examples of good quality red wines from the Bourg district are:

Château du Bousquet	Château Lagrange
Château de Boucaud	Château Grelau
Château de la Libarde	Château Mille-Secousses

The white wines such as Bayon, Lansac, Pugnac and Château de la Grave are, at the very least, worth experimenting with.

Blaye. North of the Côtes de Bourg lies the Côtes de Blaye in which both red and white wines are produced. Like those from the Côtes de Bourg, the red wines are superior, being both smooth and supple to taste. They share with the Bourg and Fronsac wines the name of the 'little red wines of Bordeaux'.

Fronsac. The Côtes de Fronsac adjoin the Pomerol district and produces spicy, well-rounded red wines, rich in colour. As already mentioned Fronsac is the third of the group dubbed 'the little red wines of Bordeaux'. The soubriquet is ungenerous because, little or not, they are usually excellent value for the price asked. They are extremely good carafe wines and can be drunk quite young, and have a minimum alcoholic strength of 10·5° G.L.

Premières Côtes de Bordeaux. The vineyards of the Premières Côtes de Bordeaux stretch for about 80 kilometres along the right bank of the Gironde and bordering Entre-Deux-Mers. They produce both red and white wines. The red wines, with about 11·5° G.L. alcohol, have a spicy taste and can be drunk reasonably young. Even so, they age well. The white wines can be dry, medium or sweet and they have an alcoholic strength of about 12° G.L. Both the reds and the whites make ideal wines for everyday drinking.

Entre-Deux-Mers. The vineyards of Entre-Deux-Mers are of course between two rivers, not seas. The rivers are the Dordogne and the Garonne. The northern vineyards (the Bonnes Côtes) produce mostly red wine of a very tolerable standard and which is sold in quantity as Bordeaux Rouge. The southern part (the Petites Côtes) produces little red wine but considerable quantities of white wine, much of which is very popular in the United Kingdom, probably because of the picturesque name and reasonable prices rather than the quality of the wine. The wine is dry by nature but is often blended to give a suggestion of sweetness. The more southerly vineyards tend to produce sweeter white wines of better quality, but here they tend to merge into the Cadillac district and the cantons that make up the Premières Côtes de Bordeaux district.

Ste-Croix-du-Mont and Loupiac. To the extreme south of Entre-Deux-Mers, opposite the Sauternes district on the other side of the Gironde river, are the two white wine regions of Ste-Croix-du-Mont and Loupiac. The wines are lusciously sweet and made from grapes which are not picked until they are overripe—similar to the effect of *Botrytis cinerea* action on Sauternes.

St-Macaire. Also on the north bank of the Gironde and opposite the Sauternes district is St-Macaire, whose surrounding vineyards once produced a large quantity of red wines. Now, however, the controlled appellation is for white wines only. These can have a dry spiciness or can be of a sweet variety.

Ste-Foy-la-Grande. East of Entre-Deux-Mers on the south side of the Dordogne river lies the hilly country of Sainte-Foy-la-Grande, from the vineyards of which are produced very useful ordinary wines, the best of which are allowed the appellation Ste-Foy-Bordeaux. Three quarters of the wine is white and the remainder red. It would be typical to find these wines sold by the glass in French bars and cafés.

Sauternes. The five *communes* of Barsac, Bommes, Fargues, Preignac and Sauternes itself make up the famous wine district of Sauternes. From this district come luscious sweet wines of exceptional finesse; indeed the produce of Château d'Yquem is rightly regarded as the greatest sweet wine in the world. The excellence and sweetness of the Sauternes wines derive from the method of harvesting the grapes, the picking of which is spread over as long as two months from the beginning of the normal vintage. When the grapes are fully ripe, the leaves are removed from the vines to allow maximum air and sunlight to penetrate to the grapes. As the autumn sun beats down, the skins of the grapes become brown and, if the weather stays favourable, some rain being essential, little brown spots form on the surface of the skins. The skins gradually become thin and then wrinkle and, slowly, the fruit dries, leaving the grapes with a rotting appearance, which is justifiably rewarded with the name of *Pourriture noble*, or noble rot. The technical name for the mould causing this is *Botrytis cinerea*. The grapes are picked, almost individually, only when they have reached this nobility. This careful and severe selection considerably reduces the yield for anything between a third and a half of the crop may be lost. Obviously the expense of production is greatly increased by this unusual harvesting and, when account is taken that in some years the weather may ruin nearly the whole crop, the making of this wine is a precarious business. However, the classical wines that are enjoyed universally justify our gratitude for the risks which the vignerons take. The official classification of the wines of the Sauternes is as follows:

Premier Grand Cru (classé depuis 1855) : Château d'Yquem

PREMIERS CRUS

Château La Tour-Blanche	Château Climens
Château Lafaurie-Peyraguey	Château Guiraud
Château Clos Haut-Peyraguey	Château Rieussec
Château de Raine Vigneau	Château Rabaud-Promis
Château de Sudulraut	Château Sigalas-Rabaud
Château Coutet	

DEUXIÈMES CRUS

Château Myrat	Château Nairac
Château Doisy-Daëne	Château Caillou
Château Doisy-Dubroca	Château Suau
Château Doisy-Védrines	Château de Malle
Château d'Arche	Château Romer
Château Filhot	Château Lamothe
Château Broustet	

Generally the *communes* are happy with the generic name of Sauternes. The exception is Barsac, which prefers to sell its wine under its own label. So although all Barsacs are Sauternes, not all Sauternes are Barsacs.

Cérons. The district of Cérons, lying between the Graves and Sauternes districts, produces an average white wine of the Sauternes type. It is less sweet than Barsac, the *commune* of which ɨt borders and in which it was once contained. Like the Sauternes, it has an alcoholic content of not less than 12·5° G. L.

ROSÉ AND SPARKLING WINES

There is quite a substantial amount of Rosé wine (always dry) made in Bordeaux, which is at last making its way into foreign markets and is found readily in Chinese restaurants and the like. While it is a pleasant wine, it should not be taken too seriously.

Entre-deux-Mers is the centre of the sparkling wine industry. Made by the *Méthode Champenoise* (second fermentation in bottle) these wines, although not nearly as fine as Champagne, make an interesting change:

Vintage guide for Bordeaux Wine

White		Red	
Great	Very good	Great	Very good
1945	1948	1947	1945
1947	1950	1949	1953
1949	1952	1952	1955
1955	1953	1959	1962
1959	1961	1961	1964
	1962		1966
	1966		1967
	1967		1969
	1969		1970
	1970		

BURGUNDY

WHEN Burgundy was a mediaeval kingdom, and later a duchy, it was customary for most of the nobility to take the wise precaution of bequeathing or donating part of their lands to the Church. With their usual inspired diligence, the religious orders who

received the lands set about cultivating the vine or improving the vineyards already established. By the 12th century, monastic orders held a considerable share of the Burgundian vineyards to the extent, indeed, that fears arose that good living was taking over from good works. But the build-up of the Church's control continued until the French Revolution when the anti-clerical ideology of the times led to the seizing by the government of the vineyards and their sale to the people. The peasants, of course, could each not afford more than a small area, many of which consisted of only part of a single vineyard. In contrast to the Bordeaux vineyards therefore, those of Burgundy are usually to this day in multiple ownership, the most frequently cited example being that of the 50·5 hectares vineyard of Clos de Vougeot that is owned by 50 proprietors. One could expect, therefore, that many different wines could be promoted under the name of one vineyard according to the different aspirations and standards of the various proprietors. For this reason the reputations or pedigrees of the Burgundian wines are likely to be less solid than the wines from the large vineyards of Bordeaux under single ownership.

The vineyards of Burgundy cover over 500 square kilometres lying mainly along the 193 kilometres between Dijon and Villefranche in five areas—Côte de Nuits, Côte de Beaune (both of them part of Côte d'Or), Côte Chalonnaise, Côte Mâconnaise and Le Beaujolais. Away 96·5 kilometres to the north-west between Dijon and Paris lie the Chablis winefields in grand isolation. For the most part, all these lands are hilly and the finer growths of grapes are cultivated towards the bottom slopes or perhaps more accurately on the bottom half of the slopes. The soil in the best producing areas is made up of limestone, marl and schist.

Because of its northerly climate, the Burgundian grapes suffer from insufficient sunshine in some years. Pressed like this, the ensuing wine would be harsh and low in alcohol, completely false to the Burgundy image. To counteract the deficiency in sugar and the overabundance of acidity, beet-sugar or cane-sugar is added to the grape juice during fermentation. The amount of sugar allowed is strictly controlled by the Government. This improvement of the wine is called in France 'chaptalisation', after Dr. Chaptal (1756–1832), who was the originator of the practice. Dr. Chaptal's idea is also used in Germany where they call it 'Verbesserung'.

About 100 million litres of wine are produced in Burgundy each year and of this 1 000 000 hectolitres has the *appellation contrôlée* pedigree. Five-sixths of the wine is red, made from Pinot Noir or Gamay grapes. The one-sixth white wine is made from Chardonnay, Aligoté or Pinot Blanc grapes. The Pinot Noir grape produces the finest red wines, and is used principally in the Côte de Nuits, Côte de

Beaune and Côte Chalonnaise. The vineyards of Côte Mâconnaise and Le Beaujolais mainly grow the Gamay grape, which yields more abundantly, if with less quality, than the Pinot Noir. The choice is not swayed so much by the abundance as by the reality that the Pinot Noir does not grow well in these areas. Sometimes red wines are made with one-third Pinot Noir grapes and two-thirds Gamay grapes, and these wines are marketed as *Passe-Tout-Grains*. The white Burgundies depend on the Chardonnay grape for quality, and this grape is extensively used in Chablis as well as for the white wines produced in the Côtes de Nuits, de Beaune and Mâconnaise, where it is sometimes used in blend with the Pinot Blanc grape. The Aligoté grape produces abundantly the lesser white wines of Burgundy.

Red Burgundy and Claret are the best red wines in the world, but which is the better of the two will long be argued. The differences between them derive not only from the differences in soil, climate and variety of grape, but particularly from their methods of production. The Burgundies are left to ferment for much shorter periods, between five and eight days. Having accumulated less tannin in consequence, the Burgundies can be drunk much earlier than clarets. Indeed, the Beaujolais wines often reach their peak within a year or two of the vintage. As already mentioned, chaptalisation is widely practised and provided it is not overdone to produce fat, lazy wines, the practice can make up for shortcomings caused by climate. But, today on the market, there are 'Burgundies' which are not true Burgundies, for they are merely admixtures from Algeria and Morocco, blended by some importers with a proportion of the native stuff. Then there are countries such as Australia and Spain which make wine à la Bourgogne and style it as such. So, what with the chopping up of the vineyards in such a way that you can have many different wines being sold under the same name, however slight the difference; the chaptalisation during fermentation; and injudicious blending; the choice of a Burgundy wine is much more of a gamble than the choice of a Claret.

Nevertheless, there are great Burgundies still being produced and sold either as *Domaine Bottled* or under the name of a reputable shipper or importer. These wines are stored and matured in oak casks. Before being bottled, the wines are clarified by the use of egg whites (three to each hogshead) which in two or three weeks carry the impurities to the bottom of the casks. White wines are also clarified in this way, although some proprietors use milk straight from the farm rather than eggs. These white wines are not left in casks for so long as the red wines, being bottled after twelve to eighteen months. This practice gives fresh and fruity wines which typify the white Burgundies —many of which are the finest white wines in the world.

In the background of these generalities, it is now reasonable to discuss the wines in more detail.

Côte de Nuits. The Côte de Nuits stretches from Fixin, south of Dijon, to Corgoloin and it produces the most notable red Burgundies, the modern monarchs of the ancient kingdom. The area takes its name from Nuits-St-Georges, an important commercial and vine-growing centre. The wines take a time to develop but, when they do, they are magnificent, especially those of the *Grand Crus*, the great growths. The wines, nearly all of them are red, have an alcoholic content of not less than 11·5° G.L. Their chief characteristics are that they are well balanced, generous, full-bodied and have a fruity bouquet. It is generally agreed that the greatest of all Nuits wines come from the *commune* of Vosne-Romanée and that the best vineyards within this parish are Romanée Conti, Romanée Richebourg and La Tâche. Hereunder is a list of the famous communes of the Côte de Nuits and their most outstanding vineyards:

Communes	Vineyards
Fixin	Clos du Chapitre
	Clos de la Perrière
	Les Hervelets
Gevrey-Chambertin	Chambertin
	Clos de Bèze
	Charmes Chambertin
	Clos St-Jacques
Morey St-Denis	Les Bonnes Mares (in part)
	Clos de Tart
	Clos de la Roche
	Clos St-Denis
Chambolle Musigny	Musigny
	Les Bonnes Mares (partly in Morey St-Denis)
	Les Amoureuses
	Les Charmes (Part in Morey St-Denis)
Vougeot	Clos de Vougeot
Flagey-Échézeaux	Grands Échézeaux
	Échézeaux
Vosne Romanée	La Romanée-Conti
	La Tâche
	La Romanée St-Vivant
	Le Richebourg
	La Romanée
	La Grande Rue

Communes	Vineyards
Nuits-St-Georges	Les St-Georges
(including the wine	Les Cailles
of Prémeaux)	Les Vaucrins
	Les Porrets
	Les Pruliers
	Les Boudots
	Les Cras

The wines from all these vineyards are red wines. Little white wine is made in the Côte de Nuits but such as Musigny Blanc from Chambolle-Musigny, Clos Blanc de Vougeot from Vougeot and Perrières from Nuits-St-Georges have decidedly excellent reputations.

Côte de Beaune. Unlike Côte de Nuits, Côte de Beaune is famous for its excellent white wines as well as red ones although 80 per cent. of the production is still red. The region stretches south from Corgolin down to Chagny.

The red wines are more delicate than those of Côte de Nuits, but they have their own elegant assertiveness. Most of them are sold under the *commune*, or parish name, for example—Beaune, Volnay and Pommard, names which roll off even the English tongue. If not by the name of the *commune*, the wines are sold under the names of the particular vineyards. A fascinating establishment in this area is the Hospice de Beaune, a mediaeval Flemish-style building where, on the third Sunday in November each year, a wine auction is held.

The wines on offer at the auction come from vineyards which from time to time have been given or bequeathed to the Hospice by appreciative donors, and the proceeds of the sales go to help the old and the sick of the locality. The Hospice was founded in 1443 by Nicolas Rolin, who served King Louis XI as a tax collector. He shares with St. Matthew our forgiveness for choosing such a vexatious profession. Some of the wines offered at the auction come from excellent vineyards, not all of them in the *commune* of Beaune. Some come from Aloxe-Corton, Pommard, Volnay, Meursault and similar areas. There are about 56 hectares of vineyards belonging to the Hospice and 85 per cent. of the wine which they produce is red, the remainder white. Very high prices are fetched at the auctions, due more to the benevolence of the bidders than to the merits of some of the wines. For each lot, the bidding starts when the auctioneer lights a candle, which he douses when the lot is sold. The French and the Belgians are very prominent among the bidders but America, England and many other countries are also well represented. The auction lasts well into the evening and is the apex of three days of jollification in the town.

The finest red wines of the Côte de Beaune come from the *commune* of Aloxe-Corton; generous and well-rounded wines. This *commune* also produces one of the outstanding Burgundy white wines—Corton-Charlemagne. However, it is generally agreed that the finest of all Beaune white wines comes from the *commune* of Puligny-Montrachet, where the eight-hectare vineyard of Le Montrachet can be relied on to produce annually about a thousand cases of wine that can fairly be described as the finest dry *still* white wine in the world. It has elegance, with a certain vigour, a fine bouquet and a suggestion of almonds to the taste. The commune of Meursault also produces white wines of excellent quality.

Hereunder is a list of the *communes* as they run from north to south through the Côte de Beaune, with the names of their finest vineyards. Generally, the more southerly the vineyard, the lighter the red wine:

Communes	Colour of wine	Vineyards
Pernand-Vergelesses	Red	Iles des Vergelesses
Aloxe-Corton	Red	Le Corton
	Red	Le Clos du Roi
	Red	Les Bressandes
	Red	Les Renardes
	Red	Les Chaumes
	Red and white	Le Charlemagne
Savigny-lès-Beaune	Red	Les Marconnets
	Red	Les Vergelesses
Beaune	Red	Les Grèves
	Red	Les Fèves
	Red	Les Marconnets
	Red	Les Bressandes
	Red	Les Clos des Mouches
	Red	Le Clos de la Mousse
Pommard	Red	Les Épenots
	Red	Les Charmots
	Red	Les Rugiens
	Red	Les Argillières
	Red	Les Bertins
	Red	La Chanière
Volnay	Red	Les Caillerets
	Red	Les Fremiets
	Red	Les Champans
	Red	L'Ormeau
	Red	La Barre
	Red	Le Clos des Ducs
Meursault	White	La Pièce-sous-le-Bois and Les Perrières

Communes	Colour of wine	Vineyards
	White	Les Charmes Dessus
	White	Les Genevrières
	White	La Goutte d'Or
	Red	Les Cras
	Red	Santenots du Milieu
Puligny-Montrachet	White	Le Montrachet
	White	Chevalier Montrachet
	White	Bâtard Montrachet
	White	Caillerets
Chassagne-Montrachet	White	Part of Le Montrachet
	White	Part of Bâtard Montrachet
	Red	Les Boudriottes
	Red	Le Clos St-Jean

Côte Chalonnaise. Côte Chalonnaise takes its name from the town of Chalon-sur-Saône. Its wines are good but not great, being much lighter than those from the Côte d'Or, and their life span is also shorter. The red wines are far superior to the white wines. The principal centres are:

Rully. Rully is the centre of a district producing sparkling wine, and some decent red and white wines such as Les Pierres, Mont-Palais and La Bressande.

Mercurey. Mercurey is the best known and most productive wine district in Chalonnais, and noted for its good standard red wines. Among the best are Le Tonnere, Les Byots, Les Crets and Les Nogues. Much of the Mercurey wine is sold in Britain simply as Mercurey—a good honest blend usually of very good value.

Givry. Givry, again, is mainly a red wine area, producing lighter and less fine wines than Mercurey. The best are Clos-Saint-Paul, Clos-Saint-Pierre and Clos-Salomon.

Montagny. Montagny is a white-wine centre. The wines are ordinary rather than inspired, but such as Les Bouchots, Les Combes and Les Carlins are well thought of locally.

Côte Mâconnaise. Côte Mâconnaise is really famous for one wine only and that is Pouilly-Fuissé (pronounced *poo-ee fwee-say*). This is a good thoroughly sound light dry white wine made from Chardonnay grapes, which must be grown in the *communes* of Solutré-Pouilly, Fuissé, Chaintré or Vergisson to warrant the name. Mâcon, itself, produces red, white and rosé wines. There is nothing distinctive about them, although the red wines are seen more outside France. Generally, they are marketed as Mâcon Supérieur or simply as Mâcon Rouge, usually at a reasonable price. These wines can be drunk young, for they have a lively and fruity character.

Beaujolais. It is said that in France alone they drink twelve times more Beaujolais than Le Beaujolais can produce. The average output of Beaujolais wine is about 41 million litres, so it is not too uncommon to find some of it speaking with an Algerian or a Spanish accent. However, the genuine red Beaujolais is a delightful wine, best drunk when it is young and fresh, say two years old. Some white wine is being marketed nowadays but it is quite commonplace. Beaujolais means many things to many people. It is a name that trips off the tongue, sounds knowledgeable and sophisticated to the uninitiated. It is often derided by the wine snob and the blasé, but it is the stand-by of the expert who shows his guests his real knowledge of Burgundy wines. The best Beaujolais wines come from Saint-Amour, Juliénas, Chenas, Moulin-à-Vent, Fleurie, Chiroubles, Brouilly and Morgon. Of these, Moulin-à-Vent (windmill) and Fleurie are best known, and Morgon has perhaps the greatest staying power. Certainly, Morgon is the fullest wine.

Chablis could be called the wine of the shellfish as they complement each other so well. The wine is greenish white in colour, light and very dry, fresh and crisp to taste. Again, like Beaujolais, the 2 600 vineyards in Chablis could not possibly produce the volume of wine marketed under the name. The genuine Chablis, classified by French law of Appellation Contrôlée, is known under the following distinctions:

Grands Crus Chablis are produced from the seven outstanding vineyards of Les Blanchots, Les Clos, Valmur, Les Grenouilles, Les Vaudésirs, Les Preuses and Bougros. The vineyard of La Moutonne, between Les Vaudésirs and Les Preuses and now a part of Les Vaudésirs, is generally considered worthy of inclusion in the Grands Crus Chablis category, whose wines have an alcoholic strength of about 11° G.L.

Premièrs Crus. There are twenty-two vineyards producing wine of the Premiers Crus category, and their wines are only slightly less great than the Grands Crus Chablis. They have an alcoholic strength of about 10·5° G.L. and are usually sold with the prefix Chablis.

Chablis. The wines in the category 'Chablis' are mostly exported in barrel. Basically they include any white wine from any of the Chablis communes. The alcoholic strength is about 9·5° G.L.

Petit Chablis. Petit Chablis is the least in quality made from any grapes throughout the Chablis *communes*. Again, much of it is sold in barrel, but most of it is drunk in France. It is this wine that is sometimes blended with other white wines and sold abroad, sad to say, as Chablis.

The best Chablis wine, a truly great white wine, will mature in bottle with correct care up to ten years, but the general run of these wines is unlikely to last much more than five years.

Vintage Guide for Burgundy Wine

White		Red	
Great	Very good	Great	Very good
1947	1953	1947	1945
1949	1955	1949	1953
1952	1957	1952	1955
1959	1962	1959	1962
1961	1964	1961	1964
1969	1966	1969	1966
	1967		1967
	1970		1970

❧ 6 ☙

CHAMPAGNE

THE old province of Champagne gave its name to, and gets its fame from, the great sparkling wine it produces. Champagne, the best known of all wines, has been renowned down the centuries and, nowadays no other wine can evoke such aspirations of the 'good life'.

The Champagne country lies about 149 kilometres north-east of Paris, and the famous winefields are found in the valley of the Marne around Épernay, in the Côte des Blancs around Cramant and in the hilly country between the Marne Valley and Rheims and further west in La Petite Montagne. These last two areas are generally known as the mountains of Rheims, though they are really no more than hills. About 18 000 of the 30 000 hectares which make up all these areas are cultivated as vineyards.

Passing through this countryside, one is continually reminded of the Marne, a quiet elegant river wending itself in and out of the famous wine villages of Damery, Cumières, Dizy, Ay and Tours-s-Marne. Away from the river are the hills, always the hills. Often thickly

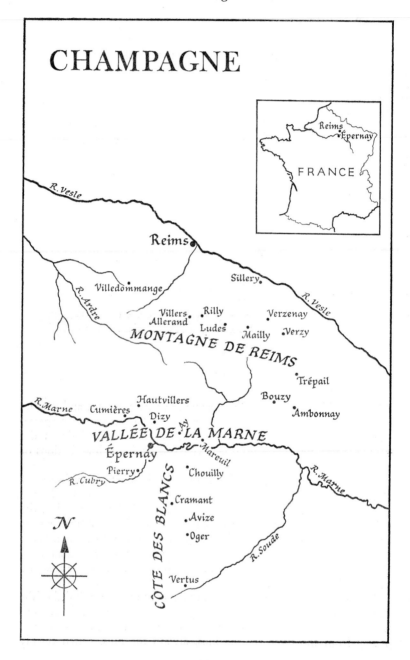

1 The vine in winter straddling the offices of a Sherry shipper in Jerez de la Frontera

3 The Pergola system of training the vines at Merano. South Tyrol

2 A landscape of vines at Bolzano, Northern Italy

5 Close-up of the terraces and the schistose soil predominant in the Douro district

◀ Terraces of Port wine vines above the River Douro

6 The Riesling vine, supported by high poles in the Moselle vineyards

7 Treating the vine with insecticides in the Côtes-du-Rhône

8 Grapes in the early stage of development being trained along wire strands in Cognac

wooded, they give solidity to the landscape and provide shelter and vegetation for the flatlands which even when not cultivated, can be richly green. Red-roofed houses, of which there are many, provide bright spots of colour and the church spires of the villages give character to the surroundings. The Route de Champagne itself is an interesting, if somewhat precarious, journey with a maze of narrow, plunging roads, pleasantly relieved at time by lengths of straight driving. The vineyards which often abut the roadside are sometimes dominated by huge buildings where the *vendangeurs* eat and sleep during vintage time. Apart from its picturesque features, the country is notable for its hospitality, for nowhere are doors opened wider than in the Champagne Houses of Épernay and Rheims.

Rheims, the panoply and glory of ancient France, is a city historically famous, but the true capital of the Champagne District—confirmed by President de Gaulle during a visit in 1963—and ten times smaller than Rheims, is Épernay. This quiet and comfortable town, on the left bank of the Marne and well stocked with deep cellars, tends to provide for the home market, although 28 kilometres of these cellars belonging to Moët & Chandon send their wines to countries all over the world. Other firms in the Épernay District, like Pol Roger, Perrier-Jouët and Bollinger (Ay) also have world-wide reputations. However, Rheims— pronounced *Rance*—provides for the commercial interests and boasts such renowned firms as Krug, Mumm, Veuve Cliquot, Pommery & Greno, the Heidsiecks, Louis Roederer and, the oldest Champagne House of all, Ruinart which was established in 1729 and which holds to this day a reputation as a connoisseur's Champagne. It is mainly in the cellars of these two towns that the delicate wines of the Côte des Blancs are blended with the wines from the twisting valleys of the Marne and the hilly slopes of the mountains of Rheims. Later we shall see that the Côte des Blancs also produces a speciality Champagne of its own, sold under the label of Blanc des Blancs—white of whites.

It is perhaps fitting that, in this District so closely associated with the history of France, Dom Pérignon (1638-1715), a Benedictine monk who for 47 years was cellarer at the Abbey of Hautvillers, carried out his famous experiments. According to legend, Dom Pérignon finding himself happily appointed as head cellarer to the Abbey, set about improving the still wine which had a tendency to sparkle in the spring. Recognising this virtue, but also noticing the wine's later tendency to become cloudy, he decided that if he could clear the wine and retain the sparkle, its quality and thereby sales potential would be increased. So he began by bottling the wines young and, aided in his blending by a highly sensitive palate and, in his bottling, by a perhaps fortuitous introduction to the Spanish cork, he was able to trap the spring effervescence and prevent the air penetrating to cause cloudiness. Prior to this, stoppers of hemp soaked in oil saved the wine from harmful bacteria, but due to their inability to seal the bottle neck hermetically, they failed to keep the air out and the sparkle in. But above and beyond all this, Dom Pérignon's greatest contribution to Champagne was in the blending of various wines according to his judgement of their vinosity, fullness, flavour, fragrance, delicacy and so on, to offer a balance of one quality against another and to emerge with a wine of all-round excellence which no wine from any particular area could give.

His own life also attained a balance, a tragic one, when his refined palate was sharpened by blindness. But we hope he could yet see, in his mind's eye, the clear sparkle of Champagne. The Abbey where all this took place is fortunately preserved by Moët & Chandon and is well worth visiting, not only in tribute to Dom Pérignon, but also for the splendid views of the Champagne countryside—hills, woods, chalky fields, busy vineyards and the long slow barges on the winding river and tributary canals.

THE COMITÉ INTERPROFESSIONNEL DU VIN DE CHAMPAGNE

To preserve the highest reputation of Champagne, strict standards and discipline, often supported by legislation, have been instituted and, since 1941, the Comité Interprofessionnel du Vin de Champagne (abbreviated as C.I.V.C.) a quasi-governmental body, has protected the interests of those involved in the production and sale of Champagne. The Committee, acknowledged by all for its sincerity in the care of the welfare and reputation of Champagne, is made up of representatives from the Champagne houses, the vinegrowers themselves and the Government and is supported by nine sub-committees which represent every shade of involvement in the industry.

The Committee's main responsibilities are:

The classification, within the delimited Champagne area of the different growths (the area was delimited by law in 1927);

acting as liaison between wine growers and Champagne firms;

fixing prices;

research and testing of new techniques and equipment;

advising vine growers on soil worthiness for the Champagne vine and other aspects of grape production;

combating parasites and aiding the fight against spring frosts which may severely damage the grape crop;

protecting the name Champagne;

promoting sales; and

social aids.

But besides the regulations and adherence to them, the factors which make Champagne so elegantly superior to all other sparkling wines are the northern climate, the soil and sub-soil, and nature of the terrain, the type of vine and human tradition and skill.

CLIMATE

The Champagne vineyards are the most northerly in all France and get no more than the minimum climatic variations necessary for the production of a grape good enough for making the wine. The average temperature is about 10° C. Winters are fairly mild, but spring is a troublesome season, with frost a great hazard. Summer is hot, usually with a generous supply of rain and autumn for the most part is fine and crisp.

Spring is an anxious time for the Champagne people and weather is their constant preoccupation. They have many interesting theories about it too, illustrated by adages such as 'Thunder in February, take your casks to the attic' i.e. you won't need them; 'Thunder in March, be careful'; 'Snow in February is as good as sheep manure'; 'Fog in March or Frost in May is very bad'; 'Rain on St. Médard's Day (8th June)—Rain for 40 days afterwards unless St. Bernabe (11th June) cuts the grass under its feet'.

But frost causes most concern. Some firms are now, at very great expense, laying pipelines through the vineyards which ignite to counteract the frost. Hail is another hazard especially when the vines have flowered, when it can be disastrous.

SOIL

The soil in Champagne is much more hospitable to the vine than to any other crop. In Roman times, when by order of the Emperor Domitian, the vines were destroyed, the grain crops which replaced them were poor. Two centuries afterwards the Emperor Probus compelled his soldiers to replant the land with vines. Great quantities of chalk or limestone are found under the topsoil of loam and gravel of varying depth. The chalk has a softness which must have made it easy initially to tunnel out of the cellars under Rheims and Épernay. Furthermore, it provides the ideal underground coolness for maturing Champagne. The natural temperature within these cellars is from 10° C. to 13° C.

GRAPES

The three successful grape varieties for Champagne are Pinot Noir, Pinot Meunier and Chardonnay. Pinot Noir is a small black grape grown mostly in the mountains of Rheims. The wine from this grape is slow to mature, but it is well rounded wine and high in alcohol. Pinot Meunier is a more robust black grape, grown in the Petit Montagne and the Marne Valley. The wine has great body and strength and is the quickest to mature. Chardonnay is a white grape grown in the Côte des Blanc. The wine takes longest to mature; it is lowest in alcohol but imparts gracefulness and elegance.

The grape breakdown within the Champagne area is 75 per cent. black to 25 per cent. white.

CLASSIFICATION OF THE CHAMPAGNE GROWTHS

The C.I.V.C. classifies each year the vineyard areas on a scale of percentage of fine quality growths. The classification (100 per cent. being the highest) is determined by previous history and the quality of the grapes at vintage time, and is reviewed annually if necessary. A typical and informative classification is that made for 1966, the most recent year of a great vintage, as follows:

GROWTH		Scale %	GROWTH		Scale %
Ambonnay		100	Brugny-Vaudancourt		86
Avenay		93	Cauroy-lès-Hermonville		81
Avize		100	La Celle-sous-Chantemerle		
Ay-Champagne		100		Noirs	80
Baslieux-sous-Châtillon		81		Blancs	83
Baye		85	Cerny-lès-Rheims		85
Beaumont-sur-Vesle		100	Cerseuil		82
Beaunay		85	Châlons-sur-Vesle		82
Belval-sous-Châtillon		81	Chambrecy		81
Bergères-lès-Vertus	Noirs	90	Chamery		88
	Blancs	93	Champillon		93
Berru		82	Champlat-Boujacourt		81
Bethon	Noirs	80	Champvoisy		82
	Blancs	83	Châtillon-sur-Marne		82
Billy-le-Grand		90	Chaumuzy		81
Binson-Orquigny		83	Chavot-Courtcourt	Noirs	87
Bisseuil		93		Blancs	88
Bligny		81	Chenay		82
Bouilly		86	Chigny-lès-Roses	Noirs	94
Bouleuse		80		Blancs	86
Boursault		81	Chouilly	Noirs	90
Bouzy		100		Blancs	93
Branscourt		86	Coizard-Joches		85
Breuil(le)		81	Coligny		85
Brimout		81	Comblizy		81
Brouillet		86	Congy		85
Broyes		85	Cormicy		81

GROWTH		Scale %	GROWTH		Scale %
Cormoyeux		83	Mancy	Noirs	86
Coulommes-la-Montagne		89		Blancs	88
Courcelles-Sapicourt		80	Mardeuil		82
Courjeonnet		85	Mareuil-le-Port		82
Courmas		87	Mareuil-sur-Ay		98
Courtagnon		80	Marfaux		82
Courthiezy		81	Merfy		82
Cramant		100	Méry-Premecy		80
Crugny		86	Mesneux (les)		90
Cuchery		81	Mesnil-le Hutier (le)		82
Cuis	Noirs	90	Mesnil-sur Oger (le)		99
	Blancs	93	Montbré		94
Cuisles		82	Monthelon		88
Cumières		90	Montigny-sous-Châtillon		83
Damery	Noirs	85	Morangis		84
	Blancs	86	Moslins		82
Dizy		95	Moussy		88
Dormans (Try, Vassy,			Mutigny		93
Vassieur, Chavenay)		81	Nesle-le-Repons		81
Écueil		90	Neuville-aux-Larris (la)		81
Épernay		88	Nogent-l'Abbesse		87
Étoges		85	Œuilly		81
Etrechy	Noirs	87	Oger		99
	Blancs	90	Oiry		99
Faverolles		86	Olizy-Violaine		82
Fèrebrianges		85	Ormes		80
Festigny		81	Oyes		85
Fleury-la-Rivière	Noirs	83	Pargny-lès-Reims		89
	Blancs	83	Passy-Grigny		82
Fontaine-Denis	Noirs	80	Pevy		81
	Blancs	83	Pierry		90
Germigny		85	Poilly		81
Givry-lès-Loisy		85	Port-à-Binson		82
Graubes	Noirs	90	Pouillon		82
	Blancs	93	Pourcy		82
Gueux		85	Prouilly		82
Hautvillers		90	Puisieulx		100
Hermonville		82	Reims (Lot Brisset)		88
Hourges		86	Reuil		83
Janvry		85	Rilly-la-Montagne		94
Jonquery		82	Romery		83
Jouy-lès-Reims		89	Rosnay		81
Lagery		86	Sacy		90
Leuvrigny		82	Sainte-Euphraise		86
Loisy-en-Brie		85	Sainte-Gemme		82
Louvois		100	Saint-Martin d'Abbois		86
Ludes	Noirs	94	St-Thierry basses vignes		87
	Blancs	86	Sarcy		81
Mailly-Champagne	Noirs	100	Savigny-sur-Ardre		86
	Blancs	86	Sermiers		88

GROWTH		Scale %	GROWTH		Scale %
Serzy-et-Prin		86	Villedommange		90
Sillery		100	Ville-en-Tardenois		79
Soilly		81	Villeneuve-Renneville		93
Soulières		85	Villiers-Allerand		90
Taissy		90	Villiers-Franqueyx		82
Talus-Saint-Prix		85	Villiers-Marmery		90
Tauxières		99	Villiers-sous-Châtillon		83
Thil		82	Villevenard		85
Toulon-la-Montagne		85	Vinay		86
Tours-sur-Marne	Noirs	100	Vincelles		83
	Blancs	90	Vindey	Noirs	89
Tramery	Noirs	86		Blancs	83
	Blancs	86	Vrigny		89
Trépail		90			
Treslon		86			
Trigny		82	MARNE (crus non côtes)		75
Trois-Puits		94			
Troissy		81			AISNE
Unchair		86	Canton de Condé-en-Brie		
Vandeuil		86	Barsy-sur-Marne		82
Vandières		82	Passy-sur-Marne		82
Vauciennes		81	Treloup Chassins		82
Vaudemanges		90	Beaulne-en-Brie		81
Venteuil		85			
Verneuil		82	AISNE (Moins les communes		75
Vert-la-Gravelle		85	ci-cessus du Canton		
Vertus		93	de Condé-en-Brie)		
Verzenay	Noirs	100			
	Blancs	86			
Verzy	Noirs	99			AUBE
	Blancs	86	Tous les crus de l'Aube		75

The percentages will be reflected in the prices and, while all farmers would like their vineyards to be on the top rung of the ladder, it is obvious that some localities are more fortunate than others in the important matters of position and soil.

CULTIVATION OF THE SOIL, CARE OF THE VINE

Work commences in the vineyards in November when manuring takes place and the earth is banked up on the vine stumps to give protection against frost. Where vines are planted on hilly slopes, holes are dug to trap the rains. The vine shoots are loosened from the wires on which they have been trained to afford easier access for pruning. In Champagne only three types of pruning are allowed; this restricts production and ensures quality. Depending on the type of soil one of the following methods is used—the Chablis, Cordon de Royat and

Guyot. The work takes place usually in March. Towards the end of March the branches are linked to the wire strands once more and the soil is levelled off.

In May the vines are sprayed with copper sulphate to prevent diseases such as mildew and oidum and to fight off parasites. When it can be afforded helicopters are used for the purpose. Also in May hoeing takes place to loosen the soil and to prevent weeds from taking a grip and stealing the precious water. Old leaves are removed and a second and third spraying take place. In June, the soil is hoed again when a fourth spraying is done. The shoots are then tied to the wire strands to support the fruit and outer leaves and thinned to enrich the remainder with sap and to allow the sun better penetration. In July and August the vines are sprayed again and the earth is hoed. In August the leaves are trimmed and in September they are thinned to afford the grapes maximum sunshine. And so to the vendange.

THE VINTAGE

Basing their judgements on the weather and the state and maturity of the grapes, with particular regard to their sugar and acid content, the C.I.V.C. decides the most favourable time for commencing the vintage. Usually the grapes are gathered during the last two weeks of September, but the harvest can be later. In 1965, for example, when the weather was bad throughout France, picking did not begin until 10th October. The grape bunches are cut off the vines with knives, scissors or secateurs, and up to 35 000 people are engaged in the work which can last from two to three weeks.

The Pinot Noir grapes are usually picked first. They are carried in baskets (paniers) to a central point where the unsatisfactory grapes are removed. This selection, known as *épluchage*, is of prime importance as grapes at peak condition only are used in the making of Champagne. The grapes are now loaded into huge wicker baskets (mannequins) of varying sizes, the ideal ones holding 40 kilos. Baskets of this size are easy to handle and when piled on top of one another do not crush the grapes underneath. The baskets are then taken in carts, with rubber wheels sprung to ensure smooth transportation, or they are taken quickly to the wine presses which are nowadays usually located within the *Champagne Maisons*. Here they are weighed and emptied into the presses, which are great heavy affairs.

THE PRESSING OF GRAPES

Each press holds 4 000 kg of grapes known as a *marc*—each marc producing 2 666 litres of grape juice equivalent to 596 gallons. In all there are four pressings but only the first three are used in the making of Champagne.

The first pressing called *Vin de Cuvée*, is the gentlest, lasts for 1½ hours and produces 2 000 litres of *must* or 2 500 bottles of Champagne. The great Champagne firms use only this for making Champagne. The next two pressings called *première taille* and *deuxième taille*—also known as *Vin de Suite*—produce a *must* of a deeper hue. This is sold to firms who manufacture less fine Champagne, which is often marketed as B.O.B. (Buyers Own Brand). After these pressings have been completed, the marc or débris is transported to a hydraulic press, located in the vicinity of the pressing house, where the last drop of grape juice is extracted. The resulting product, after fermentation, becomes a table wine and is usually given to the workers as a fringe benefit, but some is retained for distilling into Brandy, Marc de Champagne. This final pressing is called *Rebèche*.

Pressing goes on continuously throughout the day and night, the whole operation taking from two to three weeks. Because of the amount of black grapes used—as much as 3 to 1 white—care is taken to make sure that the must does not have a prolonged contact with the skins lest the wine becomes stinted, with a consequent loss of bouquet and delicacy.

FIRST FERMENTATION—IN CASK (*Fermentation de Mouts*)

Underneath each press are three vats linked by tubes. The vats are usually made of stone or cement lined with glass pannelling. Glass was first used by Moët & Chandon in 1916 and since then it has become popular because it is easy to clean and sterilise. A more recent innovation is the stainless steel vat, lined with Prodor-Glas, which is excellent but expensive to install. Each vat is labelled according to the name of the growth—Ay, Bouzy, Cramant etc. and is kept at a temperature of between 18°C. and 20°C., with complete freedom from draughts. A day or so after the *must* arrives in its appropriate vat, the natural sugar and yeast in the *must* act on each other and start fermentation. The action converts the sugar into alcohol and carbon dioxide, the latter at this stage, escaping into the air. Fermentation can last for weeks, sometimes until December, when the wine, with the approach of winter, becomes quiescent. There will be a certain loss of wine due principally to evaporation and to the racking of the wine which takes place about three times after the first fermentation. The loss is rectified by the addition of the same quality wine to the vat or cask. The wine at this stage still has a trace of sugar and has become lighter in colour.

Around Christmas the cellar doors are opened and the air allowed to circulate. This has the effect of causing the impurities—dead yeast etc.—to fall to the bottom of the vats. According to custom, the wine may or may not be racked at this stage. The changing of the wine from one cask to another is known as *soutirage*.

MÉTHODE CHAMPENOISE

The Cuvée. Champagne is not the product solely of any particular Domaine or Château. In fact a bottle of Champagne may consist of wine from the grapes of thirty-five or more different vineyards. Some of the greatest Champagne firms have no wineyards of their own and buy from the Vignerons—numbering 16 000—who, quite naturally, refuse to sell out. Each vineyard has its own attributes and is rated in excellence from 100 per cent. down to 75 per cent. as we have seen.

We know it was Dom Pérignon who conceived the idea that blending the different qualities not only improved the wine but gave interest and character far greater than if the wine were made only from the grapes of a particular vineyard. Furthermore, no firm, even the most important, uses only 100 per cent. quality grapes in the processing. Apart from economic reasons, it takes certain wines to complement others. The best firms use a minimum of 40 per cent. of top-quality grapes.

Champagne is usually made from a mixture of black and white grapes but sometimes it is made entirely from white grapes from the Côte des Blancs. These grapes on their own produce a light, elegant, yet subtle wine and the product is now being extensively promoted under the name of *Blanc des Blancs* enjoying great success on the North American market.

Before the blending of the wines, the directors and the *chef des caves* foregather to decide which wine blends best with which. The tasting of the young wines may continue for days, sometimes weeks. It is a slow process. Past records are of help but, in the end, the *chef des caves* has the last word because, after all, he is the expert. The decision made, the wines are carried by tube in the agreed proportions to huge vats powered by mixers which ensure the complete integration of the wines.

At this stage cane sugar, dissolved in old wine, is added to the blend. The amount of this *dosage de tirage*—bottling dosage—varies according to the amount of natural sugar remaining in the young wine. In a poor year, the *chef des caves* often adds old wine of high quality to the blend to give it a lift. Even in an outstanding year it is permitted to use up to 15 per cent. of older wine for the purpose. However, this is not usually done.

Preparation for the Second Fermentation. When the *Coupages* (mixings) have settled and the time is right (mysterious influences decide this, as there is a cycle when the yeasts ferments act best—it may be February, March or April) the wine is filtered to eliminate old ferments. At this time of year the Champagne wines have a natural tendency to commence a second fermentation. The tendency is given a helping hand by the addition of yeast culture, which can be purchased from the Institute Pasteur in Paris or cultivated by the firms themselves in special tanks installed on the premises. Just before bottling the yeast culture is added to the wine in vat and thoroughly mixed. The wine is now ready for bottling.

Bottling. Whatever the size, bottles must be new and perfect in every way as they have to withstand tremendous internal pressure during fermentation—up to 620 kN/m² (90 lbs per square inch)—which lasts from four to six weeks. When fermentation ends the pressure has usually fallen to 482 kN/m² (70 lbs per square inch), equivalent to an average tyre pressure of a double-decker bus.

From now onwards, the wine spends the rest of its life in its original bottle. It will, however, be corked twice—now and before the wine is offered for sale. Formerly, corks were made from the bark of the Spanish and Portuguese trees. To-day, due to the expense and scarcity of this type of cork, only the final or permanent cork is of this quality.

The First Cork. Previously corks, new or old but in good condition were used and fastened down by a metal clasp known as an Agrafe. Nowadays a polythene inlet is fitted within the bottle neck and a metal crown cap, inlaid with cork, is fastened on top. Plastic stoppers have been experimented with, but they were found to warp and loosen and to impart a flavour which spoiled the delicacy of Champagne.

The bottles are now ready to be transported to the cellars and are taken there either in baskets or by small tractors. These cellars are cool to ensure slow fermentation. The size of the bubbles is an indication— the smaller the better. The cellars are dark because the ferments within the bottles act better in darkness.

The Second Fermentation—in bottle (Prise de Mousse). The second fermentation, in bottle, lasts from three to four weeks and when it is finished the wine is Champagne with an alcohol increase of 1° G.L. acquired through the second fermentation. The wine is by now powerfully effervescent, but it is not clear, due to the presence of dead yeast cells, tannin, and other floating matter. Depending on the quality aimed at, the bottles will continue to lie horizontally—*sur lattes*—for another three to four years. Some lesser firms keep them stored like this for only one year or two years at most. In these years the wine is maturing and, from time to time, the stack of bottles are moved from place to place, the idea being to see that each bottle is shaken so as to ensure that the wine keeps in contact with those particles which give Champagne some of its special bouquet.

The Caves or Cellars of Champagne. The caves or cellars are usually low, interwinding structures carved mostly out of limestone or chalk but sometimes reinforced with brick and mortar. Dimly lit, they are rich in atmosphere and history, perhaps none more so than those of Ruinart in Rheims which are awesome in contour, in depth and in their extreme whiteness, but all Champagne cellars have their own special charm and one might easily get lost in the darkened maze. Here and there the walls are hung with plaques to Napoleon, De Gaulle, Chevalier and many others and the visitor may be told proudly and often that Napoleon visited the area five times and that he used to take Champagne and Burgundy on his expeditions. They will also tell you that, after visiting Champagne he was always successful in battle.

The cave workers are very proud of their profession which requires great skill. While attractive to some of us to see them perform, their work might appear to the casual visitor as rather monotonous. With a five-day week and eight hours a day in a cool, often damp atmosphere, their dedication, physical attributes and job satisfaction cannot be held in doubt.

Bottle Breakages. While the wine is lying *sur lattes* in the cellars, the high pressure in the bottles causes breakage of about 1½ per cent. each year. There was a time when it was actually dangerous to work in these cellars because of flying glass, especially in warm weather. Cavists were accustomed to use wire masks for protection. Now, with more precise control of yeast and sugar, before the second fermentation, breakages have been minimised.

The Remuage. When the wine has matured sufficiently or is required for sale, the bottles are given a good shaking to free the sediment and are taken to a frame known as a *pupitre*. This frame holds 120 bottles, 60 on each side, more if ½ bottles, less if magnums (2 bottles) are to be 'worked'. Here the *remuage* or riddling of the bottles takes place, the aim being to guide the sediment, which is floating in the bottle, up into the neck. The holes of the *pupitre* are of such a nature that they can hold a bottle in any position from the horizontal to the vertical.

The bottles are first placed neck inwards in the holes at an almost horizontal position. Every second day, the *remueur*, the man who performs the *remuage*, tilts the bottle 3 mm, 4 mm or 6 mm to the right and upwards until at the end of the operation, which can take up to three months, the bottles stand almost upside down. A *remueur* can attend to 40 000 bottles a day, sometimes more, giving each a little shake and a sharp twist to get the sediment moving in the right direction. In Rheims the *remueurs* favour a white mark on the bottle to indicate position, but this is dispensed with in Épernay. It is most interesting to see these skilful men at work and visitors are suffered gladly. Suffered, we repeat, because bottles nearest the passage are more difficult to control on account of the draught caused by the hundreds of people walking by each day. When the *remuage* is finished and the sediment neatly lodged within the polythene inlets in the necks of the bottles, the bottles are carefully removed from the *pupitre* and stacked upside down —*Mise en Masse*—necks fitting into punts row upon row. They are left in this position away from lights and draughts for varying times. Some firms leave them three months, others three years or more. But all keep a certain amount in this position for a long period as the wine continues to mature and keep in good condition while it stays in contact with the sediment which must later be disgorged.

Dégorgement. Apart from clearing the wine, the purpose of this disgorging is to remove the sediment with the least possible loss of wine or pressure.

Two methods are used:

(1) *à la Volée*—in full flight
If the bottles have been sealed with corks, the *dégorgeur* cuts away the steel clasp (agrafe) with a special knife and then with a pincers which looks like a lobster claw he eases the cork from the neck. The internal pressure sends the sediment flying out. If crown caps are used, the *dégorgeur* takes them off with a simple mineral water opener. In this case the pressure releases the polythene inlet which has trapped the sediment.

(2) *à la Glace*—by freezing
The bottles are placed in wire trays and immersed neck downwards in a zinc-lined tank containing refrigerated brine to about 5 cm below the cork or just below the polythene inlet, if the latter is used. They are left there for 10–12 minutes in which time the sediment freezes. Then the *dégorgeur* works as above and the sediment flies out wrapped in ice. This method is regarded as the better and it is quicker. During the actual disgorging less wine is lost—now 2 per cent. compared with up to 5 per cent. previously, and with not so much loss of pressure.

Whichever method is used, each bottle is now sniffed to detect condition and, with the aid of strong bulbs, tested for clearness. If satisfactory on both these counts, the wine is now given, depending on the country it will visit, a dosage which is called *Liqueur d'Expédition*. The purpose is two-fold—one to replenish the wine lost through disgorging, the other to add sweetness to suit the particular demand. Britain likes her Champagne *brut* or *nature*, as dry as possible, but not all countries have similar tastes. The advantage of dry Champagne apart from taste, is that defects cannot be disguised by sweetness. The dosage consists of cane-sugar mixed with the same quality Champagne. Each firm has its own recipe for the mixture which is held secret, but here is a rough guide:

Brut, Nature—Goût Anglais—very dry—up to 1% L. d'Expédition
Extra Dry	less dry—1 – 3% L. d'Expédition
SEC—Gout Americain	fairly sweet—3 – 5% L. d'Expédition
Demi-Sec—Goût Francais	sweet—5 – 7% L. d'Expédition
Demi Doux	very sweet—7 – 9% L. d'Expédition
Doux	Extremely sweet—10% L. d'Expédition

Some Champagne firms now have mechanised equipment for the whole disgorging and liquering process.

Final Stage. The wine, brought to the correct level, now gets its final cork, made always from Spanish or Portuguese cork. The name Champagne is stamped on each cork, as required by law. The bottles are passed along from the corking machine for sealing and for muzzling with wire to keep the corks in place. The bottles are washed, dried and tested and passed to a revolving machine which mixes the dosage thoroughly in the wine. After this comes a siesta of three months, to create harmony between the wine and its *liqueur d'Expédition*. Then it goes for dressing (labelling) and is once more checked for flaws. The bottles are then garbed in tissue paper and packed ready for shipment.

TYPES OF CHAMPAGNE

Super Vintage or *Tête de Cuvée* is a wine of supreme merit made from the best grapes of an exceptional year and put out under a special label, e.g. Moët & Chandon's Dom Pérignon, Ruinart's Dom Ruinart, Louis Roederer's Cristal.

The idea originated from Moët & Chandon but now most firms have a special vintage which is very expensive, is hard to come by and is usually reserved for important personages or extra special occasions. The wine can be seen in antique-looking bottles, specially labelled.

Vintage Champagne is a wine from a year when all the factors have

CYCLE OF WORK IN THE CHAMPAGNE DISTRICTS

Season	In the Vines	In the Cellars (The still Wine)	In the Cellars (The Sparkling Wine)
WINTER	Application of manures and fertilisers Pruning		
SPRING	Securing of the vine branches to the wires Hoeing Removal of the leaves from old wood Spraying with fungicides		
SUMMER	Spraying with fungicides Spraying with insecticides Trimming of the leaves Thinning of the leaves		
AUTUMN	PICKING THE GRAPES Pressing of the grapes Purging of the must	Fermentation of the musts New wines on the lees	

Season	In the Vines	In the Cellars (The still Wines)	In the Cellars (The Sparkling Wine)
WINTER		Racking Assembling together of the new wines of each vineyard Placing of a percentage of the new wines in reserve for use in the blending of future non-vintages Preparation of the Cuvées (Blends)	
SPRING		BOTTLING	Second Fermentation in bottles
DURING THE YEARS TO COME			Insertion of the bottles in the pupîtres Remuage Stacking of the bottles neck downwards Removal of the sediment The final rest period Inspection of the bottles Dressing and packing of the bottles

combined to produce grapes of perfection with the correct proportion of acidity, sugar and other characteristics. It is a wine of a single year, though 15 per cent. of a former year's wine of equal merit may be blended with it. Not all vintage Champagne is sold as such. Some of it is retained to boost a lesser year. Firms are usually reticent about declaring a vintage too early—principally for economic reasons—though they may have a good idea of the potential of the wine at harvest time. This they certainly do know in the following spring when the growths are tested for blending.

The following are some Champagne vintage years:

1900†	1933	1952†
1904†	1934†	1953†
1906	1942	1955
1911†	1943†	1959†
1914†	1945	1961†
1921†	1947*	1962
1928†	1949	1964
1929		1966*—may be the best
		1969 for 20 years
		1970

† indicates great ones
* indicates exceptional ones

It was thought 1959 was going to be a really remarkable wine but it matured slightly heavy, however, it still is a great wine.

Vintage Champagne is inevitably expensive and the purchaser is wise to reserve it for special occasions.

Non-Vintage Champagne is a blend of different years and, in relation to price, is almost the best value, provided that the bottle bears a reputable label. It is lighter on the palate than vintage which is another reason why some people prefer it.

Pink Champagne. Since the dethronement of Hollywood as the film centre of the world, pink Champagne has gone out of fashion. It used to be very popular but got a reputation as 'a woman's drink' and rather gimmicky. As a matter of fact, it is usually very good but should not be confused with other sparkling red wines. No artificial colouring is allowed in making pink champagne which is done either by allowing black grapes longer contact with the *must*, or by adding red wine to the blend.

BOTTLES

Champagne bottles are good to look at and are solid and comfortable to hold. In the early days, they were even more attractively shaped but were not practical for *remuage* or, later, for binning. They have an affinity to Burgundy bottles with, of course, thicker glass.

They come in varying sizes:

Quarter bottle or split	20 cl	(6½ fluid oz)	
Half bottle	40 cl	(13 fluid oz)	
Imperial Pint	60 cl	(19½ fluid oz)	
Bottle or quart	80 cl	(26 fluid oz)	
Magnum 2 bottles	1·6 litres	(52 fluid oz)	
Jeroboam 4 bottles	3·2 litres	(104 fluid oz)	
Rehoboam 6 bottles	4·8 litres	(156 fluid oz)	
Methuselah 8 bottles	6·4 litres	(208 fluid oz)	(1·65 gals)
*Salmonezah 12 bottles	9·6 litres	(312 fluid oz)	(2·44 gals)
*Balthazar 16 bottles	12·8 litres	(416 fluid oz)	(3·3 gals)
*Nebuchadnezzar 20 bottles	16 litres	(520 fluid oz)	(4·07 gals)

* These have not been made since World War I

Only the half, Imperial pint, bottle and Magnum go to the *pupitre* for *remuage*. Some of these when disgorged, fill under pressure the ¼ bottles and those larger than Magnums. It would be far too expensive in labour and time to put ¼ bottles through the long process of *remuage* and the large bottles would be far too cumbersome to handle.

It is considered that the wine matured in magnums is best in quality. Certainly, matured like this, the bubbles are smaller and most experts agree that this is indicative of quality. Wine filled under pressure does not hold its effervescence so long in glass and is generally considered to lose its edge through being transferred.

LABELS

Champagne labels are decorative but not loud. Besides giving the name of the firm they usually tell when the company was founded, and whether the wine is vintage or non-vintage. If a vintage wine, the year is given and whether it is *brut*, or *sec*, etc. Should the firm have royal appointment this is shown and, of course, like all French wine imported into Britain, Produce of France is indicated on the label.

WHEN IS CHAMPAGNE READY FOR DRINKING?

It takes Champagne at least two years to mature after bottling, although it is legal to sell non-vintage Champagne after one year. Champagne is at its best after three to seven years maturing. After that it is more likely to deteriorate than improve. There are exceptions, like for example old wines which are kept *surpointe* and are not disgorged until required for drinking. But, in the normal course of events, Champagne after a certain age will commence to madérize.

STORING CHAMPAGNE

Champagne should be stored at a temperature of between 10° C. and 13° C. If this is not possible it should at least be stored in the bins nearest the ground where the temperature is coolest. The storage area should be ventilated but free from draughts, strong lights and strong odours. Like all wine Champagne should be laid horizontal, making sure the wine is at all times in contact with the cork. A slightly damp atmosphere is not injurious and it helps to keep the cork full, making air penetration more difficult.

SERVICE OF CHAMPAGNE

Champagne should be served chilled. A temperature of 7° C. to 8·5° C. is ideal. People who claim that Champagne is nothing but glorified cider probably have never had the wine properly temperatured and, perhaps, drink an inferior brand anyway, but if Champagne is chilled too much it loses its bouquet and tends to get dull and lazy.

Champagne may be chilled in two ways, either by putting it into a fridge an hour before service or by placing it in an ice bucket—ice and water up to the neck of the bottle—for about half an hour before required.

In some restaurants they merely add ice shavings—which only form an igloo—a warm blanket around the bottle. The combination of ice and water is important. Apart from making the wine taste better, chilling lessens the pressure within the bottle and minimises loss from frothing over when opened.

Opening the Bottle. Champagne should be opened as silently as possible. There will be a slight pop, but if the cork flies out with a loud bang the wine has probably not been sufficiently chilled or has been carelessly handled. The bottle should be handled gently, as shaking accentuates the natural effervescence, resulting in loss of wine. Have your glass ready before attempting to open the bottle. Unwind the ring or key of the wire muzzle and take the whole lot off together with the foil. From now onwards keep the palm of your hand over the cork with a clean napkin around the bottle neck in case of accidents, stand the bottle straight. Using both hands, twist the bottle to the left and the cork in the opposite direction. When the cork begins to move, tilt the bottle to an angle of 45° and over the glass. The cork will immediately come away in the palm of your hand. Wipe the lip of the bottle and pour directly into the glass. Holding the bottle at an angle of 45° as one extracts the cork simply balances the pressure between CO_2 escaping and air entering.

Pouring. Pour against the inside of the glass as this helps to control the effervescence. Glasses should be half to two-thirds full. The void will trap the froth and the bouquet. Never add ice cubes, and swizzle sticks should never be used.

Glasses. Glasses should complement the wine they hold. Ideally they should be long-stemmed and narrow-rimmed with deep, elegant slender bowls. The old favourite, the saucer champagne glass is now out of fashion due to its failure to trap the effervescence or to concentrate the bouquet. The flute and tulip-shaped glasses meet all the requirements but, if these are not available, the ordinary 8 oz. (227 cm³ paris goblet will do very well indeed.

THE CHAMPAGNE BUSINESS

France is far and away the greatest consumer of Champagne in the world, consuming almost as much as three times the total export to the rest of the world. Since 1960 the figures for sale in bottles are:

Year	France	Others
1960	35 356 579	13 908 922
1961	38 658 873	15 528 976
1962	42 484 190	15 435 536
1963	46 831 453	17 186 806
1964	52 050 368	18 154 327
1965	58 192 955	20 428 081
1966	64 847 515	22 040 429
1967	68 562 592	24 498 455
1968	59 982 335	26 514 467
1969	67 086 841	26 896 979
1970	71 169802	31 054 288

Outside France the four greatest consumers are:

	Great Britain	U.S.A.	Italy	Belgium
1966	5 489 878	4 122 875	2 206 103	2 670 655
1967	6 249 640	4 097 155	2 835 316	2 624 144
1968	6 872 711	4 369 963	3 196 008	2 894 118
1969	5 533 566	4 286 950	3 575 170	3 163 969
1970	6 317 143	4 509 626	5 733 074	3 157 880

SOME CHAMPAGNE SHIPPERS

Épernay	Founded	Rheims	Founded
Moët & Chandon	(1743)	Ruinart Père et Fils	(1729)
Perrier-Jouët	(1811)	Lanson Père et Fils	(1760)
Bollinger (Ay)	(1829)	Louis Roederer	(1765)
Pol Roger	(1849)	Veuve Clicquot-Ponsardin	(1772)
Mercier	(1858)	Heidsieck & Co. Monopole	(1785)
		G. H. Mumm & Co.	(1827)
		Pommery & Greno	(1836)
		Krug & Co.	(1843)
		Charles Heidsieck	(1851)

ATTRIBUTES OF CHAMPAGNE

Champagne is pre-eminently the wine of celebration and festivity. Perhaps expense adds a touch of glamour but the wine's greatest attribute is that its sparkle is at once communicated to the staidest of revellers. With popping corks and the exhuberant urge of the froth to leave the bottle for the glass, the scene is set for the enthusiastic honouring of the toast and even the tolerant acceptance of the speech.

Like betting on horses, the rueful contemplation of money spent on Champagne is comforted by the memory of the gaiety. The sparkle remains as a glint in the eye to lend pleasurable endurance to the hangover. It is this effervescent delight of Champagne that gives it its characteristic value as a gentle stimulant to old age and convalescence, as the best mid-morning pick-me-up and as the accompaniment of anniversaries, opening ceremonies, christenings and weddings. Despite its reputation for these purposes, Champagne is an eminently satisfactory table wine with almost any dish from oysters to fruit. Justifiably therefore, Champagne is the King of Wines and this claim needs no other proof than its universal use for the libations poured at the launching of ships.

Note.—If the name 'Champagne' is attributed to wines from other countries mentioned in later chapters, the author will, of course, mean 'Champagne style' wines.

CR 7 CR

ALSACE

A LSATIAN wines are coming more and more into prominence
and, at last, have overcome their reputation as 'bulk' for German
wines. During the notorious occupation of Alsace-Lorraine by
the Germans from 1871 until 1918, the Alsatian vineyards were cultivated to secure the largest possible yield of grapes. Quantity took over
from quality. Since 1918, the policy has been reversed and the prolific
vines have been uprooted and replaced by more suitable species. The
Germans again interfered and during the Second World War severe
damage amounting to devastation occurred. In 1946, a fresh start was
made to make use in French style of the excellent climate of Alsace,
which allows, if properly used, the grapes to mature slowly. Although,
except for those of Champagne, the vineyards of Alsace are the most
northerly in France, the location of the vines on the eastern and
southern slopes of the Vosges mountains ensures a maximum of sunshine. The rainfall here is the second lowest in France, and it is estimated
that the mountain slopes get fifty days more sunshine a year than the
valleys. It is the special Vosges umbrella which lifts the clouds borne by
the west winds clear of the vine-covered slopes.

The vine-growing region, about 96·5 kilometres long, covers about
18 000 hectares of land on which there is a considerable variety of soils.
Limestone, granite, gravel, marl and sand are found among the com-
positions and each variation of soil is matched by the cultivation of a
suitable species of grape. The best growths of all are obtained on the
limestone slopes.

Some red and rosé wines are produced for local consumption, but
the main product of the Alsatian vineyards is white wine. Whereas
other French wines are called after place names, Domaines or Châteaux,
the wines of Alsace are named after the species of grape used in their
pressing, for example, Alsace Riesling. The principal vine species
cultivated are:

Riesling. As in the vineyards of the Mosel and Rhine valleys, Riesling
proves to be the finest species of grape for the Alsatian soil, and these

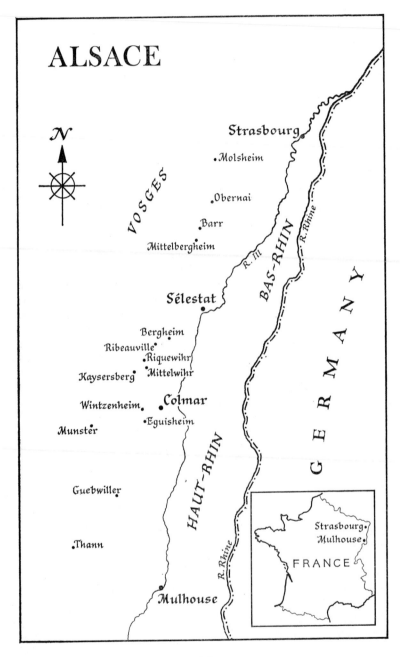

grapes make wines of excellence although limited in yield. The wines are elegant, with a fine bouquet, and are crisp, fresh and pleasant to drink. They are reasonably long lasting and have a good alcoholic content. On the table they go especially well with shellfish.

Chasselas. The Chasselas vines, also called Flambeau d'Alsace, give a good yield of grapes, which produce fresh, light and agreeable wines, akin to some Swiss wines made from the same variety of grape.

Muscat. The name of this species suggests that a sweet wine will be produced from the fruit, but in Alsace an individual wine that is dry and fruity is obtained. It has a pronounced bouquet and has a similar taste to its grape.

Pinot Blanc. The Pinot Blanc vines produce a wine that is sometimes slightly prickly and usually fairly high in acidity.

Pinot Gris. The Pinot Gris species was first imported from Hungary and is sometimes called Tokay d'Alsace, but it has been at home in Alsace since 1550. The wine is sometimes semi-sweet but always big and rich with good lasting qualities.

Sylvaner. In quality, the Sylvaner vines do not produce the finer Alsatian wines. However, the wines are refreshing, sometimes prickling and make good apéritif or light luncheon wines.

Traminer-Gewürtztraminer. After Riesling, the Traminer species of grape makes the best quality wines. The Gewürtztraminer is a variety of Traminer and its wine has gained an international reputation. *Gewürtz* means spicy and the wine is certainly that with a very pronounced bouquet, which reminds some of violets or roses and others of something very much less delicate—but the interpretation of bouquet is related to imagination. Many people, when introduced to Alsatian wines, prefer the Gewürtztraminer. It is a wine that can be enjoyed with most foods, even with curried dishes which usually destroy wines of any sort.

Other Species. The red wines of Alsace are made from Pinot Noir grapes and the rosé wine, known as Schiller wine, is made from a combination of red and white grapes. Other Alsatian wines are described on their bottle labels by Gentil, which indicates a blend of wines made from select grapes, by Zwicker, which indicates a blend of ordinary and noble grapes, and by Edelzwicker (*edel* meaning finest) which denotes a blend of noble grapes only.

In some years, when the climate has been unfavourable to some vineyards, and the grapes have not ripened sufficiently, sugaring (chaptalisation) of the *must* is allowed to increase the alcoholic content. This practice is avoided if at all possible. But if it is unavoidable the ensuing wine can only be marketed as *vin ordinaire*. Sugaring always removes the fine edges of a wine.

There is also some speciality picking of grapes, such as Auslese and Beerenauslese, in excellent years, when the grapes are left on the vine long after the normal vintage has been completed. The resultant wines are of really excellent quality with generous natural sweetness. Generally, however, Alsatian wines are either dry or medium dry. All wines produced in the specially delimited areas, provided they are made from the recognised grapes and in accordance with the true and traditional local manner (*usages locaux loyaux et constants*), are entitled to the appellation *Alsace Contrôlée*. Yet it is still the name of the grape species, Riesling and Traminer being supreme, which, along with the name of the firm that makes or ships the wine, gives the customer his best guarantee. Vintage years are also a useful guide and so is age. Alsatian wines are generally at their best when matured for from three to five years although the finer wines will keep well up to ten years.

Alsace wine labels are not complicated. The ordinary wines are usually promoted as Riesling Vin d'Alsace and the superior ones are ranked as Riesling Grand Vin, Riesling Grand Cru or Riesling Premier Cru with the best as Riesling Réserve Exceptionnelle. The ordinary wines have an alcoholic strength of at least 9° G.L., and the superior wines one of at least 11° G.L. Sometimes the name of the village and a particular vineyard is given on a label. Thus you could have, for example, Riquewihr Schoenenburg Riesling Réserve Exceptionnelle indicating in respective order the village, the vineyard, the grape and the quality.

The Alsace wineland is divided into two departments, Haut-Rhin from Sélestat to Thann and Bas-Rhin from Strasbourg to Sélestat. The Haut-Rhin produces the largest amount of fine wines with Riquewihr and Ribeauvillé as the two best producing villages. Others, like Ammerschwihr, Bergheim, Guebwiller, Eguisheim and Turckheim, produce fine wines also. Colmar is the commercial centre of the wine trade. In Bas-Rhin fine wines come from the villages of Barr, Obernai, Mittelbergheim and Kintzheim. The individual vineyards of Alsace have not been officially classified.

Vintage Guide for Alsatian Wines

White	
Great	Very Good
1947	1950
1949	1952
1953	1957
1955	1958
1959	1962
1961	1964
	1966
	1967
	1969
	1970

ᏮᏰ8ᏰᏮ
THE LOIRE

THE Loire countryside is justly known as the garden of France. The river itself, the longest in France, flows for about 1 000 kilometres from the Cévennes until it reaches the Atlantic. The vine has over 200 000 hectares of majestic homeland in this landscape of hills, châteaux, grand estates and consequential towns. Although the wines do not, perhaps, do justice to the majesty of the beautiful setting of the vineyards, they are, nevertheless, interesting in their variety and pleasing to the taste. Climatically, the area is well favoured with fairly mild winters, an adequate rainfall and long but not scorching summers. The many hills protect the vines from the cold winds, and most of the vineyards are sited on the slopes of the hills so as to obtain maximum sunshine.

Vintages usually occur late, in October sometimes November. Many Loire wines are marketed without a vintage year as they are at their best when drunk young.

As the Loire crosses twelve departments, there are great diversity in

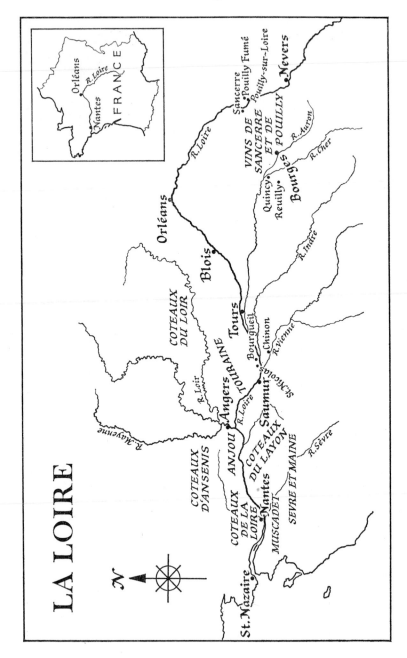

LA LOIRE

the soils of the vineyards and considerable variety in the species of grape cultivated. The principal grape species used are, for red wines, Cabernet Franc, Cabernet Sauvignon and Pinot Noir; for rosé wines, Cabernet, Groslot and Gamay; and, for white wines, Muscadet or Melon de Bourgogne, Chasselas, Chenin Blanc and Sauvignon Blanc. The vineyards of the Loire commence where the river changes its generally northerly direction to a westerly direction and it will be convenient to discuss the wines as the vineyards are reached down river.

Pouilly-sur-Loire is not far to the west of Burgundy and its important vineyards produce red, white and rosé wines. But the reputation of the district lies in one particular white wine, Pouilly Blanc Fumé or Pouilly-Fumé as it is usually called. This is made from the Sauvignon grape, which in this locality is called the Blanc Fumé grape because of the blue smokey mist reflected by the ripe grapes. Pouilly-Fumé is a delicately soft semi-dry white wine with a flinty flavour, and its name gives the knowledgeable a happy opportunity to insist that it must not be confused with the Pouilly-Fuissé of southern Burgundy.

Sancerre, in the Cher Department, produces mainly white wines, rather similar to the Pouilly wine except that they are lighter and less elegant to the taste. The best come from Sancerre itself, Chavignol, Verdigny and Bué. Bué also produces some good red and rosé wines.

Quincy. The dry white wines of Quincy have a steely flavour and it is required that they must have an alcoholic strength of not less than 10·5° G.L. to entitle them to be marketed as Quincy wines.

Reuilly lies to the south of Quincy but its white wines are very similar. Some rosé wines are also made in this area.

Vouvray, near Tours, is a very important wine centre on the Loire. The vineyards produce fairly dry or medium sweet white wines, some of which are *still*, some *petillant* (crackling) and the others *sparkling*. Most of the wine is *still*, but the area is, perhaps, better known for its sparkling wines which are made by the same method as that for Champagne.

Chinon and Bourgueil lie on opposite sides of the Loire, but they produce very similar red wines with a raspberry and violets perfume and flavour. They, along with Saint-Nicolas, are the only red wines of consequence from the Loire vineyards and are best drunk when four or five years old. They have an international reputation. Bourgueil is the more powerful wine.

Anjou. Over half the wine product of Anjou, now the department of Maine-et-Loire, is white wine, but Anjou wines to people outside France are synonymous with the pale pink slightly sweet rosé wine, the best of which is made from the Cabernet grape. Saumur is another internationally known Anjou wine, more especially the sparkling wine made by the Champagne method. Again, the area produces more still wines than sparkling wines but it is the latter that have prestige. They are sometimes sold under a trade name such as Golden Guinea. Another excellent producing area in Anjou is the Coteaux (slopes or hills) du Layon. The wines from here are generally sweet white dessert wines made from late harvested overripe Chenin Blanc grapes. The best known is Quarts de Chaume which has a beautiful flowery bouquet and is rich in alcohol. Bonnezeaux is another fine growth producing fruity, sweet white wine.

Coteaux de la Loire. The white wines from the Coteaux de la Loire are somewhat drier than the Coteaux du Layon wine, the best coming from the village of Savennières, or more specifically from the vineyards of La Coulée-de-Serrant and La Roche-aux-Moines. Although they are looked upon as dessert wines, they are not specially sweet but are full-bodied with a good alcoholic content.

Muscadet. Muscadet wines are very dry and are produced around the city of Nantes at the mouth of the Loire. These Brittany wines take their name from the grape species from which they have been pressed. They are white wines, having an earthy tangy taste, and they are best drunk young. They are very popular wines and are an excellent accompaniment to shellfish.

ᥰᥰ 9 ᥰᥰ

PROVENCE

PROVENCE wines are usually sold in attractively shaped waisted bottles with decorative labels. Unfortunately the wines do not fulfil this image of quality. Far more rosé wine is made in Provence than either red or white wine and, indeed, it is the rosé wines which uphold whatever prestige Provence wines have on foreign markets. There is a considerable diversity in the species of grape cultivated. For white wines, Clairette, Ugni Blanc, Rolle, Sauvignon and Grenache are the most popular, while Grenache, Cinsault and Mourvèdre are the principal varieties for the red and rosé wines.

The following wines of Provence are worthy of particular mention:

Bandol. The wines from Bandol are sold as Bandol or Vin de Bandol and they may be red, white or rosé. The red wines are of good quality, high in alcohol content and have a good firmness in body.

Bellet, near Nice on the Riviera, produces mostly red and rosé wines, which are very popular in their own locale.

Cassis. The rosé and white wines of Cassis have a reputation for being excellent accompaniments to fish dishes. This is fortunate as Cassis itself is a seaport located only 24 kilometres east of Marseilles, and there is plenty of fish in the Mediterranean. The white wines are considered to be superior to the rosés.

Palette. Quite good table wines, red, white and rosé, are produced at Palette which is near Aix-en-Provence. Stricter control in their production has recently been introduced and, already, there is reason to think that these wines will improve in quality.

Côte de Provence. The wines of the Côte de Provence, controlled under V.D.Q.S., are beginning to be seen on international markets. They are hardly as good as the wines already mentioned, which for the most part are drunk locally or in the cafés of Paris, but they are pleasing and attractively presented.

In conclusion, it is fair to say that the wines of Provence are never better than when consumed in their own environment—in the bars, cafés and restaurants of the Blue Riviera. Taken away from there, they become sad. Who wouldn't?

THE WINES OF THE JURA

The most famous wine of the Jura is Château-Chalon, which is a dry sherry-type wine produced from the Sauvignon grape grown in a number of vineyards situated about fifteen miles from Arbois. The vintage usually takes place in December, and, after a slow fermentation the wine is put into casks for six to eight years. While maturing in cask it develops a yeast surface similar to the Flor in dry sherries and the wine is not refreshed for at least 6 years. When bottled the wine will keep for forty to fifty years. It has an alcoholic strength of $15°$ G.L. and it is also known as Vin Jaune (yellow wine) because of its colour.

Other specialities of the Jura are the *straw wines* or vins de Paille. These are produced by drying the grapes outdoors on straw or by hanging them on hurdles in warm rooms. This evaporates some of the water and, in consequence, a deliciously sweet wine with an alcoholic strength of up to $16°$ G.L. is fermented from the grapes. Some red and rosé wines are also made in the Jura and these are often marketed simply as Arbois wine. But the wines of the Jura are generally hard to procure abroad.

THE WINES OF SAVOY (SAVOIE)

Although Savoy produces both red and white wines, it is the latter, in the Haute-Savoie, especially those of Crépy and Seyssel and Apremont, that are the more outstanding. The white wines can be still wines or semi-sparkling wines. Roussette de Savoie is also an agreeable white wine. The Chasselas and Roussette are the most popularly cultivated grape species. Of the red wines Arbin, Cruët, Montmélian and St-Jean-de-la-Porte are considered best. A little rosé wine is made in Savoy.

THE WINES OF LANGUEDOC AND ROUSSILLON

The districts of Languedoc and Roussillon form the most prolific wine-producing region of France. About 40 per cent. of the total French output of wine comes from here. The wines are generally ordinary and are used for everyday drinking by the French themselves or for blending with sundry other wines or as a base for Vermouths. They are usually called Midi wines, but within this large area, which stretches from Carcassonne to the Mediterranean Sea, there are to be found some above-average wines such as the sparkling wine Blanquette de Limoux, the table wines of Limoux, Clairette du Languedoc and Clairette de Bellegarde, which are white wines, and the table wines of Minervois and Corbières, which may be red, white or rosé.

A speciality from this district are the dessert wines called Vin Doux Naturel. These are unsweetened unfortified wines which have an alcoholic strength of not less than 15° G.L. The best-known names are Banyuls, Muscat de Frontignan, Muscat de Lunel, Rivesaltes, Maury and Grand Roussillon. They are made from overripe grapes so rich in sugar that complete fermentation is not possible, and the remaining sugar imparts their characteristic luscious sweetness. The best known is Banyuls which also produces red, white and rosé table wines. For the table wines, the Grenache is the chief grape species cultivated, and for the dessert wines, the Muscat species is the most in evidence.

MONBAZILLAC

Monbazillac is about 64 kilometres from Bordeaux and produces sweet Sauternes-type wines made from a combination of the Sémillon, Sauvignon Blanc and Muscadelle grapes. The grapes are gathered when they have reached the *pourriture noble* state and the wine, after maturing, takes on a deep golden colour. The wine is lusciously sweet and makes an ideal accompaniment to sweets and desserts.

CORSICA

Corsican wines may be red, white or rosé. The most highly regarded are Patrimonio, Borgo, Pisciatello, Calenzana and San Gavino. A feature of these wines is their high alcoholic content. Cap Corse is a famous Corsican apéritif.

THE RHÔNE

FROM Lyons to Avignon, the Rhône vineyards stretch for some 225 kilometres on both banks of the river, extending to about 10 kilometres on the left bank and about 20 kilometres on the right bank. Rhône wines are often classified as Burgundies, which they are not, although they are marketed in similar-shaped bottles. Because of their robustness and alcoholic strength, they are often described as the most masculine of French wines. In the northern part of the Rhône valley the soil is mostly granite and pebbles, while in the southern part it is mainly limestone and clay.

The climate in the valley is consistently good and for this reason vintage years have not so much importance as in other wine-growing areas. Even in winter it is seldom bitterly cold, and most of the rain falls in the spring. Summers are usually very hot and autumn is long and hot. The one great hazard for the wine grower is the mistral, the cold, dry and very powerful wind which sweeps in from the north-west. As a protection against this, cypress trees are planted and, sometimes, even the vines themselves are planted at an angle. The principal species of grape cultivated are, for red wines, Syrah, Grenache, Mourvèdre, Cinsault and Gamay; for white wines, Voignier, Marsanne, Rousanne, La Roussette and Clairette.

Some 91 million litres of wine, a good deal of it *ordinaire*, are produced a year from the Rhône vineyards, or the Côtes du Rhône, but some of them have real distinction, starting with Côte Rôtie in the north.

Côte Rôtie. It is thought by many that Côte Rôtie is the finest of all Rhône red wines. It is, indeed, excellent though not nearly so well known as Hermitage or Châteauneuf du Pape, which are mentioned below. Côte Rôtie is made from the fruits of two vines, the Syrah (red) and the Voignier (white) in the ratio of 80 per cent. red to 20 per cent. white. The wine has a beautifully rich purplish-red colour and is full bodied with a hint of raspberries in its flavour. It ages well. One time, it was customary for the wine to be matured in cask for about five years,

but, now, it is generally bottled about two years after the vintage.

Condrieu. The wines of Condrieu are white and, depending on the vigneron that produces the particular one, may be dry, semi-sweet or slightly sparkling in the fashion of the Vinho Verde of Portugal. Because of the small hectareage under the vine in this district, about 12000 bottles only are produced annually and most of this is drunk at home within a year of the vintage. If allowed to age it tends to lose the fruitiness for which it is justly popular.

Château-Grillet. With just over one hectare cultivated with the vine, Château-Grillet produces about 3000 bottles annually of full-bodied, dry, white wine. Mainly because of their scarcity they enjoy the reputation of being a connoisseurs' wine. They are certainly fashionable and they are much sought after.

Hermitage. Overlooking the riverside town of Tain on the left bank of the Rhône is the hill of Hermitage covered in vineyards. Red and white wines in the proportion of four to one are made from these vineyards. The reds are full-bodied and generous and they improve with age. The whites also age very well and are dry, powerful but mellow, with golden tinges. Some straw-coloured wine is also made, called Vin de Paille, by drying the grapes on straw mats for at least two months after they have been picked. Hermitage wines are usually categorised as Crozes-Hermitage or L'Hermitage. The latter has much more elegance than the former and are generally considered to be superior.

St Joseph. On the opposite bank to Tain is the town of Tournon, and around this town are the wineyards of St Joseph, which produce red and white wines similar to the Hermitage wines. However, the red wines have less fullness and the white wines are lighter. The wines of St Joseph are generally not so fine as those of their near neighbours.

Cornas. Cornas wines are red and, in youth, they are inclined to be rough. With age they develop a welcome mellowness.

Saint-Péray. The wines of Saint-Péray are white and may be still or sparkling. They are full, fruity and heavy and they tend to get darker in colour as they grow older.

Clairette de Die. The vine species Clairette and Muscat grown beside the town of Die contribute to produce the muscat-flavoured sparkling Clairette de Die wine. Made by the *Méthode Champenoise*, the wine is usually excellent and good value for its price.

Châteauneuf-du-Pape. Châteauneuf-du-Pape is the best known of all the Rhône wines although it is not necessarily the best wine. The vineyards are located on the left bank of the Rhône, north of Avignon, where for the most part the soil is extremely pebbly. There is a variety in the taste of Châteauneuf-du-Pape wine mainly due to the numerous species of grape allowed in the growing, 13 in all being used. The pebble or stones reflect the rays of the sun on to the grapes, which produce a wine of high alcoholic strength, usually over $12·5°$ G.L., or more consistently, 13 or 14° G.L. The selection of grapes at harvest time is strict to ensure that the pressed grapes will produce the full strong deep-coloured red wines for which these vineyards are famous. Some white wines are also made but, while they are sound and full-bodied, they are no more than curiosities in comparison with the red wines. Château-neuf-du-Pape wines bask in the attraction of their name, which stems from the time when Avignon was the Papal seat (1305-77). Clement V, the first of the Avignon Popes, was a noted wine lover and the land around the castle which he built outside the town was later planted with vines. Hence the name of the wine. Some of the better-known vineyards are Château de la Nerthe, Château Fortia, Château de Vaudieu, La Gardine, Saint-Patrice and Clos des Papes.

Tavel. The rosé wines of Tavel are probably the best-known rosé wines in the world, and to some they may also be the best to drink. But for many people they have a dry earthiness which takes getting used to. The vineyards are located in the Department of Gard on the right bank of the Rhône near Avignon. The wines have a specially beautiful rosé colour of their own, almost the colour of onion-skin. At their best the wines are fine, fresh and full-bodied.

Côtes du Rhône. Many Rhône wines are marketed under the name of Côtes du Rhône. Indeed, the appellation covers well over a hundred *communes*, some of the highest rank, throughout the Rhône valley. The wine so labelled is generally less fine and less reliable than the wines with a specific appellation such as Côte Rôtie. However, these red wines are usually good value and are particularly suitable for wine and cheese parties and similar occasions.

Although, as we have said, vintage years are not very important when considering Rhône wine the following are worth noting:

Vintage Guide for Rhône Wines

Great years   1945, '49, '52, '59, '61, '69
Very good   1947, '50, '55, '57, '62, '64, '66, '67, '70

ᚼ11ᚼ

WINES OF GERMANY

GERMANY lies too much to the north for easy cultivation of grapes in enough quantity for wine production and it is not surprising, therefore, that German wines are costly and difficult to produce. Whereas the southern lands of Europe can exploit and protect natural resources, the skill and labour of man are essential to successful vine growing in Germany.

The German vineyards, however, owe their origins to the sunnier south during the long periods when encampments of Roman legions formed an earlier 'Maginot line' for the defence of Gaul and the Empire from war-like Teutonic tribes. What more natural than that the legionaries, during the long and boring intervals between the fighting, should cultivate the vines from their homelands? But it was the Church that later moulded the soldiers' hobby into an industry from which the quality product of today has developed. From the 12th century religious orders nurtured the vines as the basis of their lay prosperity. The consciences of the dying rich and noble Germans found rest in bequeathing properties to the monastries enabling them to extend their cultivations.

In 1803, Napoleon 'secularised' the vineyards, but a perpetual reminder of the influence of the Church is seen in many of the names of vineyards such as Jesuitengarten (Jesuits' Garden), Kloster (Cloister), Johannisberg (St. John's Hill), Karthäuserhofberg (Carthusian Castle Hill) and many others. We can hazard a guess that the soldiers were keen on quantity and the monks on quality. Both succeeded but the minimal cost of their labours, presumably limited to participation in their products, cannot be found in secular industry.

Many of the vineyards are situated on hillsides or steeper slopes where no mechanical aid can operate. The soil itself is often hard and slatey, and to safeguard the vines, terraces have to be built and maintained to prevent erosion by rain and wind which would otherwise wash or blow away the earth from the roots. Most of the vineyards are on slopes facing south to trap the sunshine, and where this is not possible they face the west where at least they have the advantage of the occasional afternoon sun. Some vineyards are just patches, but others are considerable in size. They are all well tended with characteristic attention to detail. So, although Germans seem to be more at home with a tankard of beer than a glass of wine, it is obvious that there is a great feeling for wine and an even greater determination to produce a reliable and individual product.

There are in Europe more than six million hectares of land under the vine, of which only 0·8 per cent. are in Germany. France has 35 times this amount, Italy 34 times. But, lacking in quantity, Germany is justifiably famous for its quality white wines. The United Kingdom and the United States of America take more than 50 per cent. of the export, each sharing the consumption about equally.

And the German wineland is beautiful too—dominated by two rivers, affectionately known as Father Rhine and Mother Moselle. The Rhine with its choppy waters is the more impressive, grand and big in every way. Its waterways are always busy carrying barges as well as more luxurious craft. Castles of incredible architecture look down from vine-covered slopes, while below, almost at the river's edge, are the wine villages—so picturesque that they might well have been the inspiration for Grimm's fairy tales. The Moselle on the other hand is a shorter, narrower and more winding river than her spouse. It is less busy commercially and its hillsides are steeper. The soil in its valley is harder and the vegetation less green. But, with its own characteristics, it is not less beautiful, and it also has its castles and intriguing villages. Indeed, the view from the village of Ürzig looking down on to the vineyards and the river is perhaps the most spectacular in the whole German wine land. In summer, the banks of both rivers are popular with hikers and camping enthusiasts and the flags of the various nationals in residence with their multi-coloured tents make a fine contrast to the green background.

THE GERMAN WINE DISTRICTS

Wine is made in many parts of Germany, but the principal districts are:

a) The Rhine and its tributary the Nahe. The wines from these districts are called Hocks in the English-speaking world. The name came from the town of Hochheim on the river Main. Queen Victoria in her day favoured the wine from this town. Consequently its popularity increased so much that the demand could not be met from Hochheim and the name was extended to include any Rhine wine.

b) That from the Moselle and its tributaries, the Ruwer and Saar.

c) The Franconian or Steinwein.

d) The lesser wines of Württemberg-Baden.

e) The river Ahr.

GERMANY

N

WEST EAST
GERMANY
Cologne
Frankfurt
R. Moselle
R. Rhine

chheim
R. Main
Frankfurt
FRANCONIA

inz
ubenheim
ackenheim
ierstein
ppenheim
RHEINHESSEN
ntersblum
Würzburg

Worms

Mannheim
R. Neckar

R. Rhine
WÜRTTEMBERG~
BADEN

*To Bodensee and
Switzerland*

Climate. The German vineyards are the most northerly in the world and often suffer from an overabundance of rain and insufficient sunshine. They are also liable to severe frosts, especially in May, and to hail-storms. Summers are short and the sun, when it can be felt, is often obscured by the perpetual haze particularly prevalent in the morning and early afternoon. Along the Moselle, slates are built around the vines, not only for protection, but to store the sun's heat and to reflect it on to the grapes. The soil itself is of course slatey. These slates are so essential that whenever they are washed away by heavy rains or destroyed by heavy winds they are quickly replaced from a nearby quarry. In years when the weather is unfavourable and the grapes have not ripened sufficiently, a green and acid wine results, and some growers are obliged to add sugar before or after fermentation, to the *must* or to the wine. This sugaring, known as *Chaptalisation* in France, has been made legal in Germany (German Wine Law, Art. 3 (25 July 1930)).

Sugaring may only take place between 1 October and 31 January, and it is illegal to re-sugar a wine. These wines are known as *improved wines* or, in German, *Verbessert.* They can never be great wines because there is always a certain harshness about them. The opposite is *Naturwein*—a natural wine.

A new German wine law covering broader aspects of viticulture and nomenclature has been under discussion for some time. However, its promulgation has been delayed because of the adviseability of conforming with certain aspects of the general wine law of the Common Market, which has not yet been finalised. The purpose of the new law will be *to protect the drinker of German wines.*

Soil. Generally the soil in German vineyards is so poor that no other crop would flourish. Made up of decomposed granite, slate, sand, clay loam or limestone or a combination of these, it requires much 'working'. The soil is heavily manured about every three years and fertilised in between times. In the Moselle district, friable slate is predominant, and on the sheer, almost perpendicular slopes, preparing the vineyards is a treacherous occupation. In some vineyards, at vintage time, the descent is so steep that the baskets of grapes have to be eased down by ladder.

Grapes. More than 30 different types of grapes are used for wine-making, but the important varieties are: the Riesling, Sylvaner, Traminer, Müller-Thurgau and the Pinot Noir (for red wines). The Riesling is the classic. Although it has a small yield, it ripens late and it is susceptible to frost. Its grapes are small too, but its wine has fine body and bouquet. The Moselle and Rheingau favour this species. The Sylvaner yields larger grapes and bigger crops. It is popular in the

Palatinate, Rheinhessen and Franconia, but it lacks real finesse. The Traminer is no longer in favour as it does not ripen until very late. It is grown in some parts of the Palatinate and Franconia, but its vines are no longer being replanted. The Müller-Thurgau (Riesling crossed with Sylvaner) is a fairly new grape and about 20 per cent. of the German vineyards are under this vine. It has a good yield, it ripens early and it produces a light agreeable wine which is best drunk young. The Pinot Noir, or Spätburgunder, is a thoroughbred vine from Burgundy or Champagne and the grape is used for making red wine.

Some other grapes in German vineyards are—Ruländer (Pinot Gris), Elbling, Scheurebe and the more recently introduced Würzburg Perle. Hard experience determines the most suitable method of training the vines. Moselle vines are trained to two metres high or more on single poles—while the Rhine vines are kept closer to the ground and trained on wire strands. All these vineyards have known the disease *Phylloxera* and are also susceptible to *Oidium* and Mildew. Many other vine diseases, including the insect pest *Cochytis*, can cause havoc to an already precarious industry. Government inspectors are always available to advise on the prevention or cure of these diseases.

The Vintage. The gathering of the grapes takes place usually late in October or early November. It is generally so cold at the time that the workers need to wear gloves for protection. Before the vintage, a strict guard is kept on the vineyards and no unauthorised person is allowed to visit them. A Commission in each area with the aim of securing the best vintage sets a favourable day for beginning the picking of the grapes. This Commission is guided by the weather forecasters for it is imperative that the grapes are free from dew or rain when gathered. Each morning the chiming of church bells signals that picking may commence, and in the evening that work must cease. There is great refinement in the harvesting of German grapes. Besides the normal picking there are variations as follows: *Spätlese,* which is the picking of some grapes after the normal vintage to ensure ripeness; *Auslese,* which is the gathering of selected special bunches of grapes; *Beerenauslese,* which is the gathering of specially selected over-ripe grapes; and *Trockenbeerenauslese,* where the grapes are left on the vine until they have shrivelled almost to raisins. This last variation results in the evaporation of up to three-quarters of the water-content of the grapes bringing the harvest down to a small and expensive production. This process is the equivalent of *pourriture noble* at Sauternes and is known in Germany as *Edelfäule.*

Another harvesting process, special to Germany, is that of Eiswein (ice-wine) which was introduced in 1842. The grapes, completely ripe, are left to be attacked by frost which freezes the water within the grapes. The remaining juice is then more concentrated and of course very rich in sugar. The grapes are picked and pressed at a maximum temperature of − 6°C. (21·2° F.) and the result after fermentation and maturing is a delicious but expensive wine. This wine is not produced often, perhaps on average once every ten years, but it has been made more frequently lately.

The Making of the Wine. Table wines are made in Germany in much the same way as throughout the rest of the world allowing of course for local conditions and traditions. Nowadays German wines, except for the classical ones, tend to be bottled between six and eighteen months after fermentation. The method of production is briefly as follows: the grapes are pressed usually by hydraulic presses and the *must* or grape juice is separated from the skins, stalks and pips before fermentation commences. The fermentation takes place in huge glass-lined or stainless-steel tanks. In January or February, the wine is transferred or racked into wooden casks, where it is left to mature. The wine may be racked twice again, but finally it is passed through sterilisation filters. These filters are a relatively recent innovation and they have effected a great improvement on the previous systems. They have the advantage of being able to clear the wine at cellar temperature; they exclude harmful bacteria and germinating fungi; and they ensure that the wine does not change its nature by the application of heat as in pasteurisation.

Labelling of Bottles. The German labels on wine-bottles are for some the most informative, and for others the most intimidating. The simple ones usually have the following details:
1) The name of the town or village in adjectival form, e.g. *Winkeler*;
2) the name of the particular vineyard, e.g. *Hasensprung*;
3) The name of the grape from which the wine was made, e.g. Riesling;
4) the vintage year, e.g. 1959; and
5) the name of the shipper, e.g. Deinhard & Co.

The complex may have additional information such as *Naturwein* (natural wine, no sugar added); *Spätlese, Auslese,* etc. (how the grapes were gathered); *Wachstum* or *Gewächs* (growth of) followed by the name of the owner of the vineyard; *Original Abfüllung* or *Original Abzug* (original bottling by the owner of the vineyard); *Schloss Abzug* (Castle-bottled, i.e. equivalent to the château or estate-bottled tag for French wines); *Kabinett* (the proprietor's special reserve); *Fuder No., Fass No.* or *Stück No.* (cask number); *Feine* or *Feinste* (fine or finest); and

Echt (genuine). The new Wine Bill when it *becomes law* will affect some of this terminology.

THE WINES

Rhine wines—Hocks—are usually marketed in tall slender-necked brown (amber) bottles. These wines come from four district regions— Rheingau, Rheinhessen, Rheinpfalz (or Palatinate) and the Nahe Valley.

Rheingau. This classic area produces the finest of Rhines, full of bouquet, body and finish. They require long maturing before they develop their true refinements and they have considerable lasting power. The region extends from Lorch to Hochheim and among its most famous wine villages are the places given in the following list, with some best vineyards indicated in parentheses:

Assmannshausen—Noted for its red Assmannshausen Höllenberg which is regarded by many as the best red wine in Germany;
Rüdesheim (Schlossberg, Burweg);
Geisenheim (Rothenberg, Steinacker)—Here also is located the renowned Viticulture School and Research Institute;
Johannisberg (Schloss Johannisberg, outstanding, and Klaus Johannisberg);
Winkel (Schloss Vollrads, outstanding, Winkeler and Hasensprung).
Oestrich (Lenchen, Doosberg);
Hattenheim (Steinberg, outstanding, and Mannberg);
Hallgarten (Schönhell, Jungfer);
Erbach (Markobrunn, an outstanding reputation);
Eltville (Sonnenberg, Frienborn);
Rauenthal (Baiken, outstanding, and Gehren);
Hochheim (Domdechaney, Kirchenstück).

Wines from Lorch, Bacharach, Kaub and Boppard *may* also be classified as Rheingau wines although they lack the fine finish associated with other Rheingau wines.

Rheinhessen. The province of Rheinhessia from Bingen through Mainz and on to Worms, on the opposite bank of the Rhine to Rheingau, produces a vast quantity of wine most of which is good rather than great. The pedigree stretch of vineyards lie between Mainz and Worms, known as the Rhinefront, although Bingen produces good wines with a characteristic smokey taste, such as Schlossberg, Scharlachberg and Rosengarten. On the Rhinefront, Bodenheim has quality vineyards like Westrum and Burgweg. Further along is Nackenheim, well represented by Rotenberg and Engelsberg. Then to the renowned Nierstein home of Rheinhessia's best vineyards such as Rehbach, Glöck, Auflangen, Hipping and the generic Domtal. Oppenheim has Sackträger, Goldberg and Kreuz; and Worms is associated with

Liebfraumilch. Originally Liebfraumilch was a wine produced around Liebfrauenkirche (Church of Our Lady) in Worms. Nowadays it may be applied to any decent wine from any of the Rhine vineyards or from a blend of some of them. Today, however, there are three protected Wormser wines—Liebfrauenstift, Liebfrauenstift Klostergarten and Kirchenstück. Liebfraumilch is indeed a popular wine in Great Britain, but it is to German wines what Beaujolais is to French—of varying qualities. It is wise to look for a registered trade name such as Hanns Christof (Wein), Blackfriars or Blue Nun. Ingelheim, between Bingen and Mainz, is the red wine district of the Rheinhessen.

Rheinpfalz or the Palatinate. In contrast with most German vineyards, the vines of the Palatinate are generally planted on level ground, many sited on the foothills of the Haardt Mountains. The climate here is more favourable for the cultivation of the vine than elsewhere in Germany, and consequently the area produces a milder, more mellow, less acid and more luscious wine, although it never attains the finesse of the Rheingau wines. The region extends from Bockenheim to Glasweiler and is divisible into three—Upper, Middle and Lower Haardt. Only the Middle Haardt produces fine wines. The best come from Deidesheim, Först, Königsbach, Ruppertsberg and Wachenheim; while Dürkheim (red and white), Gimmeldingen, Haardt, Kallstadt, Mussbach, Neustadt, Niederkirchen, Ungsein and Winzingen are also noted for good wines. Perhaps the Förster vineyards of Jesuitengarten and Kirchenstück are best known abroad, but many feel that the finest Palatinate wines come from Deidesheim, such as Grain, Hohenmorgen, Kisselberg and Leinhöhle.

The Nahe Valley. The Nahe, west of Rheinhessia, lies between the Rhine and the Moselle—as do its wines in the matter of taste, though some may have more affinity to the Rheingau than to the Moselle. The light elegant wines from the Nahe valley mature quickly but lack depth in flavour. The most famous is undoubtedly Kupfergrube from the village of Schloss Böckelheim, but Niederhäuser Hermannshöhle from Niederhausen and Galgenberg from Bad Kreuznach are also outstanding. Norheim, Roxheim, Mönzingen and Bad Münster, also, produce some excellent wine of their type.

Moselle Wines. The Moselle wines are usually marketed in green or blue-green bottles and the category of Moselle also incorporates the wines of the Saar and Ruwer. The Moselle meets the Rhine at the Deutscher Eck (German Corner) in Koblenz. On its way it passes many great vineyards, the best being along the Middle Moselle between

Trittenheim and Zell. The wines are less in alcoholic content than those of the Rhine, rarely exceeding 10° G.L. Moselle wines are usually dry and flinty with a tendency to effervesce (*spritzig*). They also have a powerful bouquet and, mostly, can be drunk in abundance without ill effect. The most famous of all Moselle wines come from the Berncasteler Doktor vineyard, now divided into three and owned by Deinhard & Co., Dr. Thanisch and the Lauerberg Estate respectively. The name originated in 1360 when the Archbishop of Trier, Boemund II, was supposedly cured of a dreadful fever by drinking the wine. Restored to health, he is said to have exclaimed, 'This wine, this *doktor*, has cured me'. The wine was further popularised by the personal physician to King Edward VII who had, it seems, an appreciation of the wine as a medicine. Besides Berncasteler wines, which have the generic name of Berncasteler Kurfürst, the Middle Moselle produces an abundance of fine wines from the places given in the following list, with the names of some of the best vineyards given in parentheses:

Trittenheim (Laurenziusberg, Neuberg; Altärchen);
Niederemmel (Taubengarten, Lay);
Dhron (Rosenburg, Roterd);
Neumagen (Engelgrube, Rosengärtchen);
Piesport (Goldtröpfchen—an outstanding vineyard, the name meaning 'little gold drop');
Brauneberg (Juffer, Falkenberg);
Kues (Weissenstein, Herrenberg—these vineyards are just across the bridge from Berncastel on the left bank and, indeed, are often coupled with Berncastel wines);
Graach (Himmelreich, Domprobst);
Traben-Trarbach (Schlossberg, Halsberg)
Wehlen (A classic area which produces the famous Wehlener Sonnenuhr— Sonnenuhr means sundial and there is a beautiful old stone sundial situated among the vines. The vineyard is owned by a number of proprietors. The wine can be even more expensive than Berncasteler Doktor);
Zeltingen (Schlossberg, Himmelreich);
Erden (Treppchen, Herrnberg);
Ürzig (Kranklay, Urlay);
Kröv (Steffensberg, Nacktarsch);
Enkirch (Steffensberg, Edelberg) and
Zell (Zeller Schwarze Katz, Klapertschen).

The Saar Wines. The light wines from the Saar valley are noted for their steely flavour and are made mostly from the Riesling grape. Perhaps the best wine of the district is Ockfener Bockstein from the village of Ockfen. Other villages (with the names of some of the vineyards in parentheses) are Ayl (Kupp, Herrenberg); Wiltingen (Scharzhofberg, Scharzberg); Kanzem (Attenberg, Hörecker); and Oberemmel (Rauler, Agritinsberg).

The Ruwer Wines. The Ruwer wines, although generally inclining towards acidity, can be elegant and good when conditions have been favourable. The main villages and vineyards are Kasel (Nieschen, Hitzlay); Avelsbach (Herrenberg, Oberherrenberg); Eitelsbach (Karthäuserhofberg, Sonnenberg). All these produce wines of quality. The Moselle equivalent to Liebfraumilch is Moselblümchen.

OTHER WINES

Ahr Valley. The River Ahr is a tributary of the Rhine and its valley produces about equal quantities of red and white wines. The reds are considered to be the better, especially the Ahrweilers-Daubhaus and Rosenthal and the Walporzheimer-Honigberg. The vineyards of the Ahr valley are the most northerly in the world and their wines are generally thought to be very ordinary.

Württemberg-Baden. These South German wine areas near the Swiss frontier produce mostly for home consumption. Their red, white and rosé (Schillerwein) wines are little known abroad. Stuttgart is the commercial centre of this area's wine industry but, although it has its own vineyards, most of the wine is produced in the valleys of Enz, Jagst, Kocher and Rems. Baden is a prolific wine-producer, the most interesting wines coming from around the shores of Lake Constance (Bodensee). There is a speciality wine made here—a white wine with faint red tinges—called Weissherbst.

Franconia. Opinions vary about the attractions of Franconian wines or, as they are popularly known, Steinwein. Some think that they are among the finest white wines in the world. Others say that the best thing about them is their beautiful flagon-shaped bottle known as Bocksbeutel. The wines are produced in and around Würzburg on the River Main. They are made from Riesling and Sylvaner grapes and have an earthy taste. The wines keep well and, while they may be compared in some respects to Moselle wines or even to a French Chablis, they are of a much hardier nature. The outstanding wines are Würzburger Stein and Würzburger Leisten, and to a lesser degree the wines from Escherndorf and Randersacker. Klingenberg am Main produces a red wine which is among the best in Germany.

Sekt. The sparkling wines of Germany, both red and white, are called 'sekt' or 'Schaumwein', and they are made throughout the wine-producing areas. In 1826, the Germans began to make sekt around Württemberg and since then the industry has flourished. While it could not reasonably be compared with Champagne, the best of it is made by *Méthode Champenoise*—second fermentation in bottle. A great deal, especially for home consumption, is made by the tank or Charmat method described in Germany as Grossraumgärverwahren Schaumwein. By this method the second fermentation is in a closed tank, from which the wine is filtered and then bottled under pressure. Some firms use a third method whereby the second fermentation still takes place in bottle, but rather than go through the long process of Remuage (described in the chapter on Champagne) the wine is emptied under pressure into a tank where it marries with the correct proportions of sugar and brandy—liqueur d'Expédition—and finally runs through a filter into fresh bottles.

Sekt wines are usually left to mature for from one to three years. While they are sometimes elaborately labelled, they are often marketed simply as sparkling Hock, sparkling Moselle and so on.

GERMAN BRANDY

Brandy in Germany is called *Weinbrand* which means 'burnt wine'. Much of it is made from imported wine and is distilled after the fashion of Cognac. Asbach is a particularly good style of German brandy.

Vintage Guide for German Wines

Great	Very good
1949	1952
1953	1955
1959	1957
	1960
	1961
	1962
	1964
	1966
	1967
	1969
	1970

❧ 12 ☙

SPANISH TABLE WINES

I T has been estimated that for every seven bottles of wine drunk in
Great Britain one of them will be Spanish. Spain produces over 2 250
million litres of table wines each year and of these some 180 millions
are exported. The great virtue of these wines, in terms of value for
money, is their relative cheapness. They are never great wines, but they
are rarely disappointing either. Although justifiably popular, they
somehow have a public image of being second class. They are regarded
as synonomous with 'plonk', with cooking wine, with wine cups, with
bottle parties, and so on. Rarely are they offered at a good table or,
if they are, they are usually disguised in brilliant decanters. One of the
reasons for this is the senseless promoting of these wines as Spanish
Burgundy, Spanish Sauternes, Spanish Chablis and so on. Imitation in-
vites comparison and these wines do not match up at all to their alleged
French counterparts, and they do not resemble them in quality or style.
Consequently, the lover of French wines is usually sceptical about self-
confessed substitutes and the general public is misguided. However, if
one is a bit adventurous in purchasing, one can be well rewarded.
Because of the sunny constancy of the climate in Spain, vintage is not
an important consideration. Indeed, dates on Spanish wine labels are
notoriously unreliable and they may have nothing at all to do with the
year of vintage. But, as a guide, *cosecha* denotes a vintage year, *reserva*
a wine of some age and *gran reserva* a wine of considerable age. The
chicken-wire on some Spanish bottles was originally put on to prevent
interference with the labels.

THE WINE DISTRICTS

Rioja. Rioja wines are the best known of all Spanish table wines. They
take their name from Rio Oja, a little river west of the town of Haro.
This river joins the River Tirón near Anguciana and the Tirón in its
turn joins the Ebro. The Ebro passes by the finest of the Rioja vineyards,
which are divided into those from the Rioja Alta, and those from the

SPAIN

F R A N C E

GALICIA
RIBERO

Bilbao
Haro Logroño
R.Oja RIOJA
R.Ebro
Saragossa
Perelada

CATALONIA
Barcelona
Sitges
Panades
Tarragona

TRAS OS
MONTES
Peñafiel
R.Duero
Salamanca

Madrid
R.Tajuña

GALICIA

R.Tago
Toledo

Valencia

PORTUGAL

ESTREMADURA

LA MANCHA
Valdepeñas

MURCIA
Alicante

Córdoba
R.Guadalquivir
Montilla
Moriles
Seville
ANDALUSIA
Santúcar de
Barrameda
Puerto de Santa María
Jerez de la Frontera
Gibraltar
Málaga

Cartagena

N

Rioja Baja. The Rioja Baja vineyards produce wines with more alcoholic content than the Rioja Alta, but the latter produces wines of finer quality. Red, white, rosé and sparkling wines are made in Rioja, but it is the red variety which is the standard bearer, carrying the Rioja reputation—a justifiably high one. Rioja red wines are matured for quite a time in cask. If they have any affinity with French wines, it is perhaps with the Rhône wines. The Tempranillo, Garnacha and Graciano grapes make the best of the red wines, while the Viura, Garnacha Blanca and Malvasia grapes make the best white wines. The towns of Haro and Logroño are the commercial centres, and the best-known producers in the area are the Marqués de Riscal, the Marqués de Murrieta, Federico Paternina, Bodegas Franco-Españolas, Bodegas Bilbainas, Bodegas Palacio, the Compañía Vinícola del Norte de España and the A.G.E. Bodegas Unidas.

La Mancha. The best wines of La Mancha are the Valdepeñas, both red and white. The red is the more popular, it is sturdy and fruity, although sometimes because of its lack of acidity it can taste flat and dull. The grapes used for the red wines are the Garnacha, Cencibel and Tinto Basto; and those for the more popular white wines are the grapes of the Airen, Pardillo and Cirial varieties.

Málaga. Málaga produces a sweet fortified dessert wine that is made from a combination of the Pedro Ximénez and Muscat grapes. Fermentation is stopped at an early stage by the addition of grape spirit. Also added to the make-up is *vino tierno*, a sweet wine made from dried-out grapes, and boiled down grape juice called *arrope*. In days gone by, Málaga wine was popular in England where it was known as Mountain, but nowadays Málaga has gone out of favour. The better Málagas are matured by the solera system.

Catalonia. Besides the Tarragona wines mentioned below, Catalonia produces the red Alella wine and the white Casteli del Remy. Panadés is a centre for sparkling wines, where a good brandy called Mascaro is also produced. The popular tourist resort of Sitges produces an attractive dessert wine from the Malvasia grape. There is also a very interesting wine museum at Villafranca del Panadés.

Tarragona. Tarragona wines, both red and white, are essentially fortified wines made after the fashion of port wine. In fact, they have been described as the poor man's port and they used to be found on foreign markets labelled as Tarragona Port. English law has long since prohibited such description. The Garnacha and Picpoule red grapes and the Malvasia, Macabeo and Muscatel white grapes are in most general use in this region. Tarragona nowadays is very likely to be an unfortified oversweet red wine of questionable quality.

Alicante. Alicante red, white and rosé wines are produced in abundance and are sometimes sold under the appellation 'Montana'. The red wines, especially, are vigorous wines, made principally from Monastrel grapes. They have a strong alcoholic content and they age well. At one time there used to be a port-like Alicante wine imported into England called Tent, made from the Tintilla grape.

Valencia. The Valencia wines are often sweet. The best-known wine of the district is Benicarlos, a Castellón robust red wine. The red wines of the Utiel-Requeña also have a good reputation, but they are inclined to be too sweet. The principal grape species are Monastrel, Garnacha and Bobal.

Córdoba. The Province of Córdoba is synonymous with the wines of Montilla-Moriles—wines which must be *elaborado* or made in the towns or villages of Montilla, Moriles, Lucena, Cabra and Puente Genil to entitle them to be sold as Montilla-Moriles. They are made almost entirely from the Pedro Ximénez grape with some slight additions from the Moscatel and Lairén species. While they have a certain affinity in style with some Sherries they are not always fortified. To be sold in cask they must have at least one year's maturation and have a minimum alcoholic strength of 15° G.L.; wines sold in bottle have a minimum of 16° G.L. alcohol. Montilla-Moriles wines are not matured in casks as in Jerez or in huge wooden vats as in Rioja, but in enormous stone jars called *tinajas*. These are of Roman amphora shape, narrow at the base, then bulging outwards three-quarters of the way up, and narrowing again at the top. The jars are much taller than a man, being some one to three metres high and made of earthenware. They are built into the site and hold anything from 2 500 to 5 000 litres of wine.

THE SPARKLING WINES OF SPAIN

Since a famous legal decision in 1961, the Spaniards can no longer market their sparkling wines as Champagne. The best Spanish sparkling wine is made by the *Méthode champenoise*, i.e. a second fermentation in the bottle. The wines of Codorniu from Panadés and of Perelada from the Costa Brava are best known.

The Brandies of Spain. Brandy in Spain is often sold under the name *Coñac*, but it is nowhere near as good as the Cognac of France. Apart from Mascaró and Torres of Panadés, nearly all the good Spanish brandy is made in the Sherry district of Jerez de la Frontera. The more reputable brands are Lepanto, Insuperable, Veterano and Fundador.

ᏩᎦ13ᏩᎦ

SHERRY

IN the Province of Cádiz in Southern Spain, between the river, Guadalete and Guadalquivrir, lie some 10 000 hectares of undulating vineyards, encircling three centres—Sanlúcar de Barrameda Puerto de Santa María and the famous Jerez de la Frontera. From this area, Sherry, a fortified wine of historical and international repute, is produced. Unless 'Sherry' is made from the grapes of these vineyards, it is masquerading under a false description. In this connection, it may be of interest to record that, in the now-famous court case in London in 1967, brought by the Spanish shippers, Mr. Justice Cross ruled that the word 'Sherry', by itself, means only the wine from the Jerez de la Frontera area of Spain. But he also ruled that the products called British Sherry, South African Sherry, Australian Sherry, and Cyprus Sherry may continue to be so described because of the long period of time that these expressions have been used. He stated, however, that they are not Sherry and may not be called simply 'Sherry'. The hearing, which lasted twenty-nine days, involved forty-six witnesses and more than £100 000 in costs.

Through the ages, Jerez has known Phoenicians and Romans, Visigoths and Moors. In fact, the word Sherry is a simplification of Sherrisch the old Moorish name for Jerez. Restored to the Christians in 1264, Jerez helped to hold the frontier against the Moors for another two centuries, until the final liberation of Spain. In recognition, King Don Juan I, on 21 April 1380, bestowed the addendum—of the frontier—to Jerez.

During all the years of these exciting times, the vine continued to be cultivated and, from about the 12th century, Sherry wine has been the most important factor in the economy of Jerez and her two sisters. Jerez, the main centre of commerce, naturally attracted most of the merchant traders, many of whom settled and made their home in the locality. Some of these traders or shippers were British or of British origin—not surprisingly because, by the middle of the 14th century, England had become the largest consumer of Sherry in the world, sometimes taking as much as 90 per cent of the total exports; and

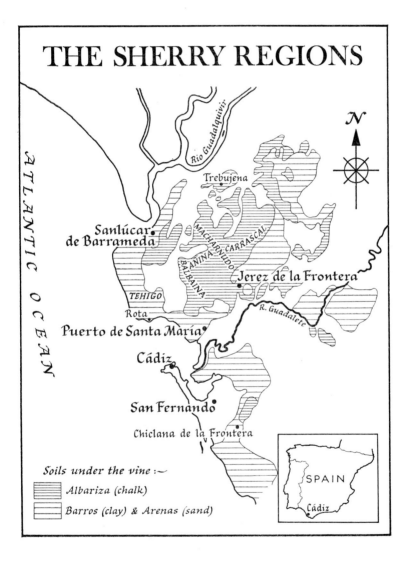

THE SHERRY REGIONS

Rio Guadalquivir

Trebujena

ATLANTIC OCEAN

Sanlúcar
de Barrameda

MACHARNUDO

CARRASCAL

BALBAINA

Jerez de la Frontera

TEHIGO

Rota

R. Guadalete

Puerto de Santa María

Cádiz

San Fernando

Chiclana de la Frontera

Soils under the vine :—

Albariza (chalk)

Barros (clay) & Arenas (sand)

SPAIN

Cádiz

England has remained its most loyal patron ever since. The renowned Manuel Ma. González Gordon of González Byass, author of a most authoritative book on Sherry, *Jerez—Xerez—Scheris*, stands as the courteous representative and the sagacious repository of these traditions.

Jerez (pronounced Hereth) is today a delightful city of cobbled streets, whitewashed façades with wrought-iron balconies and interesting alleyway markets. Orange trees abound along the sidewalks and every now and again one comes across intriguing little *tascas* (bars) where the locals eat their *tapas* (appetising morsels, mainly shellfish) and drink their very pale, very dry Sherries, known as *Finos*. Most of the proprietors promote one brand of Sherry and extensively advertise that fact in typically colourful Spanish style. And in and around the City are the famous Bodegas, huge, high, thick-walled, arched cellars or warehouses, where Sherries are matured and blended. Built high, they provide the coolness necessary for the proper maturing of most Sherries.

González Byass, one of the major Sherry shippers, have recently built a three-storey, temperature-controlled *Bodega* for the maturing of *Finos*. This is the largest *Bodega* in the world, with a capacity that can hold 29 000 butts—a butt holding 490·7 litres. However, before the wine comes to the *Bodegas*, there are many operations which should be understood and recorded, for Sherry is not simply the product of grape spirit added to fermented grape juice. The process involved is a long one.

CLIMATE

The area around Jerez has a yearly rainfall of about 635 millimetres less than 10 per cent. of which falls during the summer months. The heat in summer is torrid with the temperature often rising to 43° C. It has even been known to escalate to 46° C. in the shade. So before the rainy season commences, the Jerezanos have to take steps to conserve the rains, which when they do arrive, in late October—early November, fall like a deluge. For healthy vines, it is essential that the roots get adequate moisture throughout the year. The operation called *Deserpia* ensures this. In early October a square metre of soil is dug down towards the roots of each vine and the spare soil made into a rim around the square or serpia. When the rain comes, it lodges within the rim and later seeps through to be stored in the loose soil underneath. Through regular tilling, the soil is kept loose and porous and it is a remarkable fact that during the hottest weather, cool and moist soil is to be found under the baked soil on top. A tribute to inventiveness and care.

SOIL

Basically there are three types—*Albariza, Barros* and *Arenas*. Of the three *Albariza* is the most important. Outstanding in appearance, it is white in colour, resembling that of the Champagne area in France. It is found principally on the upper slopes of the vineyards, its composition being calcium carbonate (about 80 per cent.) and clay. The name comes from *albo* meaning white. *Albariza* produces, without question, the best grapes for Sherry and, indeed, the finest Sherry, 'Jerez Superior', is made exclusively from grapes grown on this soil.

The second type is *Barros* which is rich in iron and often has a reddish appearance. Normally clayey and darkish to look at, its composition nevertheless includes about 30 per cent. calcium carbonate. While this soil is generally found in low-lying areas it can also be found side by side with the *Albariza*, even on the upper slopes. Grapes from this soil produce good but not great wine.

The third type is *Arenas*. The yield per hectare from this soil is considerably more than that from the other two. However, while the yield is high, the quality is not as good, and, in fact, it is no longer in general use for the cultivation of the wine. It is sandy in appearance and softer in texture than the *Albariza* or *Barros*.

GRAPES

In olden times, grapes of many varieties were grown in this area. To-day only two are used for the making of Sherry—the *Listan Palomino* and *Pedro Ximénez*. The *Palomino* is the classic and indeed up to 90 per cent. of the total vines in Jerez are of this variety. The grape is medium-sized, white, sweet and low in acidity. Pedro Ximénez grapes are slightly smaller, golden in colour, and produce an extremely sweet wine which is used principally for sweetening Sherries. In the 16th century, a German soldier called Peter Siemens, brought this species of vine into the country. Hence the name.

ENEMIES OF THE VINE

The main ones are *Oidium* and *Mildew*. The former effects the shoots of the vine, the latter the leaves and fruit. Sulphur and copper-sulphate are the most successful treatments. Of course, like most other wine-growing areas, this district was devastated by the vine louse, learnedly and politely known as the *Phylloxera vastatrix*. The attack here came in 1894. As a remedy, American root vines, immune to the *Phylloxera*, were imported for grafting purposes. The plant that came from America was called *Vitis riparia*. Nowadays, there are areas in Spain which specialise in the cultivation of the American vine to meet the demand within the country for *Phylloxera*-resisting roots.

In new vineyards, grafting is done in August but, if this graft fails, grafting is tried again in February. In spite of this there has been no decline in quality or change of type but the life of the vine has been shortened from an expected 75 years or more to a maximum of 30–40 years. *Phylloxera* is still prevalent in the soil and a Spanish vine, planted without grafting, will die within two or three years.

CULTIVATION OF THE SOIL, CARE OF THE VINES

Work in the vineyards is continuous. The only respite is during the rainy season when the elements are on the side of the cultivator and his workers. At the present time very important changes are taking place in the vineyards of Jerez. Machinery has been introduced to aid the ingenuity of man. Tilling and hoeing of the soil is done by tractors and treading of the grapes is giving way to mechanised presses. It is an expensive transition, costly to the grower and, if it were not for extensive planting of new vineyards it could deprive workers of their normal livelihood. Although the tractor can till and hoe, it requires more room to manoeuvre than man and this means a certain land wastage. However, where formerly it required ten men to work an hectare of soil in one day, now a man and a tractor can complete the work of ten hectares in one day.

Another important recent innovation by some cultivators is the use of wire instead of staves for supporting the vines. Two or three strands of wire, over 30 cm apart, are strung between poles forming a fence on which the vines are trained. Gone is the monotonous labour of fixing the staves but, again, the new method is expensive to introduce. The wires are, of course, much more reliable and require less maintenance. The staves need manual planting, regular inspection, adjustment to hold the vines and grapes and, after the harvest, collection and storage. The wire fences can be left without fear of rot and have proved a great boon in labour saving. But the principal advantage is that the new fences allow the sun better access to the leaves giving increased sugar content to the grapes, resulting in greater alcohol potential.

The culture of the vine starts in October after the earlier vintage has been completed. The staves are taken out of the soil and piled into bundles. Then the *serpias* are made ready for trapping the rains. Where tractors are used, large indentations are made in the soil, especially on the slopes, similar to the old *deserpia*, and mounds are formed to prevent the rains from coursing down into the plains.

Meanwhile manuring has begun and this continues until December. Normally the vines need manuring once in four years. The practice is to treat a quarter of the vineyard each year. Where the crop has been unrewarding more frequent attention is given; the treatment being a mixture of horse manure and fertiliser.

Pruning commences in December. A vine with two arms or branches will yield good grapes but, by pruning one, the other will produce grapes of superior quality. In the following year, the branch which has been pruned is allowed to grow and the previous year's producing branch is, in its turn, treated in the same way. Thus the strength and sap of the vine is fed into one branch. The pruning continues into January when the workers, hands sometimes protected with mail-coated gloves, strip the useless and old bark from the trunks. This prevents parasites from nesting on the vines and from breeding offspring to feed on the new leaves and budding fruit. The war on parasites in this prolific climate is waged continually throughout the year.

In February the earth is tilled to a depth of 20 cm. Sometimes there are rains in March which percolate through the softened earth. Now the mounds around the *serpias* are flattened as the leaves begin to appear. Until August the vines are, from time to time, sprayed with copper-sulphate and, with tractors and their accessories in use, the vineyards give the impression of lying in dense fog. In May the vines start flowering and during this month and the next the operations known as *castra* and *recastra* are carried out by expert workers. These entail the pruning of useless buds to prevent a drain of strength from the remainder.

Early June is usually the time when the grapes begin to form and, until the harvest in September, weeding is continuous for weeds steal the precious water so necessary for the vines. In July the earth crust is pressed firmly downwards, to conserve moisture in the soil. August sees the new vineyards being prepared and the grafting of the Spanish on to the American roots. These vines will need to be tended for four or five years before they produce a grape of satisfactory quality. When the vines reach this age, they can be expected, given normal conditions, to yield from 6 000 to 12 250 kilos of grapes per hectare which, at 700 kilos of grapes for each butt of Sherry, represents some ten butts per hectare. The same vines, when they reach ten to twenty years, will produce 14 800 to 17 300 kilos per hectare, representing some eight to ten butts.

Vendange

In Jerez, the gathering of the grapes normally begins in the first fortnight in September, depending on the weather and the condition of the grapes. Within these two weeks a day is set for the picking. Sometimes it coincides with the Feast of the Nativity of the Virgin Mary, which falls on 8 September. A token pressing of the grapes is made in public in honour of the patron Saint of the Vintage, San Ginés de la Jara. This is a time for great revelry and the celebration of the Vintage Fête—*la Fiesta de la Vendimia*—is eagerly looked forward to by young and old. However, there is no fixed regulation about the date of picking for if the Agricultural Engineer, the heads of the firm and the vineyard manager feel that their particular vineyards are ready, they decide to start the Vintage. The picking lasts for about twenty days with people from the countryside converging on the Sherry areas to offer their assistance. These include the Gypsies, who, in their flamboyant fashion, contribute to an atmosphere of gaiety and lightheartedness. With knives to cut and *canastas* or *tinetas* to carry the bunches of grapes, work is soon well under way. Full baskets are carried to a central point where unsuitable grapes are removed. Piled into panniers on mules, they are transported to the *Almíjar*, the yard in which grapes are placed on mats to dry. Or, if the grapes are picked in the vicinity they are carried there, shoulder-high, in baskets by the pickers. The *Almíjar* is strewn with esparto grass mats, where the *Palomino* and *Pedro Ximénez* grapes are left to dry. The drying of the *Palomino* grapes is allowed to continue for from twelve to twenty-four hours, to enable the skin moisture to evaporate. While the drying of the *Pedro Ximénez* continues much longer, the duration can vary from ten to twenty days, depending on weather and the strength of the sun. These grapes are stacked in much smaller quantities than the *Palomino* to allow better access to the sun and to enable them to be dried almost to the consistency of raisins. Ultimately, the juice from these grapes will be tremendously sweet and the ensuing wine used to sweeten the dry wines of Jerez to suit world taste and demand. At night-time all these grapes are covered to prevent damage from falling dew.

PRESSING

The grapes are now ready to be pressed—there are two methods used:

    1. The oldest and still some think, the best way is as follows: The

grapes are put into *lagars*, wooden troughs about 9 square meters. These troughs are tilted to allow the grape juice to flow to a spout into tinas or tubs and, from these containers, into casks. In the *lagars* two, three or four men (*pisadores*) tread the grapes. They wear specially studded boots called *zapatos*, boots with nails so positioned that they puncture the grapes and free the juice, leaving everything else intact. The treaders also use wooden shovels to aid them in their work.

2. Recently mechanised presses have come into vogue but not without severe criticism. It was felt by many authorities that, for the finest Sherries, grapes should not come into contact with metal and it was argued further that presses, by their nature, could crush stalks, skins and pips, thereby releasing too much tannin. However, in spite of this and the long history and traditions of the *Zapatos* method, mechanised presses are fast gaining in popularity, to such an extent that some wine-growers are now establishing them in the vicinity of the *Bodegas* and transporting the grapes there for pressing. Furthermore, it has been proved that these presses, when lined with stainless steel, produce a *must* of equal or even better quality than has been known with the old method.

THE THREE PRESSINGS OF THE GRAPES

The first pressing is called *Yema*. The grapes are broken into pulp and a few handfuls of *Yeso*, Gypsum (calcium-sulphate), are scattered over the mass. This operation is called 'plastering'. Sometimes the procedure is omitted altogether, depending on the area in which the grapes are grown. As the treading continues, the must is run off and transferred to waiting butts. The butts are filled, leaving a 15 per cent. ullage, and taken immediately to cool *Bodegas*. The *must* from this first pressing produces the finest Sherry.

The second pressing, called *Aguapié*, produces juice from the pulp of the first pressing and makes less fine wine. In the centre of each *lagar* is a tall iron screw about $2\frac{1}{2}$ metres high. After the first pressing, the pulp is stacked around this vertical thread and bound with an esparto grass tape. Heavy wooden blocks are placed over the tightly bound pulp and pressure from the two handled screw releases the juice.

In the third pressing, called *Prensa*, the juice is extracted by an hydraulic press, the pulp being again collected and squeezed to the limit. The wine from this latter pressing is sometimes distilled into Brandy or made into vinegar.

It was the custom to start pressing in the cool of the evening so that fermentation would not start too soon but nowadays, with modern transport to take the juice quickly to the *Bodegas*, the men work by shifts throughout the day e.g.:

Unit 1 works from 8 a.m. to 12 noon; from 4 p.m. to 8 p.m.
Unit 2 from 12 noon to 4 p.m.; from 8 p.m. to 12 midnight.

FERMENTATION

Within a day after the arrival of the *must* at the *Bodegas*, a tumultuous fermentation occurs within the casks, due to the action of yeast on sugar which converts the latter into alcohol and carbon dioxide. So fierce is the action that the grape juice seems to boil. This first fermentation lasts for four to seven days and, when it ceases, a slower fermentation occurs which continues for two or three months. They have a saying in Jerez '*El día de San Andrés, el mosto vino es*', meaning that on the day of St. Andrew (30 November) the must becomes wine. Not entirely true of course, because a slow fermentation with Sherry usually continues through December.

FLOR

With the arrival of spring, *Flor* (flower) which is the yeast growth that appears on Sherries, generally starts to develop on the surface. *Flor*, which is native to Jerez and sometimes to the Arbois district of the Jura mountains in France, looks like an off-white scum forming a crust on the wine. This crust can be 5 mm thick or more and appears stronger in spring and autumn. After a time it dries and sinks to the bottom of the cask but more forms to take its place. *Flor* needs air to live which is the reason why an ullage is left between wine level and bung. It gives Sherry some of its most distinctive characteristics.

In January, when the wine has become clear (or fallen bright), the first classification is made—this classification is for quality. Each shipper has his own method and mode of operation. Hereunder is one method used. Experts, using a *Venencia*, an implement having a long whale-bone handle with a slim silver or stainless steel container at one end, extract through the bung hole of each cask a sample of the wine. Mainly by smell, they classify the wine as under:

First Classification

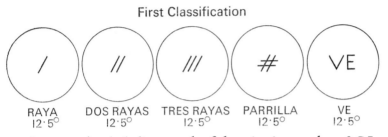

RAYA	DOS RAYAS	TRES RAYAS	PARRILLA	VE
12·5°	12·5°	12·5°	12·5°	12·5°

At this stage the alcoholic strength of the wine is around 12·5° G.L. The / stroke is found to be the best and as much as 85 per cent. of the total can come into this category. It gets top rating because it is considered likely to develop into a *Fino* or *Oloroso* of top quality which are the most highly prized in the region. It is then racked by transferring into clean but mature casks. The alcoholic strength of this wine is now raised, by the addition of grape spirit to 15·5° G.L., taken to a cool *Bodega* and left for one year.

The // stroke indicates a secondary type wine, which does not, in the experts' opinion, make the best quality Sherry. So, at this stage the *Flor* is prevented by increasing the alcoholic strength up to 18° G.L. *Flor* can grow on Sherry from 15-16° G.L. alcohol. This wine is now known as Raya and taken to the Raya Bodegas to mature. For some time it is left, by some shippers, in the open air as it matures better and faster in conflicting temperatures. Seldom sold in its own right, it is used as a blender. It has good body but lacks refinement.

The /// stroke is deemed unsuitable for making Sherry. It is put aside and later distilled into high- or low-strength alcohol which is eventually used to fortify the Sherries of the future or aged for Brandy, in its own right after distillation.

The # Parrilla is used for distillation (Burning) or washing the lees out of casks. The VE sign indicates that the wine is only suitable for converting into vinegar.

At this stage, all these wines are vintage wines—wines of one year—and are termed *Añadas*. The word is derived from the Latin *annus* (year) but later we shall see there can be no such thing as a vintage Sherry. While all the qualities of the first classification receive due attention when appropriate, the first quality wine receives the attention of a spoilt child. At the end of a year in cask, this first quality wine is again classified for type when it can be determined with some conviction, what the final type of the sherry will be.

Second Classification

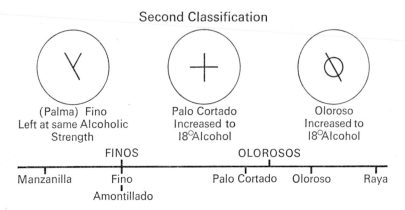

(Palma) Fino	Palo Cortado	Oloroso
Left at same Alcoholic Strength	Increased to 18°Alcohol	Increased to 18°Alcohol

FINOS   OLOROSOS

Manzanilla	Fino	Palo Cortado	Oloroso	Raya
	Amontillado			

Although there may be some reassessment of categories during the next couple of years, this is not due to error in the original classification but to the unpredictable variations which may take place in casks during maturation. By and large, however, the wines tend to remain true to their second classification. For the next two years or so, the wines are nurtured in their appropriate *Criadera*—the nursery for young wines—then, after final assessment, they are taken to be matured through the casks or scales of the *Solera*.

SOLERA

The *Solera* may be likened to a school, where the wine from the nursery is introduced to the first grade and is gradually promoted until it graduates as the final product. In the tiers or casks of the *Solera*, the entry classes are at the top and the graduating classes at the bottom. This is a system for regularly blending young wines with old so that eventually a consistent standard for any particular Sherry is obtained. The casks are placed on top of one another, usually three or four tiers or scales high, but according to facilities and the custom of the particular house, there may be more or fewer scales. Four tiers are best from the operational point of view. The operation works like this—wine for exportation is syphoned out of the bottom scale, which in fact is the *Solera* proper, (*Solera* comes from the word *suelo* and means the butt nearest the ground)—and the ullage is then made up with wine from the second scale. The cellarman makes sure in so doing that part of each butt in the second scale goes into each butt of the bottom scale. The system is continued from the third to the second scale and so on with new wine coming in to make up the ullage in the top scale. Wine is extracted three or four times each year but, to maintain quality, **no** more than two-thirds of the bottom scale is taken each year which amounts to a varying percentage of the *Solera*'s total, depending on the number of scales. When transferring Fino wine from one cask to another care is taken to extract the wine from underneath the *Flor* yeast without disturbing the *Flor* itself. For that matter, such care is always taken when extracting from or adding wine to casks. In these circumstances, wine is always treated with the utmost gentleness.

Now is a good time to mention the various types of Sherry, all of which have been through the *Solera* system since they were classified.

GROUP NO. I—FINOS

Manzanilla. This is a very pale and very dry Sherry, made at Sanlúcar de Barrameda. It is the driest of all Spanish wines and improves with age in firmness and flavour. It has a delicate taste, leaving a slightly salty/bitter aftertaste. It is possible that the sea winds may account for this as Sanlúcar is situated on the Atlantic. The wine is very dry indeed which may be why it has not become popular in Britain. Although it is an elegant wine it is rather delicate and has a reputation for not travelling well. Some people claim that it loses its quality and flavour when shipped abroad but if the wine is in good condition and is carefully bottled in Spain, it will travel with fortitude to any country, whatever the climate, whatever the distance.

The soil in the area of production can be a mixture of *Albariza*, *Barros* or *Arenas*. It is light in colour and brittle in consistency. The *Palmas* are *Finos* from Jerez and Puerto de Santa María and according to body are marked *una* |- *Palma*, *dos* |= *Palmas*, *tres* |= *Palmas* and *cuatro* |= *Palmas*. These wines are dry, without bitterness in aftertaste and are perhaps the favourites where Sherry is produced. Pleasant to smell they are clean on the palate and, although delicate, they are by no means slight. In Spain they drink their *Finos* much drier than we do. It is an ideal apéritif wine and the taste is improved when served chilled, not frozen. The renowned Tio Pepe is an excellent example. *Fino* wine is the wine on which the *Flor* has grown thickest during maturation and it is this *Flor* that gives it its pungent yet delicate flavour. *Flor* feeds on the alcohol but the strength of wine in casks is not diminished because in Jerez water evaporates through the wood at a faster rate than alcohol. *Finos* are always matured in the coolest part of the *Bodega*.

Amontillado. Briefly, *Amontillado* is the name given to *Fino* Sherries when they have lost, due to age, the delicate character of the *Finos*, and have acquired characteristics of their own. It possibly got its name because as it lost its *Fino* character, perhaps it resembled certain wines from Montilla. It is an extension or continuation of the *Fino* and is not always the product of design, that is to say a *Fino* sometimes becomes an Amontillado and nobody can give a reason for the change. Usually, however, if a *Fino* is left a long time without being refreshed by younger wine, it is possible that it will become an Amontillado. With age, Amontillado Sherries become amber in colour and develop body and a somewhat nutty nose. It is by nature a dry wine but, according to taste and demand, shippers may add a little sweetness. It is better served slightly chilled and is ideal with a biscuit at eleven or as an apéritif or with the soup and fish course, if it is dry.

Nowadays Amontillado is a misnomer as it is used to describe all pale sherries which are full bodied or not too dry.

GROUP NO. 2—OLOROSOS

Palo Cortado. This wine comes between the Amontillados and the Olorosos. It is nearer to the Olorosos, to which it has a great affinity especially regarding palate. However, it has the aroma of the Amontillados. It can best be described as the most delicate of the Olorosos. According to body, they are given the following markings by way of classification; *Un CORTADO* $+$, *Dos CORTADOS* $\neq$, *Tres CORTADOS* $\not\equiv$, *Cuarto CORTADOS* $\not\equiv$. This is a wine not often seen on the British market.

Olorosos. In Spain *Oloroso* is a full-bodied dry wine which leaves a suggestion of sweetness on the palate. It is a more golden in colour than Amontillado and its aroma is less than a *Fino*. Outside Spain one may find it deep brown in colour due to the addition of *Vino de color*. All the Cream and Amoroso Sherries that we know are, in fact, Olorosos which have had sweetening and colouring added to give them the sweet, smooth taste and rich colour, which is popular in England today. Another wine in this category is the 'East India'. This got its name from the time when casks of Sherry were used as ballast on sailing ships bound for the East Indies. It was thought that the slow rocking of the boat aged and improved the wine. Certainly the access to clean fresh air would be an advantage because Sherry thrives on it and this is the reason why *Bodegas* are located away from the roads and traffic and are enclosed by thick high walls and surrounded by gardens in the effort to keep the air as pure as possible.

East India Sherry is now a thing of the past because vibration from the engines, heat and the limited space available in the hold of modern ships no longer make it a practical and economic proposition.

9 A tonelero at work on a Sherry cask (butt)

10 Sauternes grapes in the later stage of ripeness. This is known as *pourriture noble* (noble rot)

11 Wine press lying idle awaiting the *vendange*

13 Carrying the grapes up to the collecting centre near Funchal

12 Gathering Madeira grapes grown over high trellises

14 A Champagne wine press being packed with grapes

15 (*Left*) A *remueur* at work in a Champagne cellar (*Right*) The *dégorgement* to clear Champagne free of sediment

16 Soleras of Sherry casks in the modern bodega of González Byass

These then are the various types of wine, but, of course, there are many variations of each type. Each winegrower or shipper has his own variations and blends; for example, the firm of Gonzalez Byass makes 32 brands of Sherry but they all stem from the two main types—*Finos* and *Olorosos*.

SHERRY AILMENTS

On occasions, some Sherries develop sickness of one sort or another and must be attended to, otherwise the wine becomes undrinkable. The most serious ailment is acidity, which can be developed by the vinegar microbe through over-exposure to air. The addition of alcohol normally detains this.

Another ailment is cloudiness. This is found especially in *Finos*, when minute flecks of the *Flor* are still in evidence. Fining, the process for clearing wines, cures this.

Oiliness. This often disappears of its own accord but should it not, the cure is to air the wine—pouring it out of and back into the same cask—and then filtering it.

FINAL STAGES

Usually Sherry is not sold until it is between 5 and 7 years old. A good *Fino* takes 9 years to mature. When the wine is syphoned off from the bottom scale of the *Solera* there are certain operations which must be affected before it is fit for the customer'. All these operations take place *after* Sherry has been through the *Soleras*. These may include: sweetening, addition of colour, blending, fining and filtering.

Sweetening. The wine from the *Pedro Ximénez* grapes is used for sweetening. These grapes, because they have been left to dry on the esparto mats until they become like raisins, produce a luscious *must* when pressed. The sugar content of these grapes is so high that only partial fermentation is possible, therefore the *must* remains sweet. The wine is blended and matured through its own *Solera*. While this wine is sometimes sold under its own label as a liqueur wine, its real purpose is that of sweetening other Sherries, because all other Sherries, due to complete fermentation, are dry. There is one exception—*Dulce.* This is got by running freshly pressed *must* into barrels already containing enough alcohol to detain fermentation. Once initiated in this way the sugar content is preserved. It is called *extinguished must* (*Mosto Apagado*).

Colouring (Vino de Color). All Sherries are naturally inclined to be pale in colour, they become darker through age or by the addition of *Vino de Color.*

Color is got by taking *must* before it commences fermentation, putting it into a large copper boiler and placing it over a gentle fire. Before and when the liquid comes to the boil, it is constantly stirred and skimmed so that all impurities are removed. As the boiling continues, the *must* is reduced in quantity to one-fifth of its former volume for *Arrope* and to one-third for *Sancocho.* At this stage the *must* is almost black and it is gradually removed from the fire so that the liquid cools gently. During the process of boiling, care has to be taken that the liquid does not get singed or burned. This is blended with fresh mosto and fermented and later blended into Sherry in very small amounts to obtain the correct shade.

Now it will be decided whether the alcoholic content is sufficiently high. If not, it must be increased to the required level. Sherries for sale usually have an alcoholic strength of between 16 and 20° G.L.

Blending. The *Solera* system of blending usually does a superb job but, occasionally it is decided that certain casks lack character and depth in flavour. To counteract this, a small amount of wine is drawn from a special *Solera* and blended with the wine in these casks. This *Solera* can be a hundred years old or more, into which, at many years interval, specially selected new wine is added, to make up for the loss due to evaporation. On its own this wine is undrinkable because it has in fact become a wine essence but add it to any other Sherry and it works wonders on its behalf. However, this wine must be used with great discretion, because of its value and strength of flavour.

Fining and Filtering. Fining always takes place, also filtering if the Sherry is to be exported in bulk or bottled. Fining is the operation that clears the wine of any impurities, which may still be floating about. In Jerez this is done with the aid of egg-whites and a special absorbative earth from Lebrija, a town which is located about eighty kilometres north of Jerez. When the wine settles it is racked off, usually into a cask, but sometimes into a tank, and filtered.

CASKS AND BOTTLES

The wine is now put into fresh casks or directly into bottles. If it is to be exported, it is usually shipped in casks.

Casks. All the great Sherry firms have their own workshops for making casks. Oak is the recognised wood, and the best type of oak mostly comes today from the New Orleans districts of America. The wood is imported in bulk and made up by expert workmen called *Toneleros*. These coopers are a tightly-knit guild and the sons of employed fathers get first option when jobs become available. America, however, can no longer supply sufficient oak and nowadays Spanish oak is also used. This is not as satisfactory as it is more porous resulting in greater waste of wine. Even with the American oak a wastage of 5 per cent. can be expected during all the processes because of evaporation from the bung, left open or loosely fitted, to enable air to enter freely. Access to air is necessary for Sherry, although this would turn other wines into vinegar. Over the years the satiated casks assist in the maturing of the Sherry; indeed, when seasoned they are sold to distillers for the maturing and colouring of whisky.

Bottling. Bottling of Sherries was not generally favoured in Jerez until the end of the 19th century. Now all firms sell their special brands in bottles. Jerez has long had a factory for making bottles, and recently another was built by some of the Sherry firms to meet increasing demand.

SHERRY BUSINESS

There are two types. The first when firms cultivate and market their produce under their own label as proprietary brands—example, Tio Pepe, Alfonso, González Byass, Dry Sack of Williams and Humbert and Long Life of Garvey etc. The second, when an importer asks for a special blend to be made up to his own recipe and requirements for him to sell in his own country under his own label. All Sherry firms are glad to do the second type of business under contract, and indeed it makes up a considerable part of their business.

ATTRIBUTES OF SHERRY

There is a Sherry for all occasions—with a biscuit for elevenses, before a meal as an apéritif, as an accompaniment for the various courses throughout the meal, with the Sweet Course (Cream or Brown Sherry), as a liqueur (*Pedro Ximénez*) after the meal. It is also the greatest hospitality drink, often the saviour of a dull parlour or conversation. No other wine is as useful in the kitchen for its flavouring qualities. Because it is a fortified wine, it lasts for weeks after the bottle is opened whether decanted or not. It is an acceptable drink for persons of all ages and tastes. Unlike other wines its flavour is not impaired by tobacco smoke. Its quality remains consistent in all climates.

SERVICE OF SHERRY

In England, most homes have their Sherry glasses varying from cocktail glasses to small tumblers, some of them even in coloured and ornamental glass. There is an attraction in pretty glasses that should not be criticised, but for real appreciation of Sherry, bouquet and taste, the glass should be stemmed, thin in texture, clean and polished, long and narrowing a little towards the top. Not more than half of the glass should be filled so that the bouquet can gather in the upper half as the first offering to the drinker.

Temperature also plays an important part in the expert service of Sherry. The recommendation is to serve the Finos and the Amontillados chilled but not iced, and the Olorosos and Cream Sherries at room temperature. From the normal bottle of Sherry one can expect to serve fourteen glasses.

Some leading shippers of Sherries are:

> González Byass & Co. Ltd.
> Pedro Domecq S. A.
> Garvey S. A.
> Duff Gordon & Co.
> Williams and Humbert Ltd.
> Sandeman Bros. and Co.
> La Riva & Co. Ltd.

Note—If the name 'sherry' is attributed to wines from other countries mentioned in later chapters the author will, of course, mean 'sherry style' wines.

⚭14⚭

WINES OF PORTUGAL

T HE Portuguese are not great Port-wine drinkers, as they find it too heavy and alcoholic for the climate; but they drink their table wines with gusto, consuming over 125 bottles a head a year. Portugal is the fifth largest producer of wine in the world, only Italy, France, Spain and the Argentine producing more, and it has about 3 366 square kilometres of vineyards yielding over 1 363 million litres of wine a year. Control of the production is tightening considerably and, among other things, wines for export have to have the sanction of an official body, Gremio Dos Exportadores, before they are allowed on their way.

It is not surprising that the Portuguese table wines are increasingly finding more opportunities in world markets. Deservedly so, for while they may never reach the standard of the great French and German wines, they are refreshingly reliable and good value. In Portugal itself, it is almost impossible to drink a bad wine and most of them are 'just right' for the occasion, whether as a cooling drink on a hot summer's day or as the appropriate accompaniment to the country's national dish of Bacalhau (dried salted cod).

Wine is made throughout the country and some of the grapes grown for production are:

White wines—Azal, Alvarinho, Arinto, Bastardo, Cainhos, Dourado, Gualratino, Malvasia, Rabigato and Sercial.

Red wines—Azal, Amaral, Bastardo, Tinta Carvalha, Tinta Pinheira, Ramisco, Tourigo and Preto Mortágua.

When the *Phylloxera vastatrix* scourge struck the Portugueses' vineyards, one area remained immune. The vineyards of Colares, 32 kilometres from Lisbon and close to the sea, at the foot of the Cintra mountains remained healthy. Here the top soil of the terrain and the soil to a good depth beneath are of sand, and the *Phylloxera* louse failed to penetrate the sand to attack the roots below.

THE WINE DISTRICTS

The wine districts can best be divided into three categories. First, the wines of the mountains, the Minho, the Doura and the Dão. Second, the wines of the plains, Torres Vedras, Ribatejo, Alcobaça, Almeiri and Cartaxo—often called Estremadura wines. Third, the wines of the ocean, Colares, Carcavelos, Bucelas and Setúbal—on the Atlantic coast near the estuary of the river Tagus.

The Wines of the Mountains (Minho). The Minho wines come from the province of Entre-Douro-e-Minho in the north-west of Portugal and are generally described as *vinho verde*, green wines. The greenness refers to the taste and not to the colour, which can be red, white or rosé. They are called green because they are young, eager and invigorating with definite acidity. One of their most pleasing characteristics is the prickling sensation which they give to the palate. They are a product of a designed culture. The vines are trained on such high trellises that the grapes do not benefit from reflected ground heat; thus they have a higher acid content and a lower sugar content than grapes grown nearer to the ground. After fermentation, a good proportion of malic acid remains, and when the wine is bottled, usually after five months, this acid changes to lactic acid and carbon dioxide. It is of course this gas which imparts to *vinho verde* its special *pétillant*, *frizzante* or *spritzig* characteristic. The wines, usually with an alcoholic content up to 10° G.L., are ideal for 'swilling' and for quenching thirst. Well-known names among the Minho wines are Casal Mendes, Casal Garcia, Penafiel Verde Branco, Manção, Alvarinho Cepa Velha; all these are white wines. The red wines are Barrocal, Espadeiro and Vinhão Tinta.

The Wines of the Mountains (Douro). The best of the Douro wines are produced near the Spanish border in the Tras-os-Montes region, where two-thirds of the product is used to make table wines and one-third sent away for making port wine. Of all the Douro wines, Mateus Rosé is best known in Great Britain. It is made at Vila Real and sold in flagons similar to the Franconian Bocksbeutel which has no doubt helped the success of the quality advertising which has done so much for this wine. Much rosé wine of a pétillant variety is made in the Douro region although, to achieve this quality, some of the wines are artificially injected with gas. Regoa is the main centre for red wine and Ermida produces the best white wine. Lamego is noted for its sparkling wines, made principally by the *Méthode Champenoise*. At Alijo in the Upper Douro, a speciality wine is made on the lines of the Sauternes wines of France; grapes are left on the vine until they develop the 'noble rot' or *Botrytis cinerea*, which makes them so rich in sugar that fermentation ceases at an early stage. This results in a sweet luscious wine, which is usually matured in cask for some four years.

The Wines of the Mountains (Dão). Alongside the rivers Dão and Mondega, about 48 kilometres south of the Douro and 64 kilometres inland from the Atlantic Ocean, are the terraced mountain vineyards of the Dão district. Red wines predominate in the produce of this district, and they are smooth and velvety because of a high glycerine content. Some of the very good ones, like Dão 'Cabido' and Dão 'Caves Alianca', are not too unlike the wine of Burgundy. The white wines, flinty and aromatic, lean in similarity towards the Chablis wines. Bairrada especially and Agileda, on the way to the Ocean, are centres for sparkling wines.

The Wines of the Plains. The wines of the plains are indeed plain wines, somewhat similar to the Midi wines of France. They are produced plentifully for home consumption and are usually known as Estremadura wines. The red wines, Torres Vedras, Ribatejo and Cartaxo, are full-bodied but flat; and the white wines, Alcobaça and Almeirum, are dry but they have no 'bite'.

The Wines of the Ocean. When the Colares vineyards escaped the *Phylloxera* plague, the wines from them became very well known and popular, and the name Colares, hitherto applied to almost any Portuguese table wine, became restricted to the wines from the particular district and its use is now protected by law. The red wines from Colares are considered to be among the finest in Portugal; they are strong and smoky and have an abundance of tannin. The white wines are quite dull in comparison. Like many other good Portuguese wines, Colares wines often have 'Garrafeira' printed on the labels of the bottles and this denotes that the contents of the bottle are a special reserve wine, matured in bottle before sale. By contrast, a bottle labelled 'Vindima' is put on sale as soon as the contents have been put in it.

Carcavelos wines are mainly white wines although there are some red. Both kinds have great lasting power. In the past these vineyards near the mouth of the Tagus were noted for their production of a sweet white fortified wine, but the modern wines from this region are much drier, less in alcohol and have a distinctive nutty flavour.

The Bucelas wines at first are white wines and change as they grow older to a straw colour, which given more time will turn to golden. Made from Artinto grapes, they are fresh and clean to the palate, to which they can be slightly prickly. They were once known in England as Lisbon Hock.

The vineyards surrounding the port of Setúbal are famous for producing one wine, Muscatel de Setúbal, which is a sweet fortified wine, golden in colour. The method of its making is unique to Setúbal. When a desired balance is achieved during fermentation, the wine is fortified by the addition of grape spirit. Then, fresh Muscatel grape-skins are added and allowed to macerate with the wine until the following spring, when it is racked in clean casks. A fresh but fruity wine, ideal as an accompaniment to a sweet course, is the result.

PORT

PORTUGAL provides the interesting paradox of a country which is small in area but which produces a great variety of excellent wines. Predominant among these, of course, is Port Wine.

Port has always been associated with O-Porto—the port, whence it got its name, as indeed did Portugal itself, for in Roman times Oporto was known as Portus Cale, the name which eventually became Portugal. Today, the wine and the city are called Porto by the natives.

While Port and Oporto are synonymous, the actual, delimited area for the wine is situated about 64 kilometres to the east of Oporto whence it stretches from Régua for about another 96·5 kilometres to Barca d'Alva, where the river Douro enters Portugal from Spain. This area is known as the Upper Douro Valley. It would be difficult to find a countryside more beautiful, with hills and mountains sheltering the river, as it lazily winds in and out of view, on its journey seawards. Olive, chestnut and pine trees are in abundance, giving in high summer wonderful colour and perfume. Though the road does not always accompany the river on its meandering journey, the railway, for a great part, does and the occasional chugging train only emphasises the wonderful peacefulness of the landscape.

Here then is the home of the Port-producing vines, planted on terraces of intricate pattern on both sides of the Douro and its tributaries, in the

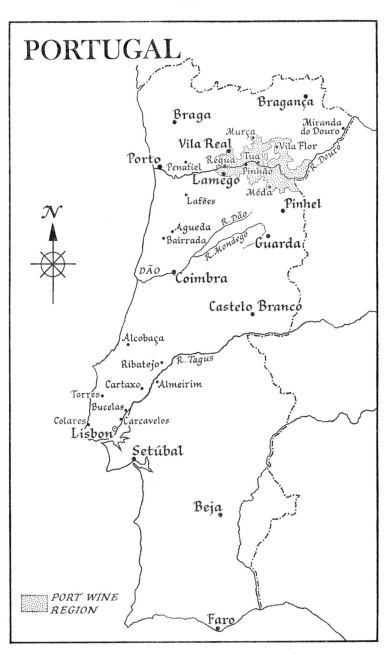

valleys, below and high up on the slopes of the hills and mountains. The village of Pinhão is the centre of the Port country, and in and around this small, tidy settlement are situated some of the greatest Quintas (vineyards). By each Quinta is a long white building with bold lettering on the roof indicating the name of the Quinta or the shipper who owns it.

Port as we know it today has had a rough passage to establish its reputation. Originally an ordinary table wine with an affinity to Burgundy, it was exported to England as early as the 14th century. As a beverage wine, it was considered rather crude and did not find much favour in Britain. However, in 1703 it got a welcome boost through the Methuen treaty. John Methuen, at that time English Ambassador to Portugal, signed a trade agreement with Dom Pedro II, which allowed Portuguese wines to be imported into England on much more favourable terms—one-third less duty—than the already-established French and German wines. In return, English woollens were allowed on to the Portuguese market for the first time. The signing of the treaty had no immediate effect on wine trade figures. The British palate, long accustomed to the refinements of the great French wines, regarded Port as uncouth. Gradually, however, fiscal-measures won the day and the wine became more acceptable by the addition of grape spirit—Brandy —and the use of the elderberry. Brandy was first introduced because the wine travelled badly. The difficulty with Port, then, was not that it was so weak but that it was so rich that even after fermentation some sugar remained, so that when the alcohol evaporated on the voyage a secondary fermentation started up with most unpleasant results. More alcohol was added to ensure that even with evaporation the alcoholic content of the wine could never fall so low as to allow a secondary fermentation. Over the years, more and more Brandy was added with the result that the wine changed from a table wine to a fortified one. The change-over was gradual, occurring, roughly, between the years 1770 and 1840. The Elderberry was introduced to improve the appearance of the wine, but this doubtful and criticised practice has long since been outlawed. The colour of the red Port of today is achieved by the natural method of bringing the grape juice (*must*), into contact with black skins of the grape during fermentation.

As the wine became more popular, far-seeing Englishmen and Scotsmen found their way to Oporto to establish themselves as wine shippers in a townland called Vila Nova de Gaia just across the river. It is here, since then, that the great wine lodges (lodge comes from the Portuguese *loja* meaning warehouse) have been located. As trade flourished, profiteering and sharp practice crept in, and eventually, the farmers, thinking they were being exploited, appealed to the Government. In fact, they themselves were the chief offenders, using generous helpings of Brandy and Elderberry to bolster up inferior wines. In their favour, however, it must be said that, while the shippers were forever demanding better-quality wines, no incentives were offered in return by way of increased prices. Furthermore, the shippers were not always diplomatic in their dealings with the farmers. Basically though, the main grievance was a matter of money.

In 1756, the Marquis de Pombal, who was then Prime Minister, set up, through a charter, a monopoly for the Upper Douro wine country. The aims were to reduce the power of the British shipper, to improve the quality of the wine and to further the prosperity of the farmers. Unfortunately, the administration which undertook to implement controls was lax and open to bribery; instead of improving, the wine became, over a period, steadily worse. But some good did materialise, principally in the demarcation of the port wine area—the first wine area in the world to be so defined—and, for the farmer, a price escalation of from £2 to £6 per pipe (a pipe = 700 bottles = 522·5 litres). Gradually the monopoly became less corrupt and indeed did some fine work in the interest of Port. Later it became known as the *Real Companhia Velha*, but was eventually stripped of its governing and monopoly powers.

Since 1933 we have looked to three Government-controlled bodies to safeguard the quality and high reputation that Port now enjoys. These are:

No. 1—The Port Wine Institute (*Instituto do Vinho do Porto*). Its duties include the administration and general promotion of Port wine. The Institute also ensures the authenticity and alcoholic strength of the wine and it will not issue certificates of origin unless it is satisfied that the wine is suitable to be exported as Port. It controls the demarcation zone and has the power to visit the shippers' lodges at any time.

No. 2—The Port Wine Shippers Guild (*Gremio dos Exportadores do Vinho do Porto*). This Guild, whose committee is elected from the shippers themselves, deals mainly with exports. To be issued with certificates of origin every Port shipper must belong to the Guild. Requirements for membership are that the shipper's lodges be located within the precincts of Vila Nova de Gaia; that the shipper has a stock of at least 300 pipes of Port with room within the lodge to hold still more; and that he pays the necessary industrial taxes. Although 300 pipes is the minimum stock allowed, a shipper must hold a ratio of 3 pipes to every one shipped.

No. 3—The Douro District Department (*Casa do Douro*). This department deals mainly with the agricultural side. It controls the planting of new vineyards and advises on all aspects of soil tillage. It ensures that the vines are planted not more than 600 metres up the slopes and that they have adequate shelter. In its research stations it carries out tests and experiments and continually seeks to make the farmers' work less arduous than it is.

The Casa do Douro authorises each farmer to make a certain quantity of port wine from his grapes and the rest must be used for table wine. If a farmer is left with any of his authorised port wine on his hands, the *Casa do Douro* buys it and stores it for at least five years and then sells it as matured Port wine to the shippers, offering them certain inducements to buy it. The *Casa do Douro* also buys up all the table wines made by the farmers and *unsold* elsewhere and *these* it distills and sells at the following vintage either to farmers who wish to make Port for their own account, or to shippers who wish to have farmers make the port for them. It also controls prices.

Consistently high standards are not easily maintained but basically, since the last war, Port has remained steady in quality with characteristics and blends, true to type. Since the first demarcation in 1756, the limitation has been revised, first in 1908 and again in 1921. In between, in 1914 to be exact, an Anglo–Portuguese treaty made Port a protected name in Britain. This treaty describes Port as 'a fortified wine produced in the delimited Douro region and exported over the bar of Oporto'.

The word 'bar' comes from the time when it was the practice to close the port each night against pirates by stretching chains from bank to bank, across the river. The limitation that the wine should be exported over this bar is obviously a political requirement—this could not possibly improve the quality of the wine—but the topographical limitation was necessary because only in the Upper Douro Valley are conditions absolutely favourable for the making of this great wine.

CLIMATE

There are extreme temperatures in the Douro Valley. The winters can be very cold with temperatures often falling below zero and snow is not unknown. Winter also provides almost all the rainfall—sometimes up to 127 centimetres—December being the wettest month. By contrast, summers are usually hot, with temperatures up to 37° C.-44° C. Oporto, on the other hand, is humid—the Manchester of Portugal—and gets double the rainfall, while the summer temperature can be as much as 16·5° C. lower.

SOIL

The soil, if it can accurately be described as such, is made up of outcrops of granite and schistose stone. Only the latter as we have seen, may be used for the growing of Port wine grapes. Granite will also grow these grapes but the result is a wine with little body and lacking the characteristics of Port. The schistose soil is brown and slaty in appearance and is fairly rich in minerals. Its cultivation presents serious problems because, due to the nature of the soil and the steepness of the vineyards, mechanisation has not been possible. The soil, in fact, is so tough that picks, crowbars and even explosives are used in an effort to bring it to the proper consistency. However, the *Centro Nacional de Estudos Vitivinicolas*, now seriously looking into these problems, will, it is hoped, one day find a satisfactory solution.

GRAPES

There are about fifteen species now in general use for the making of Port wine. Some farmers use all fifteen, some fewer, but all the species have their own particular attributes and compliment each other in different ways.

The Bastardo, Touriga, Mourisco, Souzão, Tinta Francisca, Tinta Cão, Tinta de Carvalha, and the Boca da Mina are the principal species for red Ports. For white Port, the most favoured grapes are the Moscatel Branco, Rabo de Ovelho, Mourisco Branco, Malvazia Rei and the Gouveio.

It is true to say that the least-productive vines, planted in the less accessible places of the Alto Douro, yield the best grapes for making Port and so these grapes fetch the highest prices. It is estimated that in the Alto Douro, it requires grapes from a thousand vines to make one pipe of Port, whereas a thousand vines planted in lower terrain will give five times the yield. In days gone by, the price margin between the good and less good areas was considerable. Nowadays the difference in price is slight. As the Government guarantees to purchase all wine within the demarcated area, there is a tendency for farmers to concentrate on the more productive areas, the areas of high-yielding vines with poorer but higher-producing qualities. So, as always, we have to depend on the integrity of our Port shippers in their selections.

CULTIVATION OF THE SOIL—CARE OF THE VINE

Because of the stone-like consistency of the soil and the dearth of mechanical aid, the labour involved in cultivation is hard, long and monotonous. The Douro vineyards are, in the main, a series of stone terraces built on the sides of hills and slopes. These terraces have to be diligently maintained to prevent the rains from washing away the earth from around the vines and to conserve moisture for the long, hot summer ahead. Sometimes there is a supplement of summer rains but this is regarded in the nature of a bonus and is not a frequent occurrence. Often the terraces bulge or break, and, when this happens, the work of restoration has to be swift and immediate. Pruning is carried out between November and February. In spring comes the important job of loosening the soil and piling it around the vine roots, to give protection against the sun. The vines themselves require constant attention. The roots go deep down into the crevices of the rocky subsoil where the winter moisture is contained. Before the vines shoot in March, the wire strands they are trained on must be checked for stability and, where necessary, made steady. From May to July the vines are sprayed at least three times, sometimes as many as eight times, with copper sulphate, to guard against disease: and then there is the usual weeding and watching for parasites. Grafting is another chore because after the *Phylloxera* came to Portugal in 1868, it was found necessary to graft the native vines onto the American *Phylloxera*-resistant roots. This work takes place between January and April. These new vines, when they are four or five years old, produce grapes satisfactory in quality for Port but it is not until they are seven years old that full fruiting occurs. They will bear fruit for another thirty to forty years but the bunches decrease with age although the quality always improves. In August there is somewhat of an easing-off from labour in the vineyards but this is only the prelude to the lively activity of the vintage.

THE VINTAGE

The actual commencement day for picking the grapes varies from vineyard to vineyard, depending on location, exposure to the sun and condition of the grapes. The vintage usually begins in late September or early October.

The farmer or shipper—if he owns a Quinta—will already have engaged a collection of men, women and children, the numbers depending on his requirements. This band of villagers comes year after year to the same Quinta and their own homes may be as far away as the Minho. On the specified date they appear, to their own accompaniment of drums and music. The women carry their belongings balanced in baskets on their heads while the men happily strut along empty-handed. When they arrive at their accommodation, they segregate, males in one apartment, females in another.

Work starts with the women and children cutting the grape bunches with scissors or knives and the men transporting only the perfect grapes in baskets (*cestos*) to the sheds or buildings which house the granite stone troughs (*lagares*) in which the grapes are pressed. When filled, a basket weighs about 54·5 kilogrammes. If the *lagares* are located far from the vineyards, the grapes are taken to a central point and transported from there by ox-cart.

Nowadays there are two methods of making wine in the Douro. The old or *lagare* system and the new or fermentation vat method of which there are several types and systems. Most farmers and some shippers still use and favour the old to the new methods and the principal reason for the change-over is the great shortage and cost of labour nowadays in the Douro—many of the men seeming to prefer work on the hydro-electric schemes in the area or to suffer 'exile' in France, where financial rewards are much greater.

THE OLD METHOD

Baskets of grapes are emptied into the *lagares* which are about 1 metre deep and 5 metres square. When the pile almost reaches the top, the pressure from above breaks the lower grapes and the resulting must is allowed to escape into a container. This *must* is later put back into the *lagar*, to go through its natural process.

Meanwhile bare-legged men commence cutting the *lagar*—treading the grapes, this is known as the *corte*. In a line, with arms linked, the men take their time from the leader—*um-dois, um-dois*. They work in four-hour sessions and it takes two men to work a pipe. The action of the treading releases the grape juice, or *must*, without crushing the pips and stalks which would give the *must* a bitter taste due to the excessive tannin content.

The *corte* normally takes about four hours. By the *corte* we mean the first treading, which should crush all the grapes. After that the lines are broken up the men wander about or dance about in the *must*, treading it individually without the strict discipline of the first four hours. The normal *lagar* holds enough grapes to make about twelve pipes, so that, as two men are required per pipe, it will need a line of twenty-four men for the *corte*.

As the treading continues, colour and body is being extracted from the grape skins. The treading may continue for 24, 48 or even 60 hours, according to the temperature, rate of fermentation or the type of wine required. There is always careful supervision to ensure that fermentation does not start too quickly. Treating the *lagares* with sulphur prevents this. In cold weather especially, when the *must* is reluctant to stir, the warmth from the trampling feet is a valuable asset in aiding fermentation to commence.

If a dry wine—a seco—is being made, treading and fermentation will be longer than for the *Geropigas* or the very sweet blending Ports.

In all cases, however, by the time treading has been completed fermentation has long since commenced. The men now get out of the *lagares* and have the task of keeping the manta or cap—grapeskins etc.—submerged so that all the colouring and goodness is extracted. To achieve this a *macaco* or monkey is used. This is a wooden contrivance for keeping the must moving up and down in the *lagares*, instead of continuing the treading as was normal in old times.

THE NEW METHOD

The grapes are brought to a centrifugal crusher. This crusher is so controlled that it removes the required amount of stalks, yet crushes the grapes without breaking the pips. Stalks and pips give tannin to wine, but, while a certain amount is essential, too much is bad. When the grapes are crushed, the juice and the mash are pumped into huge fermenting tanks. These tanks, made of cement or granite, are lined on the inside with a special plastic paint. Each tank has a cooling system and this aided by an addition of sulphur—in very hot weather—helps to control the actual fermentation. When the fermentation commences, the natural gas (CO_2), with the help of *must-moving machines* with propellers, forces the *must* up into a top tank, where escape valves, working on the principle of a coffee percolator, releases the carbonic acid gas. As soon as this happens, the *must* courses back into the bottom tank, mingling with, and submerging the mash on its way and, in consequence extracting maximum colour and goodness. The escape valves close automatically on top and the same procedure is repeated again and again until the wine comes over at the required sugar reading. The wine is then run off into storage vats, which are located on a lower level, where the same proportion of Brandy is blended with the wine as in the case of the classical method. The above procedure applies to the making of red Port. White Port is made in the same way except that the *must-moving machines* and propellers are dispensible and, of course, in the case of the Apéritif Ports, the wine is allowed almost complete fermentation. The residue left over after the wine has been run off is taken to an hydraulic press for two pressings. The first pressing may be used for Port, but more usually it is allowed to ferement completely and is made into a beverage wine. The second pressing is generally used for seasoning casks.

Fermentation. This is the action of the yeast—the bloom on the grape skin—on the natural sugar in the must, converting it into alcohol and carbon dioxide gas, the gas escaping into the air. Usually wines are allowed to ferment naturally right out, i.e. until the whole sugar content of the grape juice has been converted into alcohol and carbon dioxide. Not so with Port.

It should be explained that the ferments which convert the sugar to alcohol are unable to work after 16° of alcohol G.L. is reached. This would be more or less the natural strength of Port wine left to ferment out without interference. However, if during the fermentation the alcohol level is suddenly raised to above 16° G.L., the fermentation will come to an end, while there is still some natural sugar left in the must. The modern procedure when making Port wine is for the sugar-level to be tested with a saccharometer at regular intervals during the fermentation and when it is half-way through, that is to say when there are only 8° of sugar left, the must is allowed to run out through a pipe to a vat in the *adega* (the barn-like cellar of an Alto Douro farm) on a lower level. At the same time and through the same pipe, brandy, at 78° of alcohol, G.L. is also allowed to run into the vat, thus mixing with the *must* and stopping the fermentation. The quantity of brandy insisted on by the Casa do Douro is one hundred litres to four hundred and fifty litres of Port wine. Of course if a very sweet Port is required, the fermentation would be stopped much sooner and if a dry white Port is being made, the wine will be allowed to ferment nearly right out. But in any case the principle is the same and gives the result that Port wine is the only important fortified wine in the world which has its own completely natural sweetness. All other sweet wines have grape-sugar or syrup or some other sweetening material added after they have fermented completely out. The wine is then thoroughly roused and integrated—it is now, in fact, Port and will be kept in these vats until January at least, when it is ready to be taken down from the Alto Douro to its new home in Vila Nova de Gaia.

During the winter, the natural sediment falls to the bottom of the casks or tuns. In other words, the wine 'falls bright'. Cold weather has this effect on all young wines. Brandy is now added but before the wine is ready for transportation from the Douro, it is transferred into new casks or pipes, leaving behind the sediment or lees in the old. Port wine coming down from the Alto Douro to Vila Nova need only show 16·5° of alcohol G.L., as long as it has a minimum of 2° of sugar. In fact most Port comes down with 3° or 3·5° of sugar, so 16·5° G.L. or more of alcohol is the normal. If the sugar shows less than 2°, the combined strengths must equal 20°. Although Port is known to mature faster in the Alto Douro, facilities there are not adequate, so the wine is usually taken down to the lodges of Vila Nova de Gaia after the first winter and certainly before 30 June. The wine under Government seal is transported nowadays in tankers by road or in pipes by rail. This is a much faster and less expensive method than of old, when casks were piled on the beautiful *Barcos Rabelos* boats and taken downstream. These boats are now out of general use. Cockburns were the last firm to use them but some are still to be seen moored by the dockside at Oporto where, very picturesque, they lie for the purpose of publicity. Many people regret the passing of the boats in the belief that the gentle rolling of water transport was preferable and more beneficial to the wine than the cocktail shaking of the hazardous journey which the wine now endures. An attractive theory based on sentimentality as the short journey to the lodges is really not detrimental to the wine.

LODGES

The lodges of Vila Nova de Gaia are a honeycomb of overhanging buildings cluttered in a maze of steep cobbled streets which climb up from the Douro on the opposite bank to Oporto. Entering through cramped and almost shabby exteriors one is surprised at the spaciousness and gracious atmosphere found inside. Many of the lodges have several floor levels and it was traditional that the young wines arrived at the top floor and graduated to the bottom, from where they were shipped.

When the new wine arrives at the lodge, more brandy is added (Port is eventually sold at an alcoholic strength of 21° G.L.) and the wine is given time to settle before being tasted for quality and classification. This work is done by experienced and skilful people. On their judgement depends the consistent quality which Port lovers expect, when they open a bottle of their favourite brand. These professional tasters decide which wines complement others and which wines, when added to old stock, will emerge as a continuity of their firm's particular styles.

After the tasting, the wines are blended in huge vats called *Balseiros*. In the centre of each vat is a large pole attached to which are three pairs of paddles whose motions thoroughly mix the blend. Recently, firms like González Byass have started blending in large cement tanks, coated on the inside with a special plastic paint. Within each tank is a stainless-steel mixer driven by a 4 h.p. engine. This method has proved very effective. The wine is now ready to be transferred to wood tuns, vats or pipes where, except for racking (changing the wine from the old cask into a fresh one), which happens about three times the first year and less frequently after that, the wine remains and matures, until it is ready to be shipped or bottled. Port matures more quickly in smaller casks because of its greater surface exposure to oxygenation. During each year in cask there is a $2\frac{1}{2}$–3 per cent. wine loss through evaporation. Some firms are now trying to combat this by lining the roofs of the lodges with plastic foam.

TYPES OF PORT

Apéritif Port. This is a white Port, the fermentation of which has been allowed to continue until almost all the sugar has been converted into alcohol. It is the driest Port possible and has been gaining in popularity since its introduction. It is best served chilled with a slice of lemon and some ice.

White Port. This is really pale gold in colour. It is processed in the same way as other Ports except that only white grapes are used. It comes over rather too sweet for the British palate and, in consequence, extreme chilling is advised before drinking. It is not generally a popular wine, except perhaps in France.

Ruby Port. This is a blended wine of various years. It starts life almost purple in colour but the longer it is allowed to remain in cask (generally from four to eight years) the lighter it becomes, due to air penetration through the pores of the wood, and the fact that the wine is racked so often, thus coming into contact with more air. When it becomes Ruby, it is bottled for sale. Sometimes it throws a deposit (sediment) in bottle. When this happens it requires careful decanting. It is full-bodied, smooth, pleasant wine and is generally very good value for money. In the North of England they like a fat, young, rich Ruby, which is shipped from Oporto when it is a little under two years old. After a year's 'landing age', it is sold over the counter and they call it 'black-strap'.

Tawny Port. This is an extension of Ruby inasmuch as it is the same quality wine but is left in cask (over ten years), until it becomes tawny in colour. Depending on age and blending, it may be tawny, medium tawny or light tawny. It can be drunk immediately it is bottled and throws no deposit, because the crust has been left behind in many casks. It may be served chilled. For cheaper varieties, some shippers make a blend of white and red Port. The genuine tawny is the triumph of the blender and it is an all-day all-weather wine.

Vintage Port. This is the nonpareil, the *chef-d'œuvre*, the wine of one harvest of an exceptional year, when all the elements have combined to produce the ultimate in quality. Vintage Port can be made from the grapes of one Quinta alone or from a combination of the best of many. All shippers, whether they own Quintas themselves or not, buy from about 60 farmers whose standards and performance the shippers know and respect. The shipper declares whether the wine is vintage or not.

As so many shippers are involved, there is no uniformity of decision. In 1954 for example only one shipper throughout the Douro declared vintage. On average, a shipper, if lucky, will ship about three vintages in every ten years. When a shipper considers his wine to be of a sufficiently high standard to merit declaration, he will set aside and blend together the very best wines of that year. The wine is then allowed to remain in cask for two years in the lodges before being shipped to the wine merchants, who do their own bottling, though the shipper will also bottle on request. The young wine in bottle is very raw, for the wine and brandy have not yet reached harmony and will not do so for another ten to twenty years. While the wine matures in bottles lying horizontally, it throws a heavy deposit which settles in a firm crust on the lower side of the bottle. A splash of paint or a label on the upper side of the bottle indicates that the crust is lying on the opposite side. This facilitates future handling. As vintage Port is not generally fined before bottling, should the crust break, the wine becomes cloudy if not carefully decanted. As soon as the wine merchant or shipper bottles the wine, it may be sold to the trade or general public who then set about laying-down the wine to mature for *at least* ten years in their own cellars. After such a long time in bottle, the wine loses its deep purple hue and emerges red-purple in colour. Corks because of their contact with alcohol, go brittle with age and are normally replaced every 15 years or thereabouts.

The following are variations of vintage Port:

Late-bottled Vintage. As the name suggests, the wine is allowed to remain longer in cask than two years and consequently it will take less time in bottle to reach maturity. It is a quality Port, lighter in colour and less in body than the normal variety and it is sold without date of vintage as required by recent Portuguese law.

Crusted Port. A blend of young wines of different years, shipped in cask and bottled with the same care as vintage. It is sold without a date and gets its name because it throws a crust in bottle. It has almost the same colour as vintage Port but is much less expensive and extremely good value for money.

FINAL STAGES

With the exception of vintage, crusted and very old tawny Ports, all other varieties have to be 'clarified' before they are shipped or bottled. This can be done in many ways, by Isinglass, white of eggs, filtering, pasteurising or refrigeration. Even when vintage Ports are being bottled, a bright crisp October day is usually chosen because dull weather or a drop in temperature can cloud Port while it is being transferred from cask to bottle.

Based on the French technique of chilling, pasteurising or refrigeration can stabilise the wine and keep it bright and clear in bottle for at least a year. This may appear to be harsh treatment for the wine but in fact rather than suffer, the wine gains in smoothness as a result.

Should the wine remain in bottle longer than a year it will commence to throw a light deposit, proving the wine is still alive. If the wine is to be shipped, it is today usually sent abroad in five-pipe stainless-steel tanks.

CASKS AND BOTTLES

As we have seen, some Ports spend most of their lives in cask, while others, like vintage spend only two to three years in wood, at most. Whatever the time, their period in cask is of the utmost importance because casks allow wines to breathe and the wood itself imparts natural attributes such as tannin. Casks are made from oakwood which has to be imported as the Portuguese oak is brittle and apt to crack. Formerly, Polish oak was always used but nowadays, as it is difficult to procure, shippers rely on the use of Yugoslavian, British and the Memel oak from Russia. When the wood arrives from abroad it is left to season, in the open for at least two years. Then skilled cooperage comes into play, with the shaping, then steaming of appropriate lengths to make them pliable for hooping immediately they come out of the ovens. With great dexterity the tops and bottoms are fitted and the whole operation is done at surprising speed, without nails or other fittings, to complete the cask. The cask has now to be seasoned and this is done by filling it with a beverage wine or a below-standard Port and leaving it for a few months to soak.

Bottles. Port bottles vary a great deal in size. Those which we see displayed in shop windows hold ·75 litres. There is also the half bottle but less-common sizes are the magnum, equivalent to two bottles, the tappit-hen (three bottles), the jeroboam (four bottles) and the rehoboam (six bottles). The larger sizes are used mainly for banquets or great gatherings. Except on such occasions they are not very practical as Port takes longer to mature in them and, of course, once opened they have to be consumed within a few days, after which the Port becomes flat and sour. Most bottles are coloured dark green or black to prevent sun or strong light, which would alter the colour of the wine, from penetrating. There is usually, but not always, a punt at the bottom to give strength to the bottle. In Oporto there is one bottle factory, and there are many others in southern Portugal.

STORING OF VINTAGE AND CRUSTING PORT

Port wine is best stored in a cellar where the atmosphere is dry, or at least fairly dry, and of an even cool temperature. Cellars are now rarities, and it is sufficient if the bottles are kept in an even temperature, away from draughts and strong odours. Whether stored in a cellar, pantry or on the family sideboard, there should be no vibrations and no handling until required for use.

The bottles must be stacked horizontally with the label or white splash uppermost.

DECANTING

Because of the crust or sediment, some Port wines such as vintage and crusted should be decanted before they can be served. The wine is poured into the clean decanter and the crust or sediment is left in the bottle. It is a delicate operation to ensure that all the drinkable liquid is decanted without the unwanted crust and sediment. Here are some suggestions:

(i) If possible, stand the bottle for one whole day before decanting. About two hours before serving, cut the wax off the top rim and wipe around the top of the bottle. Because of age, the cork may have become weak and crumbly, so when inserting the cork-screw, a wide-spiralled one is best, make certain that it goes through the centre firmly but gently. To avoid the danger of breaking the neck of the bottle, it is best to hold the bottle by the base rather than the top. On your left, have a sparkling clean glass decanter and, in between, a lighted candle. With the neck of the bottle above the flame, pour the wines gently into the decanter until, with the aid of the candle-light, you see the sediment appearing in the neck. Now stop pouring.

(ii) There is a special gadget in the form or iron tweezers whose tongs are shaped to fit the neck of the bottle. The tongs are heated, red-hot, clamped around the middle of the neck for a minute of two, released and quickly replaced by a cold wet cloth bandage. Then with a quick jerk, the neck, with the cork within it, is separated from the bottle. The wine can now be decanted. This operation is very useful if the cork is crumbly but it is essential to use the proper tweezers which are now rather rare.

(iii) Run the sharp edge of a heavy knife a few times around the *flange* near the top of the neck. Then with the back of the knife, carry out a series of taps on the neck starting at the bottom and working upwards, and the final tap on the *flange* will sever the neck of the bottle at the *flange*. The protruding cork can then be pulled out. Decant as before.

SERVICE OF PORT

Apéritif, white and tawny Ports, if used as appetisers, should be served chilled but not iced. Ruby, vintage and other varieties are served at about 18° C. but they must never be warmed artificially. The wine should be uncorked some two hours before it is served to enable the wine to breathe.

GLASSES

Glasses should be clear to show off the colour of the wine, and be of thin texture to enable full appreciation of the taste. They should be shaped to close a little towards the rim. The tulip and dock varieties are ideal. They should not be filled beyond two-thirds capacity so that sufficient room is left to trap the bouquet. Cut crystal glasses are very popular for Port and beautiful to look at when filled. One should get fourteen decent helpings from a normal bottle of Port. Serve a second, rather than a bumper double.

PASSING THE PORT

At table, each person pours his own Port wine. The bottle, or usually the decanter, is passed from right to left starting at the host. This direction in the *passing* is because most people are right-handed so the movement is natural. It is an old English custom and there are fanciful and romantic theories how the practice originated—the fanciful having to do with the earth's rotation and the romantic with the giving of the wine from the heart. The wine-waiter, the butler or whoever is given the chore at home, will hand the decanter to the host in such fashion that the host can take the decanter by the neck. After helping himself, he will pass it to the guest on his left, who will take hold by the body of the decanter, help himself and then pass it to his left where it will be received by the neck. And so on—held alternatively by neck and body—around the table back to the host.

ATTRIBUTES OF PORT

Let us nail a lie. Port does not cause gout. At least, it cannot be blamed for this ailment any more than any other drink taken in excess.

In England Port is one of the best-known wines and this is because of its many and diverse attributes. Unlike, for instance, Champagne which conjures up revelry and celebration in an expensive environment, Port wine is known and tasted in castle, mansion, semi-detached and bedsitter; in lush hotels and lowly pubs; at mayoral banquets and by hospital beds. In its several varieties there is one for every occasion—every pocket. It is used in cookery and in cocktails, with soda for long drinks, as a tonic during illness, and as a restorative after work or play. It is a stimulant for and an accompaniment to good conversation and this last virtue gives it its pride of place at the end of dinner. With good Port circulating, conversation is always warm, witty and eloquent. It is, in short, the wine of goodwill.

THE PORT BUSINESS

Port was, we know, made to suit the British palate, but in recent years France has become by far the biggest customer, as the following percentages show:

	%
France	36·0
United Kingdom	17·0
Portugal	10·4
Fed. Republic of Germany	9·9
Belgium & Luxemburg	6·2
Holland	4·8
Denmark	3·8
Sweden	2·7
Norway	2·4
Switzerland	1·9
Ireland	1·4
U.S.A.	0·9
Other Countries	2·6

It is indeed a flattering tribute to Port, that France the greatest wine country in the world, has trebled its imports in the last ten years. Perhaps the French palate was eventually bound to recognise the virtues of vintage Port for the final glory of a well-ordered meal, but in fact, it is the vogue for apéritif, white and tawny Ports that reflect the increased sales. Clever or fortunate salesmanship has recognised the Frenchman's preference for a sweet apéritif and found its rewards. Extensions of the salesmanship to other European countries is now showing similar 'dividends'. So far, however, America has resisted the seductions of Port as a popular drink. No doubt the pioneer days were not conducive to cellarage and more recently prohibition led tastes astray to hard spirits. Nevertheless, the best vintages are now finding a demand and there should be opportunities for expanding this market. So far we have been talking of expanding markets, but what of the time-honoured British market? The pretended determination of the British to abandon their traditions and to despoil their aristocrats is seriously challenging Port wine's hold on the British market. Although apéritif Ports are beginning to make an impact and the traditional demand for vintage is being maintained, the sales of ruby and tawny Ports are not being sustained. The feeling of well-being and luxury from a choice glass of Port, will always be appreciated, despite the competition from the new sparkling substitutes for drink.

Some Leading Port/Wine Shippers

Cockburn Smithes & Co. Ltd.
Croft & Co. Ltd.
González Byass Ltd.
Mackenzie & Co. Ltd.
Offley Forrester Ltd.
Sandeman & Co.
Taylor, Fladgate & Yeatman
Warre & Co. Ltd.

Some Recent Vintages

1920	1931	1945	1958
1922	1934	1947	1960
1924	1935	1950	1963
1927	1942	1955	1966
			1967
			1969

Note—If the name 'port' is attributed to wines from other countries mentioned in later chapters the author will, of course, mean 'port style' wines.

❧ 16 ❧

MADEIRA

IN 1418, one of Henry the Navigator's captains, João Gonçalves Zarco, discovered an island some 560 kilometres into the Atlantic from the Portuguese capital of Lisbon. The island was completely wooded along its whole length of 50 kilometres and width of 23 kilometres. The island was given the name Madeira, which means wood or timber, and Zarco, popularly called the 'blue-eyed', was rewarded with the appointment as Captain-General of the island. He established his base at the site which is now the island's capital of Funchal. The blue eyes apparently saw the trees as an obstruction to colonisation, which would need good crops to support it. Zarco set fire to the forests, and for some seven years the trees were burning, but not only was the ground cleared for cultivation, the wood-ash enriched the soil. Adventurous Portuguese, Spaniards and Italians settled in the island, and their descendants prosper in this famed holiday resort and sub-tropical climate. Much of the prosperity is due to Madeira wine.

The early settlers brought the Malvasia vine from Crete and imported the sugar cane from Sicily. Soon, a market for sugar and wine was found in England, a fact that is conveniently if not specifically recorded in English history books by the sad drowning of the Duke of Clarence in a butt of Malmsey in 1478. In fact, this wine from the Malvasia grape probably came from Crete rather than Madeira, but in either case, the poor Duke was drowned in a beverage wine, for it was not until about 1700 that the wine from Madeira was fortified. Between 1580 and 1640, the island had been controlled by Spain which discouraged viticulture there. The trade with England, however, survived and was eventually stimulated, aptly enough, by the revelries which followed the end of the Puritan Commonwealth and the restoration of the Stuarts in the person of the Merry Monarch, Charles II.

English merchants established themselves at Funchal, and encouraged the natives to plant more and more vineyards to meet the growing demand for Madeira wine in England, a demand that grew when the Napoleonic Wars cut off much of the French and other European wines.

George III enjoyed this island wine, and royal patronage helps sales. By the reign of Queen Victoria the wine was a settled favourite among the wealthy and the expanding middle classes. In polite society, a glass of Madeira wine poured from a heavy glass decanter on the huge mahogany sideboard would be offered to the respectable visitor as surely as a cup of tea is nowadays offered to the welfare visitor to more humble homes.

In 1852, the first of two catastrophes struck the Madeira vines. A fungus—*Oidium tuckeii*—devastated the vineyards and for eight long years there was no wine available for export. Ten of the thirteen English shippers closed down, but the firms of Leacock, Blandy and Cossart Gordon had the fortitude and foresight to hold on. Leacock in particular took a leading part in the replanting of the vineyards when the scourge was eventually cured with sulphur. This time, it was mostly the verdelho vine that was planted, and the industry was again on the road to prosperity. Alas, in 1873, the vines were again destroyed, this time by the dreaded *Phylloxera vestatrix*. Leacock once more led the fight against the new epidemic and, as in Europe generally, the disease was overcome by grafting the American vine roots—immune to the disease—with the native vines. Leacock died in 1883 and his work was continued with courage by another English shipper, Charles Blandy. He must frequently have despaired at the slow recovery of the vines, but he was at last rewarded by a great vintage—Verdelho 1910, Verdelho being the most successful vine in that year.

GRAPE VARIETIES

Most of the grapes grown on the island are among four species— Sercial, Verdelho, Boal or Bual, and Malmsey. Verdelho is the most favoured variety, and Malmsey is also known as Malvoisie or Malvasia. Lesser varieties like the Terrantez and Bastardo are cultivated in a limited way. The vines in Madeira are grown on pergolas which reach to a height of about two metres, which is high enough to enable the grapes to be picked from underneath and at the same time provide shade and protection for the harvesters, for the sun can be very strong in Madeira during vintage time.

THE MAKING OF MADEIRA

The vintage usually starts in mid-August and sometimes lasts until late October. Grapes at sea-level, the Verdelho and Boal, are gathered first; then the Malmsey grapes; and, lastly, the Sercial grapes which are cultivated on the highest terraces where, because the atmosphere is cooler, longer time is needed for satisfactory ripening. To pick the grapes in prime condition, it may be necessary to go over the vineyards selectively as many as four times. The gathered grapes are taken to a wooden trough called a *lagar* where, to the rhythm of guitar music, bare-legged men trample them. Mechanised presses are beginning to take over from this exertion, but the traditional method of extracting the juice is still sometimes used. When the *must* is freed from the *lagars*, it is sent immediately to the lodges at Funchal, The *must* is transported in casks by lorries or in 55-litre goatskin containers carried on the backs of hardy labourers called *borracheiros*. As fermentation commences in the fermenting vats, those wines intended for dessert wine—Boal and Malmsey—have their fermentation terminated at an early stage by the addition of grape spirit, distilled from Madeira wine. Cane sugar distillate may be used instead of grape spirit. This curtailing of the fermentation has the effect of retaining the natural sweetness of the *must*. The drier varieties such as Sercial and Verdelho are allowed to ferment much longer. Alcohol is, however, added in small doses. In this way the fermenting process is slowed down but not stopped.

When fermentation is completed, the fortified wine is given a resting period in the cool lodges. The wine is now known as *Vinho Claro*. In the olden days at this stage, the wine would be carried in a sailing ship on a trip to the tropics and back. This journey, with the wine coming into gradual contact with heat and later withdrawing from it again, certainly improved the quality and taste of the wine. But these trips were soon found to be uncommercial. They were replaced by the introduction of an artificial heating system, which basically has the same effect on the wine as the tropical journey had. The system is known as *Estufagem*.

THE ESTUFA SYSTEM

An Estufa is simply a heated room or a stove. In its earliest form, when it was called Estufa del Sol, it was similar to a glasshouse, with the natural rays of the sun warming the wine in pipes (a pipe is a cask holding 418 litres). The cool night air adversely effected the wine under this system, so artificial heat was introduced. Nowadays, there are two methods of heating the wine. Either central heating is installed with hot-water pipes (plumbers' pipes—not casks) along the walls, or hot-water pipes are run through cement tanks in which the wine is maturing. Each tank has a capacity of about 40000 litres. These tanks are controlled by a thermometer which has a Government seal attached. If the temperature rises above an agreed degree, the seal breaks and Government inspectors ensure that the wine will not be offered for sale as Madeira. Individual shippers heat their wine to their own chosen, but agreed, temperature. Usually the maximum temperature is fixed between 43·3°C. and 60°C., and many consider that 50°C. is the ideal. The lower the maximum temperature the longer is the period allowed for the incubation, and the finer is the wine. The temperature is increased very gradually, never more than 2·75° per day. When the required temperature is reached, it is kept constant for three or four months and sometimes for as long as six months. During the final month, the heat is gradually reduced, bringing the wine slowly out of the 'tropics' and back to normal temperature. The wine is now called *Vinho Estufado* and it will have lost from 10 to 15 per cent. of its original volume; it will have gone darker in colour and have acquired a slightly burnt taste. After the wine has been well rested, it will be racked in fresh casks and will now be called *Vinho Trasfegado*. In these casks, the wine is fortified by the addition of an average of 10 per cent. of alcohol. Now called *Vinho Generoso*, it is ready to enter its appropriate solera.

THE SOLERA SYSTEM

Although vintage Madeiras (wine of a particular year, sometimes from one vineyard) are still available, they have become very scarce and expensive since the *Phylloxera* epidemic. It takes fifty years or more to mature a vintage Madeira in cask, a proposition not very attractive in the modern fast-sell world. The main demand is for a good-quality wine to come to one's sideboard reasonably cheaply. Solera, i.e. blended wines, can meet this requirement. The old vintages are often used to help give consequence to younger wines. The Solera system originated in the Sherry district of Spain and was introduced into Madeira during the last quarter of the 19th century. It is a maturing and blending system described in detail in the chapter on Sherry. Briefly, casks of wine rest on one another to form a kind of pyramid four or five scales high; some of the oldest wine in the casks closest to the ground is drawn off for sale; the remainder is replenished and refreshed by younger wines from the casks in the next tier and so on up the scales or tiers with the final ullage in the top casks being replenished by new wine. The Solera system is an excellent way of maturing the wine, but above all else it ensures uniformity in taste and quality, so necessary for safeguarding a firm's hard-won reputation.

The law does not allow Madeira wine to be sold until thirteen months after its time in the Estufa, and generally it is kept much longer before being shipped.

Solera Madeiras can be quite old but if, for example, Solera 1900 is indicated on a bottle, it does not mean that the wine is a vintage wine of that year, but that the Solera was started or laid down in that year. Of course there may well be traces of the 1900 wine in the bottle.

VARIETIES OF MADEIRA WINE

Most Madeira wines are named after the grape species of their production, although occasionally one finds a bottle with a vineyard-name or another geographical name. There are four dominating varieties:

Sercial. Sercial Madeira is an amber-coloured apéritif wine with a very crisp finish. It varies from very dry to not so dry, depending on the brand. Chilled, it makes a delightful preprandial drink.

Verdelho. Verdelho Madeira is gold, almost rosé, in colour. It is not quite as dry as Sercial. It is an excellent accompaniment to soup, or it can be drunk enjoyably at any time of the day.

Boal. Boal Madeira is deep golden in colour, sweet and full-bodied to taste. It has a fine balance of sugar, acid and tannin. It has a somewhat smoky taste and it goes very well with the sweet or dessert course.

Malmsey. Malmsey Madeira is almost dark brown in colour and it is the most renowned and expensive of all Madeiras. With a powerful bouquet, it is luscious and honeyed to taste, yet with a slight caramel flavour. Truly a dessert wine, it is even better after the coffee course. Like all Madeiras one of its best characteristics is its ability to dry out yet linger on the palate. It is never cloying; instead, it leaves one with a *dry good-bye.*

Others. Other less well-known Madeira wines such as Terrantez (dry with a bitter finish) and Bastardo (a refreshing sweet wine) are not so easily obtainable.

ATTRIBUTES OF MADEIRA WINE

Maderia wine has an alcoholic strength of around 20° G.L. It can outlive any other wine, possibly because of the volcanic soil on which the grapes are grown and to the 'cooking' it gets in the Estufa. It is an excellent aid in the kitchen for soups, sauces and sweets, which is one reason for its popularity in France. In Britain, Sherry has become perhaps too strong a competitor for Madeira and in fact France and Scandinavia are now the best customers for the wine.

Some well-known shippers of Madeira are
Blandy & Co.
Cossart, Gordon & Co.
Leacock & Co.
Rutherford & Miles Ltd.
Shortridge, Lawton & Co.

ᓀᔦ17ᔦᓀ

THE WINES OF ITALY

ITALY is the greatest wine-producing country in the world (over 4 545 million litres a year) although nobody could sensibly claim she produces the greatest wines. But good or indifferent her wines are drunk on a grand scale at home—an estimated 185 bottles per capita, each year—and in increasing quantities abroad.

The vine grows throughout the country usually under the most ideal conditions. However, many *vignerons* are not as disciplined as they might be and sometimes plant the vine on incompatible soil or intermingling with olive trees, or among vegetable and grain crops. This, together with some injudicious pruning has gained the Italian wine industry a reputation for carelessness. But an Act of Parliament passed in July 1963 was intended to do for Italian wines what *Appellation Contrôlée* has done for French. The Act, decree No. 930 (*Denominazione d'Original Controllata*) is divided into three categories:

1. *Semplice* (plain). This merely guarantees that the wine was produced in the locality stated. It does not guarantee quality.
2. *Controllata* (controlled). Means that the wine conforms to the conditions and qualifications indicated for it.
3. *Controllata e Garantita* (controlled and guaranteed). Guarantees high quality wines which have conformed to the most demanding regulations regarding type of vine, type of soil, yield per hectare

and so on. These wines may only be sold in bottles or in containers of not more than 5 litres.

Wine producers in order to label their wines 'controlled' or 'controlled and guaranteed' must submit detailed documentation to the Ministry of Agriculture and Forests starting with the cultivation of the vine, going right through to bottling and proposed distribution.

Outside these controls are the local consortiae comprised of growers who ostensibly *seek* to improve standards. Indeed many of them do, such as the famous consortium of the Black Cock for Chianti Classico; but many others make little impression. There are also some growers outside any control who continue to make wine in any old fashion.

There are some fine wines in Italy, some with the magical names of Barolo, Valpolicella, Chianti, Orvieto, Soave, Santa Maddalena and Lago di Caldaro. Lovers of the wines are not slaves to vintages which is understandable when one considers that climatic conditions vary little from year to year. Many wines are often named after the vine rather than the locality and there is a great diversity of vines and complexity too when the same vine stock might bear a different name throughout various districts. Below is a list of the more popular species.

White Wines	Red Wines
Cortese Bianco	Aleatico Nero
Malvasia Bianco	Barbera
Pinot Bianco	Bracchetto
Riesling-Italiano	Grignolino
Trebbiano	Nebbiolo
Vernaccia	Pinot Nero
	Trebbiano
	Sangiovese

THE REGIONS

Valle d'Aosta. This is a French-speaking region which is not particularly noted for fine wines, but Blanc de Morgex (white) Carema, Donnaz (light reds), Passito Della Val d'Aosta and Torretta Di San Pietro (dessert wines) are considered good.

Piedmont. Italian Vermouth, originated in Turin, the capital of Piedmont, in 1786. But perhaps the most international wine to come from this region is Asti Spumante. Made from the Muscat grape with help from the Pinot and Riesling its secondary fermentation takes place either in bottle (*Méthode Champenoise*) or in tank (*Charmat* or *Cuve Close* method). Piedmont is also rich in genuine table wines. The finest reds are Barolo, Barberesco, Barbera, Grignolino, Dolcetto and

Gattinara. Bracchetto is a good Rosé wine or can be sparkling, and the dry Cortese is an above-average white wine.

Liguria is on the Italian Riviera with Genoa as the Commercial Centre. Vernaccia and Vermentino are the classic vine stocks and the area is famous for white *Cinqueterra* wines both dry and fairly sweet, an excellent example being the high-strength sweet wine called Sciacchetra. *Cinqueterra* means 'five lands' and the wine comes from the five villages of Corniglia, Monterosso, Vernazza, Biassa and Tiomaggiore. The best red wine in Liguria is Rossese di Dolceacqua, a strong full wine said to be a favourite of Napoleon—what a capacity that man must have had!

Lombardy. A great many grape varieties are used in this area including Barbera, Croattina, Uva Rara and Nebbiola for red wines and the Riesling, Cortese, Malvasia, Muscat and Pinot for white. Pavia is regarded as the commercial centre. Barbacarlo, the Vatelline wines—Sassella, Inferno, Grumello—Sangue di Giuda, are better than average red wines, Chiaretto di Moniga is a decent rosé wine while Val Versa, Frecciarossa, Fraccia and Lugana are about the best white wines. Santa Maria Della Versa is a sparkling wine with a good local reputation.

Alto Adige. This is one of the most progressive and beautiful of all the Italian wine districts. Until 1918 it belonged to Austria. Even today the local people speak both German and Italian. The wines are also promoted in both languages which is somewhat confusing and intimidating for the casual explorer. More deserves to be known about these wines in Britain because they are indeed very good and travel well too. The reds are light with an affinity to fine beaujolais and, like beaujolais, they may be drunk young. The whites are rather akin to the wines of Alsace and if you find the Alsatian Gewürztraminer a bit too much, try the Traminer Aromatico from this region. Other fine white wines are Rhine Riesling, Terlaner, Pinot Bianco (Weissburgunder) and the Bressanone wines Silvaner, Traminer and Rülander located close to the Brenner Pass. Of the red wines Santa Maddalena and Lago di Caldaro are really outstanding, Colline Bolzano, Pinot Nero (Blauburgunder) Meranese di Collina, Teroldego Rotaliano, Lagrein Rosé (light ruby in colour) are also good and perhaps the finest sparkling wine in all Italy is produced here—Gran Spumante.

Bolzano, the commercial centre, is one of the chief wine towns in Italy. This is not surprising considering that the area accounts for about 45 per cent of Italy's total wine exports, Austria, Germany and Switzerland taking most of this.

Veneto. This area centres around Verona and it is difficult to say which is its most outstanding wine. It is perhaps either Soave the dry white wine made from the Trebbino and Garganega grape or the garnet red Valpolicella from the shores of Lake Garda. Both are well known outside Italy and although *Soave* means 'sweet and gentle' it is genuinely dry and firm. Valpolicella is a romantic name, reminiscent of holidays in Italy. The wine is reliable, ideal for swilling or as an accompaniment for red meats. Bardolino, another favourite red wine, quick to mature, is made from a combination of Corvina and Negrara grapes. It is soft and dry to taste. Gambellara is a white wine similar to Soave. Recioto Nobile is a good red sparkling wine made from specially selected grapes from the outside clusters and Recioto is a fulsome heavy red table wine which enjoys popularity in its own locale.

Friuli Venezia Giulia. An area around Trieste which is not remarkable for its wines. The best whites are Verduzzo, Tocai—no relation to the famous Tokay of Hungary—and Riesling Renano. The most noteworthy reds are the Cabernet, Merlot and Refosco. Piccolit di Friuli is the most interesting liqueur wine of the area and is sometimes described as the Château d'Yquem of Italy—a fine compliment.

Emilia-Romagna. This region is more noted as a gastronomic centre, and has few really good wines. The best are Bianco di Scandiano, Albana di Bertinoro (both white) and reds Sangiovese and Lambrusco di Sorbara. The Lambrusco may more accurately be described as fizzy as it is usually allowed to ferment in bottle. Poured into a glass, it makes a glorious froth which quickly disappears leaving a dry clean-tasting prickly red wine. A unique and individual wine.

Tuscany. This area is synonymous with Chianti of which the style Chianti Classico is finest of all being well rounded and velvety. Chianti Classico comes from a delimited area of some 320 square kilometres. Six regions, the Siena Hills, Arezzo hills, Mt. Albano, Florentine hills, Pisan slopes and Rufina are also entitled to call their wine Chianti. Other good red wines are Vino Nobile di Montepulciano and Brunello di Montalcino. Notable white wines are Vernaccia di San Gimignano and Bianco di Pivigliano. There are also many good dessert wines in the area such as Vinsanti and Aleatico di Portoferraio. Siena is the commercial centre.

Umbria. Orvieto, a cathedral city, gives its name to the most famous wine from this region. There are two types, Orvieto secco (dry) and Orvieto abboccato (fairly sweet) the latter made from grapes which are allowed to commence to decay after being gathered. These wines are bottled in attractive Fiasco (those bottles wrapped with matted straw). Such presentation has helped their sales abroad. Rubino di Lugnago is the most important Umbrian red wine.

Marche. This area is noted for one wine in particular—Verdicchio dei Castelli di Jesi, a fairly light straw-coloured wine with a somewhat bitter taste. It is rightly regarded as one of Italy's best white wines and is sold in sexy-shaped bottles. Verdicchio di Matelica, pale straw in colour is also a fine wine.

Lazio. The Rome District—also known as the Castelli Romani Region. From this area are two fine wines, Est! Est!! Est!!! di Monte-fiascone (light dry or fairly sweet white wine) and Frascati a clear golden dry, semi-sweet, sometimes sweet wine. Incidentally Frascati also has a good dry red wine called Frascati Fontana Candida. Est! Est!! Est!!! is an interesting name for a wine. It stems from the time Bishop Fugger of Bavaria when preparing for a visit to Rome in A.D. 1111 sent his steward, Martin, on in advance to advise him where he should make overnight stops giving special consideration to the quality of the wine. The steward, when he found a wine of good quality, marked the door of the establishment with 'EST' (an abbreviation of Vinum Bonum Est). On reaching Montefiascone he indicated Est! Est!! Est!!! So impressed was he with the wine. The Bishop and Martin never did reach Rome but stayed happily on in Montefiascone until death.

The wine does not hold such an exalted position today but it still is a considerable wine. It is made from the Muscat, Trebbiano and Rossetta grapes.

Frascati is one of the Castelli wines. Other good ones are Albano, Genzano and Marino. Grapes for these wines are generally grown on the volcanic hills outside Rome. Falerno is a dry white wine with a bitter after-taste. A similar-named but superior wine comes from the Campania region.

Abruzzi and Molise. This is not a great wine area but produces some good ones like Cerasuolo d'Abruzzo (rosé), Montepulciano d'Abruzzo (ruby red) and Peligno Bianco, which is the best white wine of the region produced near Aquila.

Campania. The popularity of this area as a holiday paradise—Naples Positano, Capri, Ischia, Amalfi—overshadows its reputation as a wine-producing centre. The best-known wine from the region is Lacrima Christi—tears of Christ—this can be either white, rosé or red though the white, dry or fairly sweet and somewhat aromatic, is the true, traditional type. The grapes for this wine are cultivated on the slopes of Mount Vesuvius. Other good white wines are Capri, Ravello and Ischia. Ravello also produces a pleasant rosé and, of the reds, Capri Rosso, produced north of Naples, are also palatable wines. The white is a full dry wine as is the red but another variety can be fairly sweet.

Puglia. An area noted for harsh rather than fine wines. Sanservo and Locorotondo (white), Castel del Monte Rosso, Torre Quarto and Santo Stefano (red) and Rosato del Salento (rosé) are the most interesting.

Basilicata. The vines are grown on and around volcanic slopes. No quality wine is produced, but the white Malvasia del Vulture and the red Anglianico del Vulture have good local reputations.

Calabria. The toe of Italy. The wines from this area are not known internationally, but the most interesting are the red table wines such as Pollino, Pellaro and Savuto and the dessert wines Greco di Gerace and Moscato di Cosenza.

SICILY

The best known of all Sicilian wines is *Marsala*. It has an affinity to Port, Madeira and Sherry. A fortified wine, it was founded by an Englishman John Woodhouse in the 18th century. The grapes used are Insolia, Cattarato which produce a dry white wine. To this is added 6 per cent. of Vino Cotto—unfermented grape juice boiled down in kettles to syrup consistency—and 6 per cent. of Vino Passito, a wine whose sweetness has been retained by the addition of grape spirit before fermentation has been completed. The wines are blended together and the best is matured by the Solera system often in the open air from 2 to 4 years. It is sold at an alcoholic strength of from 17-24° G.L. G.L. Labels may show the following abbreviations.

L.P.   —London Particular
C.O.M.—Choice Old Marsala
O.P.   —Old Particular
S.O.M. —Superior Old Marsala

Lord Nelson once ordered 500 casks of Marsala for his troops but nowadays the wine is languishing due to the fierce competition, particularly from Sherry and Port. Marsala has a somewhat burnt taste and although it is generally sweet there is also a dry Marsala called Old Virgin. It is a very useful wine in the kitchen especially for soups, sauces and sweets. It is an important ingredient in the famous Italian sweet—Zabaglione. Authentic bottles have a numbered neck label with Sicily traced in red.

Well-known shippers are Woodhouse & Co., Ingham Whittaker & Co. and Florio & Co.

Of the white table wines Corvo Bianco, Alcamo, Capo Bianco, Etna Bianco are all reliable and the reds—Corvo Rosso, Faro and Pachino Rosso—are highly considered locally. Malvasia di Lipari, sweet and golden in colour, is a very good dessert wine.

Sardinia is best known for its dessert wines such as Vernaccia di Sardegna, Moscato del Tempio, Malvasia di Sardegna and the red dessert wine akin to Port called Girò di Sardegna. However, Maristella and Vermentio—white—are considered good table wines as are the reds—Santa Maria la Palma, Oliena and Ogliastra Rosso.

ᘓᔔ18ᔕᘐ

HUNGARY

HUNGARY produces about 550 million litres of wine a year and most of it is white wine. In Great Britain, Hungarian wine is synonymous with the deep golden Tokay and the dark red Egri Bikaver, popularly and warningly known as bulls' blood. Before discussing these wines, mention should be made of the lesser known wines of Hungary.

Lake Balaton. The vineyards around Lake Balaton, the largest lake in Eastern Europe, produce much good white wine, some of which is to be seen in Britain as Balatoni Riesling and Balatoni Furmint, both named after the species of grape from which they are made. These are dry wines with a hint of sweetness and they are beginning to become very popular. Locally in Hungary, Badacsonyi Szurke Barat made from pinot gris grapes is considered to be the finest of all Balaton wines. It is an aromatic wine, yellow-gold in colour, but its difficult name will not help it to sell outside Hungary. Then there is the Badacsonyi Keknyelu wine, popularly known as Blue Stalk, and the fairly sweet dessert wine called Szurke Barat, both with excellent local reputations.

Mor. Mor, situated some 80 kilometres west of Budapest, is one of the very few European wine regions that did not succumb to the *Phylloxera* vine pest. Ezerjo is the principal species of grape cultivated and a dry golden wine called Moriezerjo is the best product of the region.
   And now the two classic wines:

Eger. The town of Eger, 137 kilometres north-east of Budapest, is the centre of the vineyards that produce the renowned Egri Bikaver wine, known and marketed abroad as Bulls' Blood. Made from a combination of Kadarka, Burgundy and Médoc Noir grapes, this dark-red wine has a forthright robust personality. Although it is a good accompaniment to highly flavoured foods, it is really in its element at bottle parties, etc. Some people prefer to drink this wine chilled.

Tokay. Tokay wine is made in the delimited area of Tokaj-Hegyalsa. It is made principally from Furmint grapes although the Muskotaly and Harslevelu species of grape are also used to a small degree. Tokay is one of the greatest wines in the world. In a great vintage year, it is a dessert wine of real excellence and an expensive one too. But Tokays vary in sweetness, some can even be dry. A Tokay needs careful choosing. One labelled simply as Tokaji is likely to have a doubtful pedigree. The name Tokay or Tokaji should be followed by one of the following suffixes:
   Pecsenyibor. This denotes a dry table wine produced from the lower reaches of the river Hegyaljai;
   Szamorodni. This indicates either a dry or sweet wine (depending on the year). The wine is made from ripe and over-ripe grapes pressed together indiscriminately, though the sweet variety will have naturally an abundance of over-ripe grapes;
   Aszu. To produce this type of Tokay, there is selectivity in the picking of the grapes, similar to the *Beerenauslese* in Germany. The over-ripe grapes are picked separately in small buckets called *puttonyos*, each of which hold about 13·5 kilogrammes of grapes. A mass of doughy pulp is made of these shrivelled grapes, and the pulp is then mixed with the ordinary ripe grapes. The mixture is trodden in canvas bags. The ensuing *must* is put into fermenting casks and the number of

puttonyos in the mixture will determine both the quality and the sweetness of the wine. The casks each hold about 155 litres, so a wine marketed as 'three *puttonyos*' will have the juice of the equivalent of three bucketsful of over-ripe grapes as part of that total. The range can be from one to six *puttonyos*, the more *puttonyos* the sweeter the wine. It is rare to find six *puttonyos* on a label, three, four or five are the usual.

Tokay Essenz. Tokay Essenz is also made from over-ripe grapes, but the grapes are not pressed. They are placed in a tub, where their own pressure gradually breaks the skins and the syrupy juice trickles out into a container. The result, of course, is a grape essence, very rich in sugar, which nowadays is not sold commercially, but often used to improve the Aszu variety.

Tokay should be served slightly chilled, if all the many qualities attributed to it are to be enjoyed. It is said to be an aphrodisiac, a mender of marriages, a restorer to health and so on. Certainly it is highly prized and highly priced.

19
SWITZERLAND

THE Swiss and their visitors drink most of the 100 million litres of the wine produced in Switzerland annually. These wines, though never great wines, are in the main good or very good. They are usually overpriced on foreign markets and this, together with unenterprising promotion, accounts for the limited demand outside Switzerland.

Most Swiss wines are dry and white and have a tendency to be prickly on the palate because of a malolactic fermentation occurring in the wine after it has been bottled. Most of the vineyards are situated on steep terraced slopes and the prolific, best ones, are located in the

French-speaking part of the country in the cantons of Vaud, Valais and Neuchâtel.

Vaud. The canton of Vaud is the most prolific producer of wines in the country, and its vineyards are set in picturesque scenery along the shores of Lake Leman. The hilly district of Lavaux east of Lausanne is particularly beautiful and its villages, especially those of Saint-Saphorin, Villette, Cully, Riex, Rivas and Dézaley, produce good quality dry white wines made from the Fendant grape. Of these wines the best known are from the vineyards Clos des Abbayes and Clos des Moines, which are owned by the city of Lausanne.
West of Lausanne are the wine villages of La Côte. Chief among these are Mont-sur-Rolle, Féchy, Vinzel, Luins and Malesatt, which produce wines that are more robust but less fine than those of Lavaux. Here the Chasselas grape is commonly cultivated.

Valais. Valais is also known as Vieux Pays (Old Country) and it produces a good selection. The white Fendant, made from the Chasselas grape, is perhaps the best known. Some people find the Johannisberg, a dry sharp white wine made from Sylvaner or Müller-Thurgau grapes, an even better wine. The Riesling and white Hermitage are also interesting wines. Pinot Gris grapes gathered long after the normal vintage produce an excellent straw-coloured sweet dessert wine called Malvoisie. Of the red wines, the Dôle with its powerful bouquet is one of the finest if not the finest red wine of Switzerland. There is also a lesser red wine called the Petit Dôle. The Pinot Noir and Gamay grapes are combined to make these wines.
An interesting white wine, unfortunately not obtainable outside Switzerland, is the hard flavoured Vin du Glacier. This wine is made in the plains below the Val d'Anniviers, but as soon as it is made it is carried by the mountaineers in 35-litre barrels to the villages near the glaciers. Here, in casks made of larchwood, it matures for ten to fifteen years.

Neuchâtel. Most Neuchâtel wines are white and made from Chasselas grapes. There are some good red wines made here, notably the Cortaillod, which is made from the Pinot Noir grape. There is also a famous pink wine made from the same grape and called Cortaillod Œil de Perdrix. Many of the Neuchâtel white wines go through a secondary fermentation in bottle. They are bottled young and the finest of them are known to make stars as they are poured into a glass—and you don't have to be hit over the head to see the effect!

SOME OTHER WINES
OF EUROPE

Austria. Austria has nearly 40 500 hectares of vineyards cultivating many varieties of grape, although the Riesling, the Grüner Veltliner, the Müller-Thurgau and the Rotgipfler are the most favoured species. Nearly 136 370 000 litres of wine are produced annually of which about 85 per cent. are delicate, fresh white wines that are at their best when drunk young. The outstanding Austrian white wine is, without doubt, Gumpoldskirchener, which is produced near Baden south of Vienna. Basically a heavy and fairly sweet wine, it is made from the Rotgipfler grape. From Badvöslav, further south from Vienna, comes the best red wine, called Vöslauer. However, the most popular red wines consumed in Austria are two from Bolzano in the South Tyrol, Italy; these are Santa Maddalena and Kalterersee. The Austrians have good taste, which may be one of the reasons why, deep in their hearts, they are sure that the Tyrol territory is rightfully Austrian, as it once was. For this reason, wines bottled in the Tyrol are allowed into Austria free of duty.

The vineyards to the west of Vienna in the Wachau district produce fine white wines such as Dürnsteiner Katzensprung, Dürnsteiner Flohaxen, Loiben Kaiserwein, Kremser Kögl and Kremser Wachtberg. The Burgenland boasts of its fine white wines such as the Neubergers and the Morbischers and of its excellent Blaufrankische red wine. There are sparkling and semi-sparkling (Perlwein) wines made in Austria but her reputation on the international market will rest on her excellent white wines. Perhaps the best known Austrian wine on English wine-lists is Schluck, a name that means 'mouthful of wine'. The gay Austrians, however, drink most of the wine they produce. Less than 22 million litres are exported each year, mostly to the United States of America. Wine for everyday swilling in Austria is described as 'Schoppenwein'.

Bulgaria. Viticulture is rather new in Bulgaria although the country now produces some 210 million litres of wine annually. Many of the wines are named after the grape species used in their production and best of all are the light Beaujolais-style red wines. The main centres of production are Trnovo, Plovdiv and the Black Sea district. Chardonnay, Riesling, Dimiat, Misket, Sonnenküste and Bulgarische Sonne are all dry white wines of good quality. Melnik, Mavrud, Kadarka, Cabernet and Gamza are the best red ones. Pamid is the best rosé wine and of the sparkling wines Perla (white) and Iskra (red) both made by the *Méthode Cuvé Close* are very pleasant. Pliska is the country's fines Brandy.

Czechoslovakia. Although Czechoslovakia produces wine in three regions, Bohemia, Moravia and Slovakia, the output does not meet even the internal demand. Consequently, little is known of the wines outside their native land. Slovakia is responsible for about two-thirds of the production. Both white and red wines are made, the whites from the Rhine Riesling, Traminer and Sylvaner grapes and the reds from the Blauer Burgunder and Portugieser grapes. The principal commercial centre for wine is Bratislavia.

Greece. It is estimated that out of the 213 000 hectares of vineland in Greece, 62 per cent. goes to produce grapes for wine. The remainder produces grapes for raisins and sultanas. We know it was the Greeks who taught the techniques and skills of viticulture to the Romans and to this day there is a great tradition for wine production throughout Greece and its islands. The annual production is about 360 million litres. To too many people, however, Greek wine is synonomous with one particular one, the famous Retsina. This is the best-known mainland wine and is associated particularly with Athens. The taste of Retsina, a dryish white or pink wine, can be very offputting at first. Its special taste is attributable to its containing 1 per cent. of resin, the sap of the pine tree, which is added to the grape juice before fermentation. The resin was probably first added at the time of the Peloponnesian wars when Athens was struck by cholera. Whether or not it was a useful antiseptic, there is no doubt that the natives liked the curious taste and the additive has been used ever since. Also in the environment of Athens, good white wine such as Hymettus, San Helena and San Marino are produced.

In Macedonia and Thrace, the Popolka, Cinsault and Limnio vines are cultivated and red wines are the usual produce. Good examples of these are Naoussa and Arnaia. The best wines of the Peleponnesus come from around Patras. Particularly well known are the dessert wines, Mavrodaphne and Muscat of Patros. Other good wines from here are the white Santa Laura, the rosé Tegea and the red Demestica. An interesting carafe wine is the red Arakhova.

Among the isles of the Aegean Sea and the Cyclades the most famous of the wines produced is the Muscat of Samos. Samos wines can be sweet or dry. The island of Lemnos produces good wines such as the red Kalamnaki and the white dessert wine Muscat of Lemnos. Cyclades is well known for its sweet wines such as Vino Santo and Niclteri. The Ionian islands are noted for red table wines like Ropa of Corfu and Robola of Cephalonia.

However, besides table wines, there are other Greek specialities such as *Ouzo*, *brandy* and *Mastika*. Ouzo is an aniseed-flavoured brandy which makes an excellent apéritif if taken in the proportion of one part of Ouzo to three parts of water, with some ice added. Greek brandy, without ever having the refinements of French brandy, is quite an acceptable accompaniment to coffee. The better-known brands such as Cambus and Metaxas compete favourably with all but the French brandies. Mastika is a type of liqueur. It has a base of grape spirit and is given extra flavouring from the sap of the Mastika trees that grow on the island of Chios only.

Luxemburg. The wines of Luxemburg have an affinity with the wines of the Moselle and of Alsace. The vines are grown mostly on the banks of the Mosel river, a river which starts in France then forms a border between Luxemburg and Germany before it enters Germany. It is natural therefore that the wines are somewhat similar to the Moselle wines. All these wines are white and they impart an agreeable prickly sensation on the palate as one drinks them. Belgium is the best customer for them; while Holland takes a goodly share too. The better-quality wines are made from the Riesling, Traminer, Rulander and Auxerrois grapes, and they are graded in the order Cru Classé, Premier Cru, Grand Cru, Réserve and Grand Réserve. The bottles of the better Luxemburg wines will show these gradings and will also show a Marque Nationale with an official number on the neck-label.

Rumania. Rumanian wines are usually named after the districts in which they are produced, such as Murfatler, Tirnave, Dragasani, Odobesti, Cotnari, Teremia and Valea Calugaresca. There are, of course, individually named wines such as Segarcea Cabernet, a sweet red wine, Sadova, a medium sweet rosé wine, Nicoresti, a fine full-bodied red wine, Cotnari 5, a sweet white dessert wine, and Kadarka, another fine red wine. Red and white vermouth-style wines are also produced, and the Rumanian spirits include Slibovitza, a plum brandy, and

Tzuica, a fruit brandy. Rumanian wines are exported to many countries and one of their attractions is that they are usually reasonably priced.

Russia. In the days of the Tzars, Champagne flowed freely in Russia, not that the peasants noticed it, but it was all bought from France in which an extremely sweet Champagne was willingly made to suit the Russian taste. Today, the Russians (perhaps the peasants still don't notice it) drink their own natively produced Champagne and they even export some under such names as Kaffia and Krasnodar, both of which they describe as Champanski as if some English schoolboy had been asked to suggest a name. The Russians also export a pink sparkling wine. In one of their celebrated programmes, the Russians planned to produce 1 136 million litres of wine a year and they have probably now attained about four-fifths of this ambition.

The principal wine regions are in Moldavia, in the Crimea, in Georgia and in Armenia. The chief wines of *Moldavia* are Negri de Purkar, a full red wine, Kabernet, a red wine made from the Cabernet grape, Aligoté, a fairly dry white wine, and Fetyeska, a quite dry white wine. The best *Crimean* wines come from Yalta with its limestone slopes. The southern Crimea is noted for its dessert-type wines after the styles of Sherry, Port and Madeira. The main centre of prodcution is Massandra, where lusciously sweet Muscatel-type and Tokay-type wines are produced. It is from the Crimea that Kaffia, perhaps the finest of all Russian sparkling wines, hails from.

Besides the sparkling Krasnodar, *Georgia* ships to Great Britain both red and white wines. The best known of the red wines, Mukuzani No. 4 and Sapervani No. 5, are both very dry but strong in alcohol in the region of 14° G.L. The best of the white are Tsindali and Goorjuani, two straw-coloured wines, which are not great wines by any standard, but they are interesting and good value for the price usually asked. Much of the wine from *Armenia* is sold as 'Caucasian'. This region is known for its sparkling, fortified and dry white wines, but its best export is its very dark brandy, which is very palatable indeed. Pamid is the best and the best-known rosé wine from Armenia. Perla, a white sparkling wine, and Iskra, a red sparkling wine, are both made by the *Méthode Cuve Close*. The better-known red wines are Cabernet, Gamza, Melnik, Mavrud and the sweet wine, Kadarka.

Yugoslavia. The white wines of Ljutomer and Maribor in Yugoslavia are being increasingly appreciated on world markets. Besides their style, their prices are so reasonable and their promotion so enticing that more and more people are being attracted to them. Many of these wines are sold simply as Yugoslavian Riesling, Riesling being the name of the grape species from which the wines are made. Another grape, the Sipon, produces a sweeter variety of wine. The Sylvaner, Traminer, Ranina and Sauvignon grapes are also popularly used in Yugoslavia for making white wine. The straw-tinted GRK, a robust, dry white wine is deservedly well thought of and a sweet white wine, from the Radgona district, called Tiger Milk, has recently become very popular in Britain. The grapes for this wine are late-gathered (spätlese) and consequently have a high sugar content. Yugoslavia also produces some fine red wines such as the very dry Prokupac, Dingač, Prošek Cabernet Brda and Opolo. Some of these are fairly sweet and rich in alcohol, Cviček and Kavadarka are rosé wines that are well suited to summer drinking. All in all, Yugoslavia has a wide variety of honest wines which merit experimentation and patronage.

Turkey. Turkey has some 728 000 hectares of land under cultivation as vineyards, which yield sufficient grapes to produce about 20 million litres of wine a year. The export of wine is under state control but there are some esteemed private producers like Feltu and Kutman from Istanbul and Metin And from Ankara. Usually Turkish wines are named after places although there are some which are named after the species of grape from which they have been made.

West of Istanbul is the town of Tekirdag which produces a good fairly sweet white wine. Other wines above average in quality produced in Thrace are the red wines, Papazkarisch and Buzbag, and the dessert wine, Misbag. Bursa is a strong red wine which takes its name from the town of that name, and Kalecik, Cubnik and Hasandede in Ankora make very acceptable red and white wines. Sergikarasi from the town of Gaziantep near the Syrian border is a robust red wine, and from the east of Turkey in the town of Elazig comes the powerful red Okuzgozu. Fortified wines, such as sweet muscatels, are also produced in Turkey as are carbonated sparkling wines. Of course, Turkey is famous for its anise-flavoured Raki, rather like Ouzo in taste, and for its orange-flavoured liqueur Portakal. The native brandy is not too bad either.

⊂❧ 21 ❧⊃

SOME MEDITERRANEAN WINES

Malta. About 1 620 hectares of land in Malta are cultivated as vine-yards, but these have to do their best with a climate which can vary between torrential rain and scorching sun. For this reason the wines are very ordinary, some even harsh. All types of wine are made, and many hold the opinion that the best of them is the Altar wine, the wine of the Church. Dessert wines, made from muscat grapes, are establishing themselves, and there is a growing popularity for Verdela, a rosé wine. In London, the Capitan Wine Agencies have an extensive list of the Maltese wines. Maltese wines have an alcoholic strength of about 11–12°. Marsovin is the winery generally associated with Maltese wines.

Cyprus. It has been estimated that nearly a half of the farming population of Cyprus is involved in the making of wine. The main market for the produce is in England, and the wineries are at Limassol and Papos. About 85 per cent. of the wine is red and the best known is Commanderia. This dessert wine in early life is a rich red in colour but, as it ages, it becomes tawny. The basic wine is made from dried-out grapes and this is then flavoured with cloves and resin and with scented woods that are suspended in the wine within a bag. Aphrodite emerges from the vineyards as a semi-sweet red wine with a good reputation, and who would sully such a name? Then there are Olympus, a full-bodied red wine; Othello, somewhat similar; Kokkineli, a deep rosé wine; Arsinoë, a white wine and a sparkling wine called Duc de Niçoise. Of all the Cyprus wines, none are more extensively advertised than the sherry-type wines produced from grapes grown in vineyards allegedly planted by the Queen of Sheba in her rare spare time. Great Britain is the principal market for these wines. Although they are mainly of the sweet variety and pleasant to some tastes, they hardly match up to the Spanish sherries. The three grape-species usually cultivated in Cyprus are the Mauron, for red wines, the Xynisteri, for white wines, and the Muscat, for dessert wines.

Israel. After the *Phylloxera* scourge of the vineyards in 1890, Baron Edmund de Rothschild by his generosity and counsel caused the re-establishment of viticulture in Israel on a firm basis. Ever since, vine growing and wine making has flourished, with the result that there are now some 4 450 hectares of vineyards producing a variety of types of wine under the alert supervision of the Wine Institute of Israel, established in 1957. The aim of the Institute is to increase production as well as to raise the already high standard of quality and to market the wines advantageously. Experiments are carried out with soils, machinery, vine-crossings and so on. At present, the principal grape-species in use are the white Sémillon, the Muscatel, the Alexandre and Clairette Égreneuse and the black Carignan and Alicante Grenache. The varieties of wine produced include the white wines—Palwin, Carmel Hock, Massadah, Château Montague, Graves and Sauternes; the red or white wines Ben Ami and Avdad; the red wines Primor, Adomatic, Carmelith and Château Windsor; the sparkling wine President; and the dessert wines Vered and Partom (both port-type wines), Topaz, Savion and Tivoa (similar to Tokay), and Sharir (a sherry-type wine). A variety of vermouth is also made and brandy, of which the brand known as 777 Richon, is excellent and expensive.

Algeria. Most of the 1 360 million or so litres of wine produced in Algeria annually is either red or rosé. The red wines are made from the Carignon, Cinsault or Alicante Bouschet black grapes, sometimes from a blend of all three species. The rosé wines have the Cinsault, Grenache and Aramon grapes in the blend, while for white wines the Ugno Blanc and the Clairette de Provence species are the most favoured. There are three principal regions of vine cultivation, Alger, Oran and Constantine, and these vineyards cover some 360 000 hectares. From Alger come the red or white wines of Ain-Bessem-Bovira, Côtes du Zaccar, Haut-Dahra and Médéa; and from Oran come the red, white or rosé wines Ain-el-Hadjar, Coteaux de Mascara or the inferior Mascara, Monts du Tessalah and Deud-Imbert and also the red wine Mostaganem. The wines from Constantine are very poor wines from a very poor area.

Morocco, also, produces an abundance of red wines somewhat similar to those from Algeria. A sufficiency of white wines is also produced there but these are inferior in quality to the red wines. Fez and Meknès are the chief wine-producing regions and Vin le Fez is considered to be one of the best wines produced in the country. Most of the wine is exported to France or the former French possessions.

Tunisia also exports wine to France, but most of it is of *vin ordinaire* quality. Nearly all of it is red wine but as a speciality some white wine such as Muscat de Tunisia is also made.

22

SOUTH AFRICA

GRAPEVINES were first planted in South Africa in 1655 and, by 1824, 4½ million litres of wines were being exported. Nevertheless, it was not until 1918 and thereafter that the industry of wine production began to show dividends. This was the result of the formation of the K.W.V. or *Ko-operatiewe Wynbouwers Vereniging* (Co-operative Winegrowers' Association), which greatly improved the organisation, production methods and marketing of the industry. About 90 per cent. of the exports of wine from South Africa now comes from the member's wineries. The two main regions where the grape is cultivated for wine making are the Coastal Belt and Little Karoo.

The Coastal Belt. The coastal belt stretches from the coast to Drakenstein, with wine centres at Paarl, Constantia and Stellenbosch. Here the climate is temporate, although the winters may be severe. Spring and autumn are mild and the summer is long and hot. The annual rainfall is about 60 centimetres. The soil varies in composition with shale, sandstone and granite dominating. Vineyards are usually located on the hillsides and on the lower mountain slopes.

Little Karoo. The main centres of wine production in the Little Karoo are Worcester, Montagu, Oudtshoorn, Robertson and Ladysmith. The region stretches from the Drakenstein Ranges to the Swartberg Ranges. Here the climate is hotter and drier, with more severe winters, than in the coastal belt. The annual rainfall averages about 30 centimetres. Consequently the region is more suited to the production of sherries, dessert wines and brandies. Every year is regarded as a vintage year in South Africa, so that the year of production is often not included on the labels.

White Wines. The best white wines of South Africa come from Stellenbosch, Paarl and Tulbagh. Because of the hot climate, special attention is given to inducing a slow fermentation in order to procure white wines of quality. This is usually done by circulating the *must* through a refrigeration unit or by having atemporators in the fermenting vats. These wines are bottled young, probably at six months or a year. They do not improve much by keeping. The species of grapes used are the Riesling, Stein, White French and Clairette Blanche, and the wines have an alcoholic strength of about 12 per cent.

Red Wines. These red wines are classified as light-bodied or full-bodied. The Constantis valley, Somerset West and Stellenbosch produce the light-bodied wines, while Paarl, Durbanville and Stellenbosch make the full-bodied wines. The favourite grapes for the light wines, which have an alcoholic strength of about $12\frac{1}{2}$ per cent., are the Cabernet, and the Shiraz (also known as the Hermitage), the Gamay, the Pinot, the Pinotage, the Pontac and the Shiraz are the most popular species of grapes used for the full-bodied wines, which have an alcoholic strength of over 13 per cent. The red wines are usually matured in bottle for three to four years.

Sherry. Over one-fifth of the Sherry wine imported into Great Britain comes from South Africa. Matured by the Solera system, it is a very good sherry wine and ranks in quality only second to the authentic sherry from Spain. The finest of them are the dry sherries and the medium sherries whose production is carried out on the same lines as that for the Spanish sherries. The 'Flor' or wine yeast also forms naturally in South Africa and this, of course, gives the wine its special characteristics. Grape spirit is added to fortify the wine. It spends about two years in a *criadera*, which is a wine nursery of oak casks where young sherries begin to show their styles, and is then put through the solera system for six years or more for blending and maturing.

The best dry and medium sherries come from Paarl, Stellenbosch, Twibagh and Goudini, while the heavier and sweeter ones come from Worcester, Robertson, Montagu and Bonnievale. The grape species used are the French grape (the Palomino of Spain), the Stein grape, the Green grape and the Pedro Ximénez. The variations of South African sherries are Fino (very dry), Amontillado (medium dry), Oloroso (golden and full-bodied; sweet), Old Brown (darker and sweeter than Oloroso) and Walnut Brown (darker and sweeter still).

Dessert Wines. For dessert wines South Africa produces muscatels and ports, all fortified wines with an alcoholic strength of from 16½ to 20 per cent. Most of the muscatels come from Robertson, Montagu, Bonnievale and the Nuy districts; and the ports from Stellenbosch and Paarl. The muscatels are made from the muscat grape and are matured in cask for up to seven years. They range in colour from amber to deep red. The ports are made from some authentic Portuguese varieties of grape and also from Hermitage, Shikas, Mataro and Pontac grapes. They are matured in casks for up to ten years and then bottled. Their styles are Ruby Port, Tawny Port and Vintage Port. The Ruby is matured in cask for five years, the Tawny for eight years and the Vintage for two years in cask and then up to fifteen years in bottle. White Port, made from the Stein and Muscatel grapes, is matured in cask for less time than any of the others.

Brandies and Liqueurs. An outstanding brandy called Oude Meester is made at Stellenbosch. It is really fine. The K.W.V. produce an assortment of delicious liqueurs of which the brand Van der Hum is best known.

AUSTRALIA AND NEW ZEALAND

AUSTRALIA

THE Australians have only themselves to blame that their wines are not highly thought of and in fact have a rather poor reputation. To the strong outdoor beer-drinking Australian all wine is just 'plonk' and this may be the reason why they have neglected to make full use of the opportunities provided. The natural propensities of many parts of the country for the building up of a wine industry could have been as renowned as any in the world. Despite the fact that the vine was one of Australia's earliest imports, having been brought over in 1788 and planted on the site that is now Sydney's botanical gardens, Australians have not made the most of the vine-growing qualities of their land.

These comments are not intended to imply that the production of wine has been neglected. There are some fine wine regions which produce some excellent wines but the vintners parade most of these under the names of French wines. This practice may well be because of the successful export industry built up by one firm in selling burgundy-type wines to Great Britain. The names may be reasonably descriptive, but who will not tend to think that Australian burgundy, Australian bordeaux or Australian chablis are just about in the same class as British sherry. Some wines were sold to England as far back as 1854, but between 1872 until well after the First World War practically all the exported wine was of the burgundy-type. This burgundy became a popular and respectable drink among that section of the English people which in those precise days was known as the lower middle class. As this class expanded in numbers, so the sale of Australian burgundy prospered, with the consequence that knowledgeable and regular wine-drinkers have relegated all Australian wines to an inferior class.

Australia produces about 155 million litres of wines annually. About a half of this is made into table wines or fortified wines. The other half is distilled into a spirit for fortifying wines, or distilled into brandy. The Australians are wise enough to drink the best of their wines themselves, still calling them 'plonk', and the others are exported, mainly to Britain, Canada and New Zealand. Largely because of the energetic abilities of James Busby, who arrived in Australia in 1824, the wine growers of Australia have an extremely good understanding of the cultivation of the grape, and their good efforts are supported by ideal climates and soils. What has been lacking has been the inability of the middlemen to get proper appreciation for the products. It would be an interesting piece of research to find out why exports approaching 18 million litres in 1927 are now down to less than half that figure. The 1927 figure resulted from the success, or rather the rescue from failure, of a scheme for providing soldiers returning from the 1914–18 War with a livelihood. Settled on lands along the Murray River in the borders of New South Wales and Victoria, the veterans, few of whom could have been experts, produced a bountiful crop of luscious grapes. The industry could not cope with the glut until the Government granted a bounty and excise concessions, the effect of which gave an impetus to the export of fortified wines which has not been sustained.

Once again the excellent cultivation potential of Australia was illustrated, but so was the lack of efficient marketing. The principal areas of production are the Hunter River area, the Murrumbidgee Irrigation area and Corowa in New South Wales; the Murray River area in Victoria; the areas in South Australia of Southern Vales, Coonawarra, Barossa Valley and Adelaide Metropolitan; the Roma area north-west of Brisbane in Queensland; and the Swan Valley area near Perth in Western Australia. It has been found that, except in Western Australia, the great wine-grape species cultivated in Europe are not suitable to the climatic and economic needs of Australia and the most cultivated grapes are those such as Frontignac, the Riesling, the Hermitage, the Pedro Ximénez, the Sémillon and the Rosaki. In the Swan Valley of Western Australia, however, Cabernet Sauvignon grapes are grown, mainly for claret-type wines and it is from this area that a world reputation for quality wines may be some day gained.

Fortified Wines. There are some very good sherry-type wines produced in Australia of which the dry varieties known as Flor Fino, Fino Palido and Special Fino have good reputations. Medium-sweet and cream sherry-type wines are also made in some quantity for the Australians have a sweet tooth. A number of ruby, tawny and white port-style wines are sold under registered trade or brand names. The fortified wines are usually made from the Palomino, Doradillo or Pedro Ximénez grapes.

Red Wines. The Australian red wines have an alcoholic strength of 10 to 14 per cent. They are usually marketed either as clarets or Burgundies and they are deep red in colour. The best are made from the Cabernet Sauvignon grape and the next best from the Shiraz or Hermitage and the Malbec grape. Some of the wines reveal on the labels of their bottles the grape species from which they are made, such as Coonawarra Cabernet and Mount Pleasant Hermitage. But, by and large, the red wines are sold as Australian burgundies or Australian bordeaux with little to differentiate among them except the brand name which is unlikely to have been heard outside Australia.

Rosé Wines. The Grenache grape makes the best Australian rosé wine and much of the other rosé wine is made from the Hermitage, Cabernet or Merlot species. Although often marketed simply as rosé wine, the labels sometimes carry the producer's name and the grape species.

White Wines. The Australian white wines have an alcoholic strength of 11 or 12° G.L. They are usually sold as Chablis, Mosel, Riesling,

Hock of White Burgundy, though they may often show a vineyard or a registered name on the label such as Penfolds Private Bin Riesling. Just as the Australian Bordeaux wines are generally lighter in body than the Burgundies, so the Australian white wines such as Chablis and Mosel are lighter in body than, say, the Hock varieties. Sometimes the grapes for white wines are picked later than others, so that the extra bit of sunshine will make the wine more fulsome. Such a wine is Gramp's Orlando Barossa Riesling Spätlese. The wines do not improve much with age.

Sparkling Wines. When wine people begin to consider Australian sparkling wine, they must always think of the best known of all, Great Western, produced in Victoria. The sparkling wines are marketed as Champagne in Australia, but this practice is forbidden by law in Great Britain and many other countries. Brands with registered names are also marketed, such as Barossa Pearl. But, often Australian sparkling wines are promoted as sparkling Moselle or sparkling Burdundy. The best of the sparkling wines are made after the fashion of Champagne's *Méthode Champenoise*, but much of it is made by the tank or '*cuve close*' method which produces a less satisfactory wine.

In Australia today, big and powerful firms and co-operatives are taking over from the smallholders, and one day this may result in a greater appreciation of Australian wine in the markets of the world. Perhaps the most general criticism of Australian wines is that they lack the acidity that gives good wines their bite. Because of the difference in climate and taste between Britain and Australia and the great distance between the two countries, it is fair to assume that Australian wines are best drunk at their source. With the expansion of economic interests across the Pacific Ocean, Australia may well try to develop large sales of wine in the United States.

The best Australian brandy is made by the pot still method. It is very dark in colour and quite palatable to drink.

NEW ZEALAND

Most New Zealanders drink beer in preference to wines and spirits as the annual average individual consumption shows—80 litres of beer, 3·1 litres of wine and 3 litres of spirits. But since 1950 there has been a considerable growth in the wine industry, although the total production is still not much more than 5·5 million litres a year. The momentum of the industry's growth is confined to the two centres of Auckland and Hawke's Bay. Auckland is the more important centre from which come the firmly established wineries such as Mount Lebanon, Pleasant Valley Vineyards, Mazuran, Panorama and the Western Vineyard, Ltd. Hawke's Bay is associated with such wineries as Macdonalds, which has been taken over by the renowned firm of McWilliams of Australia, and with the Marist Mission and the Wohnsiedler Wine Company, Ltd.

In all there are about 350 hectares of land under the vine of which both hybrid and *Vitis vinifera* species are cultivated. Most of the wines produced are dessert wines, which are marketed as ports, sherries, hocks or madeiras. The table wines also are sold under descriptions which indicate their similarity to the traditional European wines such as claret, sauternes and hock. In fact, none of these wines, to a cultivated palate, resemble their European counterparts—the New Zealanders have a better taste for beer.

THE UNITED STATES OF AMERICA, SOUTH AMERICA AND CANADA

THE U.S.A.

THE cultivation of the vine for making wine has had a history of ups and down in the United States of America. Some of the earliest settlers in the East planted vines and today many of the eastern states have some vineyards but the climate with its rugged winters on that side of the continent will only permit the hardy native grape vines, Catawbas and Concords, to flourish. These produce wines which are really palatable only to the inhabitants of the region. The most successful cultivations are in Ohio where the industry was greatly encouraged by the enormous immigrations from Europe last century. Competition from California was almost overpowering, prohibition destroyed the trade legally and the avoidance of the law and then the reaction when prohibition was repealed have all had their influence. Today there are vineyards which are commercially important in the Hudson River valley, Finger Lakes, Chautauqua and Niagara areas of New York state and along the shores of Lake Erie in Ohio. Some wine is also produced in Maryland, Michigan, New Jersey and Washington and there are a few vineyards in Arkansas, Georgia and Illinois. From the point of view of the European taste the best thing that can be said about the wines produced in these areas is that they have the honesty not to borrow European names. The wines are usually called after the varieties of grape-vines cultivated, Concord, Delaware, Catawba or Norton. While not giving much credit to the wines produced from these vines, it must always be remembered that it was cuttings from these vines that saved and have since preserved the vines of Europe from the scourge of *Phylloxera*. Unfortunately, Europe has not been able to repay the debt because attempts to graft species of *Vitis vinifera* from Europe have been unsuccessful.

Quite different conditions obtain in California with a climate that might have been specially designed for the cultivation of fruit and in particular for the best species of wine-producing grapes. Originally introduced by the expert Spanish missionaries and later strongly reinforced by the importation of European vine species, the cultivation of the vine in California has now grown to a large and important industry, quite outshining in quality and quantity the brave efforts of the eastern cultivations. The annoying thing is that the Californians have used the European names for their wines, which creates the impression that they are unworthy to have an individual christening. Still, there is the advantage that some idea of the wines may be obtained by their naming after the well-known wines.

Californian claret and burgundy have a higher alcoholic content than their namesakes, but they usually have less acidity and the red wines are darker. Californian chablis is not even made from the pinot Chardonnay grape, and although a reasonable wine, it is very far from being a French chablis. Sauternes has lost its final sibilant in crossing the Atlantic and sauterne can be a dry white wine and haute sauterne a sweet wine. Riesling, Moselle and Hock, in their Californian dressing are white wines without much body. Californian Tokay would not be recognised by a Hungarian, but perhaps the name has been accorded as a tribute to a Hungarian nobleman named Haraszthy who settled in California in the middle of the last century. He brought the expertise of a long line of wine-making forbears, together with great energy and generosity to the diffusion of European species of vines throughout the State. It must have been he who developed the Zinfandel grape, hardly ever found outside California, which produces an unusual but full and fruity red wine, which has the honour of being sold under its own name of Zinfandel. The stupidity of prohibition did grave harm to the industry in two ways. First the abolition of wine-making for about fourteen years and secondly the destruction of American taste by bootleg spirits. The trade has now completely recovered and modern methods of production and marketing are ensuring that Americans and, through increasing exports, the rest of the world, can appreciate these wines at a very reasonable cost. Perhaps the very finest of French and German wines cannot be competed with in quality, but California is producing in abundance good wine reasonably available to all. In the marketing of the wine American independence is asserting itself, and the wines are now being sold under true American or grape-species' names without pretending they have anything to do with the snob wines of the world. Another innovation which is of considerable importance in securing that the wines will be properly appreciated with some expert pretensions, is the practice of printing on the labels the pedigree of the wine, its year and vineyard, its grape and other details of the making. It can be confidently anticipated that California will become one of the really great wine regions of the world, and that its capacity for large production will help to ensure that the increasing demand for good wine will not have to be met by debasing the traditional wines as has recently been alleged in regard to some Burgundies and Chiantis.

The recovery since prohibition and the promise for the future have both been greatly stimulated by research at the University of California, which has been wise enough not to limit itself to the time-honoured processes of the Old World for the cultivation of grapes or the manufacture of wine. The varying soils of California permit the prolific production of nearly all kinds of grapes and therefore the making of nearly all kinds of wine. Some enterprises are so huge that the traditional methods of harvesting the grapes would not be capable of gathering the vast quantities of grapes. Nor would traditional pressing processes manage the quantity. American technical expertise is solving these problems, largely by university research, so that mechanical harvesting, pressing in enormous tanks and all the other processes of wine-making can be carried out economically without impairing the quality of the wine.

The types of Californian wines have been classified by the Wine Institute and Wine Advisory Board, both of California, in five categories, appetiser wine, red table wine, white table wine, sweet dessert wine and sparkling wine.

Appetiser Wines. These carry the names made famous in the old established European wine regions. California sherry varies from pale dry wines to very dark amber rich sweet wines and all of them have a somewhat nutty flavour. California Madeira and Marsala are like sweet sherries. California vermouth is usually sold under the brand names of the producers and vary with the particular flavour imparted. They can be dry and light coloured and sweet and amber coloured.

White Table Wines. Most of these are sold under the European name that seems to suit them. The descriptions are reasonably accurate except that Sauterne is a full-bodied dry wine although there are some sweet wines called Sweet Sauterne, Haute Sauterne or Château Sauterne. The alcoholic content varies between 10 and 14° G.L.

Red Table Wines. The red table wines also have an alcoholic content not exceeding 14° G.L. Californian clarets and burgundies are the best known, the former being dry, red, medium wines and the latter being more ruby in colour with more body and flavour. Some of these are bottled under names that indicate the grapes that they have been made from, such as Carignane, Grignolino and Mourestel all claret-types and Charbono, Gamay and Pinot Noir burgundy types. California Chianti is even bottled in the Italian basket style but the wine is probably a bit softer than the Italian wine. Zinfandel wine has already been mentioned (page 175). Barbera and Barberone wines are full-bodied and very dark in colour and the flavour of the barbera grape is very noticeable. Aleatico wine is sweeter than the others and has the muscat bouquet and flavour of its grape. The rosé wine is dry and light, somewhat pink in colour, and is a pleasant drink in hot weather.

Dessert Wines. There are Californian sherries, ports, muscatels, tokays, màlagas and angelicas. Except for the angelicas and tokays, they all resemble their European namesakes. The tokay is a blended wine which is sweeter than sherry but has the nutty flavour of the sherry included in the blending. Angelica is light coloured but very sweet, having up to as much as 15 per cent. unfermented sugar.

Sparkling Wines. The Californian sparkling wines include 'Champagne', 'Pink Champagne' and a variety of almost any other of the

Californian wines that can also be made to sparkle. The 'champagnes' vary in sweetness and follow the French fashion in their description as *brut* etc. The 'pink champagne' is made from rosé wine. Quite a lot of the ordinary wines are made to sparkle by carbonation, but these are cheaper than the natural sparklers.

SOUTH AMERICA

Chile. French and German immigrants to Chile established the pattern of vine cultivation there. They were greatly helped by the fact that Chile, sheltered by the Andes and wrapped around by the Pacific, was isolated enough to miss the *Phylloxera* scourge that devastated most other vineyards of the world. The *Vitis vinifera* vine flourished in Chile and grafting with American roots has not been necessary. The red wines are made after the style of Bordeaux wines, using the Cabernet grape, or of Burgundy, using the Pinot Noir grape. The best dessert wines are made from Muscat grapes and for white wines the Riesling, Sauvignon Blanc and Sémillon grape species are mainly used. The best Chilean wines come from the Maipot and Aconcagua Valleys. Near Santiago is the excellent vineyard of Undurraga, the wines from which are exported in attractive flagon-shaped boxbeutel. Under Government control, wines for export are classified as 'courant', 'special', 'reserve' or 'gran vino' according to whether they have matured for one, two, four or six years, respectively.

Argentina. About three-quarters of the wine produced in Argentina is red vin ordinaire. The many Italians who settled in the country after the Second World War have had a decided influence on Argentinian viticulture. Most of the vine species cultivated are now the European Riesling, Sauvignon Blanc and Pinot Blanc grapes for white wines and Cabernet Sauvignon, Merlot and Malbec grapes for red wines. The Mendoza district is the best region, its output being responsible for three-quarters of the national total of 2 490 million litres a year. Other good districts are San Juan, Rio Negro, La Rioja, Jujuy and Salta. Some good brandies are made at Catamarca.

Wines are made in Bolivia, Brazil, Ecuador, Paraguay, Peru and Uruguay but the majority of them are consumed in their native lands.

CANADA

Canada produces about 22 million litres of wine a year. As the winters are very cold, the *Vitis vinifera* vines do not thrive in Canada, so American-type vines are used such as the Delaware, Duchess and

Niagara species. These are known as 'fox' grapes as they give the wine produced from them a taste described as foxy, although a vixen would not agree with the description. Most of the vines are trained on trellises. The Niagara Peninsula of southern Ontario is the chief wine-producing region and the wines are mostly port-type or sherry-type.

❦ 25 ❦

THE WINES OF ENGLAND

A FEW pockets of vineyards still battle against the climate in England, the brave survivors of the many vineyards cultivated as the result of the introduction of viticulture by the Romans and, later, by the spread from the 9th century onwards of monastic orders into Britain. Not all monks were fat and jolly, but wine was essential for the Mass and the more that was produced provided a surplus for sale to provide a revenue for the upkeep of the monasteries. By these communities, wine making was gradually extended from the southern counties until there were vineyards even in Stirlingshire. When his matrimonial troubles led Henry VIII to dissolve, some would say plunder, the monasteries, the vineyards fell into decay. To-day most people would guess that no grapes are cultivated in England for wine making but, in fact, there are reasonably successful vineyards in Hampshire, Lincolnshire, Norfolk, Surrey and Sussex and a few elsewhere. Perhaps the most outstanding of these vineyards are in Hampshire, one on the estate of Sir Guy Salisbury-Jones at Hambledon and the other owned by the Gore-Brownes at Beaulieu. These vineyards produce white wines after the style of German white wines and the Beaulieu vineyard also produces a good rosé wine. The produce is not abundant although some of the wines are exported to America and even to the Continent.

Of course, viticulture is not easy in England. The grapes are gathered late in October or early in November and even then a satisfactory degree of ripeness is not always obtained because of the unpredictable climate. Even in the bright, sunny and long summer of 1969 with its warm Indian summer, the grapes in a Norfolk vineyard produced a maximum potential of only 8·8° alcohol G.L. This indicates that in a bad or normal year the grape must would need considerable sugaring if a reasonable alcoholic strength were to be achieved. We have seen already that sugaring never produces wines of fine quality.

Birds, especially blackbirds and starlings, are another hazard, for they seem to take to grapes like a child to ice-cream. The only protection from their greedy devastation is to cover the vines with netting, but this is an expensive and laborious task.

At Oxted in Surrey, there is a research station for viticulture where much good work is being done, but, by and large, each individual grape-grower has to make his own experiments by trial and error. It is to be hoped that the research and experiments will soon effect a reconciliation between grape species and soil and weather conditions. At present the grape species usually favoured are the Riesling-Sylvaner or Müller-Thurgau, the Seyve-Villard and the Teleki.

Merrydown in Sussex has given itself a notable reputation for the production of 'wines' made from fruits other than the grape. The producers also make a very good authentic wine from Riesling-Sylvaner grapes, but their sound reputation rests on their fruit wines such as apple wine, blackberry wine, elderberry wine, raspberry wines and so on. They are all well worth trying.

From the commercial angle, the most important development in the making of wine in England stems from the enterprise of Alexander Mitsotakis and Emmanuel Rodie. These two gentlemen in 1900 hit upon the idea of importing concentrated grape juice, free of revenue duty, from the Continent. On arrival, the evaporated moisture is replaced, fermentation takes place and the end result is wine which attracts much lighter taxation from the Excise men than imported wine. A company was formed in 1904 and since then the production of British wines has flourished. About 90 per cent. of the product is of the fortified wine variety and the acknowledged favourite with the British public (we cannot bring ourselves to say the British palate) is the rich ruby port. British made sherries and vermouths are also popular. The great virtue of British wines is their cheapness and their consistency in colour, taste and flavour. It is estimated that one in every four bottles of wine drunk in Britain today is a British wine. Perhaps President De Gaulle was wise to keep Britain out of the European Common Market! Britannia might still rule in a liquid environment.

ᏫᎦ 26 ᎧᎦ

WINE AND FOOD
HARMONY

THE fortunate people who live in wine-producing countries have
not, as we know from our holidays abroad, worried too much
about their water supplies. When thirsty, they drink the local
wine. In other countries, where wine has to be imported and is therefore
somewhat expensive, the drinking of wine is almost always associated
with the eating of food. Just as we like to change our menus, so we also
like to change our wines. Although perhaps too much can be made of
the fetish of linking particular foods with particular wines, there can be
no doubt that both food and wine will be enjoyed all the more if they
are both selected in relationship to each other. The marriage of wine
and food depends on many factors. Most people are content to follow
the conventional rules that red wine goes with red meat, white wine
with white meat, rosé wine when one is in doubt and champagne
when one can afford it. There is merit in a simple rule for the lazy
minded and that is about all that can be said for this conventional rule,
which ignores some other important considerations.

It ignores, for example, the time of day. It is no use indulging in full
big red wines, whatever the fare, in the middle of the day if serious work
is to be done in the afternoon, whether by brain or muscle. Heavy wines
make the imbiber heavy also, and it is better to leave them for evening
meals, which are eaten in more leisurely fashion and which give more
time for both the consumption and the digestion of both food and wine.
The time of year is also important. In hot sweltering weather, a nicely
chilled white or rosé wine is usually a far more acceptable and sensible
choice than a luke-warm red one. In contrast, cold weather demands
warming red wines, and menus should be organised accordingly.

Whether a wine is chosen to suit the food, or the food to suit the
wine, is a matter of personal preference, but few people realise that it is
also important to choose wines to suit the guests. Old friends will
create no problem, but it is worthwhile giving some thought in
advance to the likes and dislikes of newcoming guests. This is a useful

courtesy. There is rather a dreadful snag of particular and exquisite concern to the wine-loving host. How sad it is for a host if his keen desire to be at his entertaining best is continuously hampered by the polite necessity to brush from his jogging memory that vulgar proverb about *casting pearls*. It may sound harsh, even rude, to suggest that a bottle of a favourite wine should not be *cracked* for the benefit of the undeserving, but think of watching a noble wine being quaffed, without comment, as if it were water, and obviously without recognition. A domaine-bottled Romanée-Conti has gone when a Spanish Burgundy would have been enjoyed just as much.

The proportion of men and women in a party is also a matter for deliberation. Unless the choice is a single wine such as a rosé, it is better to provide a red wine and a white wine and to offer each guest a choice. But whatever you do, do not attempt to order a pedigree wine for the discerning and at the same party order a routine wine for the others. That is really bad manners.

The atmosphere and environment of a restaurant should be allowed to help you choose a wine. It is difficult, for instance, not to choose Italian wines in a typical Italian restaurant. A Tuscan wine, say, will go so well in the atmosphere of the establishment and with the fare. Yet taken out of this environment into a restaurant where English or French cooking is the rule, such a wine will seem quite limp. But it is always the host who has to make the final choice of wine, although he may consult his guests. If in doubt he must be guided by his own palate.

As in life, so in wine, it is best to follow tradition until you know what alternative you want or until you feel experimental. The 'set' rules for the appropriate wine to have with a dish have been developed over the centuries and have been well proven. Even so, they are not the be all and end all. It is wise not to be too academic because unconventionalities sometimes rub each other the right way. The main thing is that the marriage of wine with food should be harmonious. It would be a waste of time, for instance, to try to match a delicate white wine with a grilled steak, or to have a full-bodied red wine with boiled fish. In the first case the wine would be completely dominated by the food, and in the second the food would be overpowered by the wine.

There are some dishes which no wine can accompany satisfactorily and almost any wine will be ruined to the taste if the food is vinegary. The word vinegar comes from the French *vin aigre* meaning sour wine. It is best to avoid drinking wine with hors d'oeuvre or dressed salad when their ingredients include vinegar. Even mint sauce, with its vinegar content, can spoil an accompanying wine. Eggs do not go well with wine, probably because of their sulphur content, although this does not by any means apply to cheese omelettes. Carrots are too sweet for the enjoyment of a dry white wine. Curries are too spicy and highly flavoured to go well with wine, although it would not hurt to try a Gewürtztraminer wine; *Gewürtz* means spicy and the wine is certainly that. Sweets made with chocolate are obnoxious to wine.

White wines go best with white meats. An exception would be stuffed hot chicken or turkey which deserve light red wines. Red wines are best to accompany red meats. Sweet wines should accompany sweet dishes. In the order of service, dry white wines are served first and sweet white wines are served after red table wines. Young wines are served before old and dry wines are served before sweet wines. Good wines are served before great wines for it is best to finish with the finest.

Another generality is that, if you are having wine with your meal, your drink before the meal ought to be a grape apéritif. Cocktails and spirits dull the palate and destroy its receptivity for what is to come. There is also less likelihood of unwanted after-effects if you do not mix the grain with the grape. The following notes give some suggestions for ensuring harmony between food and wine:

Apéritifs: Dry Champagne, dry sherries, dry white port, dry madeiras, vermouths, dry white wine;

Hors-d'œuvre: No wine if the dishes include vinegar;

Oysters: Dry Champagne, Muscadet, Chablis;

Smoked salmon or trout: Pouilly Blanc Fumé, Muscadet, Traminer;

Pâtés: Dry vigorous red wine;

Snails: Dry white wine;

Fish: Dry Moselles, Alsace Riesling, white Burgundy;

Shell fish such as lobster: Hocks and Graves;

Lobster Thermidor or Lobster à l'Américaine: These can stand up to a rosé wine, but not Anjou, which is too sweet, or even a very light Beaujolais; a semi-sweet white wine is also a good choice;

Egg dishes: No wine, or at least not a good quality wine. Eggs have the effect of neutralising the taste of wine;

Farinaceous dishes (spaghetti etc.): A light red wine; nothing to beat Italian wines for these dishes;

Poultry (cold): Dry to medium dry white wine such as Graves;

Poultry (stuffed, hot): Light red wine such as Beaujolais or a light claret;

Meat dishes: A light red wine such as claret goes best with lamb cutlets, saddle of lamb, leg of lamb, sweetbreads, roast veal, roast pork and venison. Mixed grills which include bacon and kidney are not flattered by wine.

A heavy red wine such as the Burgundies and the Rhône reds go best with steaks of all description and with roast goose, roast and braised duck, chicken chasseur, chicken marengo, haricot of lamb and ragoût of lamb.

17 Modern distillery seen through the windows of the control gallery at Le Peu, Cognac

18 Château Margaux – first growth Médoc

19 Château Beychevelle – fourth growth Médoc

20 The entrance to the cellars of Château Ausone, St-Émilion

21 Birthplace of Champagne – the Abbey of Hautvillers

22 Hospices de Beaune founded in the 15th century to help the sick, the poor and the aged

23 A Hennessy Château and the River Charente

24 Berncastel-Kues
and a sweep of
the River Moselle

Game: Light red wines are best with quail, partridge, pigeon, and the heavy red wines go well with pheasant, teal, snipe and woodcock. Of the four-legged game, rabbit and venison, go well with light red wine, while kid, wild boar and hare go better with full red wine.

Vegetables: With light red wine—spinach, potatoes cooked in milk (maître d'hôtel), new potatoes, green peas and braised lettuce. With heavy red wine—braised celery, turnips, haricot beans, roast potatoes, buttered cabbage and mushrooms. With dry white wines—cauliflower and braised chicory. With semi-sweet white wines—asparagus with Sce. Mousseline; and haricot beans.

Sweets: Sweet Champagne, Sauternes, Tokay and the wines made from the late gathered German grapes.

Cheeses: Red wines, especially the clarets and port, go excellently.

Dessert: Port, cream Sherries, Bual and Malmsey, Madeiras, Málaga, Marsala and the Vin Doux Naturel.

Coffee: Cognac, Armagnac, sundry liqueurs and malt whisky.

CR 27 CR

THE SERVICE OF WINE

As soon as guests are seated comfortably in a restaurant, they are usually approached by a gentleman with a chain hanging from his neck and at the end of it there is a small silver cup or *tastevin* with which he sometimes tastes the wine before serving it to guests. He is called the *sommelier* or wine butler. He holds an important position and a very responsible one within the hierarchy of restaurant personnel. A good sommelier is an asset to customer and to management. Knowledgeable about the wine list and the cellar, he is able to guide and advise the customer, helping to make their meals more pleasantly memorable. Also, as he is the expert, he will do the job well and this should result in increased sales.

Many people sit in awe of the wine butler and are guided by his least murmur. Others are in such a command of the situation that they do not require his advice, but simply make their choice and he takes their orders and serves their drinks at the appropriate times and in the correct manner. Unfortunately there are many people also responsible for the service of drink in restaurants, who have so little knowledge of and feeling for what they are doing that they might as well be serving water. These people can undo in five minutes what vignerons, shippers, importers, middlemen and cellarmen have spent years striving to do—to produce a bottle in perfect condition for the customer. A good sommelier will ensure that their work has not been in vain.

The first consideration in serving wine is the handling of the bottle. The bottle must be handled with respect, for the wine inside is alive and does not like rough treatment. Champagne, for example, must get very little disturbance or shaking because of its effervescent characteristics. Old red wines and vintage and crusted ports, during their maturing in bottle have thrown a deposit or crust to the bottom or side of the bottle where it has settled reasonably firmly. To disturb this deposit before decanting or service would spoil the delicacy of the wine and impart a coarseness to the taste and a spoilt appearance in the glass. The best way to bring such wines from the cellar is in a wine-cradle which will hold the bottle at the same angle as that at which it was stored, thus keeping the sediment undisturbed. Even so, the cradled bottle must be carried steadily and not swung, as is sometimes done by the careless wine butler or his commis (junior assistant).

Temperature. Dry Sherries, dry Ports, dry Madeiras and similar wines, when served as apéritifs should be served pleasantly chilled. Thirty minutes in a refrigerator will provide the right temperature. In a restaurant, the order for apéritifs is taken before the order for food. After the food has been ordered the sommelier again approaches the host with the wine list and takes the order for wine. Ideally the experienced and wise host will have ordered the wine well in advance of his arrival at table, perhaps by telephone or by early arrival at the restaurant. This will give the sommelier ample time to ensure that the wine is served at the right temperature. Advance ordering, however, implies either that the host will have some control over the food which his guests will order, or that his instructions to the sommelier have allowed for alternative wines chosen to suit the selected food. Most good restaurants have a ready stock of wines available at the appropriate temperatures. This satisfies those customers who want to deliberate over their choice of food and wine when they have arrived at table, and may possibly only require a single bottle.

Dry white wines and rosé wines are served at a temperature of about 13° C. Champagne and sparkling wines at about 7° and sweet wines at about 10°. Red wines are served *chambré*, that is at the temperature of the room, about 18° C.

White wines are served before rosé or red wines, unless they are of the sweet variety. Young wines are served before old wines. Always build up to a climax by serving the good wine before the great wine.

White Wines. One of the most appealing characteristics of white wine is that they are or can be so refreshing. Chilling helps to impart this quality. Severe chilling must be avoided as this will dull or kill the bouquet. Sweet white wines, because of their initial blandness, require extra chilling. There are two basic methods of chilling wine. The simplest way is to place the bottle in mild refrigeration for about half to three-quarters of an hour, or longer still for the sweeter varieties and Champagnes. The other and quicker way is to use an ice-bucket in which there is a mixture of ice and water which will reach to the neck of the bottle. This method chills the wine properly in about 20 minutes for dry wines and 30 minutes or so for the sweet wines and Champagnes. If salt (sea salt is best) is added to the water and ice, the chilling will be effected in a shorter time, though not necessarily more satisfactorily as the salt reduces the temperature considerably. Too much of a contrast in temperature is not good for wines.

Rosé Wines. Rosé wines may be treated similarly to white wines, but there are many people who prefer them served at room temperature. Incidentally, there are those who enjoy sweet white wines such as Sauternes and Tokays only when served at room temperature. These preferences and any other idiosyncracies should be made known to the sommelier as soon as possible if he is to allow for them.

Red Wines. 'Serve red wines at room temperature', can be a misleading injunction. Some restaurants and domestic dining-rooms are kept, perhaps unwittingly, almost as cold as their caves or cellars. Everybody knows such places. Red wine will mature ideally at such a temperature, but it will not reach its full bloom or taste in such conditions. Cold red wine always tastes retarded. It needs warmth so that its ethers can become volatile. These, on being released, produce the splendid bouquet and aroma associated with these wines.

We can be thankful that most restaurants and homes nowadays are properly heated to a temperature which is suitable for red wines. A good way to chambrer these wines is to keep a stock in the dispense bar attached to the restaurant. Another is to put an attractive display of the wines within the restaurant itself. The bottles are always decorative and they can contribute to a convivial atmosphere, and to sales.

Unfortunately there are restaurateurs and hosts at many a private dinner table who do not trouble to bring their red wines to a proper temperature. They may adopt the dubious practice at the last minute of plunging the bottle into hot water, or wrapping the bottle in a hot cloth or putting the bottle near a fire or radiator, but these methods create too sharp a contrast in the temperature of the wine, which will lose its character and become limpid and flat. If there is insufficient time to bring the wine gradually to room temperature, there is a reasonable but ideal way of dealing with the problem, and this is to serve the wine into warm glasses. Otherwise the wine can be poured from the bottle into a warmed decanter that has been dipped into hot water. To do this in a restaurant, the sommelier should first seek the permission of the customer. Despite these possibilities, wine may sometimes be served at its cellar temperature into cold glasses. The wise drinker will then warm the glass between the palms of his hands before he drinks.

Service. Having ensured that the wine to be served has been handled properly and is at the right temperature, the sommelier takes the bottle to the right-hand side of the host. Using a clean, white and neatly folded cloth as a contrasting background, he presents the wine to the host, indicating verbally at the same time the name of the wine and its vintage year. The host, being satisfied that this is the wine he asked for, nods his approval and the sommelier proceeds to open the bottle. He first produces a wine-knife, often called 'the waiter's friend', which is nothing more than a penknife with a corkscrew and clamp. The clamp can also be used for removing crown caps and sometimes the knife may also have a little cutter for dealing with any awkward wires on Champagne bottles. The sommelier, using the blade of the wine-knife, cuts the tinfoil or lead foil about one quarter of an inch below the lip of the bottle, and then removes the cap. This practice allows the wine to be poured without coming into contact with the foil, which would affect the taste of the wine or might just possibly lead in time to lead poisoning. The cork is now showing and, along with the neck, it is wiped free of mould or dust. Some corks do show a bit of mould which is usually more unsightly than harmful. A clean table-napkin is then wrapped around the neck of the bottle to protect the hands just in case the bottle is faulty. The corkscrew is pushed gently but firmly into the centre of the top of the cork, penetrating deeply but on no account so far as to protrude through the other end. Should it do so, some cork residue will get into the wine, and the metal of the corkscrew, if it reaches the wine, might have an adverse effect on the wine. The best corkscrews are the wide spiralled variety. The thin ones are likely to make a hole in the cork, damaging it without getting a grip. The separate clamp on the knife is fastened by the left hand to the rim of the neck of the bottle, and the cork is gradually eased out of the neck with pressure from the right hand. The extraction must be firm but gentle, the last few millimetres being extracted by hand in order to allow air to reach the wine more steadily. If a less-than-perfect job has left some cork fragments floating on top, this should be poured into a separate glass and taken away. If the job has been badly done or a cork of poor quality has tended to crumble with the result that the cork has been pushed into the wine, there is a special instrument, shaped like a pair of stilts but joined together at one end, which will extract the cork. The long legs, pressed together, are pushed into the wine below the floating cork. By releasing the hand pressure, the legs spread apart and their sharp curved ends grip the cork, which can now be pulled right out.

When the cork is out, it should be nosed by the sommelier, who should find that it smells of wine, not of cork. If the cork has a musty or fungoid smell, the wine itself has probably been contaminated. This is generally known as 'corked wine', wine affected by a faulty cork. If the wine is good, the inside and outside of the neck of the bottle is wiped free of dust or cork particles. The wine butler, with the host's permission, may pour a sample into his *tastevin* and taste it to make double sure that the wine is in good condition. The wine is now ready for pouring.

Pouring. All beverages are served in a restaurant from the right-hand side. This practice allows the food waiter to continue his service of food from the left-hand side. The bottle is held in such a way that the label is clearly visible to the person who is being served. Some people are shy of asking their hosts what wine they are having and the host himself, for other reasons, may be shy of telling them. If the bottle is held correctly there will be no need for asking or telling. A decent mouthful is poured into the host's glass first. This is known as 'giving the say' because after tasting the sample the host will *say* whether everything is right or not. The host is given this tasting for three reasons. First, to ensure that the wine is in good condition; second, to check that the wine is correctly temperatured; and third, if there has been a mishap with the cork and some fragments still remain in the wine, to ensure that all the fragments are contained in the small tasting, which can then be discarded with relatively little loss of wine.

After the 'say' has been given, the sommelier does not at once fill up the host's glass but he moves round the table to the right serving each guest in turn until he finally fills the glass of the host. But he does not in fact fill any of the glasses, but only pours enough into each glass, say a half or two-thirds full, to allow the wine to be gently swirled around the glass and to allow it to be nosed without risk of dunking the drinker's nose. After pouring into each glass, the sommelier gives the bottle a quick twist to the right as he finishes pouring. This prevents tears or drips of wine from falling onto the tablecloth with unsightly results or, worse, onto someone's clothes. The rim is then lightly wiped with the service napkin.

White wines, if chilled in an ice bucket, are opened while immersed in the water and ice in order to maintain the chilled temperature. Before serving, the bottle is dried completely with the clean cloth which is tied to the bucket for the purpose. After serving, the wine bottle is returned to the bucket.

Wines brought in a cradle are opened in front of the host. It is essential that the front of the cradle is elevated slightly while the cork is being drawn, or else some wine will gush out following the cork. A side plate turned upside down on which the front of the cradle can be propped will prevent such an accident.

Decanting. All red wines that have been a long time in bottle require decanting, which is simply the transference of a wine from its original bottle into a glass decanter or some other clean fresh container. The object is to draw the wine off its lees or sediment formed during the ageing process. The wine in its new receptacle should be perfectly clear and bright and sediment-free. The techniques of decanting are discussed in detail in the chapter on Port and the special techniques of serving Champagne are dealt with in the chapter on Champagne.

Before decanting wine in a restaurant, the sommelier must always have the permission of his customer, and as decanting is usually done in the cellar or dispense bar, the original bottle and cork must afterwards be brought to the table for the host's inspection.

Glasses. Wine-glasses should be large enough when half full to hold a decent helping of wine. The stemmed tulip-shaped glass is an excellent one as it is attractive and its narrowing rim concentrates the bouquet as it rises in the glass. There are speciality glasses for wine of different regions. Some sketches of these and of some special bottles are given on page 189. Above all other considerations, wine-glasses should be of good quality glass with plain bowls. Coloured stems are permissible and indeed are attractive features on hock glasses (brown stems) and Moselle glasses (green stems). In years gone by there was a vogue for coloured bowls which were useful for disguising fliers or floating sediment. But sparklingly clear bowls are essential for the showing of the true colour and clarity of a wine.

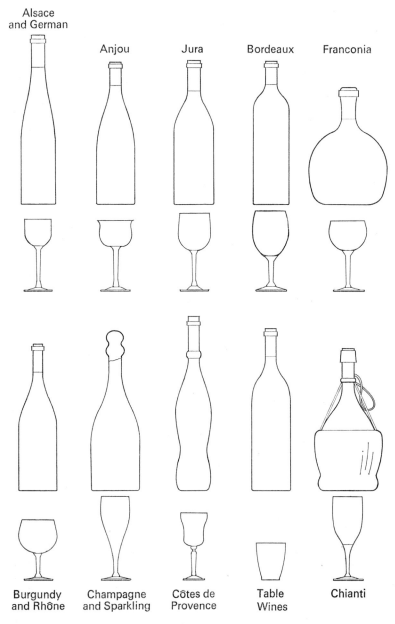

Alsace and German · Anjou · Jura · Bordeaux · Franconia

Burgundy and Rhône · Champagne and Sparkling · Côtes de Provence · Table Wines · Chianti

Bottles and their Special Glasses

The long stems on some glasses are particularly useful when drinking white wine, for then there is less temptation to handle the glass by the bowl, a misdemeanour which would automatically raise the temperature of the wine. So, when drinking white wine always hold the glass by the stem.

Finally, wine is meant to accompany food during a meal. It is an escort and should be served with the dishes and not after the dish has been consumed. It is better to serve wine too early rather than too late.

THE WINE LIST

A Wine List is a list of drinks, both alcoholic and non-alcoholic, which are available for sale in an establishment. Wines make up the bulk of this list, hence the name.

Although there are many styles of Wine Lists, there are in catering two basic types—the Restaurant List and the Banquet List. Restaurant wine lists show the complete range of drinks held for sale, while the Banquet list displays a more modest selection, concentrating on those wines and drinks which experience has shown are popular at large functions and banquets. But whatever the type of list, one rule must not be ignored—the wine list must never show items that are not actually stocked. It is most irritating for any host who has spent time considering the list and has made his selection to be told that his choice is no longer available. It is much better to delete rather than deflate, even though the deletion may adversely affect the appearance of a particular page.

Wine lists are silent sellers and even on their own they can persuade people to buy what is on offer. To do this, however, they must be informative, legible and attractive. Too often they are just plain dull, the only distinguishing feature being the name of the premises. A wine list that is distinctive will stimulate sales, therefore money spent on design and presentation will quickly be recouped.

Of course, there is also the extreme case where a wine list is so overpoweringly lavish that it intimidates inexperienced guests and unless the wine butler is sympathetic to the situation a possible sale will be lost and another glass of water will be served.

Wine Lists vary in presentation and in the information they give. Some include maps of the wine regions and photographs of wine making. Others have Bacchanalian drawings and very often introductory notes on the different wine regions and descriptive writing on individual wines. Brief notes on the different wines can be helpful to a guest when making his choice and in fact are rather better and more interesting than the fallible wine and food harmony charts that one sometimes sees. There once was a vogue for wine lists to be interspersed with well-known sayings and proverbs such as:

In vino veritas.
'A day without wine is like a day without sunshine.'
'Eat, drink and love, the rest's not worth a fillip.'

These usually appeared on the bottom of each page but they are now thought to be *passé*.

The size of the wine list is very important. It must not be so large that it is cumbersome to handle or likely to cause accidents when being used. Some are so gigantic that they dominate everything else on the table. Yet on the other hand, it is essential that they look consequential enough to appeal to the 'ego' of the diner. The texture of the cover of the list is also important because it is handled a great deal. A durable cover is essential if the wine list is meant to last for any length of time.

It is a waste of time and money to include drinks which past experience shows there is no call for.

For a large list it is a good idea to have a thumb index enabling the customer to go immediately to the area he is interested in. It is also helpful for the busy wine butler who's time is always at a premium.

The list should, where appropriate, give the following information about each wine:

The Bin No.
The name of the wine together with any descriptive comments necessary.
The Vintage Year.
The shipper of the wine.
Whether the wine is château bottled or otherwise.
The price of the wine per magnum, per bottle and per half bottle.

The Order in which Drinks appear on a Wine List. There is no guideline as to the order in which drinks should appear on a list, although it is customary to begin with Champagne. This practice is due possibly to the exalted position Champagne holds amongst wines together with the fact that it is one of the most expensive and versatile of drinks.

Here is a suggested sequence of drinks, the order is a personal preference:

Champagne	Red Bordeaux
Sparkling wines	White Burgundy
Apéritifs	Red Burgundy
White Bordeaux	Rhône wines

Loire wines	Málaga
Alsatian wines	Marsala
Other Regional wines of France	Liqueurs
Rosé wines	Cognac
Carafe wines	Armagnac
Wine Cups	Other Brandies
Moselle wines	Gin
Rhine wines	Rum
Italian wines	Vodka
Spanish wines	Whisky—Scotch, Irish,
Portuguese wines	American, Canadian
Hungarian wines	Other Spirits
Yugoslavian wines	Beers and Lagers
Wines of other countries	Cider
Sherry	Mineral waters
Port	Aerated waters
Madeira	Minerals, Juices and Squashes

Cigars (a selection of cigars is normally included on a wine list)

The following are some Key Points to consider when Compiling a Wine List

Will the list reflect the character of the establishment?

Will it suit the type of clientele frequenting the premises giving a sufficient variation of drinks to suit their tastes and spending power.

How much will the wine list cost to produce?

What size is it going to be?

Are illustrations going to be used?

Can it be printed locally?

Will it have a balanced selection?

Has the staff the necessary knowledge and experience to serve correctly all the drinks to be listed?

Will the cellar manager and his present staff be able to cope with the range to be listed?

Is there sufficient cellar space to accommodate the wines to be offered?

Has the storage area the temperature variations necessary for the different styles of wine?

Has the establishment the necessary equipment for serving the different drinks—sundry glasses, ice buckets, wine baskets, decanters, coasters and so on?

Are the suppliers' trading terms attractive and will the suppliers help towards the compilation of the list by giving advice and perhaps financial assistance?

Are the suppliers reliable?

Do they give frequent and prompt delivery?

Is the cover of the list going to be plain or otherwise and how durable must it be? Will its colour blend in with the rest of the décor?

Can the list be kept up to date regarding prices, vintages, shippers and so on?

Will the list be flexible, can it be used in other dining-rooms?

Will it be easily understandable?

Will it be attractive?

Will it have eye appeal?

Will it be easy to handle?

Will it help to sell the wines?

❧ 28 ❧

APPRECIATION OF WINE

IN some circles, the appreciation of a wine, its qualities and defects, takes on the sombre ritual of a grim religion where sometimes apparently meaningless phrases, issued as from a pulpit, sanctify or condemn the ceremonially imbibed liquid. This is a very pleasing ostentation to those taking part and is, of course, a utilitarian requisite for the expert. We cannot all be experts but all of us in our infancy learn to recognise our likes and dislikes in the matters of food and drink. We soon apply our experience by risking raids on the biscuit barrel or by kickingly protesting against the approaching spoon of physic. But at that time we rarely find, and are never given, a real opportunity to form an opinion of the merits of alcoholic drinks.

Having reached an age of independence, we correct this gap in our education, some of us perhaps too readily, but find that, with wine, there is more to it than liking or disliking. Different occasions require different wines; particular foods solicit this, that, or the other kind of wine; it matters whether the wine is chilled or decanted and even whether it has 'breathed'. The girl friend expects you to pretend to some knowledge; there is the palate of your guest or your own, and there is always price. Even a modest cellar demands some expertise in storing and temperature. Some wines should be drunk as soon as you can get the bottle open; others should not be opened for years.

So the pastime of wine appreciation cannot be left entirely to the esoteric connoisseur. Some knowledge is essential and this is best obtained by the enjoyable practice of judging wines by all their attributes, colour, bouquet, viscosity and taste. Wine does not do much for the touch or the hearing, although the feel of good glass and the pop of withdrawing corks are quite agreeable. It is the senses of seeing, smelling and tasting that are generously pandered to by wine. Noting and remembering the colours of various wines, they are nearly all beautiful, the liquidity and, for sparkling wines, the bubbles will help not only in the enjoyment of the particular wine but also provide training in the recognition and pedigree of wines. The bouquet, or the nose as some would call it, of a wine is almost as important as its taste, and glasses which are tulip-shaped or narrow towards the top will trap the bouquet. Taste is, of course, the principal sense on which wines can be judged but the most difficult to describe. Nevertheless, it is the easiest to recognise and to remember.

It is sensible and enjoyable to get full value from a glass of wine by allowing the three senses concerned to be satisfied. It is essential to do so if a fair judgement is to be given or stored in memory and it is the whole purpose of the proceedings to do so at a session for wine-appreciation whether it is a social occasion or as part of a marketing programme.

It is therefore useful to have some knowledge of how the senses work. It is the brain that notes the sight, smell and flavour from the signals sent to it from the eyes, nose and palate. During the whole time when we are awake our eyes are busy sending numerous and continuous messages to the brain and we are all very familiar both with the process of seeing and of describing what we see; so by looking at wines we automatically note its colour and clarity, by tilting the glass a little we can see whether it is of thin or thick liquidity. The nose sends its messages to the brain only after the particular nerve impulses concerned have been stimulated by being in contact with particles of the wine. The sense we call taste is partly also the work of the nose; the tongue can only depict sweet, bitter, sharp (acid) and salt.

The wine in the glass is affected by chemical changes, which themselves are affected by temperature as warmth increases molecular activity. Large quantities of air are released onto the surface of the wine and will tend to bring the wine to the temperature of the air.

These factors bring about good and bad chemical changes. If a wine is chilled the bouquet is reduced because the rate of particle escape from the wine's surface is small and the olfactory organs are given little stimuli. A wine at a warmer temperature will release particles at a reasonable rate thus producing the bouquet. If the glass is right most of this will be trapped above the wine titivating the nasal organ while the wine is being drunk, or presenting itself for sniffing independently of drinking. The latter enjoyment of the bouquet is important in the identification of the wine. What is the bouquet? Wine consists of water, alcohol, minerals and complex organic compounds. The water obviously does not contribute to the bouquet. Ethyl alcohol does have a bouquet and it may be detected in wines which are described as having a spirity bouquet. But, when wine is analysed, the matter considered responsible for creating the bouquet and flavour rarely exceeds 0·375 grammes per standard bottle. The chemical or biological changes caused to this tiny quantity of organic substances in the wine by the exposure to the air yield volatile esters and aldehydes for the nose to inhale. To inhale, but it must be a positive sniff for the bouquet to reach the effective part of the nose, and the sniff must not be prolonged because the cells are sensitive and over-exposure to a smell seems to cause them to lose interest or to seek competing stimuli.

The wine in the mouth signals a flavour to the brain through specialised taste buds or nerve endings on the tongue. The floor of the mouth, the back of the throat and even the epiglottis can detect temperature. So a small sip of wine will not give all these sites a fair share and, as it is a combination of their signals that indicates flavour, a reasonable mouthful is a requisite for tasting. The common cold and its variations affect the efficiency of the nasal and oral nerve endings and lingering pungent flavours and smells may interfere with precise appreciation. Nevertheless, for the average person taste will not brook much interference and even tobacco-smoking may not spoil the palate.

Besides flavour, the palate also feels and it seems that taste is sorted out in the brain by the information it gathers from the smell in the nose and the flavour and feel in the mouth, possibly supplemented by what the eyes have already seen.

When this sensory mechanism is suitably applied, a wine will reveal its autobiography, but in a language that only experience can teach. The translation of this language is the object of wine appreciation. The language is complex but tradition has provided a detailed glossary of terms descriptive of the characteristics of wine, appearance, bouquet and flavour.

Firstly, appearance. Everyone's familiar with the three basic characteristics of red, white and rosé and the two of sparkling or still. Red wines range in hue from a youthful purple to an amber-brown senility. Purple in its cask, it will gradually lose this tincture in bottle developing according to type to ruby, say, for a young port or for a matured but youngish Claret or Burgundy. Red itself is used to describe the colour of a red wine between youth and maturity. Red-brown indicates maturity and mahogany more maturity and mellowness. Amber-brown, if it is not a prematurely-aged or oxidised wine, indicates very considerable age. Tawny and ruby are colours usually applied to port or port-like wines. White wines are, of course, never the colour of milk, nor are they colourless like water. They all have a yellow tint varying from the deepest shades of gold to the almost colourless palest yellow-green. Unlike red wines, white wines increase their colouring with age. Sweet white wines start with a strong yellow tint, turn to gold in maturity and have a brown tinge in age. Dry white wines follow a similar course but they start as almost colourless wines. Unless they have been deliberately coloured during their manufacture like the dark sherries, white wines that have turned brown are past drinking. So are those which look dull with a yellow-brown pallor, probably overmatured or oxidised. At their best time for drinking, white wines will have a variety of pale yellow colours according to where they were produced, the paler being the drier until gold indicates lusciousness and sweetness. A slight tinge of green usually means youthfulness although sometimes it may show the presence of chlorophyll. The colour of rosé wines varies with the district from which it comes. Avoid those that look like red wines diluted with water, and those which have a slightly blue tint. A clear firm rather dark pink is perhaps the best general description of the colour of rosé wines, but the particular shades of particular wines at their best can only be gathered from experience.

After colour, the clarity and the depth or tone of the wine should be examined. The main point in judging clarity is to avoid confusing genuine sediment, which settles and may be unavoidable in red and fortified wines, with a dull mistiness which betokens a bad wine. White wines, except that some of them may have the pleasing bubbles of effervescence, ought to be quite clear, although a sudden change of temperature may produce very temporarily a few crystals. Perhaps the best criterion of clarity is that the wine should look beautiful right through, and who can define beauty except as it can be seen? Bits of floating cork are a criticism of the decanting rather than of the wine, and they have nothing to do with the condition of a wine when it is 'corked'. Ideally the sediment in fortified or red wines should not leave the bottle or decanter when the wineglass is being filled, but lack of care or an accidental shaking before service may result in some sediment reaching the glass, but it will settle and should not interfere with the limpidity of the wine. Depth or tone is best described as consistency in appearance in the glass. Here again only experience can differentiate among the subtle richnesses of different wines. Lastly, by slightly tipping the glass, the opinions already formed on the maturity and depth of the wine can be tested by the colour and action of the wine at its rim within the glass.

It is simple to sniff the bouquet of a wine, but extremely difficult to describe the impression. Fortunately smell has a good memory on which the experienced wine-taster can rely. Assuming that there is nothing radically wrong with the wine, the experienced nose should be able to detect the species of grape from which the wine was made and the youth or age of the wine. Grape aroma, naturally, can only be recognised after experience and comparison of wines of which the basic grapes are known. Youth is revealed by a sharpness or rawness, which maturity will gradually modify. Other qualities to be detected from the bouquet are fruitiness and depth. Fortunately many terms have been standardised by tradition or convention to describe most of the characteristics indicated by a bouquet, and these are included in the glossary given at the end of this chapter.

Lastly, the wine is to be tasted, and again experience has to be the chief guide. The factors to be considered at this stage may be summarised under the headings of dryness or sweetness, acidity, tannin content, body, flavour and quality. Dryness or sweetness is easy enough to judge, although too much acidity may cause an underestimate of sugar content. Acidity gives wine its kick, but too much will ruin the flavour. Body is largely a matter of the feel of the wine in the mouth. Flavour is, of course, the essence of the wine as a drink and is the final arbiter of whether you like the wine or not. Quality will probably already have been estimated from the price, but it will also be recognised by its richness and subtlety and by the lingering of the flavour.

Wine Tastings. A very pleasant and efficient way to get to know and judge wines is to take part in a wine tasting. Wine tastings were once the province of the experts but today amateurs and professionals alike take part in such pleasant occasions. In the trade, there are two categories of wine tasting. The first is organised by shippers and importers for the benefit of the retailers and a selected public including the Press. Attendance is by invitation only and there is no charge for admission. The second is organised in their turn by the retailers for their customers and others. All are welcome to attend provided they pay for their ticket at a price which will usually cover the cost of the wine and the buffet-meal provided after the tasting. Obviously, the intention of both functions is to provide customers with a sampling. By tasting, the retailer or the customer can assess the style and qualities of the wines. For the retailer who has to stock wines that will be acceptable to his customers, this is an important duty. For the customer, it will be essential if he proposes to keep a reasonable cellar unless he is satisfied to be guided, as most of us are, by his wine-merchant. Of course, high-class hotels will also be concerned in taking part in the tastings, to ensure that their cellars maintain their reputations.

The best time to taste wine is when the palate is receptive, not when it is tired and jaded. A slight hunger sharpens the senses. Morning, mid-morning or just before lunch are good times for those in the trade and for leisured customers, but for the general public a more convenient time is in the evening, provided it is before dinner. While these occasions are planned as social occasions and are meant to be enjoyable, they are not intended to be 'booze-ups', even when the Press is there! The object is to distil or obtain knowledge, so that a degree of discipline is necessary. The organisers should emphasise the serious purpose of the gathering and lead the tasters to drink the wines in proper sequence. The best way is for the wines to be served by attendants to the tasters seated at convenient tables. Stand-up tasting can develop into a free-for-all. Tables should have a white background as the white linen will reflect the colours of the wines. Table-spacing should allow good elbow room, for the taster should not be cramped and certainly not jogged as he is tilting his glass. The ideal lighting for wine is daylight, and when artificial lighting is necessary it should be as much like daylight as possible. Smoking should be forbidden and the ban strictly enforced because smoke will hamper the enjoyment of bouquet or even ruin it for those who do not usually smoke.

There has never been complete agreement about the number of wines that should be *shown* at one tasting. It is generally agreed that less than six wines at a tasting is a waste of time. Eight to ten wines are reasonable, but there can be more. It is better to have rather fewer great wines than a numerous selection of lesser wines, particularly as the latter tend to become grey and insignificant as the tasting progresses. When, instead of being seated, the tasters circulate, the bottles of the different wines should be well spaced and arranged in a convenient order; they should be kept away from corners where people would tend to congregate.

Poured carefully, one can get twenty tastings out of an ordinary-sized bottle of wine, but the total stock available should provide for up to a bottle per head. The better the wine, the greater will be the call for refills and the stocking should allow for this. In arranging the order of the wines it is better to serve first the less good wines and end with the best. Prices should not be revealed until after the tasting is finished, as knowledge of the price will tend to influence opinion of the wine. Later, the price can be put against the notes one has made on the characteristics of the wine. A wine tasting is not a sales room, but an assessment of quality. Whether the quality justifies the price is a matter for later consideration.

A selection of dry bread and plain biscuits should be within easy reach for the purpose of cleaning the palate before sampling a different wine. Often small cubes of cheese are also available but it should be remembered that cheese is flattering to wine. The French have a saying 'Sell (wine) on cheese, buy on apples', and very good advice it is.

Glasses are always a problem at wine tastings. Of all the varieties there is perhaps none more suitable than the copita, which because of its narrow mouth and tall tapering body, can, when about half full, concentrate the wine's bouquet and display the colour to perfection. The number of glasses required per person is dependent on the number of different categories of wine on show. For example, reds and whites deserve different glasses as do sweet and dry wines. However, there is usually a pitcher of water for the purpose of guests rinsing out their glasses as they finish with each wine. In the circumstances it is essential that paper napkins are available for drying the glasses. All anxieties about glasses can be overcome if a minute quantity of the wine about to be tasted is used simply to rinse out the glass. With that in mind, large empty bottles with a funnel in each should be placed in advantageous positions around the room. These will also be useful for the reception of any surplus from those who have demanded or been given lavish helpings.

When there are many wines on show, it is obvious that if the taster drank all he tasted he would end up at the end of the tasting-line in good spirits but with a dulled palate no longer keenly receptive to the wines on offer. For this reason, the keen professional or the experienced amateur will rarely be seen to swallow the wine they taste. Instead, after savouring the wine, which tells him all he needs to know, he will ejaculate the wine from his mouth into spittoons or boxes of sawdust or sand, which ought to be specially provided for the purpose. This is not to say that these people never swallow wine at tastings. They do, but it is done with great discretion and discipline.

Besides the discipline necessary in successful tasting, it is essential that the taster should record his impressions of each wine immediately he has assessed its merits or defects. It is no use waiting until going home to try to recall the impressions. Indeed a delay of even fifteen minutes or so is too long, because to be entirely accurate, as far as the palate is concerned, judgement should be noted on paper immediately. A marking system is well worth while, and this is a good guideline for people who find descriptive writing difficult. Allow, say, a maximum of twenty points for each wine, then award up to ten for taste, up to six for bouquet and up to four for colour. Outlined below is a sample tasting sheet; it includes a column for food dishes in which to record

Country of Origin	Name and Vintage of Wine	Colour Max 4	Bouquet 6	Taste 10	Total	Food	Remarks

the food a particular wine would best accompany. This can be a good and valuable discussion point at a wine tasting, and eventually the notes will relieve the less experienced host of the anxiety of marrying wine to the Sunday lunch or whatever.

And so to the actual tasting. A small quantity of wine is put into your glass. Hold the glass by its foot, thumb on top and fingers underneath, and look at the colour of the wine against the light or against a white background. Having appreciated its clarity and colour, use your wrist to swirl the wine gently about the glass. This releases the bouquet through evaporation. Next get your nose right inside the rim of the glass and take a good deep sniff. Make a note of your impressions of colour and bouquet, and then taste. Don't take a large mouthful but don't restrict yourself to a sip. Let the wine rest in your mouth for a few seconds, then roll it over your tongue and around your mouth. Then chew it and take in a little air through your teeth at the same time, as this sharpens the impression of the taste and highlights the variety of flavours in the wine. Spit out the wine, but continue to savour its taste. When the wine has been completely savoured, record your opinions of it, and continue with the tasting. Spitting out the wine is not common practice. So much depends on the seriousness of the people concerned and what they want to get out of a tasting. The number of wines on offer and the location are points to consider in deciding whether to drink the wine or not. A commercial tasting is not the same in this context as a tasting in your own home, and such matters as whether each guest has brought his own bottle for the others to appreciate, make other points to consider.

For true appreciation the temperature of the wine is important. Dry white wines should be nicely chilled. About thirty minutes in a refrigerator will do this. Sweet white wines and sparkling wines need an hour in the refrigerator. The deep freeze should be avoided as the severe contrast in temperature ruins the wine and may even crack the bottle. Red wines are served at about 18° C., or room temperature, and the bottles are opened in advance to allow the wine to 'breathe'. Hardy young red wines can be opened about two hours in advance, and the mellower and mature wines for about an hour.

The experts have a long glossary of terms with which to describe the colour, bouquet and the taste of wines. Others will wish to use their own vocabulary but the following terms will be useful to all.

Terms for describing Colour

Brilliant   Showy or striking appearance.
Broken   Diseased wine that has turned an unsightly dark colour.
Clear   Well defined, no obscuration.
Cloudy   Looks in a state of gloom. May be due to the wine being badly made or badly handled, or to bad storage, or to too drastic a change in temperature.
Dull   Lustreless. The wine lacks any exciting colour tinges.
Faded   Rich appearance has disappeared due to old age or bad storage.
Gleaming   Sparkles with interrupted brightness.
Jolie Robe   Well turned out. A wine with an attractive appearance.
Loaded   Heavy appearance which may be due to overloading with sugar or alcohol.
Impeccable   Faultless appearance.
Over-dressed   False looking. Happens sometimes with poor-quality rosés and white wines.
Scintillating   The wine has a sparkle and gaiety about it. It does not mean that it is effervescent.
Sumptuous   Rich or expensive-looking appearance.
Veiled   Troubled looking. May be due to disease or faulty handling.

Terms for describing Bouquet or Nose

Acetic   Undrinkable and needs to be thrown away because of the smell of vinegar.
Almond   Sometimes called almond paste or almond kernels. The almond smell suggests poor fining, or the wine may have been handled badly.
Baked   The grapes have had too much sun and this has given to the wine a smell of burnt grapes.
Clean   The wine has no smells that it should not have.
Cooked   Too much sugar has been added to the wine to try to offset a poor vintage.

Deep A full and rich bouquet that promises that the wine will keep well.

Fragrant A pleasant odour of herbal and similar additions to the wine.

Fruity This word explains itself.

Grapy The variety of grape used for the wine is revealed. Most grape varieties have a distinctive smell that experience will recognise.

Green No maturity. Acidity is noticeable because of the youngness of the wine.

Little Almost odourless. The wine won't be interesting in its existing state.

Meaty Even deeper than deep, but not necessarily a wine that will improve with age.

Musty An easily recognisable smell denoting a bad wine unless the smell is only temporary because there was stale air in the bottle between the wine and the cork.

Pear-drops Army instructors used to teach that Lewisite poison gas smelt like pear-drops. Well pear-drop wine smells like Lewisite poison gas. Don't drink it.

Peppery If a smell can be sharp, then it might be described as peppery, indicating that the components of a wine have not blended thoroughly, and it needs maturing.

Piquant A sharp but not unpleasant acidity.

Pricked Excessive acidity. Hardly drinkable at present, but it might be possible to let it improve in the cellar.

Spicy This word explains itself.

Stalky A twiggy autumnal smell, which may or may not be indicative of a poor wine.

Sulphury A slight smell of bad eggs which may have lingered from the space under the cork. If it does not disperse quickly, too much sulphur has been used in bottling or even at an earlier stage.

Tart Extremely piquant to the point of revulsion.

Woody The cask has given an aroma to the wine because the cask has not been sufficiently seasoned.

Volatile A useful word when you can think of no other. It doesn't sound uncomplimentary but you are inclined to pass its acidity by.

Terms for describing Taste

Acid Nothing to do with vinegary but a description of the basic taste of all wines, so it is not very descriptive on its own. An acid taste is essential for the bite expected from wine, but the degree of acidity is the revealing factor and this can vary from wine to wine and between the same wine at different ages.

Bite A refinement of acid, acknowledging the tannic acid of which too much is undesirable.

Bitter Self-descriptive of the wine and self-destructive of a taste for the wine. Probably contaminated.

Body You can't taste weight, but when you imagine that you can, the wine has body.

Breed Definitely an upper-class wine. All the qualities that can be expected from a famous vineyard.

Cloying Hangs around in the mouth.

Coarse An honest but rough wine, ideal for wine cups and bottle parties. Not to be used to describe immaturity.

Delicate The word describes itself.

Depth The wine has the great quality of producing the tastes of its ingredients but still they are all thoroughly blended.

Dry No sweetness.

Fat A good body, but inclined to be a bit podgy.

Full-bodied A small sip seems to fill the mouth with flavour. A strong alcoholic content.

Finish Crisp. The taste of the wine does not fade into lesser flavours.

Grapy The expert will frequently recognise the variety of grape that has made the wine. It is the easily recognisable ones that can be described as grapy in taste. Not the same as a fruit flavour which describes a fleshy characteristic derived from the grapes, any kind of grapes.

Green Still too young to drink.

Hard Too much taste of tannin or other acid. The wine is not yet mellow enough, or it never will be.

Heavy Fuller than full-bodied.

Light The alcoholic content is not strong.

Luscious Like a lovely woman—sweet, soft, rich and fruity.

Medium A prefix to other descriptions, e.g. medium dry, medium sweet.

Piquant A sharp but not unpleasant acidity.

Rich Luscious, but not sweet.

Robust Nothing delicate, but a good honest satisfying mouthful.

Silky Not really soft, but very smooth to the tongue.

Soft The wine feels at home in the mouth because of its maturity and good blending.

Superficial Nothing much to say either in favour or against the wine.

Sweet Plenty of sugar in the wine.

Tannin The mouth is inclined to screw up if there is too much tannin, but the tannin has to be prominent in young red wines if they are to age well.

Tough Rough and old but still not mature.

Unctuous Softly, winning, grows on you.

Vigorous   A good wine which promises to be even better as it ages.
Well-balanced   Nice combination of all the virtues, likely to be found
    in the particular type of wine.
Woody   When a wine has been kept too long in cask, it often takes on a
    woody flavour.

INTRODUCTION TO
SPIRITS

ONE of the definitions of spirit given in the Oxford Dictionary is 'the element in man regarded as separable from and animating the body'. So far as we know, nobody has succeeded in separating this element but, from early times, reasonably successful methods have been used to separate what were thought to be the 'animating' elements in various inorganic substances. This was done by numerous processes of distillation which, briefly, is the making use of the knowledge that different substances vaporise at different temperatures. Thus by heating a substance, the early-vaporising parts of it would be given off first. By collecting and cooling the early vapours, the 'spirit' of the original substance was obtained.

The early distillations do not seem to have been made with a view to producing inebriating drinks. Who would have wasted their primitive wines and beers by boiling them? And nowadays distillation is not confined to the production of alcoholic drinks. The process is used for many industrial purposes such as the production of petroleum and chemicals. But we are concerned with the distillation of alcoholic drinks. These were probably first made from distillations of weak wines, wine dregs and beer wash, but by the Middle Ages recognisable brandies or grape spirits and other spirits were becoming established.

A short account of these beginnings is given in each of the chapters on the individual spirits.

The distillation of alcoholic spirits depends on three main factors. First, that alcohol has a lower boiling point (78·3° C.) than water (100° C.). Second, that water is constantly vaporising to some extent without waiting to boil and the distillation includes water as well as alcohol. Third, that the minor constituents, including higher alcohols, aldehydes, ethers, esters, volatile acids and organic compounds, which give the product its individual characteristics of taste and smell are retained either in the vaporising or by extraction from the residue. The art of distillation, therefore, is the devising and management of appropriate stills in which to heat the fermented beer or wine wash and convenient condensers for collecting and liquifying the vapours. There are two types of *still* in general use, the *pot still* and the *patent*, or continuous, *still*.

The *pot still* is associated with separate distillations. The fermented wash is put into the still, the fire underneath heats the wash and the vapours rise and are collected in the condenser. The still is then cleaned out and recharged for the process to be repeated. The rate of distillation in the pot still is slow and consequently can be easily controlled. Unwanted elements can be rejected and essential elements which contribute to the characteristics of the final product can be extracted from the original raw material. This still is used in making brandy, most whiskies and some rums.

The *patent still* is used in the making of gins, some rums, vodkas and the light whiskies for blending. A more economical type of *still* than the *pot still*, the *patent still* has two cylindrical columns, one an analyser and the other a rectifier. The fermented wash is pumped into the top of the analyser and, as the wash descends, it meets a current of raw steam that removes all the alcohol. The alcohol vapours are passed through the rectifier, which consists of a patent still-head where fractional condensation takes place. Whereas the *pot still* conserves the secondary constituents, the *patent still* produces comparatively pure spirit that contains very little of the secondary constituents. It is a high-strength spirit, almost a neutral spirit. These *stills* are discussed in more detail in the chapters on individual spirits, the *pot still* under brandy and whisky and the *patent still* in the chapter on whisky. It is not surprising that the *pot-still spirits* are more likely to be drunk neat or diluted with water or soda water, while *patent-still spirits* are usually accompanied by a taste-giving supplement.

The factor mentioned above that water as well as alcohol vaporises into the condenser is the reason why several distillations are sometimes made in order to strengthen the alcoholic content by reducing the water content. This leads us to the complex problem of the strength of spirits. Proof is the standard of strength of distilled alcoholic spirit.

PROOF

The word proof derives from what must have been a very entertaining method of testing alcoholic strength. Some of the spirit was mixed with a little gunpowder. If the mixture could be ignited with a mild explosion the alcoholic content was too strong for drinking, i.e. over proof. If the mixture burnt with a gentle blue flame or failed to ignite, it was 'proven' as suitable for drinking, i.e. under proof—proof being taken to be 100°. It is obvious that proven spirits could be very weak or, by modern standards, very potent. Apart from judging by the taste, or watching for the effect on the drinker, there was no other method of estimating the strength of a spirit until a man named Clark, late in the 17th century, invented a weighted float. When dropped into a spirit the depth to which the float sank revealed the density of the liquor and from this the alcoholic strength could be calculated. He was thus able to calibrate a particular strength as proof and any with a greater or less concentration of alcohol was over or under proof respectively.

This gadget led to the introduction in 1816 of a hydrometer, invented by Bartholomew Sykes presumably to assist him in his work at the Board of Excise. Mr. Sykes was certainly not a supporter of the process for decimalising measurements, but he was sufficiently ingenious to lay down a standard, designed to protect the public and the Exchequer but none the less incomprehensible to all but the expert. He had the satisfaction of seeing the use of his apparatus adopted under the Hydrometer Act 1818. It is deservedly in standard use in the U.K. today, for its measurements are accurate when adjustments are made for temperature and for the sugar content in some spirits. The scale of the measurements devised by Sykes takes advantage of the difference in the specific gravity of alcohol and water. Proof spirit thus came to mean that, at a temperature of 51° F. (10·16° C.) the spirit weighs exactly twelve-thirteenths of a volume of distilled water equal to the volume of the spirit. This works out that proof spirit is a mixture of spirit and water of a strength of 57·1 per cent. of spirit by volume and 42·9 per cent. of water. This proof spirit is then taken to be 100° proof. The strength of 30° under proof spirit is therefore spirit of 70° proof, i.e. it contains 70 per cent. of spirit of proof strength which on the ratio given above means that it contains 40 per cent. pure spirit and 60 per cent. water by volume. On this scale pure alcohol is taken to be 175° proof or 75° over proof. The figure for pure alcohol is thus $1\frac{3}{4}$ times the figure accorded to proof spirit and this fraction of $\frac{7}{4}$ is used if you want to know the percentage volume of alcohol in a spirit. Thus whisky as it is usually sold in the United Kingdom at 30° under proof or 70° proof (both meaning the same) contains a percentage of pure alcohol in volume of four-sevenths of 70, which equals 40 per cent.

The French found the Sykes hydrometer an excellent invention, but they were not mad enough to accept his scale of measurements. Gay Lussac simply thought that 100° should represent 100 per cent. of alcohol in volume and nought should represent the absence of alcohol. Thus the United Kingdom's proof spirit (100°) becomes 57·1° G.L. in France and our 70° proof whisky would be labelled as 40° G.L. if it had been manufactured in France. The Americans adopted a third scale of measuring and they were reasonably logical in deciding that proof spirit should be an exact balance of alcohol and water and that pure alcohol should be 200° proof. So, American whiskey labelled as 80° proof has the same percentage volume of alcohol as the United Kingdom's 70° proof.

The above explanation of alcohol strength conversions is simplified by the following six examples.

1. To convert British proof (Sikes) to degrees Gay Lussac (i.e. by % volume of alcohol) one multiples the British proof by 4 and divides by 7.

e.g. 70° British proof $\times \frac{4}{7} = \frac{280}{7} = 40°$ Gay Lussac or 40% Alcohol.

2. Conversely to convert Gay Lussac to British proof (Sikes)

40° Gay Lussac $\times \frac{7}{4} = \frac{280}{4} = 70°$ British proof

3. To convert British proof (Sikes) to degrees USA proof, one multiples the British proof by 8 and divide by 7.

e.g. 70° British proof $\times \frac{8}{7} = \frac{560}{7} = 80°$ USA proof.

4. Conversely to convert USA proof to British proof

80° USA proof $\times \frac{7}{8} = \frac{560}{8} = 70°$ British proof

5. To convert degrees Gay Lussac to USA proof one multiplies by 2
e.g. 40° Gay Lussac times 2 = 80° USA proof.

6. Conversely one divides by 2 to convert degrees USA proof to degrees Gay Lussac.

e.g. 80° USA proof $\times \frac{1}{2} = 40°$ Gay Lussac

The following table is a useful summary:

BRITISH SYSTEM	FRENCH SYSTEM	AMERICAN SYSTEM
measured at a temperature of 51°F (10·56°C.)	measured at a temperature of 15°C.	measured at a temperature of 15°C.

Zero ——0° proof	——0° Gay Lussac	——0° U.S.A. proof
—70° proof (30° U.P.)	—40° Gay Lussac	—80° U.S.A. proof
—100° proof (Proof)	—57·1° Gay Lussac	—114·2° U.S.A. proof
—158° proof (58° O.P.)	—90·3° Gay Lussac	—180·6° U.S.A. proof
Pure Alcohol ——175° proof (75° O.P.)	——100° Gay Lussac	——200° U.S.A. proof

U.P. = Under proof, i.e. Number of degrees under 100
O.P. = Over proof, i.e. Number of degrees over 100

ᗑ 30 ᗒ

COGNAC

RIVERS or the Atlantic Ocean seem to have a considerable influence on the pedigree wine areas of Europe. Cognac, located beside perhaps the greatest wine district in the world—Bordeaux—has the benefits of both yet produces very dull, common, below-strength table wines. It is only when these wines are reduced by distillation that their potential is realised giving us, without question, the greatest and finest Brandy in the world. The word Brandy is usually associated with the name Cognac but, in fact, Brandy is made in almost all wine districts. Cognac, however, reigns supreme, acknowledged as the best by all except the devotees of Armagnac, a neighbouring district.

Cognac was not always a spirit. Like many other wine areas the history of the change from a table wine into a made wine, in this case a wine spirit, is somewhat obscure. Certainly the Dutch had a say somewhere, because the name Brandy is an anglification of the Dutch *brandewijn* (Burnt wine). There is a story told that the Dutch who were already doing trading business from the port of La Rochelle on the River Charente, liked the wine so much that they decided to ship it to their homeland. As their standard cargoes, salt and corn, occupied most of the space on ship, it was decided to reduce the volume of the wine by distillation with the intention of adding water to the spirit on arrival at its destination. However, the folk at home liked this new drink so much that no attempt was made to bring it back to normal. As if they could! Another story is that they liked the wine but because of its low alcoholic strength which would not allow it to travel well, they distilled it to give the necessary strength for the journey, planning as before to add water on arrival. It seems obvious that the Dutch would not go to such trouble with the poor wines of Cognac when far superior ones were to be had in nearby Bordeaux. So the stories carry little weight.

The most likely reason for the original distilling is the fact that the increase of Government taxes on all wines reduced the sales of the rather crude ones considerably with the result that much was left on the farmers' hands. The farmers themselves, rather proud of the wines but

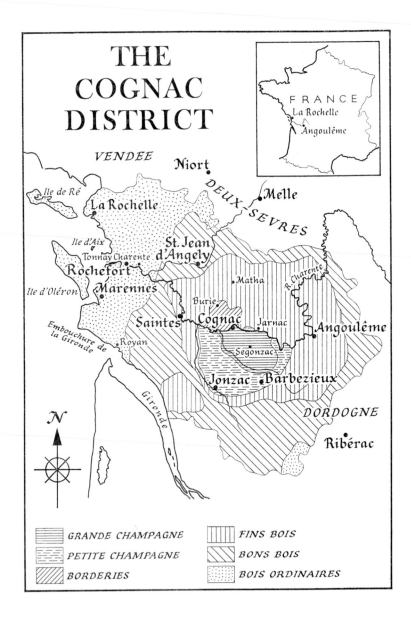

THE
COGNAC
DISTRICT

FRANCE
La Rochelle
Angoulême

VENDÉE
Niort
Ile de Ré
DEUX-SEVRES
La Rochelle
Melle
Ile d'Aix
St. Jean
Tonnay Charente
d'Angely
Rochefort
Matha
R. Charente
Ile d'Oléron
Marennes
Burie
Saintes
Cognac
Jarnac
Angoulême
Embouchure de
la Gironde
Royan
Ségonzac
Jonzac
Barbezieux
DORDOGNE
Gironde
Ribérac

N

	GRANDE CHAMPAGNE			FINS BOIS
	PETITE CHAMPAGNE			BONS BOIS
	BORDERIES			BOIS ORDINAIRES

acknowledging the fact that they were weak in alcohol (8°-10° G.L. whereas normal wines are 10°-12° G.L. or more) and that consequently they would have a short life, reluctantly decided to distill. We can assume, however, that distillation before this was not entirely unknown because based on the old Egyptian method of double distillation, the results were immediately satisfactory. In fact very little has been changed in the mode of operation since. By contrast, outside the Charente area, others tried to alter the stills to make the whole unit work quicker but results were so disappointing that herbs and other flavourings were added to disguise defects—which was of course to lead to the flourishing of liqueurs. In the meantime, the spirit of Cognac was gaining an outside reputation and in 1730, 25 000 barrels were shipped abroad. This considerable business soon came to an end with the blocking of trade routes in the Wars of the Spanish Succession. But this turned out to be a blessing in disguise because with the restoration of commerce, the shippers around Cognac found that the spirit had become almost golden coloured and had mellowed and gained harmony with a considerable improvement in flavour. And so the ageing of Cognac began by accident. Later blending was to give further improvement. It was a far cry from 1610 when Dutch, Norwegian and British merchants first started exporting the raw harsh white spirit. At this time Cognac was shipped in casks but by 1870 the firm of Hennessy was already shipping their own brand in fair quantities, in bottle. To this day, Cognac is shipped both in cask and bottle. Most shippers prefer to ship in bottle but customs duties in some countries are more favourable for spirit imported in cask. In this case, to safeguard his own reputation, the shipper may feel obliged to establish a Bottling Plant at the receiving end with all the expenses of installation and operation.

The City of Cognac from which all this business emanated is situated in South West France about a two hours car journey from Bordeaux. It has 22 000 inhabitants and, according to the natives, ranks second only to Paris in importance and fame. Certainly, of all the agricultural products exported, Cognac is one of the biggest money earners for France. However, to the visitor, it comes across just as a charming small town with an atmosphere as tranquil and unhurried as the beautiful and lazy Charente River it is built on. It has its share of factories, glass and paper being the main ones.

A feature of the city is the sooty appearance of some of its buildings—not caused by factory chimneys, but by escaping Brandy vapours which steal away at the rate of 25 000 or more bottles per day! This is known locally as *the angels' share*.

Around the city and on both sides of the river are the vineyards with wooded countryside in between. The vines are planted in straight lines, row after row, sometimes extending as far as the eye can see. Most well-known shippers own vineyards. Hennessys for example, have 485 hectares under the vine. Here and there are great farmhouses, distilleries and buildings, sited on the actual vineyards, normally surrounded by high walls to deter prying eyes. Inside are picturesque square courtyards with the traditional well in the centre. Some distilleries look antiquated, others extremely modern—with furnace automation being introduced, but, new or old, the ensuing produce is always of the highest quality.

The Cognac vine area covers 64 750 hectares presently in production, the area having been delimited by law in the year 1909. Since then, only Brandy produced within the demarcated area can legally call itself Cognac.

What makes Cognac so special? Without doubt, farmers, distillers and shippers contribute a great deal. But there are other important factors.

CLIMATE

Because of the influence of the Atlantic and the Gulf Stream, winters are generally mild, although in some years snow appears. Winter also has a regular rather than heavy rainfall as does spring. Frost is a spring hazard, but this is now being counteracted by planting high-growing vines.

Summer is fine and hot, but not excessively so, while autumn is usually fine and crisp. The average yearly temperature is 12·4°C.

SOIL

The Cognac has six distinct regions. In order of quality they range as follows:

> *Grande Champagne*
> *Petite Champagne*
> *Borderies*
> *Fins Bois*
> *Bons Bois*
> *Bois Ordinaires et Bois Communs*

The first two are the classical areas. Together they produce the ultimate in quality—a Brandy known as Fine Champagne. For a Brandy to glory in this name at least 50 per cent. of the grapes must come from *Grande Champagne*, the remainder from *Petite Champagne*.

Grande Champagne. Covers 14·4 per cent. of the Cognac District. It is a hilly country with chalk-land of up to 75 per cent. limestone—loose and porous like sponge—able to conserve rain and build a reserve to fight against summer drought. Segonzac is the important village, perhaps the richest in France.

Petite Champagne. 14·7 per cent. of District.
The soil is less chalky but firmer. Jarnac is the best known town.

Borderies. Regarded as equal to *Petite Champagne* in quality, covers 4·7 per cent. of the Region. Less chalky, it gives body to spirit. Burie is one of the important villages.

The best firms only use the grapes from these three regions and perhaps also the grapes from the *Fins Bois* Region.

Fins Bois (35·5 per cent.), *Bons Bois* (24·7 per cent.), *Bois Ordinaires et Bois Communs* (6 per cent.).

The *Bois*, as they are known, get their name from the woodlands which originally occupied these sites. The soil is mostly sand and clay and does not absorb the weather as well as the *Champagnes* and *Borderies*. Each *Bois* Region touches the sea and the soil is far richer than in the classical areas. However, the spirit from them has a somewhat earthy taste, lacking the finesse which suits refined palates.

GRPES

Eight species of grape are allowed by law to be used in the manufacture of Cognac. Only three in fact, the *Folle Blanche*, the *Colombar* and *Saint-Émilion* are in general cultivation—all white grapes.

Saint-Émilion. A thick-skinned sturdy grape which produces a rather, sour wine of about 8° G.L. of alcohol., it is a smooth maturer and does not rot. Now more than 85 per cent. of the total yield for Cognac is of this grape.

Folle Blanche. Thin-skinned grapes low in alcohol, high in acidity. A big yielder it is prone to disease and makes a bad table wine.

Colombar. Sensitive to *oidium*, it especially needs much sulphur spraying, resulting in a harsh spirit. It is high in alcohol.

Before the disease of *Phylloxera* came to Cognac, the *Folle Blanche* was the principal species. Grafting onto the American Root Vine was undertaken but this caused the grapes to grow closer and, because of their thin skins, they became more susceptible to rot. Experiments are being continually carried out and one at present in progress is the crossing of the *Saint-Émilion*, which is hardy but ripens slowly, with the *Folle Blanche* which is fragile but ripens quickly. The concentration on taller growing vines is general now, for, besides escaping the worst of the frost, they are more easily worked at harvest time and have easy access to the sun.

CULTIVATION OF THE SOIL, CARE OF THE VINE

In November and December, potassium-based fertilisers and animal manure are spread on the land and the general maintaining of equipment and machinery is undertaken. In Cognac, the vines are trained on wire which needs regular attention. The vines are pruned in February and March and in spring the land is ploughed. From now onwards until August, the soil is hoed and weeded at least four times. Once the leaves appear on the vine a constant watch is kept for disease and parasites. Some vines are sprayed with copper sulphate as often as nine times between now and vintage time. The common enemies are *oidium mildew, black rot* and the *red spider*.

THE VINTAGE

Grapes in the higher country are picked first and the *Folle Blanche* variety first of all because of the delicacy of skin. The danger lies in these grapes getting too ripe and fermentation starting within the grape itself.

Another hazard is that should rain arrive when the grapes are very ripe the skins get punctured and the crop ruined.

The vintage commences about 20 September—each farmer decides exactly when—but the general vintage usually starts between 1 and 10 October and takes from three to four weeks to complete.

PRESSING OF THE GRAPES

There are three pressings. The first is a light pressing which is transported by tube into a large cement tank where fermentation takes place.

The *Rappe*—left over after the first pressing—is then taken to the hydraulic press where two further pressings are made. These are sometimes made into wine for distillation. Depending on the weather, fermentation which is the action of yeast cells on the natural sugar in the grape, converting the latter into alcohol, may or may not start immediately. When it does commence it lasts for about three weeks and when it ceases, the grape juice has become wine.

DISTILLATION

Distillation can beneficially start immediately after fermentation is finished. Distillers are allowed by law to continue this work until the early spring.

Stills in Cognac are made of pure copper. Wine under distillation throws off acids which dissolve metals, those acids having less effect on pure copper than on other metal. Old stills gradually build up a resistance to this effect but spirit coming from young stills almost always show traces of copper.

A Cognac *pot still* normally consists of a boiler (which can hold between 790 litres and 1 820 litres), topped by a *chapiteau*, from which a pipe shaped like a swan's neck leads the vapours through or past a pre-heater, into a condenser; there the pipe takes a serpentine form and is kept immersed in running cold water. Here the vapours are changed into a liquid, which is released through a tap and filled into casks. Some firms dispense with pre-heaters. The firm of Hennessy prefer to use them as they speed up the process of distillation, save fuel and, most important of all, prevent the scalded taste which is noticeable when cool wine has been put on a hot surface.

There are two separate distillations. The first is called *Première Chauffe*. The brick furnace is made ready with sufficient coal to last eight hours. The wine is taken—sometimes with its lees—from the fermentation vats and put into the boiler. The slow, regular heat brings the temperature up to 76° C. when the alcoholic vapours come off—water vaporises at 100° C. These vapours are taken by tube through the pre-heater, thereby heating the new wine about to be distilled, and from there into the condenser, where the vapours are converted into liquid. The liquor that first comes over is called *Produit de tête* ('heads').

This product contains ethers, is in fact very unpleasant and has to be purified. The next or middle part is technically known as the *Brouillis*—boiling—but is generally called the 'heart' and this accounts for one-third of the total. It has 25 to 30° G.L. of alcohol G.L. and is put immediately into cask to await a second distillation. At this stage, it has no distinctive bouquet or flavour. What emerges finally is known as *Produit de queue*. This has too many impurities. So, the heads and tails are mixed back with the new wine about to be distilled. It takes three hearts to fill a still for

The second distillation

The *Bonne Chauffe*

The tanks are cleaned out and the hearts of three *Brouillis* are distilled together. This distillation requires careful supervision. Each minute detail must be attended to, to ensure the complete extraction of alcohol and flavourings. Whereas the first distillation takes 10 hours to complete, this second one takes 14 hours or more. Hennessy were the first to introduce automation successfully in feeding the fires. This time too there are heads and tails. Heads usually amount to 1 per cent. of the total and spirit falling under 60° G.L. alcohol forms the tails. These are put back again to be distilled with the on-coming *Brouillis*.

Now we have Cognac Brandy, white and raw, with a definite bouquet and an alcoholic strength of 70° G.L. At this stage the spirit is harsh to taste, often with strong accents of copper. Cognac is eventually sold at an alcohol strength of 40° G.L. Strength is reduced both by adding distilled water and by years of ageing in cask when the alcohol content evaporates through the porous wood.

The new spirit is known locally as *la Vigne en Fleur*—the vine in flower.

THE MATURING OF COGNAC

When distillation has been completed, the young spirit is generally put into new casks which are made from the oak of the Limousin Woods located close by. This wood is particular to Cognac and imparts special characteristics to the spirit. The new wood absorbs a liberal quantity of the spirit and it is essential that the spirit is not left too long in new casks—six months is usual—otherwise it absorbs too much tannin from the wood. Some tannin is essential for mellowness and flavour. On the other hand an older Cognac matured in a young cask will develop a woody taste. The casks hold about 272 litres and cost from £10 to make. The wood is matured for 7 years, 4 years in the open, 3 under cover but with access to air.

BLENDING

Cognac is blended either early or late in life. If a spirit has all the qualities necessary it is given a chance to find its own way. After about 5 years, constantly under supervision, it gets the marking R.N. (*Réserve Nouvelle*). It is then left alone, but, checked once a year and if it maintains progress, some of it is taken, after many years, from the nursery and put into what is known as the *paradise* where all old and fine Cognacs continue to mature. It is then a vintage Cognac, stored by shippers in a special section of a warehouse. The shippers depend on these fine spirits to bolster up inferior brandies with less bouquet and elegance.

Generally, however, shippers buy young spirit from smaller distillers of repute and blend them early with their own. When the nature of the blend has been decided upon the spirit is poured from casks through iron grills in the floor into blending vats located on the floor underneath. There, machine-motivated-paddles integrate the blend. The spirit is then transferred to casks, first into new ones, next into older ones where it ages and matures. During these years Cognac loses some of its strength due to absorption by the wood. The Government allows a 6 per cent. yearly loss for absorption and evaporation but in fact the shippers loss is seldom as much as this, except on very young Cognacs. As the spirit matures, it becomes golden, almost orange brown in colour and becomes mellow and round to taste. The blender checks the spirit from time to time and, when necessary, blends again to counteract deficiencies. Brandy only matures in cask, never in bottle, and reaches its peak between 25 to 50 years of age. Brandy, maturing in Cognac is under strict government control but no age certificates are given after it reaches five years of age. That is why 'vintage brandies' are no longer found.

FINAL STAGES

Refrigeration and Filtering. After each blending the spirit is filtered through filters of paper pulp or felt. Filtering may be effected possibly six times in the life of a Brandy. A short time before bottling a very fine and final filtering takes place—particularly to eliminate cloudiness. In Cognac Brandy, oils are prevalent and a sudden change in temperature may put these oils out of solution with consequent clouding.

Filtering is easier when the spirit is cold and to get rid of insoluble bodies the spirit is first refrigerated.

Refrigeration brings down most of these bodies to the bottom of the tank and filtering disposes of the rest. When the spirit is bright it is gradually brought back to the correct temperature and tested again for clearness, colour and alcoholic strength. It is then left to rest for six months and checked again before being bottled, corked and labelled. Colour is not always a true indication of age and some young brandies are darkened artificially with the addition of caramel.

AGES OF COGNAC

After about 75 years of age in wood a Cognac is on the decline unless of course, it is refreshed with younger Cognacs. Napoleon Brandy is now non-existent unless it is found on some rich sideboard as an antique. In any case, it would not now be drinkable. It must be remembered that all Brandies nowadays are blends of many single products of different distilleries and different years.

Cognac is not sold in America until at least 2 years old or, on the English market, until 3 years old. Stars and letters mean nothing today as a guide to age. Hennessy, who originated the starring system, have now disbanded it as they feel their estimation of what stars should indicate is not generally reflected throughout the brandy trade. Furthermore, foreign brandies, and even other spirits, are now using stars to denote quality which makes the whole system ridiculous. The only genuine guide is the name of a good shipper and the price charged. In days gone by the following table was fairly accurate, although even then each shipper had his own interpretation of what appeared on his label.

*	3 years in cask
**	4 years in cask
***	5 years in cask
V.O.	(very old) 10–12 years in cask
V.S.O.	(very superior old) 12–17 years in cask
V.S.O.P.	(very superior old pale) 20–25 years in cask ⎞
V.V.S.O.P.	(very very superior old pale) 40 years in cask ⎟ liqueur
X.O.	(extra old) 45 years in cask ⎟ brandies
Extra	70 years in cask ⎠

Special Brandies

Fine Maison	A brandy specific to a hotel or restaurant.
Fine Champagne	Brandy made from *Grande* and *Petite Champagne* grapes.
Grand Fine Champagne	Brandy made from *Grande Champagne* grapes only.
Liqueur Brandy	Brandy of great age and refinement.

STORING OF BRANDY

Whereas wine in bottles is laid horizontally to keep the cork moist and full, Brandy is stood upwards to prevent the spirit from rotting the cork. A brandy bottle thick with dust and cobwebs does not indicate age or quality but rather bad management. Once a Brandy is bottled it will not improve further. Bottles should be stored at a temperature of between 15–18° C, away from penetrating light and strong odours.

SERVICE OF BRANDY

Brandy may be served neat, or as a long drink, for example, with ginger ale. If served unaccompanied, the brandy balloon glass—not the large one but one small enough to be cupped in one hand—is ideal. The heat of the hand will then warm the contents and the fumes will rise in the bowl to be trapped underneath the slender rim. The large balloon, while attractive, is wasteful of spirit.

THE BRANDY BUSINESS

Over 75 per cent. of Cognac Brandy is exported. Particular firms have almost a monopoly of the business in certain countries. Martell does almost 70 per cent. of the English trade and Hennessy 85 per cent. of the Irish business and 50 per cent. of the American business. England is far and away the best customer taking almost 1000000 cases per year. America comes next with 600000 cases.

Some of the best shippers are:
> Jas. Hennessy & Co.
> T. Hine & Co.
> Martell & Co.
> Bisquit Dubouché & Co.
> Courvoisier & Co.
> Remy Martin & Co.

ATTRIBUTES OF BRANDY

Many people find that the attraction of spirituous drinks is their alcoholic stimulation, a fact that has gained for spirits the title of 'hard drinks'. Brandy, a great stimulant and highly alcoholic too, is rescued from being an imbiber's tippler by its maturity and refined power on the palate. It is not a drink for gulping. Rather it is a drink to sip and savour. Being a wine spirit, it is not antagonistic to wine and, for this reason and also because of its digestive qualities, it is the acknowledged post-prandial companion to coffee.

While no one would suggest that brandy should accompany the meal itself, it can add flavour and distinction to many dishes when used with discretion in the kitchen. Great Chefs have a bottle constantly by them, not only as a cooking aid but also to calm fragile temperament. Frequently, the culinary use of brandy is in evidence in the restaurant where it is favoured for Flambé creations.

Outdoors, the flask ensures that this strong comforter is available to the hunter and sportsman. On market days, many a farmer will have rescued his astute haggling ability from the depression of his cold early start by a warming glass of brandy at the Market Inn. And in bars and lounges, despite the keen competition from whisky and gin, the discerning visitor still finds a preference for brandy.

Brandy is used medicinally—whether prescribed or not—for colds, troubled stomachs and those frequent little ailments which give rise to the desire for cosseting. Nowadays, brandy is the first recourse in the home for resuscitating the faint, and a small tot can do a lot of good when mild stimulation is a desirable and immediate remedy.

With these many uses brandy must be, except to Scots, Irish and Russians perhaps, the King of Spirits, a status recognised by its price and sustained by the high quality of the Cognac product.

31

ARMAGNAC

ABOUT 113 kilometres south-east of Bordeaux lies the province or department of Gers and it is here, specifically in the regions of Haut-Armagnac, Ténarèze and Bas-Armagnac, that the excellent Armagnac brandy is produced. Of the three regions, Bas-Armagnac with its clay and fine sandy soils called *boulbène* makes the finest brandy, one with an attractively smooth finish and an outstanding perfume. In this region Eauze is the important town. Ténarèze, with Condom as the commercial centre, produces a much lighter brandy that matures quite quickly. Haut-Armagnac produces the poorest quality of Armagnac brandy, some of it tending to be almost crude. This is surprising because chalky soil exalted in most vine-growing districts, is predominant in the region. Although sold also as brandy, much of it is used as a base for liqueurs. Auch is the commercial centre of Haut-Armagnac.

Many grape varieties are used in Armagnac. Among the more popular are *Picpoule* (also known as the *Folle Blanche*), *Saint-Émilion*, *Jurançon* and *Colombard*.

The Armagnac still is a continuous-feed-type having two, sometimes three, heating platforms. The still is heated by a mixture of oak and alder timber.

The chief difference between the making of Armagnac and the making of Cognac is that where the latter undergoes two separate distillations the former gets just one, although it is a continuous one at a low temperature. Young Cognac brandy has an alcoholic strength of 70° G.L. after distillation, but Armagnac brandy may not exceed 63° G.L. More often it trickles from the *pot stills* with 50 to 52° G.L. of alcohol. From its single distillation, the brandy is transferred to casks made from the black-veined oak of Gascony. The superior Armagnacs are left in these casks to mature for about ten years and, during the maturing, they absorb colour and other special characteristics from the wood. Some, of course, are matured longer in cask, but although Armagnac mellows rapidly, they never completely lose their glow of fire to the taste—a taste much approved of by those with a wider horizon than just Cognac.

A date shown on a bottle of Armagnac brandy does not indicate that the spirit is solely of that age, but more surely that the youngest spirit in the blend is of that age.

The Armagnac countryside can claim many associations with the Three Musketeers and it is not surprising that their Gascon comrade, D'Artagnon, provides the appellation on many Armagnac labels.

RUM

GENERALLY speaking women do not like rum! Even in the Rugby club bar, where the huntresses tolerate the beer-laden exhalations of the coarse singing, they will not accept the seductive phrases of even the god-like fly-half, if these are wafted to them on the aroma of rum. It is a pity! For rum is perhaps the smoothest and healthiest of distilled drinks and certainly the most amenable to a digestion somewhat strained by a surfeit of beer.

Generally speaking men like rum! Either as a drink or as a romantic notion. If they drink it, it is often because they first tasted 'Nelson's Blood' in some virile boon companionship such as the navy, or as a grog which had encouraged their heroics in some battle they had won. If they do not drink it, they still can imagine casks of it rolling on the gory desks of the good ship *Hispaniola*, or flinch pleasurably on the thought of the exploding arteries of apoplectic pirates of the Spanish Main in their final rum-soaked delirium.

All this is because the sugar-cane, in the wake of Columbus, discovered the West Indies; and cane sugar, hitherto an expensive rarity, could be produced there abundantly and cheaply. What could be a more natural sequel than the development of an alcoholic distillation? Rum is made today wherever the cane grows freely—in Jamaica, British Guiana, Martinique, Hispaniola, Trinidad, West Indies, the Virgin Isles, the East Indies, Puerto Rico, Madagascar, the U.S.A., Cuba, Bolivia, Australia and South Africa.

Rum is a distillation of cane-sugar products, principally molasses, produced in cane-growing countries. It was probably the result of experiments carried out by the early Spanish settlers in the West Indies. Its name has an echo of the Spanish Main where it was known as Rumbullion or Rumbustion.

HOW RUM IS MADE

Freshly cut cane, with the leaves discarded, is crushed by huge heavy-roller mills. The resulting juice is boiled and as the water evaporates it leaves behind concentrated sugar. This is clarified and becomes a thick heavy syrup. The syrup is then pumped into centrifugal machines which revolve at great speed, crystalising the sugar and separating it from the molasses. The sugar is removed and the molasses—sometimes reboiled to obtain second sugars—is taken to a rum distillery. There it is mixed with water and allowed to go through a slow or a quick fermentation, the former being associated with the big heavy rums such as Jamaica rum.

Slow Fermentation. To the molasses and water is added the skimmings, called dunder, from the previous distillations. The natural yeasts in the air then settle on the surface of the mixture causing fermentation to commence. Depending on climatic conditions and the density of the substrate, the fermentation can take from 12 to 20 days to complete.

Quick Fermentation is associated with the lighter rums, like those from Puerto Rico and Cuba. Cultured yeast is added to the molasses and water and this fermentation lasts for about two days, perhaps a little longer.

Distillation. After fermentation the liquid has an alcoholic strength of about 7° G.L. This is now distilled—the slow fermenting liquid in a pot still; the quick usually in a patent still. The pot-still product—after two distillations—usually comes off at 150° British proof (86° G.L.) or under and contains a generous proportion of congenerics—esthers, acid and higher alcohols, flavour and bouquet agents. Only the heart or middle cut of the distillation is sent for maturing. The heads and tails are always sent back for re-distilling. The patent-still product will be light in body with an alcoholic strength of not less than 160° British proof (91° G.L.). It will also contain very much less congenerics.

Maturing. Rum is matured in cask for at least three years before it can be offered for sale in these Islands. In its early stages it is colourless but gradually it extracts colour from the wood. When deeper hues are required, caramel (burnt sugar) is added before marketing, the rum is reduced to the appropriate alcoholic strength by the addition of distilled water and clarified by filtering through alternate layers of charcoal and sand.

SOME TYPES OF RUM

Jamaica rum can be lightly flavoured, medium flavoured or highly flavoured. The first is drunk locally, and the second is generally popular in Britain and the third is favoured on the Continent where it is blended, usually with a neutral spirit, and is known as *Rumverschuitt*, especially in Germany.

Trinidad and *Barbados* generally produce light rums usually by the patent-still method though the pot-still method is also used. They are soft and somewhat smokey to taste.

British Guiana rums are either light or dark in colour. The light is usually consumed locally and the dark known as *demerara* is mainly exported—a great deal coming to Britain, where it is mostly matured in London warehouses and, if re-exported, is highly considered abroad.

Cuban rums are light and delicate. Bacardi is the name synonymous with these rums. But since Castro took control, this style of rum is now also being made elsewhere, e.g. Barbados. A golden-coloured rum called Ronoro is also made in Cuba.

In *Puerto Rico* rum is generally made by the *patent-still* method. These light rums are exceptionally popular in the U.S.A. where they are sold as white label (light bodied) and gold label (less light bodied).

Martinique produces aromatic rums mainly in *patent-stills* and they are usually dark in colour and medium in flavour.

New England rum is a rich heavy dark rum made in Massachusetts. It is aged in charred oak barrels. It is greatly favoured by those who like strong and full-bodied rums.

❧33❧

WHISKY

THE Irish were the first to make whisky. From the abundant surplus of grain, they made a beer wash which with the heat of turf fires, they distilled into a spirit and named *Uisge Beatha* —Water of Life.

Probably ancient traders from the Mediterranean brought the art of distillation to Ireland. Anyway, in the 12th century there was sufficient of the spirit to make it a popular and large part of the booty taken back to England by the soldiers of Henry II. The Irish forever emigrating took their welcome skills to the Gaelic-speaking Scots and eventually the English made the Gaelic name comprehensible as whisky. Today the spirit is made in many countries including Germany—*Kornbranntwein*—Japan and Australia. However, the four main producers are America and Ireland who spell the product whiskey—Scotland and Canada who leave out the 'e'—whisky.

HOW WHISKY IS MADE

Each country has its own refinements in making whisky but the basic method is fairly consistent in all countries. Barley is malted, then finely

ground to be mashed with hot water to make wort. The wort, with the addition of yeast, ferments, and the resulting wash or beer is distilled two or three times, first giving low wines and eventually raw whisky, which is put in oak casks to mature.
The details of this process are as follows:

Materials. Any cereal may be used to make whisky, but for Irish and Scotch barley is the principal ingredient with some use of wheat and rye. In the U.S.A. maize and rye are used and in Canada rye is the main ingredient. There are two basic types of whisky—Malt or pot still whisky and grain or patent still whisky.

Malt Whisky When the grain comes from the farmers it is screened—removal of extraneous matters, cleaned and, to prevent deterioration during storage, kiln-dried to reduce the natural moisture content to 12 per cent. for malting barley.

Malting. The dried grain is steeped in water for two or three days, sufficient time to enable it to take 40 per cent. or more moisture. The remaining water is then drained off, and the swollen barley is spread out on stone floors at a depth of about 15–20 centimetres, where at a temperature of about 15° C. it begins to germinate.
Germination is a complicated chemical process and in the production of whisky involves the encouragement of growth, yet the restriction of growth at the appropriate time. By the application of moisture and gentle heat the grain starts to grow. The germinating grain produces diastase—an enzyme complex—which converts some of the starch into fermentable sugars—maltose and complex dextrines. This malting period varies according to climate and the practice of the particular distiller or maltster. The barley during this period must not be left to its own resources for as the roots spread it is essential that the grain is disturbed from time to time with wooden shovels so as not to allow overheating and to prevent the roots entangling with each other. It is related that in a well-known Dublin distillery 'during the troubles' this part of the work had to be discontinued for several days, during which time the floor of malt had become a mat which was subsequently rolled up like a carpet and given away.

Kilning. The aim is to dry the grain to check the sprouting of the barley and to facilitate grinding and storage. In Scotland the grain is spread on perforated steel floors over peat fires which it is said contributes the characteristic smokey taste to Scotch. In Ireland it is spread also on perforated floors and dried by smokeless anthracite or oil-fired

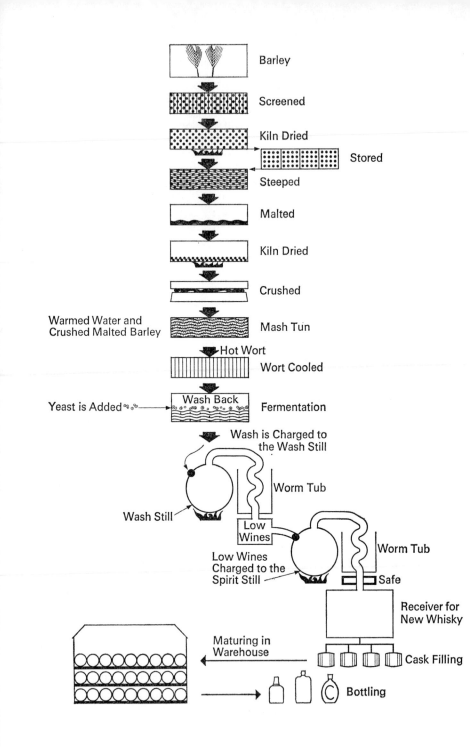

The Making of Pot Still Whisky

furnaces to about 3 per cent. moisture. It is dried gently at first so as not to destroy the enzymes and then it is finally cured by raising the temperature to 51° C. or more. The drying used to take three to four days, but modern methods can complete the job in 24 hours, and when complete, stops further growth.

Grinding. After kilning the ears of grain have become prominently chalky and soft and are taken to be stored in airtight bins to mature and await further processing, when required, the barley is screened, that is the rootlets—malt combings and dust—are removed. The combings are usually sold for fodder. The grain is now ground in roller mills and becomes grist. Both malted and unmalted barley is finely ground in Ireland to make the grist.

Mashing. The grist is then introduced to the mashing vessel called a mash tun along with the appropriate amount of hot water which has a temperature of not less than 65° C.—the water having been previously boiled in coppers. The mixture is continually stirred with revolving rakes for about 2½ hours. The Irish also use a proportion of coarsely ground oats to facilitate subsequent draining from the bottom of the mash tun. After settling for about half an hour a liquid called worts—which is a solution of sugars principally maltose produced by the conversion of starch from all the cereals by the action of enzymes in the malt—is drained from the mash tun, cooled to about 20° C. and pumped into a fermenting vessel—wash back. The grain left behind—draff—is sold as cattle food.

Fermentation. To the cooled worts is added specially cultivated yeast which works on the sugars converting them into alcohol and CO_2. The temperature during fermentation may rise to 32° C. But it is controlled by cold-water pipes called attemperators at the bottom of the tank. Fermentation is rapid and is completed in three days. The liquid is now known as wash, similar to beer without the flavour of hops. It has an alcoholic strength of from 7–10°G.L.

Distilling. The liquid is transferred to a wash-still where it is heated by fires underneath or steam coils inside and brought to the boil. Inside the still are mechanical scrapers called rumagers, which prevent solid matter sticking to the bottom and imparting a burnt taste. As the liquid boils, vapours comprising of alcohol, steam and other constituents pass through the still head and through a worm—which is a coiled pipe immersed in a large vessel of cold running water—and this reduces the vapours to liquid. The first result is known as low wines, because it is low in alcohol. Altogether this first distillation takes about 13 hours and the spent wash left behind is sold for cattle feeding.

In Scotland the low wines are collected in a low-wines receiver and then transferred to spirit stills, which look like giant onions and after a second distillation emerge as raw whisky with a strength of 20° O.P.–70°G.L.

In Ireland the low wines are distilled twice further, the final distillation in a spirit still. The result will give a whisky 50 O.P.–86°G.L. Whatever practice is used there will be a continuous pool of heads and tails—pungent crude spirit not suitable without further refining, for whisky. These are held over to be added to the oncoming low wines. The aim is to make the product as pure as possible but still retain flavour and characteristics. At this stage the raw whisky has a powerful aroma and is completely colourless. It is pumped into spirit store vats.

Grain Whisky. Gets its name because raw grain as well as malted barley is used in the production. Grain whisky is made by the *Patent* or *Coffey still* process—the still was developed and patented by an Irish Excise Officer, Aeneas Coffey in 1832. Whereas for the pot still method, described above, there are entirely separate distillations, the patent still method is one continuous operation. The still, cylindrical in shape, consists of two columns—one the analyser, the other the rectifier. Perforated plates divide each column into horizontal chambers.

The Method. Warm, fermented wash is pumped into the top of the analysing column and as it descends it meets a current of raw steam which has been introduced into the bottom of the analyser. On contact, the steam boils the wash and produces alcoholic vapours. These rise and are led by a pipe into the bottom of the rectifier. The used wash is taken out of the bottom of the analyser. Meanwhile the alcoholic vapours rise in the rectifier, meeting at certain points, the cold wash being carried down the rectifier by the wash coil. As they meet, partial condensation takes place—the vapours getting cooler, the wash getting warmer. At the point when the wash enters the top of the analyser, it has become very hot indeed. When the spirit vapours reach the top of the rectifier, they are finally condensed on a water frame. The foreshots—spirit first emerging—are taken out and sent back to the analyser and the comparatively pure spirit which follows on is drawn off into a receiver. The stillman decides when the foreshots have finished.

This spirit is lighter in body and lacks a great deal of the congenerics —esters, acids, aldehydes and higher alcohols—which contribute so

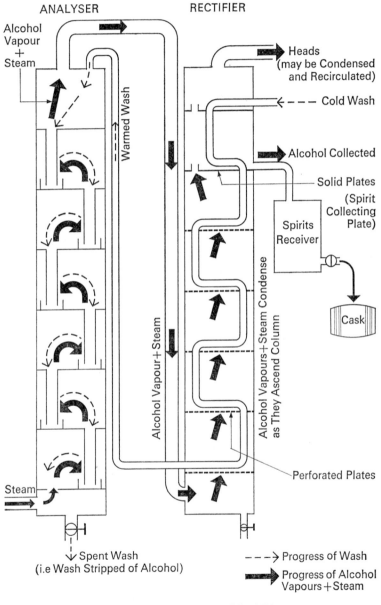

ANALYSER   RECTIFIER

Alcohol
Vapour
+
Steam

Heads
(may be Condensed
and Recirculated)

Cold Wash

Warmed Wash

Alcohol Collected

Solid Plates
(Spirit
Collecting
Plate)

Spirits
Receiver

Cask

Alcohol Vapour + Steam

Alcohol Vapours + Steam Condense
as They Ascend Column

Perforated Plates

Steam

Spent Wash
(i.e Wash Stripped of Alcohol)

- - -→ Progress of Wash

Progress of Alcohol
Vapours + Steam

Coffey Patent Still — Simplified Diagram
(size varies, up to 17 metres high)

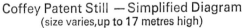

much to the bouquet and flavour of the pot still product. It is used as a blender with the pot still product, especially in Scotland.

Maturing. The whisky is now raw and colourless but with a very pungent aroma. It is pumped into spirit store vats and reduced in strength by filtered water to between 10 and 25° O.P. (63-72° G.L.). At this strength, it is filled into oak casks under Excise supervision and stored in bonded warehouses often underground and left in Scotland at least three years to mature, in Ireland at least five years to mature. The casks will be of different sizes. Some firms, like John Power in Dublin, use plain casks, old Sherry, Rum and American oak casks for maturing whisky and it is most interesting to see the distinct colour difference and lesser taste difference resulting from this practice. As the whisky rests in cask, air penetrates through pores in the wood to mellow the raw spirit. The type of warehouse will also influence maturation. A damp atmosphere will reduce the alcoholic strength but will likely increase the volume content. A dry atmosphere reduces volume greatly and to a much lesser extent, strength.

Age is important. Like people, whisky maturing in cask gets mellower as it gets older. Some whiskies mature in casks up to 15 years, sometimes more. Left too long there is a danger that it may become 'woody' in flavour. The age eventually appearing on a label always indicates the age of the youngest whisky in the blend.

Blending. The marrying together of different single whiskies with grain whisky is very much part and parcel of the Scottish industry for this past 60 years. The blender, a man of great judgement and wisdom 'noses' the whiskies under selection and having made his decision the whiskies are passed through a blending trough and into a blending vat in the approved proportions. Here they are thoroughly roused by air jets inside the vat and finally they are discharged into oak casks once more to harmonise.

In Ireland whiskies from different warehouses, from different types of cask and from different sizes of cask and of different ages are vatted together to produce the consistent flavour of the brand.

Final Stages. After blending and harmonising the whisky is filtered through asbestos and carbon sheets and its strength is reduced by the addition of pure metallic free water to suit different markets.

30°   U.P. (40°G.L.) for U.K., Ireland and Canada

23·8° U.P. (43·5°G.L.) for U.S.A.—i.e. 87° U.S.A. proof
(13° U.P. U.S.A.)

24·2° U.P. (43·4°G.L.) elsewhere.

It is tested for colour—colour comes mainly from the cask the spirit matures in but generally some caramel is added at the very end to give the correct tone.

The whisky is ready for marketing, be it in bottle or cask. It will be seen on its way by the Excise man who has meanwhile looked after the Government's considerable interest and benefit.

THE MAIN DIFFERENCES BETWEEN IRISH AND SCOTCH

Irish is produced from home-grown cereals. As well as native cereal, grain from other countries is used in the making of Scotch.

Irish pot still whiskey is made from malted and unmalted barley as well as other cereals. Scotch pot still is made only from malted barley. The Irish use hot air produced by anthracite and oil-fired furnaces for kilning.

Scots use peat which imparts the famous smokey flavour.

Irish pot stills are much larger than those used in the Highland distilleries.

Irish is distilled 3 times.

Scotch is distilled twice, sometimes 3 times in Lowland malts.

Irish is matured at least 5 years in cask.

Scotch is matured at least 3 years in cask.

Most Irish whiskey is made by the pot-still method.

Blended Scotch is usually a combination of pot and patent still.

IRISH WHISKEY

In 1770 there were over 1 000 licensed distilleries in Ireland and it's anybody's guess as to how many unlicensed ones there were. Then the law was changed to militate against the smaller distilleries and encouraged larger units which made for easier Excise supervision. By 1885 there were 28 distilleries operating. Today there are just 5 (incorporating many smaller ones), 4 in the south and 1 in the north.

In 1966 a merger of the 3 most powerful companies took place. Cork Distillers Co., Ltd. (C.D.C.), John Jameson & Sons Ltd. and John Power & Son Ltd. came together to form the United Distillers of Ireland with the aim to promote their product in world markets. With the home market secure—over 80 per cent. of the total consumption—sales promotion is now directed with great vigour abroad.

Irish whiskey is a spirit made from barley and to a lesser extent other grain. The distillations are carried out mainly in pot stills for maturing in cask for at least 5 years. There are, of course, Scotch-type whiskies made also, notably the brands Hewitts and Bushmills. But the

Irish reputation lies in their traditional whiskey, which is marketed as straight unblended or single whiskey.

These whiskies although distinctive in flavour are very smooth to the taste due no doubt to their long maturation period.

Irish whiskey has been a useful trading commodity and much of it found its way to England in the pre-gin era to sustain the English as a change from Claret. We do not know whether any claimants to thrones were drowned in a cask of Irish whiskey but Queen Elizabeth certainly liked it and Peter the Great while studying in Deptford, thought that 'of all the wine Irish whiskey is the best'. Later competition from Scotland transferred the greater proportion of the trade to Scotland. Nevertheless, a greatly expanding market for spirits resulted from the prosperity of the industrial revolution and the contemporary increase in the population of England.

SCOTCH WHISKY

The Scots fought their wars on whisky. But when they were finally defeated by the English their hero Bonnie Prince Charlie went as an exile to France and Brandy became the fashionable drink at all social gatherings. This vogue lasted until late in the 18th century. Meanwhile the English sent their Excise men to Scotland to impose duties on the national spirit. The Scots refused to knuckle under, ignored the demands and illicit distilling flourished. Farmers and fishermen promoted sales by every possible means and their cunning to outwit the 'gaugers' was ingenious. One method was the staging of funerals, with the coffin concealing bottles of wholesome whisky. It is estimated that at this time half the whisky output came from unlicensed stills. But in 1823 the Government saw sense and reduced the duty to 2/3d per proof gallon, and relaxed many illogical regulations. Some proprietors immediately took out licenses to distill. They were not popular locally but gradually the more enterprising followed suit. Illicit distilling stopped. Then ambitious distillers started to grow and on their way absorbed lesser firms. Following experiments with a new type of still called the *Patent* or *Coffey* still, the firms of Andrew Usher in 1853 started to blend malt (or pot still whiskies) with grain (or patent-still whisky). This gave a whisky lighter in body than the traditional malt whisky and a taste which was eventually to appeal to a world public. It was and is today the basis of the phenomenal success of Scotch whisky. Of course Scottish salesmanship contributed too and in 1877 the Distillers Co. Ltd., was formed by six companies in and around Edinburgh. This Company has grown ever since and it is possibly rightly regarded as the power force behind the rampant sale of Scotch today. It had to defend its reputation once when in 1905 due to the objections of the pot-still malt distillers a Bill was passed which forbade the patent-still product to be called whisky. The D.C.L. and others contested this and in 1909 a Royal Commission reported as follows: that the name whisky should not be restricted to the product of true pot still and defined Scotch as a 'spirit obtained by distillation from a mash of cereal grains, saccharified by the diastase of malt and distilled in Scotland'. How grateful the Scotch Distillers are now for such a conclusion. Sometimes as much as 60 or 75 per cent. grain whisky is blended with malt to give the finished article. And grain whiskies are less expensive to make and also take less time to mature. There are still single Scotch whiskies on the market but they are fairly rare and are made to cater for a small but faithful following.

There are about 102 malt pot-still distilleries and 12 grain or patent-still distilleries operating in Scotland today. The areas of production are:

> The Highlands
> The Lowlands
> Islay
> Campbeltown

CANADIAN WHISKY

There are around 20 distilleries operating in Canada, all privately owned but under strict Government supervision. By law Canadian whisky may be made from any cereal grain. Although it is mainly made from rye, it may be distilled from maize, wheat and barley, malt or a combination of them. The distillation takes place in a specially temperature-controlled multi-column patent still similar to the *Coffey* still. This gives a whisky light in body making it an ideal mixer especially for cocktails. Although it may be bottled at 2 years of age, it is normally matured 5 or 6 years usually in charred oak casks. It is normally sold at 70° proof (40° G.L.). But it may even be bottled as high as 90° proof (51·3° G.L.) depending on its eventual destination.

AMERICAN WHISKEY

Irish and Scottish settlers brought the art of making whiskey to America when they made their homes in Pennsylvania in the middle of the 17th century. Early in the 18th century the spirit started to become generally popular. But in 1794 there was a whiskey rebellion when George Washington's Government, short of finance, imposed an Excise duty on whiskey. Many of the distillers, rather than face the demands, moved out of these districts and spread further west into Pennsylvania and into Kentucky, California, Georgia, Indiana, Illinois and Ohio. They again started to distill and business prospered. Throughout the 19th century whiskey played an important part in the opening up of the west. The distillers provided the main drink in the boom-town saloons, refreshing the cowboys and miners and even inflaming the redskins when whiskey was sold to them illegally by the 'bad' men.

The industrial settlements in the east, growing with the entry of thirsty immigrants from Europe, also provided widening markets. By 1911 over 370 million litres were produced. These zooming sales led to the ruin of the industry. They led to attacks from the sober minded, leading in turn to the notorious Fourteenth Amendment of November 1920, which led to the thirteen dry years of prohibition. The distilleries were closed and the quantity of whiskey made and sold in that period can only be assessed by bathtubs, if they could only speak and bootlegging gangsters, if they had not been shot. But all came well in 1933 when distillers were allowed to distill once more.

Making of American Whiskey. The grains used are maize, rye, millet and barley. The grain is ground, mixed with water and cooked in pressure cookers to convert the starch. The wort is allowed to cool and then fermentation which converts the wort into beer takes place. This fermentation is induced by either of two methods:
(1) The sweet mash process—the adding of fresh yeast to the wort.
(2) The sour mash process—the adding to the wort of a substantial amount of spent beer from a previous fermentation, together with some fresh yeast.
The beer or wash is then introduced into a *Patent* still and the resultant whiskey comes off at just under 160° U.S.A. proof. This is now diluted to 103° U.S.A. proof—51·5° alcohol G.L. and put to mature in charred oak barrels, which are credited with imparting colour and quality.

Some Types of American Whiskey
Bourbon First made in Bourbon county, Kentucky. Hence the name. Made from a mash containing not less than 51 per cent. maize. Matured in new charred oak barrels for not less than 4 years.
Rye Made from a mash containing not less than 51 per cent. rye and aged in new charred oak barrels.
Corn Whiskey A fiery whiskey made from a mash containing 80 per cent. maize or more. It gets little ageing.
Straight Whiskey Unblended whiskey, aged 2 years in new charred oak casks.
Blended Straight Whiskey are mixtures of 2 or more straight whiskies.
Bottled in Bond Whiskey These are straight whiskies bottled at 100°

U.S.A. proof. They have been matured in cask at least 4 years in warehouses controlled by the Government—hence the name.

Blended Whiskey An inexpensive whiskey, being a blend of straight whiskey and neutral spirit. It is light in character and is especially useful as a cocktail ingredient.

Attributes of Whisky

Whisky is a universal social drink in reasonably prosperous societies. Indeed, in France, the home of wine, it is now considered a most fashionable drink. In the home, it vies with Sherry as the standard offer to visitors and whisky and soda is as much a household term as bacon and eggs.

Whisky has the advantage of being a welcome drink at almost all times. In moderation it is a reasonable apéritif and a most comfortable drink for after meals. As a nightcap it is probably unsurpassed.

Although it mixes well in some cocktails it accords better with mineral waters or spring water products and many like it best with ginger ale. More, of course, prefer it neat and consider it humiliated when accompanied with minerals.

However, its most outstanding qualities are stimulation and warmth. It is also a comforting refuge from the disabilities of the common cold, even if the poor sufferer has to disguise it in hot milk or lemon drink. Many doctors recognise that a tot of whisky is a solace to people in pain and a help to those with a heart condition as well as a useful stimulant for those getting on in age.

It is not used to a great extent in the kitchen but it goes beautifully with coffee and cream.

❧ 34 ❧

GIN

WHEN, at the battle of Zutphen in Holland in 1586, the wounded Sir Philip Sydney, the Elizabethan officer and poet, waved on the water to the soldier whose need was greater, the latter was no doubt grateful. But one suspects that he would have preferred a swig of 'Dutch Courage' or Genièvre which had become popular with the troops during that campaign. For in the Low Countries this spirit had a reputation for useful medicinal properties as well as a comforter for more obvious reasons. Indeed it was purposely introduced by its creator, a Dutch Professor of chemistry called Sylvius Van Leyden, as a medicine, in the 16th century. He made distillations from Rye adding the flavourings from juniper berries, those dark-blue berries whose oils were known to be a palliative for such illnesses as gout and kidney troubles. The French had already used the juniper berries to flavour poor wines, which were aptly called 'the wines of the poor' and the Dutch used the French word for the berry to name their spirit. Later they called it Genever, then Geneva, which the English later on shortened to Gin.

Doctors had soon begun to prescribe Genièvre which was offered for sale in chemist shops throughout the Netherlands. The healthy too began to appreciate its qualities and the English soldiers, always seeking among the warming spirits of the Continent for some comforter in the wretched battlefields of the Low Countries, adopted it. Carried back by them to England, it quickly became popular under the name Geneva and the English almost at once began making it themselves. There was no control over its manufacture and some products were really foul. In the reign of Charles I, the Worshipful Company of Distillers was formed and later, under the Stuarts, distilling from native grain was encouraged by charters which gave brewers the right to distill. However, other spirits like brandy and Irish whiskey already had a following on the English market and it was not until 1688 when Dutch William came to the Throne that Gin began to establish itself as the Englishman's spirit. To drink Gin was an agreeable way of waving the flag. Further encouragement came from Queen Anne who, before she died, raised the taxes on wine and brandy and lowered those on English spirits. Consumption rose from 2·2 million litres in 1690 to 22·7 million litres in 1729.

Whereas beer and cider had to be sold in licensed premises, Gin was sold by grocers, barbers and tobacconists and pedalled on street corners, market places or wherever there was a chance of business. It was very cheap, very plentiful but some of it was very bad. Illicit stills abounded where distillations were made from beer dregs, rotten vegetables and worse. It is said that in the Cities of London and West-minster one house in four sold Gin and no writing on Gin is complete without quoting the slogan displayed at a house in Southwark. 'Drunk for a penny, dead drunk for tuppence; clean straw for nothing.' Not only over-indulgent men sought the comfort of the straw but women and children too. In 1729 Parliament imposed a tax on Gin and required a licence of retailers. This only regulated the sales of good Gins and bad unflavoured stuff continued to flourish. This legislation was repealed after four years, when a new Act took its place prohibiting the sale of spirits outside dwelling houses. This merely converted these houses into spirit shops. A new Gin Act in 1736 sought to put the spirit beyond the pockets of the poor, but the increase of retail licenses to £50 and tax to £1 a gallon, simply caused wholesale evasion. There were some arrests but generally prosecutors were afraid to prosecute, fearing the angry mobs who roamed the streets to seek them out. There were riots and drunkenness everywhere and murder too. Informers suffered heavily. Nothing it seemed could stop the poor from seeking the solace of Gin. For it was the poor who were the real advocates of this drink. The upper classes regarded it as the drink of common people, although they were happy enough to dole it out in part-payment for wages. But over-indulgence reaped reward. Mental illness was prevalent and the alco-holic death toll rose. But the consumption of Gin rose also. Between 1733 and 1743 sales almost doubled, mostly of the illicit, gut-rotting variety. It was hawked from door to door, sold in chemist shops disguised in medicine bottles and bootlegged and smuggled to every den of vice. The Gin Act was repealed in 1742 and an Act in 1743 reduced the taxes. Another in 1747 again allowed distillers to sell retail. At last it was recognised that prohibition was not the answer, that fair taxes on the manufacture of Gin, an increase on wholesale prices and the licensing at moderate fees of retailers under Government super-vision encouraged responsible people to enter the business. Higher prices had inevitably a sobering effect on the masses. Gradually there was a fall in the consumption of Gin and an improvement in the spirit itself, although there were still bad concoctions to be had.

At this time the three centres of manufacture were London, Bristol and Plymouth. Trade became more respectable, taverns became more comfortable and, with industrial prosperity, workers converged on the Cities, which saw the emergence of the famous Gin Palaces, large Victorian buildings, bright, glossy and invitingly comfortable. These Palaces were, in their turn, criticised by Legislators and reformers including the Temperance Society, a movement then gaining in strength. As a result, an Act of harsh severity was passed in 1871, designed to close half the public houses. But an outraged and influential public spoke through such journals as *The Times* and *Morning Post* and in 1874 the Act was withdrawn. In the 1880's the Americans began to move in with their Gin-based mixed drinks and about forty years later they flooded the world with their cocktails. At last Gin, with diplomatic trimmings, had reached the drawing-room! The corridors of compromise! Gin must be a good drink to have survived its one-time appalling reputation. From its respected birth in Holland where, intended by its father to pursue a career in medicine, and after a quiet childhood spent under the kindly name of Genièvre, it was carried away by returning soldiery to become a sturdy English native, the darling of the working classes. Here it started a rake's progress into Gin alley rolling around as mother's ruin, Dutch courage, Bryan O'Lynn, Cockold's comfort and Royal poverty. The affluent society of the Industrial Revolution introduced it to extravagance in tavern and Gin palace and prepared it to make its fortune in America from bootlegging and bathtub during prohibition. Small wonder it became a good mixer.

THE MAKING OF GIN

Gin is a rectified spirit distilled from malted barley, maize and rye and flavoured with a choice of or an admixture of juniper berries, coriander seeds, orris roots, angelica, cassia bark, Calamus, almonds, cardamoms, bitted orange peels, fennel and liquorice.

Gin has also been known to have been made from a mollasses spirit when there was a grain shortage—but nowadays it is principally a grain spirit.

Method. An almost pure spirit is purchased from a central distillery by the Gin distiller. This is reduced by distilled water to about 10°o.p. (62·7°G.L.) and rectified (re-distilled) in a *patent still* together with a proportion of the flavouring ingredients (the formula being secret). The resulting vapours are condensed and run off as a very high-strength Gin, with the heads and tails being returned for distillation.

There are other methods of imparting flavour to the spirit. One is by steeping the botanicals in a proportion of raw spirit and distilling the mixture in a pot still. The result is then added to the rectified spirit from the patent still. Another method is to place a basket of botanicals inside the still. As the spirit vapours pass through the botanicals they become impregnated with the flavourings. The least satisfactory way of all is to buy flavouring essences from chemists and add them to the spirit.

Because all impurities have been removed by rectification, Gin, when it passes from the still is, after diluting with water, immediately drinkable. However, it is usual to give the spirit and flavouring a little time to harmonise—about 1 month—in oak cask—then it is tested for taste, clarity and strength (it is normally sold at 70° British proof [40°G.L.]) and bottled for sale.

TYPES OF GIN

Holland or Dutch Gin. This is a full heavy gin principally because distillations were made in the pot still which imparts more flavouring essences than the patent still. It has a malty flavour with an individual personality. Too definite a taste to become a good cocktail mixer. It is made principally in Amsterdam and Schiedam. Drunk neat, it can be pleasantly followed by a lager.

Old Tom. A gin sweetened by the addition of sugar syrup. It derives its name from the time when Captain Dudley Bradstreet, a government informer, in order to evade the Gin Act of 1736, purchased a sign of a cat and nailed it to a ground floor window of a rented house. Underneath the cat's paws protruded a lead pipe which was connected to a funnel on the inside. The passers-by soon came to recognise the sign which changed back and forth from district to district. Twopence put into the cat's mouth secured a mouthful of gin. Not much of this gin is made nowadays but it should be the Gin used in a Tom Collins Cocktail.

London Dry Gin is dry gin originally made in London, hence the name. It is now also made in America, either by licence from a London distiller or simply as a blank name. It has a clean crisp taste and in London is sometimes aged in Sherry casks to give it a golden colour. English gins are distilled at slightly lower proof than the American gins.

Plymouth Gin is made in Plymouth by the firm of Coates & Co. In taste it is somewhere between a Holland and a London gin.

Sloe Gin is made by steeping sloes (fruit of the Blackthorn) in gin and adding sugar syrup with a very small amount of bitter almonds.

Orange Gin, Lemon Gin, etc. are mostly artificially flavoured gins. They are easily made at home by adding the appropriate flavouring essences to gin.

Ᏸ35Ᏸ

VODKA

Russia and Poland both lay claim to having given the world Vodka. It is thought to have originated in the 12th century and has appeared under such names as Wódka, Wodki, Vodki, Vodky, Votku, Votky and now Vodka. The name translated means 'little water'. A name derived from the fact that it is colourless, tasteless and odourless. This last characteristic has gained for the drink a reputation of being a wife's-deceiver—or a deceiver of whoever is the appropriate person one wants to deceive—a conception which has undoubtedly made sales soar.

Young people also favour vodka as an introduction to spirits and they usually help the flavour and appearance along with additions of lime juice, tomato juice (Bloody Mary) or ginger ale (Moscow mule).

While vodka is native to Eastern European countries, America really made the drink fashionable. The vogue started in California, in the 1940's, and swept America when it was realised that vodka was such a versatile base for mixed drinks and cocktails. America began making it and from there it came to Western Europe. Britain was slow to accept its qualities but now it enjoys a thriving trade. Today it is truly an international drink.

In order to counter a wave of drunkenness in her country, Russia in fact banned the production of vodka between 1914 and 1925.

THE MAKING OF VODKA

Vodka is a neutral spirit and may be made from barley, rye, maize and other grain or from potatoes, sugar-beet or a combination of them. It is distilled and rectified in a *patent still* into an almost pure spirit and then slowly passed through vegetable charcoal or activated carbon, which process ensures absolute purity by removing any remaining traces of colour and flavour and so it achieves complete neutrality. Then, without maturing, it is reduced in strength to suit a specific market. In Britain vodka is sold at about 65·5° proof (37·4 G.L.). Other countries require a higher alcohol content.

There are other variations—some distillers mature their vodkas for three years or more in cask, others add herbal infusions. But generally vodka is an unflavoured, immature pure spirit which has been filtered through charcoal and reduced by water to make it palatable. Some well-known brands are Stolichnaya (Russia), Vyborova (Polish), Cossack and Smirnoff (English) and Saratov and Nordoff (Irish).

Zubrowka is a Polish drink similar to vodka but yellow/green in colour, quite aromatic and slightly bitter in taste. Its name and characteristics come from the fact that Zubrowka grass is used in the spirit. It is marketed in an attractively shaped bottle which has also a blade of the grass floating about inside. Vodka is best served chilled in ice-cold glasses.

❧36❧
OTHER SPIRITS

A *quavit or Akvavit.* Aquavit is a spirit associated with the Scandinavian countries. It is made from potatoes or grain and often flavoured with aromatic herbs and spices. It is also popularly known as Snaps or Schnapps. Denmark and Sweden produce most of this spirit and the Danes and the Swedes take care to consume most of it themselves. It is not unlike gin. For preference, it should be chilled and it is usually drunk neat. One is supposed to swig it in one gulp.

Arrack. Arrack is a distillate of fermented palm sap, specially associated with Jamaica and the East Indies. Rice and molasses is sometimes added to the liquid while it is fermenting. There is a rum taste about the spirit when molasses has been added. Otherwise there is no particular taste.

Calvados. Calvados is distilled cider and carries the name of the place in Normandy where it is made. It is twice distilled in *pot stills* and then matured sometimes for as long as twelve years in oak casks. The Americans have their own version and call it applejack brandy.

Fraise. Fraise is an Alsatian brandy from both wild and cultivated strawberries. It is an excellent drink, when genuine.

Framboise. Framboise is another Alsatian brandy but made this time with raspberries. It is estimated that it takes 13·6 kilogrammes of fruit to make one bottle of spirit.

Grappa. Grappa is a great favourite with the Italians, and this is not to be wondered at because it is their own brandy which is similar to the French marc brandy. Grappa is made from the residue from the normal pressings of grapes. It can emerge from the still with a very high alcoholic content.

Marc. Marc, a type of brandy made, like Grappa from the grape-residue pressings, throughout the vine-growing regions of France. The best known are Marc de Bourgogne and Marc de Champagne. Marc is not inexpensive for what it is.

Ouzo. An aniseed-flavoured brandy made and popular in Greece. It turns milky when water is added.

Quetsch. Quetsch is a brandy distilled from plums and is quite similar to Mirabelle, which is generally classified as a liqueur. It comes from Alsace where so many fruit brandies are produced.

Raki. Raki is a spirit like ouzo and pernod which goes milky when water is added. Associated with the Balkan countries, it can be made from potatoes, plums, grain and so on. It is best drunk neat in one straight swallow, which might easily make a summer for those not used to it.

Schnapps. Schnapps is a spirit made principally from potatoes. It is particularly popular in Germany and Holland. It may be flavoured with aromatic herbs. It is much the same drink as aquavit.

Slivovitz. Slivovitz is a popular spirit in Yugoslavia and other Balkan countries and it is a popular trophy for tourists to bring back from those countries. It is made from fermented plums, and it is distilled twice in the making. After about a year in cask, more plums are added to give extra flavour. It needs to be allowed to mature for a few years.

Tequila. A colourless Mexican spirit made from the juice of the heart and head of specially cultivated cactus plants. After fermentation the juice is distilled once or twice in a *pot still* and the result is usually aged in cask for sometime. Similar in some ways to a 'lesser' brandy, it is drunk with fresh lime-juice with a pinch of salt added. A wedge of hot chilli may also be added for good measure. *Mescal* made from wild cactus plants is a similar spirit but usually inferior in quality. Both have a fiery flavour.

Tiquira. Tiquira is a Brazilian rectified spirit which is distilled from tapioca roots. They like it locally but there is not likely to be much call for it elsewhere.

Poteen. A colourless spirit made specially around the west coast of Ireland (and Connemara specifically) from potatoes. It is of very high strength and prohibited by law to be made. However, if one knows who to approach there is plenty to be found. It is fiery, warming and comforting too, in a damp and misty climate.

ভৈ 37 ৈ৯

APÉRITIFS

HUNGER is the best appetiser, but the sharp edge of appetite is not always available to those who are used to regular meals, or to those who are obliged to eat out. But it is not only jaded appetites that enjoy the practice of preparing for a meal by a tipple of an alcoholic drink for it will help the conversation even if it does nothing for the gastric juices. Whatever the effect on appetite, it is obvious that some drinks will be more acceptable before a meal, just as soup is more acceptable before rather than after the roast. It is only fair, therefore, to accept the definition that an alcoholic drink taken before a meal for the purpose of stimulation is an apéritif, a word culled from the Latin *aperitivus* meaning to 'open out', in this case the appetite, and from what has been written about ancient feasts the Romans must have needed some encouraging preliminaries.

Different peoples seem to have different ideas on the best preparation for a hearty meal. Many Englishmen find a few pints of beer to be an essential preliminary to Sunday lunch, but that may really be to ensure the success of the post-prandial nap. On the Continent, and particularly in France, a more cultivated disposition leads to a convivial meeting with friends before the important meal of the day, when it is only reasonable to imbibe drinks specifically designed to assist the appetite. Sad indeed is the Frenchman who cannot join his confidants in a café before his meal while he drinks his Lillet or Pastis or St. Raphaël. The world has always been wise to take its civilising leads from the French, and whatever the effect on one's keenness for food, there is no doubt that a favourite drink or two disposes of the workaday strains and provides an unworried environment for a meal.

Ideally apéritifs should be clean-tasting, have a reasonable alcoholic strength, have a dry tartness in the after-taste and not have too much bulk. These qualities will generally be enhanced if the drink is chilled on ice. The dry Sherries, dry Madeiras, dry white Ports and sundry cocktails are all favoured apéritifs, but there are many other worthy and excellent pre-prandial drinks.

Vermouth. The name Vermouth is of German origin. In the 16th century it was not unusual to flavour local wines with wormwood and the flavoured wines were called *wermutwein*. The name was taken over by the Italians and the French in what would have appeared to them to be the less uncouth form of Vermouth. Something taken from the Germans had to have a scientific aura, and Vermouth was introduced for its therapeutic and digestive properties. The production of Vermouth settled in Turin and Marseilles and, since then, there have been two traditional types of Vermouth, the sweet red variety associated with Italy and the dry white one associated with France.

However, today there is no national demarcation of type, because both countries make sweet and dry, red and white, varieties. Still, gin-and-It. is still in common parlance a sweeter drink than gin-and-French.

Basically, Vermouths are aromatised wines which have been fortified. The basic wine is usually of ordinary quality, blended to a set style. Besides the wine, the ingredients are *Mistelle* (unfermented grape juice with the addition of brandy), assorted flavourings, sometimes sugar and of course alcohol. The flavourings may include herbs, roots, barks, fruits, flowers, peels, quinine and so forth.

Making Vermouth. An example of the ordinariness of the wines used in the manufacture of Vermouth is that nearly all the wines used in the making of the famous French Vermouths come from the Midi. But wherever the young wines come from they are all blended in oak vats and matured there for up to three years. Then the *mistelle* is added in varying amounts up to as much as one part of *mistelle* to four parts of wine. Meanwhile, the flavouring agents have been macerated and steeped or infused in alcohol until the correct degree of flavouring has been extracted. This may take at least a week. Then the flavoured alcohol is added to the mixture of wine and *mistelle* and the whole lot is blended well together in large tanks in which there is machinery that thoroughly rouses and agitates the mixture. Some tannin for depth and some gelatine for clarifying are then added. Later, the Vermouth is fined, filtered and pasteurised. Finally it may be refrigerated to make absolutely certain that any tartrates remaining will form into crystals and fall to the bottom of the container. The Vermouth is then stored for some time before it is bottled, for it does not improve in bottle and it is meant to be drunk when it is fresh and crisp.

Types of Vermouth. The principal dry Vermouths are Martini Dry, Cinzano Dry, Chambéry and Noilly Prat. The principal sweet ones are Cinzano Red, Cinzano Bianco, Martini Sweet Red, Martini Bianco and

Noilly Prat Red. Punt e Mes is a sweet Italian Vermouth with a bitter after-taste. Carpano is similar but less bitter.

It is usual to serve dry Vermouth chilled, with a slice of lemon or an olive. The sweet ones may be served at ordinary temperature, although many prefer them chilled. They are usually decorated with a cherry.

Dubonnet. There are two kinds of the famous French apéritif of Dubonnet—Rouge and Blonde. The white, Dubonnet Blonde, is rather sweeter than the red. They are flavoured with quinine as well as various herbs. They are best served well chilled and with a squeeze of lemon to offset the sweetness.

St.-Raphaël. Red, bitter-sweet quinine-flavoured French apéritif favoured greatly in France.

Byrrh. Byrrh is another French apéritif and it is made near the Spanish border. It is a red wine flavoured with quinine and unspecified herbs and it is fortified with brandy. It is not necessary to have a brogue to pronounce the name, just call it Beer.

Lillet. Lillet is an extremely popular French white-wine apéritif that has been fortified with Armagnac brandy.

Campari. Campari is a pinky red bitter-sweet Italian apéritif. It is flavoured with gentia, quinine and the peel of bitter oranges, among other ingredients. Usually served with ice, a squeeze of lemon and a dash of soda-water, it is also a well-known *bitters*.

Cap Corse. Corsica produces the apéritif Cap Corse. It is a wine-based apéritif and flavoured with herbs and quinine.

Bitters. There are a number of apéritifs known as bitters, and the name indicates their principal characteristic. *Amer Picon* is a very black and bitter French apéritif. Grenadine or Cassis is often added to make the flavour more acceptable. Traditionalists like it served in water, twice as much water as bitters. *Fernet Branca* is the Italian version of *Amer Picon* and it is supposed to work wonders for a hangover. Even so, it is best diluted with water.

Underberg is a German bitters which looks like and almost tastes like iodine and is in many ways similar to the French and Italian versions mentioned. The most well-known bitters, is *Angostura* which takes its name from a town which used to have that name but is now called

25 The famous Berncasteler Doktor vineyard

26 The Moulin de Verzenay dominating some Champagne vineyards

27 Boating on the Moselle, a good way to visit the wine villages and vineyards

28 Well-tended Moselle vineyards

29 Rhine vines seen from the river

31 A dray man bringing in the supplies

30 Spit-roasted mackerel to work up a thirst at the Munich Beer Festival

32 Wine tasting in a London hotel

Ciudad Bolivar in Venezuela. The town lost the bitters as well as its name, for Angostura bitters are now made in Trinidad. These bitters are justly called the Worcester Sause of the drink business. They are used in the preparation of pink gins, pink ice and so on. If you have a strong constitution, a half-teaspoonful added either to rum or wine can provide an excellent apéritif before breakfast. There are other bitters such as *orange* and *peach bitters* used principally as cocktail ingredients.

PERNOD

In 1797, a French doctor, Pierre Ordinaire, sold to a Monsieur Pernod his recipe for making a special medicinal drink which he had been promoting as a cure for gastric ailments. This drink, later to take M. Pernod's name, was a distillation from aniseed and numerous herbs, and it soon became popular throughout France, especially in Paris and Marseilles. It was drunk as an apéritif or as a long cooling drink during the day. Soon, other anise-based drinks came onto the market. These *pastis*, as they were generally called, included the notorious Absinthe, which after a lively life at least on the left bank in Paris, was banned in France in 1915.

Absinthe had nearly all the characteristics of Pernod with the attraction of a higher alcoholic content. Its flavouring agents, however, had included wormwood which, in combination with the very high alcohol content, it was claimed France's birth rate reduced, caused a reduction of potency, and which certainly contributed to nervous complaints. The Spaniards do not seem to agree with these harmful effects, or at least are not worried about them, for Absinthe is still manufactured in Spain without legal restraint although the original formula has been modified.

MAKING OF PERNOD

Pernod has remained a popular drink, and no accusation has been levelled at any of the fifteen herbs and other plants which are used in its distillation. Of the fifteen, Badiane, Aniseed and Fennel are the three main ingredients. The extract from these is called *Anethole*. The anethole and other plant extracts, with a proportion of beetroot spirit, are steeped in a still overnight to macerate. Next day, the still is heated by steam and the alcohol extracts the flavourings from the plants. As the vapours rise, they are condensed and this extract is mixed with more spirit, distilled water, colouring, Badiane oil and sugar. These are put into the mixing vat in the following order—spirit, Badiane oil, and the flavouring extract, the colouring (liquorice dye), distilled water and sugar (beetroot). When the mixture is well blended, the liquid is filtered and then bottled.

SERVICE OF PERNOD

Pernod is served with about five parts of water to one of the pastis. A measure of Pernod is put into a 227 cm³ (8 oz.) tumbler, and diluted by dripping the water into it through a special strainer or perforated spoon which holds a lump of ice and a cube of sugar. As the water joins the spirit, the drink changes in colour from a timid yellowy green to a cloudy white. This change occurs because the weakening of the alcoholic content by the water brings the natural oils of the flavouring agents out of solution into suspension.

SUZE

Another very popular French apéritif is Suze, produced by the firm of Pernod since 1964. It is a gentian-flavoured drink, and gold-yellow in colour. It has a bitter-sweet taste with an alcoholic strength of about 16° G.L. Suze is made in either of two ways from gentian roots, alcohol and water. The roots may be infused in the alcohol, or they may be distilled with alcohol. A little orange flavouring and sugar are added to sweeten it, and some caramel is added to give the desired colour. It is then left in the vats for a month after which it is filtered and bottled for sale. The taste takes some getting used to.

ℭ 38 ℭ

COCKTAILS
(and other mixed drinks)

COCKTAILS are short stiff unstiffening drinks particularly associated with the American way of life. It was the Americans in
the 1920's and '30's who brought the vogue for cocktail drinking
to Europe. During those decades they were all the rage. Wine purists
tend to look down on cocktails in their realm of appetisers, but there is
little doubt that one before a meal can sharpen the appetite. The
drawback is that it is too easy to succumb to the temptation to indulge
in more than one. But this endeavour to improve the party spirit is
liable to stultify and dull the appetite for food.

It would seem that the drinking of cocktails is on the wane, although
cocktail parties are as popular as ever. They are now wrongly named
because such parties are more correctly today associated with tray-
loads of sherries, vermouths and hard spirits rather than of *mixed*
drinks.

The true characteristic of a cocktail is that it should be made from a
mixture of different ingredients so blended that no single one dominates
the rest. The name cocktail has an obscure origin. There are many
claims to the origin of the name, but the one most worthy is associated
with Betsy Flanagan, a forthright Irish lady who kept a tavern in
America. Her husband, of course, had fought against the British in the
American War of Independence, had been killed but he had had the
foresight to leave his widow with the tavern which had the advantage
of being much frequented by the American and French officers of
Washington's army. It also had the annoying drawback of having a
loyalist as a neighbour. This loyalist kept chickens which enabled the
officers to chide Betsy about the plumpness and delectibility of her
neighbour's poultry compared with the meagre produce from Betsy's
kitchen. The Flanagan honour was saved when one evening in 1779
Betsy provided a sumptious spread for the officers and included in the
fare some of her neighbour's fine fat fowl. Before starting their meal
the officers called for their usual bracers, or mixed drinks, and when

these were served Betsy triumphantly decorated each glass with a tail feather from the ill-gotten cocks. A Frenchman, gallantly toasting Betsy for her ingenuity, cried '*Vive le Cocktail*' and so named Betsy's bracers for evermore.

There are thousands of cocktails on the market today and new ones are being invented almost hourly. It seems to be the ambition of all notable barmen to devise their own special concoctions. In Great Britain the cocktail bible is the book of the United Kingdom Bartenders' Guild entitled *The U.K.B.G. Guide to Drink*. Under almost every cocktail bar, very discreetly, one of these books is kept and no wonder, for it would need a computer rather than a human memory to remember all the recipes. Despite this useful book, the make-up of many cocktails may vary from bar to bar. For example, dry Martini has numerous variations and can give rise to vehement argument about its mixing. Most people agree that this particular cocktail should be stirred and not shaken, but James Bond in the popular films created a new vogue by insisting that his dry Martinis should be shaken.

Mixing cocktails is not a difficult operation and can easily be accomplished with success by the careful amateur as well as the flamboyant professional. The latter will, of course, seem to do the job with more skill and flair and his expertise undoubtedly encourages the imagination of the customer to add another excellence to the taste. Both amateur and professional must have certain equipment and a number of ingredients to hand.

The equipment should include cocktail-shakers, glass mixing jugs with lips, strainers (Hawthorne) with springy and wiry edges, long mixing spoons, fruit knives, forks, ice-tongs, wine-knife, spirit measures, ice-buckets, ice-pick, ice-scoop, ice-crusher, fruit squeezer, fruit board, grater and muddler for mint and sugar, cocktail sticks and sundry glasses.

The ingredients necessary are a variety of drinks appropriate to the recipes and include Angostura, orange and peach bitters; castor, lump and brown sugar; eggs; fruit such as lemons, oranges and cherries; cream; mint; sugar syrup; borage; cucumbers, Worcestershire sauce, nutmeg; cinnamon; cloves; ginger; salt and pepper.

There are a number of points to be remembered in the making of cocktails. The ice should always be clear and clean, but not snowy as this kind rapidly deteriorates. The cocktail-shaker should not be filled more than about four-fifths of its capacity so as to allow sufficient room for efficient shaking. Effervescent-type drinks should never be shaken. Glasses should not be filled to the brim as this will lead to spilling. If an egg is to be used, it should be broken into a separate container before adding it to the mixture, for eggs are sometimes bad. If at all possible, cocktails should be served in chilled glasses as this will retain their temperature better. The operation of shaking should be carried out with a short and snappy action; the mixture does not want to be rocked to sleep and prolonged shaking will merely melt the ice and so dilute the drink. Ice is used in almost all cocktails and, for the exceptions, the omission of ice is part of the recipe. The recipe should also state whether the cocktail is mixed in a mixing glass or in a shaker. If in a mixing glass, which as a general rule is used for drinks based on liqueurs or wines, *the ice should go in first*, before the other ingredients. The stirring should be brisk and continued until the mixture is cold, when it can be strained into the glasses and served. *The ice should also be put first into a shaker*, which is used for mixtures that include fruit juices, cream, cordials, sugar and such-like ingredients. After the short snappy shaking, the cocktail can be poured into the serving glasses.

Liqueur   Collins   Cocktail   Highball

Cocktail   Old-Fashioned   Sour

Cocktail and Mixed Drinks Glasses

Port   Sherry   Brandy

Other Special Glasses

However the ingredients are to be mixed, it is always best to add the alcoholic liquor last. It is, of course, axiomatic that cocktails should be mixed just before they are to be consumed.

One of the important virtues of the cocktail is that it can look attractive, and a second that it usually has a name with a sophisticated edge to it. No cocktail has been called 'mud'. Cherries, olives, lemon peel and orange peel are favoured garnishes. When peel is used, its oil should be squeezed into the cocktail and then the peel dropped into the drink. These garnishes are added after the cocktail has been mixed, not into the mixer but into the serving glasses. When fruit is used it must be in perfect condition, and it is useful to know that oranges and lemons will yield more juice if they are soaked in warm water before being squeezed.

The making of a good cocktail requires meticulous attention to detail. Measures should be used for the drinks as inaccurate amounts will spoil the balance of the taste. The same ice should not be used twice, and any remains or 'dividends' in the mixing shaker or glass must never be used as part of a new mixing, or the new cocktails will suffer. Finally, the mixture should be strained before serving as a cocktail.

The adventurous will often try to invent new combinations to make new cocktails. Until a new cocktail has been safely and repeatedly tried by its inventor, the wisest course is to rely on the mixed drinks which have been consumed with reasonable safety for a long time. The recipes for most of the well-known cocktails and other mixed drinks are set out below:

BRANDY-BASED COCKTAILS AND MIXED DRINKS

Alexander $\frac{1}{3}$ cognac, $\frac{1}{3}$ crème de cacao and $\frac{1}{3}$ fresh cream. Shake thoroughly with ice and strain into a cocktail glass.

American Beauty $\frac{1}{4}$ brandy, $\frac{1}{4}$ grenadine, $\frac{1}{4}$ dry vermouth, $\frac{1}{4}$ orange juice and a dash of crème de menthe. Shake with ice, strain into a 143 cm³ (5-oz.) goblet and top up with a little port wine.

Bonnie Prince Charlie 1 oz. brandy, $\frac{1}{2}$ oz. Drambuie, 1 oz. lemon juice and ice. Shake and strain into cocktail-glass.

Bosom Caresser 1 oz. brandy, $\frac{1}{2}$ oz. grenadine, 1 oz. curaçao, the yolk of one egg and ice. Shake and serve in a 5-oz. goblet.

Brandy Cocktail $1\frac{1}{2}$ oz. cognac, 1 oz. cointreau, $\frac{1}{2}$ teaspoon of sugar syrup, two dashes of Angostura and ice. Stir and strain into a cocktail-glass.

Brandy Hum   Half and half of South African brandy and Van der Hum. Serve on the rocks.

Brandy Smash   In a tumbler crush mint into a teaspoonful of powdered sugar, add 1½ oz. Hennessy brandy and top with soda water. Stir.

Klondike   1½ oz. calvados (apple brandy), 1 oz. dry vermouth, two dashes of Angostura bitters and ice. Shake and strain into a cocktail-glass.

Sidecar   ½ brandy, ¼ cointreau, ¼ lemon juice and ice. Shake and strain into a cocktail-glass.

Stinger   Two parts of brandy to one part of crème de menthe (white). Shake with ice and strain into a decent-sized cocktail-glass.

GIN-BASED COCKTAILS AND MIXED DRINKS

Alaska   ¾ gin, ¼ yellow chartreuse and crushed ice. Shake and strain into a cocktail-glass.

Bronx   ½ dry gin, ¼ sweet vermouth, ¼ dry vermouth, the juice of ¼ orange and crushed ice. Shake and strain into cocktail glass.

Clover Club   ⅔ dry gin, ⅓ grenadine, the juice of ½ lemon, the white of one egg and ice. Shake sharply and strain into a 5-oz. goblet.

Dry Martini   ⅔ dry gin, ⅓ dry vermouth, a dash of orange bitters and ice. Stir in mixing glass and serve in a cocktail-glass with a twist of lemon. The original recipe was ½ dry gin, ½ dry vermouth and ice. Stir in mixing glass.

Gimlet   ½ dry gin, ½ limejuice and ice. Shake and strain into a cocktail-glass.

Gin and French   ½ dry gin and ½ French vermouth. Pour over ice into a cocktail-glass and decorate with a twist of lemon.

Gin and It   ½ gin and ½ Italian vermouth. Pour over ice into a cocktail-glass and decorate with a cherry.

Gin Fizz   1 oz. dry gin, the juice of ½ lemon and a half-teaspoonful of powdered sugar. Shake with ice, strain into a 5-oz. goblet and top up with soda water.

Gin Rickey   2 oz. gin, 1 oz. lime/lemon juice, some lime/lemon rind. Put these into a small tumbler, add lump of ice, stir and top up with soda water. A dash of grenadine may also be added.

Gin Sling   1½ oz. dry gin, the juice of a small lemon, a dash of Angostura bitters and a heaped teaspoon of powdered sugar. Mix in a tumbler with ice cubes and top up with water.

Gin Sour.   2 oz. dry gin, ½ oz. lemon juice, a teaspoonful of sugar syrup and a dash of orange bitters. Shake with ice and strain into a large cocktail-glass.

John Collins   1 oz. Holland's gin, the juice of ½ lemon, a half-teaspoonful of powdered sugar. Pour over ice cubes in a tumbler, top up with soda water, stir and serve with a slice of lemon.

Medium Martini   ⅔ dry gin, ⅙ dry vermouth, ⅙ sweet vermouth and ice. Stir in a mixing glass and strain into a cocktail-glass.

Negroni   2 oz. dry gin, 1 oz. sweet vermouth and 1 oz. Campari. Pour over ice into a tall goblet, top up with soda water and decorate with a slice of orange.

Orange Blossom   ½ dry gin and ½ orange juice. Shake with ice and strain into a cocktail-glass.

Pink Gin   Into a 5-oz. goblet, shake a few drops of Angostura bitters, roll the bitters around the glass, shake out the surplus and add a measure of gin and a couple of ice cubes.

Pink Lady   2 oz. gin, 1 teaspoonful grenadine, ½ white of egg. Shake with ice and strain into a large cocktail glass.

Sweet Martini   ⅔ dry gin, ⅓ sweet vermouth and ice. Stir in a mixing glass, strain into a cocktail-glass and decorate with a cherry.

Tom Collins   Same as a John Collins except that traditionally 'Old Tom' gin is substituted for Holland's gin.

White Lady   ½ dry gin, ¼ cointreau and ¼ lemon juice. Shake with ice and strain into a cocktail-glass.

Cocktails

RUM-BASED COCKTAILS AND MIXED DRINKS

Bacardi Cocktail   ½ Bacardi rum, ¼ grenadine and ¼ lemon juice or lime juice. Shake with ice and strain into a cocktail-glass.

Daiquiri   Made as above but with Daiquiri rum.

Fish House Punch   2 bottles of Jamaica rum, one bottle of brandy, ¾ lb. brown sugar, 3 pints of water and 2 teaspoonfuls of peach bitters. Blend thoroughly and pour over a large chunk of ice in a bowl that is big enough.

Planter's Punch   2 oz. Myers rum, 1 teaspoonful of grenadine, 1 oz. lemon and a dash of Angostura bitters. Shake with ice and serve into a cocktail-glass.

Rum Nog   1½ oz. dark rum, one egg, ⅔ pint milk, one level teaspoon of powdered sugar and ice. Shake well, strain into a tall glass and add a little grated nutmeg.

Shanghai.   ⅔ rum, ⅓ Pernod, ½ teaspoon of castor sugar, the juice of ½ lemon and ice. Shake and serve in a cocktail-glass.

VODKA-BASED COCKTAILS AND MIXED DRINKS

Balalaika   ½ vodka, ¼ cointreau and ¼ lemon juice. Shake with ice, strain into a cocktail-glass and serve with a twist of orange peel.

Blenheim   ½ vodka, ¼ Tia Maria and ¼ fresh orange juice. Shake with ice and strain into a cocktail-glass.

Bloody Mary   1 oz. vodka, one split-sized tomato juice, a touch of red pepper, a touch of celery salt and one teaspoonful of Worcester sauce. Stir all together with some cracked ice in a tall glass.

Gipsy   ⅔ vodka, ⅓ Bénédictine and a dash of Angostura bitters. Shake with ice and strain into a cocktail-glass.

Iceberg   Into a small tumbler put ice cubes, pour over them 2 oz. of vodka and a dash of Pernod and stir.

Muscovital   1 oz. vodka, 2 oz. ginger wine and 1 oz. Campari. Mix with ice in a tumbler and decorate with a cocktail cherry.

Screwdriver 2 oz. vodka, 1 oz. orange juice and a half-teaspoonful of powdered sugar. Shake, strain into a medium-sized glass, add ice and a slice of orange.

Twister 1½ oz. vodka and one teaspoonful of unsweetened lime juice. Pour over ice in a tall glass and top up with 7-up.

WHISKY-BASED COCKTAILS AND MIXED DRINKS

Atholl Brose 1½ oz. Scotch whisky, 1 oz. clear honey and 1 oz. pure cream. Mix well in a warm glass and then allow to cool. Sometimes hot milk is substituted for the cream and fine oatmeal is also often added to the recipe.

Brainstorm 2 oz. Irish whiskey, two dashes of dry vermouth and two dashes of Bénédictine. Serve in an old-fashioned tumbler with ice and a twist of orange peel.

Bobby Burns 1½ oz. Scotch whisky, ¾ oz. sweet vermouth and one teaspoonful of Bénédictine. Stir with ice, strain into a cocktail-glass and squeeze a lemon rind over.

Bunny Hug Equal parts of whisky, gin and Pernod. Shake well with ice and strain into a cocktail-glass.

Highball A name of American origin which now means a long iced whisky which is topped up with mineral water or plain water.

Irish Coffee Into an 8-oz. goblet, put two heaped teaspoons of brown sugar and a measure of Irish whiskey; leaving the teaspoon in the glass, pour in hot strong black coffee up to 1 cm from the top of the glass; mix all together until the sugar is completely dissolved; then, on the back of the same teaspoon, float some *double cream* onto the surface of the liquid until there is a generous and attractive collar. If double cream is not available, whipped cream can be used instead. Serve the glass on a coffee plate without a d'oyley or spoon.

Loch Lomond 1½ oz. Scotch whisky, two dashes of Angostura bitters and one teaspoonful of sugar syrup. Shake with ice and strain into a cocktail-glass.

Manhattan 1 oz. Bourbon whiskey, ½ oz. dry vermouth, ½ oz. sweet vermouth and a dash of Angostura bitters. Stir with ice, strain into a cocktail-glass and decorate with a cherry.

Manhattan (Medium) ½ oz. rye whiskey, ¼ oz. Italian vermouth, ¼ French vermouth, a dash of Angostura bitters and ice. Stir and serve in a cocktail-glass.

Rob Roy Equal parts of Scotch whisky and sweet vermouth and ice. Shake and strain into a cocktail-glass.

Mint Julep 2 oz. Bourbon whiskey, one lump of sugar, four sprigs of mint, one tablespoonful of water and crushed ice. Muddle the sugar, mint and water in a tall glass; fill with ice, add the whiskey; do not stir but garnish with fresh mint. Leave until glass is frosted. Serve with straws.

Old Fashioned Into an old-fashioned tumbler pour 1½ oz. of Bourbon whiskey and one teaspoonful of sugar syrup, add three dashes of Angostura bitters and a couple of ice cubes, stir and leave the stirrer in the glass, and decorate the drink with a cherry or a twist of lemon rind.

Serpent's Tooth 1 oz. Irish whiskey, 2 oz. sweet vermouth, ½ oz. kümmel, 1 oz. lemon juice and a dash of Angostura bitters. Stir with ice and strain into a 6⅔-oz. goblet.

Shamrock Equal portions of Irish whiskey and dry vermouth and three dashes each of green chartreuse and crème de menthe. Stir with ice, strain into a cocktail-glass and decorate with a green olive.

Whisky Mac Equal portions of Scotch whisky and ginger wine. No ice.

Whisky Sour 1 oz. whisky, the juice of half a lemon, a half teaspoonful of powdered sugar and one teaspoonful of the white of an egg. Shake with ice and strain into a large cocktail-glass. Sometimes a squirt of soda water is substituted for the egg white, but it is then added to the drink in the glass.

Whisky Toddy Into a warm glass put a heaped teaspoon of sugar and a little boiling water to dissolve the sugar; add 2 oz. Scotch whisky and stir; then add some more boiling water and top up with more whisky. No ice.

OTHER COCKTAILS AND MIXED DRINKS

Adonis 2 oz. dry sherry, 1 oz. sweet vermouth and a dash of Angostura bitters. Stir with ice and strain into a cocktail-glass.

Americano ⅔ sweet vermouth, ⅓ Campari and a lump of ice. Pour into an 8-oz. goblet, top up with soda water and add a twist of lemon and a dash of Angostura bitters.

Between the Sheets ⅓ Cointreau, ⅓ Cognac, ⅓ light rum and a dash of lemon juice. Shake with ice and strain into a cocktail-glass.

Champagne Cocktail Place in a Champagne glass one lump of sugar dampened in Angostura bitters; pour on well-iced Champagne; float one teaspoonful of brandy on top and decorate with a slice of orange and a cocktail cherry.

Charlie Chaplin 1½ oz. sloe gin, two teaspoonfuls of unsweetened lime juice and ½ oz. apricot brandy. Shake with ice and strain into a cocktail-glass.

Coronation 1 oz. dry gin, 1 oz. dry vermouth, 1 oz. dubonnet and ice. Stir and strain into a cocktail-glass.

Glogg A bottle of medium sherry, a bottle of red wine, a half-bottle of brandy, 3 oz. powdered sugar and eight dashes of Angostura bitters. Heat but do not boil. Into small mugs which have been warmed put a couple of raisins and an unsalted almond. Pour the warmed mixture on top. No ice.

Jamaican Wonder ½ oz. Tia Maria, 1 oz. Lemon Hart rum, 1 oz. unsweetened lime juice and a dash of Angostura bitters. Place in a tall glass and top up with chilled bitter lemon. No ice.

Kiss Me Quick 1½ oz. Pernod, four dashes Cointreau and two dashes of Angostura bitters. Shake with ice and strain into a tall goblet.

Portwine Flip One generous glass of port wine, one yolk of an egg, and one teaspoonful of powdered sugar. Shake and strain into a small tumbler and sprinkle a little cinnamon on top.

Snowball Into a tall glass put ice cubes and a decent measure of advocaat, top up with fizzy lemonade and decorate with a slice of lemon.

Syllabub 2 oz. sweet sherry, 1 oz. double cream, 1 oz. milk and one teaspoonful of powdered sugar. Beat together and serve with a teaspoon in a shallow glass.

Cocktails

MIXED DRINKS ASSOCIATED WITH BEER

Apple Cocktail ⅓ sweet cider, ⅙ dry gin, ⅙ brandy and ⅓ calvados, ice. Shake and strain (when cold) into a large cocktail-glass.

Black Velvet Half Guinness stout and half chilled Champagne. Pour simultaneously into a chilled silver tankard, taking care not to allow frothing over. No ice.

Mulled Special Ale Dissolve a teaspoonful of powdered sugar in water in a half-pint tankard, add a touch of powdered cinnamon, top up with a dark beer such as brown ale or stout, insert a white-hot poker to heat the drink and then enjoy it. No ice.

MIXED DRINKS FOR THE MORNING AFTER

Bullshot 2 oz. vodka, one teaspoonful of Worcester sauce, the juice of half a lemon, a touch of red pepper and a can of Campbell's condensed consommé. Mix vigorously together with plenty of ice, strain into a large glass and be brave enough to drink it.

Hair-of-the-Dog Cocktail 1 oz. Scotch whisky, 1½ oz. of double cream and ½ oz. of honey and shaved ice. Shake well and strain into a cocktail-glass.

Prairie Oyster Together with ice, mix 1 oz. cognac, one teaspoonful each of wine vinegar and Worcester sauce and a touch of red pepper. Pour over the unbroken yolk of an egg in a 5-oz. goblet, close the eyes and swallow without breaking the yolk.

NON-ALCOHOLIC COCKTAILS AND MIXED DRINKS

Limey 1 oz. lime juice, ½ oz. fresh lemon juice and one teaspoonful of the white of an egg. Shake with ice and strain into a cocktail-glass.

Parson's Particular 2 oz. fresh orange juice, 1 oz. lemon juice, four dashes of grenadine and the yolk of an egg. Shake briskly with ice and strain into a large cocktail-glass.

Pussyfoot ⅓ lemon juice, ⅓ orange juice, ⅓ unsweetened lime juice, a dash of grenadine or a half teaspoon of powdered sugar, and one egg yolk. Shake well with ice, strain into a 6⅔-oz. wine glass, top up with soda water and decorate with a cocktail cherry on a stick.

Temperance Mocktail   3 oz. lemon juice, 1 oz. sugar syrup and the yolk of one egg. Shake with ice and strain into a large cocktail-glass.

MULLED WINE AND WINTER WARMERS

Dr. Johnson's Choice   One bottle of claret, one wineglassful of orange curaçao, one wineglassful of brandy (4 oz.), a sliced orange, twelve lumps of sugar, six cloves, one pint of boiling water and grated nutmeg. Heat the wine with the orange slices, together with the cloves and sugar until it is nearly boiling; then add the boiling water, curaçao and brandy; pour into glasses and grate the nutmeg onto the top of each drink.

The Bishop   1½ bottles of ruby port, 2 oz. lump sugar, two oranges, two cinnamon sticks, cloves and one pint of water. Prick one of the oranges all over with cloves; place this in a medium oven for about half an hour; put the port into a saucepan and bring nearly to the boil; boil the water with the cinnamon sticks and the baked orange in it; rub the sugar lumps against the skin of half of the second orange and put them into the serving bowl with the juice from the remaining half orange; combine the heated port and the boiling water and pour into the serving bowl over the sugar lumps; allow the cinnamon sticks to remain in the mixture and float the orange hedgehog in the bowl as a decoration. In the absence of a serving bowl or tureen, the mixture can be put into bottles, and if these are stood in a basin of hot water they will be kept piping hot. When serving, wrap a clean table napkin around each bottle.

Mulled Wine   Equal quantities of Spanish Burgundy and water, add to taste castor sugar, lemon, an orange pricked with cloves, a broken cinnamon stick, grated nutmeg and mint. Heat slowly, stirring all the time until the sugar is dissolved (about thirty minutes). Do not boil but serve very hot. Strain into a glass jug and serve in 5-oz. goblets. A tepid mulled wine is insipid, but boiling the mixture will evaporate the alcohol.

FRUIT CUPS AND WINE CUPS

Sangria   A drink associated with Spain. One bottle of red or white wine, one orange and one lime each thinly sliced, a half cup of sugar and one cup of water. Make syrup by adding the sugar to water; heat and stir until the sugar is dissolved. Remove from fire, add the orange and lime slices and allow the mixture to marinate for four hours. Into a glass jug put a dozen ice cubes, six marinated slices of fruit and a half-cup of syrup. Then add the wine. These amounts should serve eight 4-oz. portions. Place a slice of orange and a slice of lime in each glass and pour the sangria over them.

Burgundy Cup　Pour into a glass jug a half-bottle of Spanish Burgundy or an inexpensive Burgundy and one measure of curaçao; add slices of orange and whole maraschino cherries, add ice, top up with soda water, stir well and decorate with a sprig of mint.

Cider Cup.　Pour into a glass jug two bottles of cider, one measure of brandy and half a measure of maraschino, add slices of assorted fruit and ice, top up with soda water, stir well and decorate with slices of apple and cucumber rind.

Fruit Cup (non-alcoholic)　Into a glass jug half-filled with ice, pour three measures each of orange squash, lemon squash and lime juice and three teaspoonfuls of grenadine; top up with soda water; stir well; taste and decorate by placing a thin slice of orange between two cherries on a cherry-stick.

Hock Cup　Pour into a glass jug a half-bottle of hock, one glass of medium sherry and one measure of curaçao; add slices of lemon and rind from cucumber, add ice, top up with soda water, stir well and decorate as desired.

Pimms Cups　Pimms are very popular drinks and there are six different Pimms cups each based on a different spirit. Pimms No. 1 is based on gin, No. 2 on whisky, No. 3 on brandy, No. 4 on rum, No. 5 on rye whiskey and No. 6 on vodka. No. 1 is the most popular. The spirit required is put into a tall tumbler or silver tankard with some ice, topped up with a fizzy lemonade of good quality, and the drink is garnished with a slice of lemon, a little cucumber rind or borage. The garnishing should not be overdone or the cup will look like a fruit salad.

Note—Metric Equivalents

$$1 \text{ fl. oz.} = 28 \cdot 4 \text{ cm}^3 \text{ (millilitres)}$$
$$2 \text{ ,, } = 56 \cdot 8 \text{ cm}^3$$
$$3 \text{ ,, } = 85 \cdot 2 \text{ cm}^3$$
$$4 \text{ ,, } = 113 \cdot 6 \text{ cm}^3$$
$$\text{etc.}$$

ᏨᏗ39ᏕᎧ

LIQUEURS

A LTHOUGH connoisseurs of wines and spirits tend to frown upon liqueurs as an intruder into drinking habits, they are widely favoured as polite, attractive and digestive drinks with which to finish meals. Certainly they are attractive for they display a galaxy of beautiful and exciting colours; and they are polite in that, although often stronger in alcohol than many spirits, they are not fiery, being always mellifluous to the taste. They seem to be digestive because, after a meal, they have the ability to reconcile the conflicting turbulances of agitated or fragile stomachs. Their syrupy sweetness is anathema to some, but this is not a good enough reason for dismissing them, as they often are, as inconsequential. Liqueurs are nothing more than *sweetened and flavoured spirits,* but they should not be confused with liqueur spirits which are, for instance, brandies or whiskies of great age, quality and refinement. It is certainly advisable to be able to differentiate between a brandy liqueur and a liqueur brandy. The former is a liqueur with a brandy as its basic ingredient, while the latter is a brandy of excellence and maturity.

Although liqueurs of a sort were known in Greek and Roman times, those we know today originated from the abbeys and monasteries of France and Italy. They were made originally as curatives for colds, fever and similar ailments that were doubtless prevalent in the draughty if beautiful buildings. The monks were not looking for a tipple but for a remedy. Even today the curative qualities supplement the commercial appeals to the palate. Certainly, the claim that liqueurs are an aid to digestion is a valid one when it is appreciated that some of the flavourings used are carraway seeds, peppermint and so on. By the 15th century, Italy was the leading liqueur centre of the world, but their production is now almost universal.

MAKING LIQUEURS

There are two basic methods of making liqueurs; one *the infusion or heat method,* the other by *maceration or cold method.* For all liqueurs, a spirit base is necessary, be it brandy, whisky, rum or neutral spirit. The *heat method* is the better when herbs, peels or roots are being used in the admixture. These are rich in oils, which heat can extract together with their flavours and aromas. The *cold method* is better when ingredients such as soft fruits and resinous substances are to provide the flavours and aromas. For some liqueurs a combination of the two methods is employed.

The Heat or Infusion Method. Each producer of a liqueur has his own secret recipe. If he is using the *heat method*, he will proportion out the ingredients of his recipe and immerse them for about a day in the particular spirit he uses. The spirit extracts a fair proportion of the flavouring elements, and then the lot is put into a *pot still* where it is heated. As the alcohol reaches boiling point, the rest of the flavours, the aromas and the oils are extracted from the ingredients. The vapours given off go through the worm of the *still* and are recondensed. What comes first and last from the *still*, known respectively as foreshots and aftershots, is very pungent and unsuitable for liqueurs. The middle fraction—what comes in between—is then distilled again, and once more the middle section only is separated. This is now of high strength, colourless and full of aroma and flavour. However, instead of the *pot still*, a kind of percolator may also be used to blend the flavour into the alcohol. The ingredients are placed in the upper part of the apparatus and the spirit in the lower. As the heat is applied the alcoholic vapours rise to pass through the ingredients extracting their qualities on the way to the recondensation. Or the spirit may be motivated as is the water in a coffee percolator, and then the spirit, with the application of heat, is sent up to merge with the ingredients, percolating through them and extracting the oils, aromas and flavours.

The Cold Method or Maceration. When employing the *cold method*, the spirit is usually brandy at about normal drinking strength, which is much weaker than the spirits used in the hot method. The fruits are crushed and put into oak casks with an appropriate amount of brandy. These casks are kept at room temperature for months or years, while the ingredients are stirred from time to time. Gradually colouring matter is being extracted from the fruit, giving the liqueur a natural colour, which is sometimes reinforced with some artificial colouring. When this maceration is finished, the liquid is drawn off and filtered.

Final Stages. The colourless liquids produced by the *heat method* are nearly always artificially coloured for psychological and commercial reasons. Whichever method of production was used, and whatever artificial colouring was added, the product is tested for taste, colour, density, sweetness and clarity. It is then mixed in vats with a complementary spirit and finally sweetened with either beet-sugar or honey. After a thorough mixing, it remains in the vat or cask for at least a year where it matures. Air penetrating through the pores of the wood lends mellowness to the blend and enhances the flavour and the fragrance. Before it is bottled, the liqueur is given more filtrations and cold treatment. This ensures the clarity of the drink for the future.

The flavouring ingredients used in the manufacture of the many liqueurs are aniseed, arnica, caraway seed, kernels of almonds, cherries, blackcurrants, apricots, peaches, raspberries, strawberries, bananas, peel and rind of citrus fruit, gentian, wormwood, rose petals, violets, hyssop, myrtle, cinnamon, sage, coriander, nutmeg, angelica, honey, vanilla and quite a lot more. The following is a list of the better-known liqueurs:

Abricotine   A French apricot brandy made at Enghien-les-Bains;

Advocaat   Originally made in Holland, its ingredients include egg-yolks, sugar and brandy;

Anisette   Strongly flavoured with aniseed, this liqueur is made in many countries particularly France, Spain, Italy and Holland;

Aurum   A pale gold liqueur, orange flavoured and made in Italy at Pescara;

Bénédictine   A very famous liqueur, first made in the early 16th century at the Bénédictine Monastery of Fécamp in France, where it was originated by the monk, Dom Bernardo Vincelli. In 1793, the Abbey was destroyed during the French Revolution, but the secret recipé was saved. Some seventy years later, Alexander le Grand, obtained the recipé and commenced to make the liqueur once more. The distillery where it is now made stands on the site of the old abbey. The bottles are similar in shape to those of yore, and the DOM on their labels stands for *Deo Optimo Maximo*, meaning 'To God, Most Good, Most Great'. The liqueur has a brandy base, is flavoured with a variety of plants, peels and herbs and is yellow-green in colour;

B and B   B and B is a mixture of bénédictine and brandy to suit people who prefer a drink drier than bénédictine itself;

Cassis   This is the liqueur of Dijon in France and it is made from blackcurrants;

Cerasella   An Italian liqueur made from cherries and certain herbs. It is dark-red in colour;

Chartreuse   The Carthusian monks make this famous liqueur at Voirin in France and at Tarragona in Spain. It has a brandy base and is flavoured with many herbs and plants. It is marketed in two colours. Green Chartreuse is imported at 96° British proof (55° G.L.), and although sweet it has a dryish finish to the taste. Yellow Chartreuse is sweeter and softer than the green and is imported at much less strength, about 75° British proof (43° G.L.);

Cherry Brandy   A sweet liqueur made from an infusion of cherries and some of their kernels in brandy. It is made principally in Denmark and Cherry Heering is a brand name liqueur made by the firm of Peter Heering in Copenhagen;

Cointreau   A colourless orange-flavoured liqueur originally named Triple Sec. It has a fairly dry finish and is made in Angers in France by the Cointreau family;

Cordial Médoc   A brandy based liqueur which is highly aromatic and is made in Bordeaux; Flavoured with old claret, it is red-brown in colour;

Cuarenta-y-Tres   A golden yellow liqueur from Spain. Made, as the name suggests, from 43 different ingredients, mainly herbs;

Curaçao   Originally made in Amsterdam, and flavoured with unripe orange skins from Curaçao in Dutch Guiana. Cointreau and Grand Marnier are of the same basic family;

Crème de Bananes   A banana-flavoured liqueur with a pure spirit base.

Crème de Cacao   A chocolate liqueur made from the finest cocoa and vanilla beans;

Crème de Cassis   Another name for Cassis mentioned above;

Crème de Menthe   This had the reputation of being the favourite drink of prostitutes, but it now has very respectable associations. It is flavoured with mint. The best has a good Cognac base, it is especially good when served frappé;

Crème de Noyau   Flavoured with bitter almonds and other fruit kernels;

Danziger Goldwasser   Made in Danzig, Poland, it is flavoured with aniseed and carraway and has gold flakes floating around in the bottle. There is also a Danziger Silberwasser with silver flakes in place of the gold.

Drambuie   A golden-coloured fairly sweet liqueur promoted by the MacKinnon family in Scotland. The base is fine aged Scotch whisky with a secret blend of herbs and heather honey;

Forbidden Fruit   A brandy-based liqueur, betrayed by its name as coming from America, flavoured with Shaddock, which is a citrus fruit similar to grapefruit;

Fior d'Alpi   An Italian liqueur, yellow in colour and sold in tall narrow bottles containing a small twig on which rock-sugar crystals have formed, reminiscent of a Christmas tree.

Gallweys Irish Coffee Liqueur   Rich smokey coffee flavoured liqueur with a whiskey base. Honey and herbs are also used in the blend.

Grand Marnier   Made mostly from cognac and oranges;

Glen Mist   A whisky-based liqueur from Scotland, flavoured with herbs, honey and spices;

Glayva   Also a whisky liqueur from Scotland, flavoured with herbs and spices;

Irish Mist   A whiskey liqueur. Ireland's answer to Drambuie;

Kahlúa   An original coffee-flavoured Mexican liqueur. An excellent accompaniment to ice-cream. The combination makes a delicious sweet;

Kirsch   A pure-white liqueur from Alsace and South Germany which has a bitter almond taste. It is distilled from cherries together with their stones. It is a recognised accompaniment to pineapple and fruit salads;

Kümmel   A colourless liqueur native to East European countries. It has a neutral-spirit base and is flavoured with carraway seed;

Maraschino   Another white liqueur which originated in Dalmatia. It is made from maraschino cherries and almonds, and it is also used to flavour fruit salads;

Mirabelle   A white plum-flavoured liqueur from Alsace, France.

Parfait Amour   This is usually violet in colour, but it can be red. It is, of course, a sweet spicy and highly scented liqueur from France and Holland;

Royal Liqueur   A chocolate liqueur with a peppermint flavour.

Sambuco   White Italian liqueur flavoured with liquorice. Coffee beans are often added especially in Italian restaurants. Then the liqueur is flamed to extract their flavour and to create atmosphere.

Strega   An Italian liqueur from Milan, but very well known in other countries. It is pure yellow in colour and orange flavoured. *Strega* is the Italian for 'witch';

Tia Maria   A Jamaican rum-based liqueur flavoured with Blue Mountain coffee;

Van der Hum   A South African liqueur, which is brandy-based and flavoured with a type of tangerine called naartje. It has an orange-tangerine flavour.

Vieille Cure   This aromatic liqueur comes from the Gironde in France, being made at L'Abbaye de Cenon. It has a brandy base, Cognac and Armagnac, and is somewhat similar to Bénédictine in style. The name has sometimes been abbreviated to V.C. to accommodate those who find it difficult to pronounce the full name.

ᕙ40ᕗ

BEER

BEER was probably discovered by accident when some of the nomadic tribes of the Middle East decided to settle and establish an agricultural life dependent on the cultivation of grain. One can imagine that in times of plenty some of the grain would be stored in reserve for times when the harvest might fail. If the storage happened to be damp, the grain would sprout or start to germinate. In his desperation to salvage his store, the cultivator would probably make a porridge from the sprouting grain. This would release enzymes which, in turn, would convert the starch in the cereal into maltose. The result would be a sweet-tasting porridge. If this was not eaten immediately, wild yeasts from the atmosphere might settle causing an active fermentation within a short period. The resulting mass would contain a small quantity of alcohol—in other words, a crude beer mash. Presumably, this or the effects of its consumption were sufficiently enjoyable to encourage a repetition of the accidental brew. A more sophisticated process would be developed, so we find that a brewing process was well established in Babylon at least as early as 6000 B.C. The orderliness of the Egyptian civilisation improved the process, and the knowledge was diffused along the trade routes, especially by the Greeks and Romans.

The Romans started brewing on a commercial basis to provide a substitute for wine, and it is hardly likely that the Vandals in scourging Europe would have wished to destroy that particular facet of civilisation. The Normans brought a brewing industry with them when they conquered England, and the home-made mead of the Saxons gradually disappeared. The waters of the English rivers and the plenteous grain of the countryside formed an excellent partnership and it is not too much to claim that, since those days, the best beer in the world has been made in England. Countries which cannot cultivate the grapevine adequately for wine-making are naturally more interested in the brewing of beer. Thus Belgium, for instance, consumes more beer than England even. An exception is Germany which produces both wines and beers in quantity. Wine countries that concentrate on white wines often also produce beer, presumably because they would otherwise miss the strong taste and internal warmth of red wines. Countries which are traditional spirit drinkers are now encouraging beer production, as the long-term effects of over-indulgence can be a national disaster (e.g. Russia, France, Africa).

The term 'beer' nowadays covers all beer-like drinks such as ale, stout and lager. The traditional conception was that ale was made without the addition of hops, and that beer was made with hops. The addition of hops, to sharpen the taste with a bitter tang, in the middle of the 16th century, met with a stormy reception, and the practice was not really popular until the 17th century.

Beer can now be correctly defined as any hop-flavoured fermented beverage made from cereals, be they barley, wheat, maize, rye, rice or any other cereal, although the best and most favoured cereal is barley. Apart from the cereal, the ingredients of beer are water, hops, yeast, sugar and finings, although this latter is not a real ingredient.

Barley. There are several varieties of *Hordeum sativum* or barley and those chosen for the brewing of beer are those with a low protein content, because protein causes cloudiness. The best barley comes from good agricultural soil. Why is barley the best grain for brewing? Simply because the plumules, which are the embryo leaves of the plant, are protected by the husks of the barley grain. The plumule of other grains grow on the outside without protection and are thus liable to be damaged during growth, whilst raking on the malting floor. A damaged plumule will cause a cessation of the germinating process and the grains are open to attack by micro-organisms and fungi. Another reason, leaving scientific fact aside, it is generally agreed that beers made from barley malt have an unrivalled taste.

Malting. Home-grown barley from the farms will be brought to the brewery where it will be weighed, cleaned, dried and stored. The first essential stage in processing is the malting. The dormant grain has to be activated, and this is done by steeping the barley in water for a period between 50 and 68 hours at a temperature of about 10° C. Some brewers change the water, allowing the grain a dry resting interval during which air can be absorbed. The change of water also provides an opportunity for extraneous matters to be washed away. The swollen grain is next spread out to a depth between 15 and 30 centimetres on a hard malting floor. By varying the depth of the grain, the prevailing air draught will help the grain to achieve a uniform temperature throughout, although during the whole process the temperature of the grain may vary between 12 and 21° C. To prevent matting and to aerate the grain, it is turned over with wooden shovels. This stage will take between six and fourteen days, the length of time depending on humidity, type of barley and floor temperature. The grain must not dry out too much, but if it is allowed to remain too wet, destructive fungi will be encouraged. More modern, automated methods speed up the process.

Many modern malting floors are equipped with air-conditioning plants. During the malting process, the grain will sprout and tiny rootlets appear and this is the time when the enzymes start to convert the starch within the grain into dextrins and maltose. This process is arrested at the appropriate time by kilning, for the maltose must be preserved by preventing the grain from using this sugar for its own respiration and growth.

Kilning. To start kilning in beer brewing, it is customary for the grain to be spread on perforated tiled floors with a furnace beneath. Today, the furnaces are normally oil-fired and the temperature is kept at about 49° C. The drying of the malt is often assisted by the use of an extractor-fan, which sucks a good draught of air through the grain thus enabling the temperature of the heating to be kept to a minimum. Raking the grain also is used for this purpose. In these ways the moisture in the malt is drastically reduced, the whole process taking about one day. Towards the end, the temperature is allowed to rise slowly to as much as 85° C. and this dries the grain thoroughly and gives it a biscuit or toasting-bread texture and a different taste. This will yield a malt suitable for mild ales. For pale and lighter ales, the temperature is not raised above 65° C. at the end, and this leaves a crystal malt, so called because of its thin brittle texture. For darker beers, such as stout, some darker malts are added which are made along the same lines as the malt for pale ale, except that the heating is carried out gently in cylinders; this deepens the colour. The darkest of all, black malt, is made by heating the malt up to 225° C., when care is essential to prevent charring.

The malt is now in a preserved state and the next step is to remove the rootlets. This is done by sieving. The rootlets at this stage are known as malt culms and sold for cattle fodder.

Flaked Maize. Flaked maize, which is made by crushing maize through rollers, is purchased by brewers as another source of starch. It is steamed and is then useful in the brewing process because it is clean. The non-starch matter is removed, the starch granules are broken down and the moisture content is reduced by this process. Flaked rice is also similarly used, and for drinks such as oatmeal stouts, oats are substituted for some of the barley in the malting process.

Water. Known in breweries as liquor, water is of course an essential for brewing. Plenty is needed and, historically, breweries have drawn on the local supplies by way of wells. The great variety of local well-waters is reflected in the great variety in the quality and other attributes of local beers. The very high reputation of beers from Burton-on-Trent is based on the high gypsum (magnesium sulphate) content of the water available from wells in the valley of the River Trent. It is particularly good for the manufacture of pale ales. London well-water has a high carbonate content due to the chalky sub-soil, and this is excellent for the brewing of sweet stouts and mild ales. Of course water can now be treated to provide any ingredient missing from the local supply. In this way, the famous Guinness firm of Dublin can now produce its 'Liffey Water', as its popular stout is sometimes called, at Park Royal in London. The uses of water in breweries can be summarised as being essential for the steeping of the grain, for liquor for the mash tun, for sparging and for cleaning and washing. Many a sturdy customer in the public bar may argue that too much water comes out from the breweries, but the strength of beers depends not only on the taste of the customers but on the appropriate ratios in the contents convenient to the tax-gatherer.

Hops. *Humulus lupulus*, better known as hops, is a plant and a member of the *Cannabiaceae* family. It is a perennial plant which lasts for ten to twenty years growing each year to a height of five metres in clockwise-twisting vines. The hop plant may be male or female and even, on occasion, it may have the attributes of both sexes except that one of them will be sterile. In England, it is normal to plant one male hop plant *up wind* of a hundred or two female hops, relying on the prevailing winds to carry the pollen with distributive discretion. In Europe, male hops are not allowed near the hopfields and because of this a more delicate and seedless hop is obtained.

The two main types of hops are the Golding and the Fuggles. The former is superior but it is difficult to grow and is liable to disease. Its famous habitat is in the light loam soil of the hop fields on either side of the A.2 road in Kent. The Fuggles is a larger hop, growing best in clay soil found in the Weald of Kent. It yields more than the Golding and, when well cultivated, is of very good quality. There are a number of hybrids such as Northern Brewer, Bullion, and Brewer's Gold, and these are being developed to give a better flavour to the beer. European hop plants are seedless, which is an advantage as seeds tend to block brewing equipment. There is a moisture content of between 65 and 80 per cent. in fresh hops and, by drying in oasthouses this content is reduced to 10 per cent. This enables them to be stored for a year usually in a cold store until the next crop is available.

Hops are used in the brewing of beer for four main reasons. The hops impart a bitter delicate flavour and aroma, the resin extracted from the hops acts as a preservative giving the beer a longer life; the tannin in the hops helps to precipitate barley proteins, thus preventing a protein haze in the beer; and the hops form a filter bed in the hopback to enable bright wort to be fermented later.

Hop gardens were known in Germany in the 7th century but they were haphazardly cultivated. Hop growing was introduced into England in 1525 from Flanders, but the cultivation was not organised for another century. Nowadays, some 8 100 hectares in the United Kingdom are used for growing hops and well over half (4 450 hectares) of these hop gardens are in Kent. Most of the others are in Sussex, Hampshire, Worcestershire and Herefordshire. The chief hop gardens abroad are in Germany, Poland and Czechoslovakia, and in the United States, particularly in the states of California, Oregon, Washington and New York.

Yeast. The yeast used in the brewing of beer is specially cultured, being of the species *Saccharomyces cerevisiae* for ordinary beer and *Saccharomyces carlsbergensis* for lager beer. These unicellular fungi are added to, and live off, the sugars in the sweet wort to yield by-products of alcohol and carbon dioxide. When this fermentation is finished, the yeast is removed and the resultant product is beer. The yeast may be used again to activate fermentation, but most of it is sold to food industries which extract vitamin B or use it for the manufacture of vegetable extracts and soup concentrates.

Fining. Beer is fined in cask in order to make it clear. Traditionally, isinglass (bladder of the sturgeon) is used for this purpose. It is dissolved in a mildly acidic solution which is added to the beer in cask. Nowadays, there are of course many good proprietory finings on the market and available to the brewers. But it should be mentioned that fining is not always necessary.

Sugar. The sugar used in the making of beer is invert sugar, usually bought from a specialist firm, and which, being a product of cane-sugar, is readily fermentable. It can contribute to the sweetness of mild ales in the form of a priming solution, and it is acted upon by the yeast cells to increase the alcoholic content. Sometimes burnt sugar (caramel) is used to add colouring and taste to the darker beers.

THE BREWING PROCESS

The process of brewing begins with the crushing of the malt in a mill.

The grist is then mashed (mixed) with hot liquor (water) into the mash tun. A good brewing mash will contain at least 75 per cent. of malted barley, the remainder being made up of other sugar sources such as barley, flaked maize and wheat flour. This mixture of grist takes about two hours to be infused by the liquor which is heated to a temperature around 63° C. Mechanical rakes within the mash tun having stirred the mixture. The enzymes work on the starches to convert them into maltose and dextrins (types of sugar). A hot sweet liquid results and this is known as wort. The wort is then filtered through finely slotted plates in the bottom of the mash tun and collected in a vessel known as an underback. While this filtering is taking place, a gentle spray of hot liquor is rained down onto the grist, and this 'sparging' ensures the washing-out of all the wort. The spent grain left in the mash tun is removed and sold as cattle fodder as it has a high food value.

From the lagged underback, the wort is pumped to a copper vessel, a sort of massive kettle, which may be pressurised. In this vessel the hops and sugar are added, the quantity of hops varying from 191 to 907 grams for 100 litres of wort according to the type of beer being made—more hops for bitter beer. The wort, with its additives, is now boiled for one or two hours. This will sterilise the wort and stop any further enzyme action. It will also extract substances, flavouring and preserving resin mainly from the hops, and, with the help of the tannin from the hops, coagulate the proteins.

The fluid is now run into a hopback, which is a vessel with slotted plates forming a filter bed. The contents of the hop back are allowed to stand for 40 minutes, allowing the hops to settle and form a filter bed. The wort is re-cycled back through this filter bed again and again until it becomes bright and clear, which takes about 15 minutes. The bright wort is drawn off for cooling. The filter bed of hops may be very lightly sparged to extract the last drop of wort. The spent hops are sold as garden fertiliser.

Cooling may be carried out in a refrigerator known as a paraflow, which is an enclosed box with cold water flowing in an opposite direction to the hot wort, the liquids being separated by many thin plates or tubes. Sterile air may be injected in the wort to ensure sufficient oxygen for an aerobic yeast fermentation later in the fermenting vessel. The wort is cooled to a 'pitching' temperature between 14 and 16° C., and it is then run into fermenting vessels. The wort in the filled fermenting vessels is tested by dipping to gauge the amount of wort on which duty is payable. The sugar content is measured by a hydrometer to give the specific gravity on which duty is paid and the particulars are declared to the Excise Officer by entry in a brewing book. The Excise Officer almost always makes an independent check.

The duty is calculated from the entries in the book at the end of the month. Sugars added later are also taxed according to volume and content.

In the fermenting vessel, the yeast is added, a process known as 'pitching', either while the vessel is being filled or when it is full. The pitched yeast is used at the consistency of single cream and it contains any additional yeast food that the brewer may require. In large breweries, the vessels may be filled from different coppers via the hop backs to enable a specified gravity and quality to be sustained. The yeast, at first, reproduces aerobically in which no alcohol is produced, but the vat rapidly becomes blanketed with carbon dioxide, which seals off the air in the atmosphere. Without air, the fermentation continues anaerobically to produce alcohol. At first a light frothy head develops on the surface. Cauliflower heads of frothy yeast penetrate the light head and the sides of the vats may have to be extended by boards to prevent an overflow. The cauliflower heads eventually ease into a rocky formation, which may be up to 1·5 metres thick. About the third day of fermentation, the desired alcoholic content is reached and the excess yeast is taken off, normally by suction from what is known as a parachute funnel. After this, a dark tan-coloured dense yeast head with a wrinkled surface is formed, and this protects the beer. The process in the fermenting vessels lasts for seven days, during which time the temperature is controlled by a series of circular or spiral pipes, known as attemperators, within the vessel and through these cooling liquid is passed.

After the seventh day, the beer is racked into a reception vessel known as a racking-back, and the yeast head is left unbroken behind. The next step in the processing of the beer depends on whether it is to be sent out in casks, kegs, bottles or cans.

Casks. From the racking-back the beer is run into wooden casks into which a small quantity of hops has already been put. This is known as dry-hopping, and the hops give the beer a delicate flavour and aroma and assist in its conditioning. The hops used for this are very carefully selected. Priming sugars (dissolved sugars) are added to the cask to take the dry edge off the raw beer, to improve flavour and to encourage a slight further fermentation. This extra fermentation imparts some carbon dioxide to the beer and thus gives the beer a sparkle. Finings are added before the beer is sent out to the publican or other customer.

Kegs. Beer which is to be sold in kegs is usually given the priming and dry-hopping treatment in conditioning tanks. It is then filtered, sparkling bright, into sterile kegs under slight pressure.

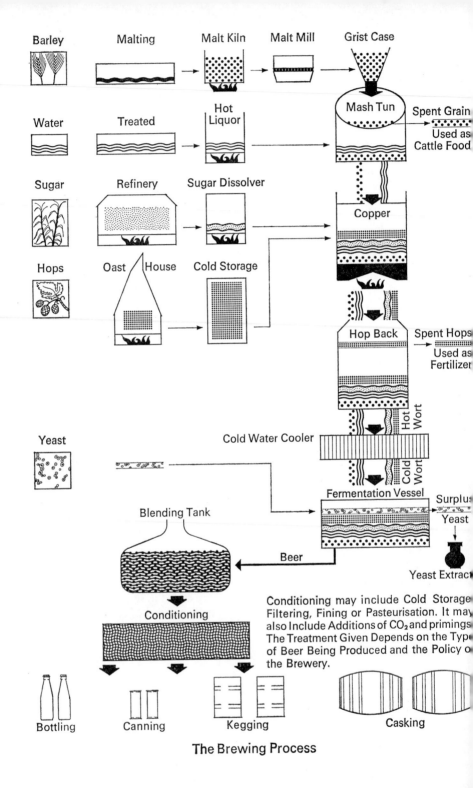

The Brewing Process

Bottles and Cans. Beer for bottling or canning is prepared in the same way as the beer to be sold in kegs. It is then run into a refrigerated conditioning tank, where it may stay for several weeks, the period for high-gravity beers being longer than for the others. It is said that the beer gathers flavour during this period, after which it is filtered into the bottles or cans under pressure where it is pasteurised. Pasteurisation prevents any further development of micro-organisms in the beer and ensures a high standard and consistent taste and condition in the beer. In some cases of bottling beer, pasteurisation is not carried out.

The brewing process can be summarised as follows, the ingredients being barley, sometimes with some flaked maize or barley, water called liquor, hops, yeast, sugar and finings:

1. The grain is weighed, cleaned, malted and kilned to become malt. The malt is blended and ground in a mill resulting in grist;
2. In the mash tun, the liquor and grist are mixed and sweet wort is extracted;
3. The wort is put into the copper where it is boiled with hops and this gives a sweet hopped wort.
4. The hopped wort is cooled and transferred to the fermenting vessel;
5. Yeast is then added, and the mixture ferments and seven days later emerges as beer;
6. The beer is racked off into cask where a small quantity of priming sugar is added; and
7. The beer is fined or filtered ready for sale.

THE STORING OF BEER

However well the brewer does his work, the customer will not get good beer unless the publican or other salesman knows his job in looking after his cellar and caring for the stored beer. Beers ought to be kept at a temperature between 10 and 12° C., and cellars must be kept clean throughout, with no fungi or cobwebs on the walls and in the corners. They must have good drainage. The piping leading the beer to the bars should be of the shortest length that the cellar site will allow, and they should not be fixed to run across the ceiling. Heat rises so the lateral pipes should remain at the lowest practical level. The piping and, of course, the joints of tubing, usually plastic nowadays, ought to be cleaned as frequently as possible and certainly not less than once a week. Draught beers used always to be delivered to the cellars in wooden casks or barrels, but increasingly metal casks and kegs are being used for this purpose. From the brewer's point of view, metal kegs last much longer than wooden ones, the cost of cooperage on the wooden casks is saved, and the quality of the beer can be controlled as it is virtually impossible to tamper with beer in metal kegs and there are no dregs. From the publican's point of view the metal kegs are simple to bring into use, they are merely stood upright, the pipe from the bar pumps is inserted neatly into the top of the keg to draw the beer off through a fitted internal tube from the bottom of the keg, while another pipe, also to the top of the keg, introduces carbon dioxide to maintain the pressure. The beer can be drawn through a simple refrigerator and this is particularly useful for draught lager. Nevertheless, metal containers can get heated during transit on a hot day, and there is perhaps always a small risk of pressure kegs exploding. Traditional beer drinkers would agree that beer is best when it is drawn from the wood but that the pressurised beer from the metal kegs is far much more reliable in quality. This is because the expertise of cellarman varies from pub to pub and sometimes from day to day. The care of beer in wooden casks is certainly not simple but filtered beer in a sterile metal container should be perfect as long as the simple rules of hygiene are observed.

When beer arrives in wooden casks in the cellar, the casks must first be stacked securely on their sides horizontally and left to allow the beer to settle and to undergo a gentle secondary fermentation. Casks must be placed so that the spiling bung in the middle of one side is on top, and so that the main bung in one end of the cask (in the head of the cask) will be accessible to the pipes or tap. After the beer is settled, the cask is spiled by hammering a spigot peg into the spiling bung. This peg is porous and allows excess gas in the cask to escape. For the larger casks, this operation is best done in two moves; first driving in a hard peg to clear the bung and provide an air space; second replacing the hard peg by the porous peg. When the cask is to be tapped it may be better to have the hard peg in the spiling bung, unless the tapper is confident that he will do his tapping by one clean blow. Tapping is driving the tap or pipe connection through the main bung thus providing the connection by which the beer can be drawn. If there is a quick sale for the beer, no further action is necessary, apart from drawing the beer, until the cask is empty. If sales are slow, the porous spigot should be changed for the hard peg at times to prevent the beer going flat through the escape of too much gas.

When the level of the beer in the cask has dropped, the cask will need to be tilted in order to draw off the beer which otherwise would be below the level of the tap. This operation requires care, first of all to ensure that the sediment that has drained to the bottom of the horizontal cask is not disturbed. Secondly the titlted level of the beer must be lower than the porous spigot, otherwise the beer will seep through this peg and spill and the seeped beer will be liable to infection which will be passed back into the cask. Obviously, the level of the tilted beer must be above the tap, but the cask must not be tilted so far that the sediment reaches the level of the tap. When all the clear beer has been drawn off, the cask, undrained of sediment, is sealed with a non-porous peg and bung and returned as soon as possible to the brewery, where it is cleaned by stem-injection and hot water jets.

Section 163 (1) of the Customs and Excise Act 1952 makes it a legal offence for beer to be returned to a cask, although some publicans may pretend not to know this. It is also an offence to mix beers other than in a glass or tankard and only then at the customer's request. Beer which is unsaleable should be sealed in its cask and returned to the brewery, which can arrange in some circumstances for a refund of Excise duty on the spoilt beer. The sediment dregs are of course not eligible for this refund.

Bottled beers, now that most of them are pasteurised, do not need such expert care, provided that they have been rested for about a week after pasteurisation to restore themselves and to gather flavour. Heavy beers such as stout need a longer rest. These rests are usually provided at the brewery and the salesman has little to do except to ensure that the beer is kept and served at an even cool temperature. The practice sometimes adopted of stacking the crates of bottled beer in open yards must be condemned as the beer will suffer from the changes in temperature. The rare non-pasteurised bottled beers need more care. They should be allowed at least a month's rest between bottling and delivery, although practice may vary in this respect to take account of the continued fermentation of the beer in the bottle, the probable life of the beer in the bottle and the formation of sediment. Some control of these factors may be secured by filtering the beer into the bottles. The proper storage of these beers in cellars and bars is important to avoid too much disturbance and to provide an even cool temperature.

THE SERVICE OF BEER

The service of beers is a simple subject but one that ought to have close attention, because the customer is usually eagle-eyed to see that he gets the full quantity in the right condition. Few men will look at the scales in ordinary shops, but fewer still will tolerate short measure in their beer.

Beer is served in a variety of containers such as pots, tankards, Toby jugs, pitchers, mugs and tumblers. But the common practice nowadays is for glass tumblers or glass mugs in pint and half-pint sizes to be used. These are usually stamped with the Imperial measure, because the publican is obliged to serve an exact measure if the customer so specifies.

This requirement is the reason why so much beer is slopped about while it is being served. For the glass has to be brimful, the beer must have a head but not too much of a 'collar' which is the vernacular for too much froth. Recently glasses and mugs are being made which have a little more capacity than the Imperial measure. The Imperial measure is marked by a line near the top of the glass and the beer fills the vessel up to this mark. This method can ensure correct measure and avoid the customary spilling. Most beers other than the darker beers (porters, stouts and brown ales) benefit by being served at a cool temperature, which is usually controlled from the cellar. To make sure that the quality of the beer remains consistent, pumps and bar taps must be frequently cleaned. Proper treatment and good cellar work ensures this.

Pouring. The pouring of beer is complicated by the facts that customers have the habit and most of them feel it a duty to secure their full measure to the last drop, and that beers are very frothy. It is necessary therefore to pour in such a way that the liquid trickles down the inside of the glass. A direct jet to the bottom of the glass followed by direct jets into the liquid already in the glass will cause too much froth to be produced. The liquid should be poured against the side of the glass whether it is being drawn from the tap, by pump or otherwise, or from the bottle. If, by this method, the beer appears to be pouring flat, that is without any froth, the outpouring should be directed to the liquid already in the glass to encourage some frothing. If more encouragement is necessary the glass should be held further away from the tap or bottle so that the beer has further to fall. Now that ladies use pubs as much as men, the sloshing of beer over bars and tables ought not to be so prevalent and the marked glasses will help to stop this. Bottled beers have to be served carefully, or else too much froth will leave insufficient room in the glass for all the liquid. This can be ensured by pouring gently down the side of the angled glass, and adjusting the speed of pouring to obtain a full glass with a reasonable head. The bottle must never be allowed to come in contact with the beer in the glass. Non-pasteurised bottled beers involve a further complication in that the sediment should be left in the bottle, yet the customer will want all the clear beer. Finally, all glasses must be clean, which means that after each use they must be washed, rinsed, dried and polished. In a busy bar at times this may be somewhat impractical but the bar must be so organised that thorough washing and drying can be rapidly carried out. There is no excuse for the lazy practice sometimes seen of just swilling the dirty glass in a sink of used water. There are proprietory antiseptic solutions specially produced for washing glasses. Household detergents tend to reduce the beer head if not rinsed from the glass properly. Finally, glasses must be regularly inspected for cracks and chips. Chipped or cracked glasses can be unhygienic and they are certainly dangerous; if they are not thrown out, justifiable complaints and claims for damages will come from the customers.

Canned beers are mainly sold for consumption 'off the premises', and they are very useful for picnics, travelling, storage and home consumption. Their storage in bars or shops is simply a matter of space but they must, like bottled beers, be kept where they are not subject to variable temperatures.

TYPES OF BEER

Lager. Lager was first produced in Central Europe. The word comes from the German *lagern*, to store. The process of the fermentation of lager can take a long time to complete. Bottom yeast is used and it is so called because, unlike other yeasts, it stays at the bottom of the fermenting vessel, instead of rising to the top. The first fermentation lasts for about a week and then the beer is stored in stainless steel tanks where a secondary fermentation at a low temperature takes place. This can last for as long as six months. Pasteurisation follows, when the bottles or cans are put through a steaming-chamber in which any yeast cells are destroyed. This prolongs the life of the lager.

Ale. In years gone by, ale was made without hops flavouring, but now there is no real difference between ale and other ordinary beers.

Stout. The names of Guinness and Mackeson are the two most known among the various brands of stout. Stout is a strong beer, on the sweet side, highly flavoured because of a rich content of hops. Stouts have a definite malty tang. Probably no drink is advertised with greater originality and ingenuity than Guinness's stout.

Porter. This drink, a weaker kind of stout, got its name because it was a favourite beverage with London and Dublin porters. It is a dark beer, brewed from brown or charred malt.

BEER-LIKE DRINKS

Cider. Cider is made from small apples which are rich in sugar and tannin. The apples are crushed and pressed, and the juice, left to itself, will ferment. Better results, however, are obtained by adding cultivated yeast. Complete fermentation gives a dry cider, but if a sweeter variety is required, the liquid can be filtered free of yeast before the fermentation has run its full course. Cider is a still drink, but some are carbonated, and some others, known as 'Champagne' ciders, are sparkling because they are bottled before the completion of the fermentation. In these last varieties there will be some sediment, so it is best to stand the bottle upright for a time before serving.

Mead. Mead is diluted honey which has been fermented by the addition of cultivated yeasts. Quite likely, mead is the oldest fermented drink in the world and was probably first made by a store of honey-attracting natural yeasts. Nowadays essences as well as fresh fruit juices are added, and in fact it is frequently promoted as a style of wine.

Pulque. Pulque is fermented from the sap of a cactus known as the Magwey. The drink is very popular in its native Mexico. It is a little stronger than the average beer and it has a sweet/sour taste. Sometimes it is artificially sweetened.

ᏔᎡ41ᏔᎡ

MINERAL WATERS AND SYRUPS

MINERAL waters are natural waters which have extracted mineral properties from the rocks and soil through which they have passed before emerging in a spring. Sufficient mineral salts in solution have been assimilated to impart a special taste and other properties to the water. The waters are often reported to have curative capacities and they are used therapeutically either internally or externally. Where mineral waters have emerged naturally, spas have been profitably established around them. The minerals solvent in the waters are made up of various combinations of alkaline potassium, calcium, magnesium, sodium, chlorine and sulphur.

The best-known water springs are at Bath, Malvern and Harrogate in England; Vichy, Vittel, Perrier, Badoit, Dax and Contrexéville in France; Baden-Baden in Germany; Solares and Marmolejo in Spain; Baden in Switzerland; Spa in Belgium; Karlovy Vary (Karlsbad) in Czechoslovakia; and S. Pellegrino in Italy. All these mineral waters are best served chilled. Bottled mineral waters are especially popular and are indeed essential from a health point of view in countries where it is wise not to trust the tap.

An important industry has been built up for the sale of artificial mineral waters. These are made up by dissolving the particular minerals in water and then impregnating the solutions with a gas carbon dioxide. It is these artificial waters that are usually used to accompany alcoholic drinks. Although it is quite easy to secure for yourself a Perrier water, say, to dilute your drink, it is generally the usage for manufactured waters to be chosen. The most common of these are soda water, Indian tonic water, bitter lemon, ginger ale and so on. The other artificial mineral waters are those collectively known to the schoolboy as pop, such as lemonade, orangeade and the coke and pepsi colas. The principal virtue of artificial mineral waters is that they have been given specific flavours which are not related to the natural salts of the natural waters. This is important because many natural waters are far from pleasant to the taste, whereas the artificial ones deliberately aim at providing an enjoyable drink.

Syrups. Syrups also are manufactured to provide concentrates for hot or cold non-alcoholic drinks. These are also used, mainly in the concentrated or syrupy form for the flavouring of alcoholic drinks. The syrups are solutions of sugar and the juice of fruit, or simply a solution of water and sugar. In all cases the solution is concentrated until the liquid is reduced to a syrupy consistency. The most widely used syrups are:

> *Sirop de Cerises* (Cherry syrup)
> *Sirop de Cassis* (Blackcurrant syrup)
> *Sirop de Grenadine* (Pommegranite syrup)
> *Sirop de Framboise* (Raspberry syrup)
> *Sirop de Groseilles* (Gooseberry syrup)
> *Sirop d'Oranges* (Orange syrup)
> *Sirop de Gomme* (Gum syrup)

The last-named syrup is made by dissolving washed white gum in water, then adding sugar and bringing all to boiling point. When the solution begins to bubble, it is removed from the heat and strained into a container. It is useful for some cocktails and mixed drinks and some 'lamp magicians' in restaurants use it as an ingredient in fruit flambée creations.

The fruit syrups are made by dissolving sugar in filtered fruit juice in a copper container. When the sugar is dissolved the container is put on to a slow heat and left there until it boils. The syrup is then strained into a container such as a wine bottle. The amount of sugar used depends on the amount of natural sugar in the fruit. Usually the ratio is in the region of three parts of sugar to five parts of fruit juice.

⊂⊃42⊂⊃

CIGARS

ROLLED tobacco leaves wrapped in a maize or dried palm leaf were being smoked by the natives of the Cuban jungle when Columbus and his explorers came upon them in 1527. Earlier evidence of this crude cigar smoking is attributed to the Mayan priests of the 4th century. They simply had a roll of tobacco leaves tied with string or some such binding. The Mayan word for smoking is *sikar* and the Spaniards, who incidentally were the first to introduce the cigar to Europe in about 1600, adapted the word to *cigarro*, from which name we can assume the word cigar originated. Europeans were slow to adopt the smoking habit but eventually it caught on. In the 1780's there was a thriving cigar-making industry in Hamburg and another in Rome.

Soldiers returning from the 1814 Peninsular War in Spain against Napoleon introduced cigar smoking to Great Britain. However, it was an expensive pleasantry, which only the few could afford to enjoy. In 1823, an import duty made cigars even more expensive.

There is no evidence of cigars being made in Great Britain before

1840, but by 1851 an industry had sufficiently established itself to enable some manufacturers to exhibit their tobacco products at the Great Exhibition of that year. Today about 90 per cent. of the cigars smoked in Great Britain are manufactured there, albeit from imported tobacco.

The true homelands of cigars are of course Cuba and to a lesser extent Jamaica. During World War II, Havana cigars were not imported to Britain and, by the time trade had been re-established in 1952, Jamaica had a firm hold on the British import market. It is, however, only fair to say that quality against quality there is no cigar on the market today to compare with a genuine Havana. The attraction of Jamaican cigars is their relative mildness and their relative cheapness due to less duty being charged on them. But, for the masses, the vogue seems to be for the smoking of cigars with less of a 'pedigree', especially the thin and small-sized varieties. This trend in taste has been responsible for extending cigar-smoking from a rare occurrence to an everyday habit.

The Cigar Leaf. The cigar-leaf is produced from tobacco seed and the leaves which will produce the finest quality, while being cultivated, are often protected from hot sun-rays by being grown under screens of cloth, and these are consequently described as 'shadegrown'. The finest quality leaves are grown in Cuba, the East Indies (Java, Borneo and Sumatra) and Jamaica. Fine leaves are also produced in the United States of America, Puerto Rico, the Philippines, the Dominican Republic, Brazil, Indonesia, Columbia, Japan and South Africa. The Dutch East Indies were once the choicest producer of fine wrapper leaf and, when the Dutch were in authority, so jealous were they of this reputation, it was a crime to export the tobacco seed. When the Dutch were expelled by Sukarno, they took with them some of the choice seeds and planted them wherever they resettled. So Sumatra-type plants are now being grown in many countries.

The Composition of a Cigar. There are three parts to a cigar, the *filler*, the *binder* and the *wrapper*. The tobacco for the *filler* is usually a blend of a variety of tobaccos to form the inner core of the cigar, and it is this which accounts for the basic flavour of the cigar. The *binder* is a single leaf which binds the *filler* together. It is the inner covering of the cigar. The *filler* and the *binder* together form the 'bunch'. The *wrapper* is the outer covering of the bunch and it completes the cigar. It is an exceptionally fine quality single leaf, which must have elasticity and strength. It must, besides, have an outstanding appearance and a fine flavour. The wrapper leaf is so important that it is grown under cloth. The finest example of this leaf comes from Havana. Wrapper-leaf tobacco is classified according to colour:

Claro (C.C.C.) denotes a light-coloured cigar;
Colorado Claro (C.C.) denotes a medium-coloured cigar;
Colorado (C.) denotes a dark-coloured cigar;
Colorado Maduro (C.M.) denotes a very dark-coloured cigar; and
Maduro (M.) denotes an exceptionally dark-coloured cigar.

It should be noted that these colours, which are all shades of brown, do not indicate the strength of the cigar. A dark-coloured wrapper does not mean that the cigar will smoke pungently. An example is the dark Indian cheroots or Brazilians which are very mild indeed.

Manufacture. The process of manufacturing cigars begins with the picking of the leaves, which are tied on lathes and hung from poles in a huge airy shed where they are cured. Then, a chemical change known as fermentation or sweating takes place. This sweating of the leaves minimises the bitter harsh content and develops the mildness and the aromatic characteristics of the leaves. As the wrapper leaves are so important and the most expensive, they are given special attention. They are tied in bundles of forty to fifty, known as hands, which are piled on top of one another in a store which has a warm and humid atmosphere. The piles are turned from time to time. The binder leaves are packed in wooden cases and transferred to a room with a temperature of about 38° C., where they ferment and mature for months or years until they are required. Some binder leaves are also matured loose-leaved in piles. The filler leaves are usually cut into different sizes to suit the various markets, and broken leaves are treated in the same way.

The making of cigars started as a cottage industry, with the cigars being made at home by hand and sold from door to door, usually by the womenfolk. Gradually commerce took over and the great majority of cigars are now made by machinery. However, the finest cigars are still hand-made and those imported to Great Britain from Cuba are all hand-made. Briefly, the stem is removed from the leaf and the filler is laid on the binder and rolled to a uniform size. The wrapper is then rolled over the binder starting at the end which is to be lit so that the veins run lengthwise. The shape is tapered off at the other end where the leaf is stuck firmly with a tasteless gum called *tragacanth*.

In manufacturing by machine, the scrap or ribbon filler is made ready and the binder leaves are cut and shaped to requirements. Nowadays, especially for the cheaper cigars, the binder is often reconstituted tobacco in sheet form. The machine then firmly and fully encloses the filler in the binder. The wrapper, cut narrower than the binder, is spirally wrapped around the bunch with the diagonal veins lying lengthwise along the cigar. Because every leaf has a left-hand side and a right-hand side, diagonal wrapping is a necessity. To complete the job, the head, or the mouth-end, of the wrapper is sealed as before with *tragacanth*.

Cigar Sizes. The sizes of cigars are classified under the following names:

Corona A straight-shaped cigar about 5½ inches (14 centimetres) long with a round top;

Petit Corona or Corona Chica Like a corona but 5 inches (12·5 centimetres) long;

Très Petit Corona The same but about 4½ inches (11·4 centimetres) long;

Half a Corona The same but about 3¾ inches (9·5 centimetres) long;

Lonsdale The same shape as corona but about 6½ inches (16·5 centimetres) long;

Ideales A thin torpedo-shaped cigar about 6½ inches (16·5 centimetres) long and tapered at the lighting end;

Bouquet A small torpedo-shaped cigar;

Londres A straight cigar about 4¾ inches (12 centimetres) long;

Panatella A long thin cigar, open at both ends and about 5 inches (12·5 centimetres) long;

Stumpen or Cheroot Stubbier than a panatella, open at either end, sometimes slightly tapered;

Whiff Small cigar about 3½ inches (8·9 centimetres) long and open at both ends.

Storing. The storing of cigars needs considerable care. They are despatched to customers in prime condition and much the best way to store them thereafter is by keeping them on slatted shelves of unpainted wood at a temperature of 18 to 19·5° C., or better still 16·5° C. with a relative humidity of 55 per cent. or at least between 53 and 57 per cent. Boxes made of cedar wood provide the most satisfactory form of storing larger cigars. The aroma of cedar blends well with cigars and, the wood being porous, allows the cigars to breathe. It is still essential that there should be a free circulation of air around these boxes and that is why slatted shelves are so important. Glass, metal, hard gloss paint and cement are prone to the effects of condensation and are thus liable to damage the cigars.

Many cigars are packed with a cellophane covering, which helps to protect the humidity level. Air-tight glass jars, lined with cedar, are used to keep cigars moist or green. Cedar-lined aluminium tubes are also good protectors, provided that the cigars have first been conditioned in the country where they have been so packed. These tubes are especially useful by the seaside as they guard against moisture and sea salt. They are also, of course, deterrents against breakages and strong odours, and they will keep each individual cigar in good condition almost indefinitely. Smells, including cooking smells, central heating and draughts are all injurious to cigars. Cigars should not be displayed in open boxes and, if proper storage facilities are not available, a humidor should be an essential and sensible purchase to keep the cigars in prime condition.

Cigar Ailments. Cockling or crackling happens when a cigar which has been conditioned is exposed to dampness. The smooth finish of the cigar will be lost, but reconditioning by the manufacturer would make the cigar smokeable and pleasurable once more. Bloom occurs when cigars are stored in an over-humid atmosphere and is nothing more than a greyish mildew. This can soon be taken off with a soft brush but the cigars may need reconditioning in a dry atmosphere. 'Salts' are grey specks caused by rapid drying of moist cigars. They are seen next to the veins of the wrapper leaf. These too can be brushed away with a soft brush. They are more unsightly than harmful. Sometimes, yellow and green spots may be seen on the wrapper leaf. These occur quite naturally and are even considered by some as demonstrative of authenticity of leaf. The yellow spots occur because of the sun's shining down on drops of rain or moisture resting on the leaf. The green spots usually mean that the leaf had an overabundance of oil in these particular spots. Spots do not affect the smoking of the cigar in any way.

Some Guides to Cigar Smoking. In appearance cigars should be smooth, firm and even and be of the same size and colour as others in the box. They should not be soft, but always firm to the touch. A brittle cigar will not give a good smoke. Cigar boxes should be opened carefully, preferably by a blunt instrument rather than a penknife or other sharp tool which could damage the cigars. Those cigars which are tied in bundles should be lifted from their containers by their ribbons. If the cigars lie flat in a box, each cigar as required should be tilted upwards by pressing carefully with the thumb on the rounded head. The other end will thus be elevated to afford easy and safe extraction. Once in the hand, the cigar should feel firm and springy. Smelling a cigar or crackling it against an ear will reveal very little if anything about its qualities. The outer leaf of the wrapper—which should have a healthy sheen—and the open or cut end—which should be smooth and even— of the cigar will tell you all you can know at this stage.

The band of the cigar, which is nothing more than an identification tag, is best removed immediately as it tends to get in the way as the cigar is smoked, but it must be removed carefully so as not to damage the wrapper leaf. If the wrapper leaf is damaged the cigar will not draw properly. Some cigars are pre-cut, but if not a clean V-shaped cut with a cigar-cutter is the recommended method of opening the end of the cigar. The cut must be generous to allow maximum free draught. Cigars of fine quality should not be pierced because this would give an inadequate draught and a bitter taste on the tongue would be caused by a moisture and tar concentration in the small aperture.

Holders are not popular with cigar smokers as they take away the sensual satisfaction of gripping the cigar with one's teeth. Cigars should be lighted with the broad flame of a match or gas-lighter, never with a petrol-lighter as its fumes would contaminate the cigar. When lighting, rotate the cigar onto the flame to effect even burning. As the cigar burns, the ash should hold together well and not flake off. A grey ash may indicate an Havana wrapper, and a white ash a Sumatra wrapper. Some people mistakenly say that a re-lit cigar never tastes the same. If, when relighting, you first remove the ash with an un-lit match, then blow through the cigar onto the flame of the lighted match, the burnt leaf will be removed without infiltrating its taste into the unsmoked part of the cigar. A perfect smoke can then be enjoyed. Careful lighting and slow smoking ensure that a cigar will burn easily and regularly. When carrying cigars on one's person, there is nothing better as a container than a leather case with separate tubings for the individual cigars.

❧43❧

BAR AND CELLAR
CONTROL

Bar sales in hotel and catering establishments can be likened to a repackaging and retail distribution exercise. Because the splitting of the bulk affects security, consideration of bar and cellar control becomes the critical factor in a profitable operation.

There is no disguising the fact that drinks offer temptation to those concerned with their sale, particularly perhaps because each depredation in itself might appear a minor one. But an occasional bottle smuggled out, a comforting nip on the side and fiddling even in coppers when cashing in, can accumulate into serious losses and can lead to more ambitious thefts. No reasonable employee will object to a system of control especially if it is designed to protect his own as well as the firm's interests. Control, therefore, must be impersonal, a scheme built on the assumption that errors, accidental or deliberate may occur, but that they will be quickly revealed. The staff should know the system and be aware of its function.

First then, bar and cellar control requires that the person in charge should have the quality of honesty and that this be a major consideration at the time of selection for the vacancy to be filled. His skills must include complete knowledge of storage and cellar work and its operation, a good working knowledge of liqueurs, wines, beers, spirits, etc., and adequate knowledge, according to his responsibilities of accountancy, administration and purchasing techniques.

The scheme of control has to take account of two major problems—*supply* and *security*.

SUPPLY

The aim is to ensure that sufficient stock is readily available without carrying an excess which results in the non-profitable investment of capital. The greater the cash tied up, the greater will have to be the profit margin needed to justify it. Not only is it of little use having money lying idle on shelves but the larger the stock held the more stocktaking and figure work there will have to be, and the more difficult it will be to notice small pilferings. The stock held must be based on an analysis of consumption and a standard purchasing amount for delivery at regular intervals should be fixed for each commodity as far as possible. In other words, a regular stock level is set for each item, but a watch for changes in customer tastes is essential so that the standard may be revised when necessary. Apart from considerations of space and likely sales, the possibility of quantity discount should be considered. For instance, if two cases of whisky are sold each week and the best discount and credit terms are for a minimum order of ten cases, then the standard fixed should be a regular five-weekly order of ten cases, thus the overall inventory will at no time exceed five weeks' supply. However, the value of the net quantity discount must be greater than the rate of interest obtainable should the money be otherwise invested.

A useful trade principle for drink-stock management is that stock turnover of fifty times a year should be established. This is indicated in the following formula:

$$\frac{\text{Total annual purchases}}{\text{The average stock held}} = 50$$

The reason for the figure of fifty is that standard range items are available on a weekly supply basis.

There are, of course, the 'pedigree' wines, to which the above formula cannot be applied. These come on the market only at certain times, and one has to bid at the right time to get them at advantageous prices. Usually and except for very large and grand caterers, it will not be a practical proposition to lay down wines in quantity for consumption after some years.

Some items of stock will turn over on a daily basis, others on a four-weekly basis or even longer, thereby achieving the fifty times a year formula.

A standard stock, again based on usual sales, should be fixed for each bar. It should be a daily norm and each bar should be stocked to this amount each morning. This quantity must be sufficient to ensure that the supply on hand will not run out during the day. For example when the usual sale of an item equals two per week, the norm should be two units of this item restocked to that amount each week. Items sold at the rate of two units a day, should be kept at a daily standard of three units, thereby allowing a margin in excess of usual consumption. Some establishments only issue stock on the return of empties, which bear a secret mark or special stamp, but this is a cumbersome and easily defeated method.

SECURITY

From the security point of view, it would be best for the cellar or storeroom to have only one door and only one key to that door. In any case only one door should be used, and only by or under the supervision of the person in charge. Any other doors should be kept locked and only used for their particular purpose, e.g. deliveries. The one key, without any available duplicate, should be kept in the manager's office, and its use forbidden except to the person in charge. No unauthorised person should be allowed into the cellar or store, and a notice to that effect should be posted on the door. A cellar manager should be a person of integrity and his duties can be listed as follows:

To review supply standards.

To place orders for stock.

To receive deliveries and thoroughly check them with the order form.

To enter accurately records of goods received in the proper book and on the appropriate bin cards.

To record in the book and cards all issues from the store.

To issue items from the store only in return for the written requisition.

To train other staff in the handling of liquor, including the necessity of stock rotation in the cellar and bars.

To make sure that drink is stored properly with reference to position, temperature, rotation and so on.

These general observations apply in all cases of premises where alcoholic drinks are sold or served, although there will, of course, be variations in detail according to the size of the establishment. The owner who runs his own place with a staff of two or three will no doubt be his own cellarman, stock-keeper and book-keeper. He will save himself a lot of trouble if he keeps to a fixed routine on the lines indicated. At the other end of the scale, a large hotel will need a whole department of staff to perform the duties, where the responsibility of the man in charge can only be fulfilled efficiently with proper delegation and records.

Routine systems are essential for the *control of cash* and the *control of stock*.

CASH

Bar staff fulfil the dual function of service personnel and cashier. Profits in an establishment are the balance between revenue and expenditure and it is therefore essential to control both aspects. The problem of cash control is to reconcile the two factors of the handling of the money by staff and the collection of it into the central till. There are two methods for this control. Firstly, the use of cash registers which record the details of each transaction, and, secondly, the paying in of cash equivalent to stock consumed.

Cash shortages usually happen for several reasons:

> Floats may not have been properly checked
> Sales may not be accounted for
> Errors may have occurred in handling change

To counteract such eventualities all cash floats should be checked by the bar manager and double-checked by the barmen or lounge waiters, who then assume responsibility for the amount. All sales must be rung-up in the cash register as soon as the transaction is made. To enforce this policy spot checks at irregular intervals may provide the only satisfactory control. If an employee knows that a check may be made at any moment he is less likely to deviate from honest practice. Staff should be trained in the handling of change. Decimal currency, which may at first add to confusion, will eventually make the calculations easier. Nowadays some cash registers incorporate a 'change due' mechanism.

STOCK

The control of stock needs consideration under seven headings as follows:

> (1) Control of stock inwards
> (2) Stock in store or cellar
> (3) Control of empties outwards
> (4) Ullages and breakages
> (5) Issues to sales points
> (6) Issues to production points
> (7) Drinks to staff at reduced or no charge

(1) *Incoming Stock.* The emphasis should be that goods must not be signed for as accepted in any way until they have been properly checked against the delivery note invoice. The delivery must always equal the quantity on the order, a copy of which should be available when deliveries are being made. A check must then be made for breakages, leakages, faulty crates and also such details as vintages and shippers, according to the specifications of the order. Only when these checks are complete should the acceptance note be signed. There must also be the financial checks: obtaining a credit note for items not delivered; checking prices on the invoice against the price list, and

ensuring appropriate credits for returned empties and rejected items. The appropriate entries must then be made into the books and bin cards.

(2) *Stock in Store or Cellar.* When goods arrive at the cellar of an hotel, entries are recorded on the appropriate bin cards and in the stock ledger. A double check must ensure that the physical quantity equals that on the order and that the prices charged equal those on the price list. This done, the invoice may be sent to the accounts department

---

Invoice   Ref. Order No. 0101

SCURJON WINE CO. LTD.
Wimbledon, London, S.W.19.
Telephone 496 2511, 2011

To: The Cohall Hotel,
Manor Mews,
Louisburgh,
London S.W.

Date: 13.1.71

A/C No. .... 69 ....   Invoice No. ....

Quantity Doz.	½ Doz.	Size	Description	Price per Doz.	Value
				£	£
1	0	BOT.	Chateau Pontet-Canet, 1962	20.80	20.80
	6	BOT.	Tio Pepe	14.60	7.30
			Total		£28.10

Cheques and Money Orders to be Made Payable to
Scurjon Wine Co. Ltd.

Order Form

THE COHALL HOTEL

Manor Mews,
Louisburgh,
London S.W.
Tel. 20II, 25II

Ref. 0I0I
Date 1, 1, '7I,

To: Scurjon Wine Co. Ltd.,
Wimbledon,
London, S. W. 19,

Please Supply

Description	Qty.	Size	@	£
Moët & Chandon, Dry Imperial '66	4 doz.	Bots.	£25.10	£100.40
Authorised By L.M.C.F.			Total	£100.40

Goods Received Book

Week Ending............

Date	Delivery / Invoice No.	Order No.	Detail (Supplier)	Value of Total Delivery	Remarks

Bin Card

Item.		
Bin No.	Re-Order Level........	

Goods

Date	In	Out	Balance

for payment. The cellarman should enter the hotel order reference number on the invoice for cross reference purposes. Depending on the premises, different people may be responsible for the administration and control of cellar stocks. It may be left to the accounts department, the food and beverage manager or the hotel cellarman himself.

Control of the Cellar: There are two basic methods for the control of the cellar. The first is to make random spot checks to reconcile stock in a bin with the bin card entry. The second is by weekly stocktaking which seeks to establish the physical consumption and reconcile these figures with the records as shown in the stock ledger.

(3) *Empties Outward.* Many containers nowadays are disposable and non-returnable and while this *alleviates* the problem of control, it adds to the problem of refuse disposal. However, there are still barrels, casks, beer bottles, soda siphons, mineral bottles and crates which have to be returned, as these are chargeable containers. Deposits on containers must be charged on the value of goods inwards, and classified as returned material cost on the way out. A book should be kept to list all returns and this checked against credit notes given by the delivery driver.

(4) *Ullages and Breakages.* Faulty wines, corked wines, weeping wines come into the category of ullage. An ullage is the unnatural void between the surface of the liquid and the top of its container. This can be caused by faulty corks. Sub-standard commodities must be certified

Cellar Control Sheet

Week Ending 27.3.'71

Bin No.	Item	Unit	Cost	Opening Stock	Purchases	Sub Total	Issues M T W T F	Total Issues	Returns	Balance of Stock C/F by Book	Balance by Stock Take	+	−	Value of Issues At Cost	Value of Bal. C/F At Cost	Remarks
1	Bourgogne Aligoté	½'s	30p	20	12	32	2·2·4·8	8	·	24	24		·	£2·40	£7·20	
	''	1's	50p	12	12	24	2·2·4·2·	10	·	14	14		·	£5·00	£7·00	
2	Chablis	½'s	40p	5	12	17	1·1·3··	5	1	11	11		·	£2·00	£4·40	CN to value of 40p attached
	''	1's	70p													
3	Meursault	1½'s														

from Invoice

from Balance (see last Stock Check)

from Invoices

from Requisition Notes

from Credit Notes

to Cross-Check with Bin Cards

Physical Stock Check

Balance to Carry Forward to Next Control Sheet

Deviation for Explanation

295

Vendange

Item	Size	Qty.	Unit Cost	Total Cost

Ullages and Breakages   Ref. No.

Bar:

Member of Staff: Date:

Remarks

Food and Beverage Manager

Goods Returned Book

Ref No. . . . .   Week Ending . . . .

Date	Credit Note Ref.	Supplier	Description	Cause	Cost per Item	Total Cost

as being such by the departmental head who authorises their return to the supplier and subsequent amendments to records and ledgers.

Control is necessary on the volume of the breakages that occur and this in turn will control careless handling. In the breakages book entries must be counter-signed by the head of department. The general practice is that the neck of the bottle with seal unbroken is held as evidence of a breakage.

STOCKTAKING

What is stocktaking? It is a physical exercise whereby a count of stock remaining after a given trading period is established in terms of quantity and of value at cost price in the cellar but at selling price in the bars. The object of stocktaking is to verify the accuracy of the written documentation with the actual stock as counted. The frequency of stocktaking depends largely on the time available for this function to be carried out. Cash bars should have a stocktake at least once a week and cellars once a month. The stocktaker should be a person who is not associated with the buying, storage or sale of liquor. (Some firms contract stocktaking externally.)

The Method. Ideally stocktaking is carried out on the quietest trading day of the week or at night time. A fixed time should be rigidly adhered to, and during the actual stocktaking no goods should be permitted into or out of the department. A *dissection* sheet alphabetically listed (wines according to bins) is used to determine the quantity of stock in hand. On completion, the total stock is valued, in order to verify that consumption has been accounted for by sales. This last check is carried out by the control department.

(Consumption equals opening stock, plus purchases, minus returns, minus breakages, minus closing stock.)

Action after Stocktaking. Stocktaking may reveal discrepancies of a physical or clerical nature. Differences of a physical nature arise where the figure of stock as shown on the bin card differs from the actual amount held. This could be an error in recording movement on the bin card. Alternatively it could show the unauthorised removal of stock. Subsequent action by management depends on the cause. Clerical errors may be shown whereby a returned bottle has not been recorded on the bin card. So the physical stock will show an excess over the recorded inventory.

Summary. Stocktaking performs two major functions. It equates consumption with sales and reveals any discrepancies. Secondly, because of its regularity in controlling stocks, the stocktaking function acts as a psychological deterrent to pilfering.

(5) *Issues to Sales Points.* Sales points cover Banqueting (credit or cash sales) and sundry bars (all cash). It is also customary to give the night porter or head floor-waiter a limited range of stock to issue to night guests (residents).

'A Distribution of Stock' timetable must be issued to staff responsible for sales points, so that issues of stock may be made in a progressive and orderly manner from the cellar. Each sales point must have a specific time at which to come to the head cellarman in order to replenish its stock. It is important that each department has a container for collecting its requirements. The container should have its own marking and baskets on wheels are ideal for this function. All orders for requisitions should be in duplicate. The barman specifies the quality and quantity required, by brand name and size of bottle. It is essential that the quantity requisitioned should approximately equal the daily consumption.

When drawing stock, both requisition copies are given to the cellarman who issues the quantity required, checking that the requisition

THE COHALL HOTEL			
Cellar Requisition			
Date	Dept.		No.
Description	Quantity	@	£
Signed _____			

note bears the signature of the food and beverage manager, if the system so requires. The cellarman prices out the value of the issues at the selling prices. One of the requisition notes is kept by the barman to hand in with his takings, the other copy is retained by the cellarman to enter in the stock-ledger and bin cards and subsequently to give to the control office together with the other cellar records. It is imperative that only responsible people should be entrusted with the collection of stock from the cellar as mistakes or misunderstandings between the cellar and the bar must be rectified before the goods leave the cellar area.

Each bar should operate a similar policy relating to breakages and spillages to that operated by the cellar. While it is recognised that careless handling can and does lead to breakages and spillage, the management's function of control is very applicable in this area of control.

BAR CONTROL

The control of bar stock hinges on equating consumption with revenue thus:

Opening stock at S.P. valuation (last closing stock)	£100
Requisitions received at S.P. valuation	£150
Sub-Total	£250
Less closing at S.P. valuation (by stock check)	£80
Less returns and spillage etc. at S.P. valuation	£10
Consumption at S.P. valuation must equal Receipts as per Cash till Summary	£160

Discrepancies may occur through barmen dishonestly bringing in their own stock, through short measurements, overcharging the customer or omission of the ringing up of sales. A cocktail bar is more difficult to control because of the composition of the drinks.

BANQUETING BARS

Orders for these are in bulk. An accurate control of all sales is essential and returns must be checked back to the cellar carefully, so that costs and consumption on each function can be worked out accurately. Issues from the cellar are normally made on a sale or return basis. Cash or credit receipts must equal consumption as per stock take. Stock is not kept permanently in banqueting bars, but all unsold stock is returned to the cellar. Detailed information about the function should be prepared and filed, giving details relating to:

The name and address of the organiser or host
The date and the day of the week
The number of guests
The type of function
The amount and kind of liquor sold
Whether it was a cash and/or credit sale.

This information will be very useful to the banqueting manager for subsequent functions of a similar nature.

(6) *Issues to Production Points.* Issues from the main stock are made to the *kitchen* for use in cooking and to the restaurant for flambée dishes. Requisitions for kitchen requirements should be made to the cellar in duplicate on the authority of the head chef. Both copies are priced by the cellarman at cost prices and one copy is returned to the kitchen with the goods. Entries in the main store or cellar records is made from the retained requisition note which eventually finds its way to the food and beverage control for verification. The *restaurant* draws issues from

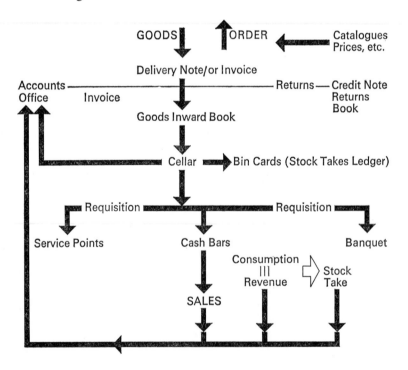

Stock, Service and Accounting Flow Diagram

the dispense bar in measure quantities against the head waiter's check, and it is issued at selling price value, which is of course included in the price of the dish.

(7) *Drinks to Staff at Reduced or no Charge.* These are checked out at cost price and the value of the ingredients is included in Labour cost.

The general rule for all issue of stock ought to be 'no check—no goods'. For ease for control it is useful in big establishments for each department to have different colour coded requisition notes.

❧44☙

FERMENTATION

THOSE lucky primitives, many centuries ago, who recompensed their harsh lives with indulgence in barley beer or some such drink probably were not aware that the process of fermentation on which they had stumbled could be described in chemical formulae. Or even, shortly, as the process whereby organic material is converted into a useful produce by the action of a biological agency. They would probably have been indignant if told that fermentation is a similar process to putrefaction, except that the end-product of the latter is not obviously useful and, indeed, may be very objectionable. They may have preferred the explanation that fermentation is the process of obtaining energy in the absence of air. The modern student will have less difficulty in appreciating the points in these notes and diagrams.

Fermentation for alcoholic drinks for the most part is the story of the action of yeast on sugar. Sugar in numerous different forms is produced by plants to provide sustenance for growth and proliferation. Yeast is a name applied to a collection of micro-organisms, a loose name because it covers many botanic micro-organisms. So we have varieties of sugar and of yeast, but they all have a common relationship in that the organisms that make up the yeast can readily use most sugars for their own vital processes. The recognition of the chemical reactions involved is of absorbing interest to those interested in the production of alcoholic drinks, for the reason that, as in chemical reactions generally, environment may help, hamper, vary or prevent the reaction and changes in the environment may alter these effects. Thus the fermentation will depend not only on the variety of sugar and the genus of micro-organism, but also on the temperature and the absence or presence of air and other factors at the time when the yeast is metabolising the sugar. For these reasons it will be seen that the storage of the fermenting liquids (e.g. in bottles or casks) and matters of climate and temperature are as important for the yeast, as climate, sunshine and rain are to the sugar.

The following paragraphs give a general description of the fermenting process although it does of course not include all the ifs and buts that the pure scientist would require.

Sugars are produced by plants which can produce chlorophyll. The vine does this, the green chlorophyll being mainly in the leaves. The sugar is made from water absorbed through the roots and carbon dioxide absorbed from the atmosphere. The energy required for the process is provided by sunlight absorbed by the chlorophyll. The vine stores its sugar in the grapes—whence it is stolen by beast and man for the succulence of the fruit. The mobility and digestive processes of the beast provide the vine with a wide seed-dispersal mechanism. Man's habit of storing food led to the discovery of wine since the grapes carried yeast in the form of bloom on the skin, into the storage vessel.

The barley plant produces sugars and stores complex sugars known as starch in the barley grain. The starch 'feeds' the germinating plant until the latter can send out roots and a green blade by which the plant can begin to feed itself, rather like the egg yolk providing food for the chicken embryo until the chicken hatches and can scratch for its own food.

When the stored sugar-material is released, e.g. by the breaking o the skin of the grape or the husk of the barley-ear, the micro-organisms of the air will break the sugars down in order to produce energy for their own vital processes; breakdown to the original building blocks, water and carbon dioxide. We are interested in the micro-organisms known as yeast. The name yeast is normally applied to a type of unicellular fungi called *Saccharomyces*, a genus of which there are many within the plant kingdom. There are many species of *Saccharomyces*. Three of these are important in the production of common alcoholic beverages—*Saccharomyces cerevisiae*, *Saccharomyces carlsbergensis* and *Saccharomyces ellipsoideus*. The first of these is the beer and ale yeast— a yeast of good activity and preferring to ferment at the top of a vat (producing a layer). The second (*carlsbergensis*) is the lager yeast—a bottom fermenter. The third (*ellipsoideus*) is the wine yeast containing varieties each suited to its native wine region. The yeasts of Champagne have the characteristic of not sticking firmly to each other or to the containing vessel. If this was not the case the process of *remuage* would be difficult and probably impossible. In other wine regions, it is an advantage to have yeasts that cling to each other and to the vessel, as this property assists in the production of clear bright wines.

The process whereby yeast cells break down glucose (a mono-saccharide) can be memorised by two over-simple equations:

1. Aerobic—in presence of oxygen—air:
   $C_6H_{12}O + 6O_2 = 6H_2O + 6CO_2$
   (one molecule of glucose, plus six molecules of oxygen, give six molecules of water and six of carbon dioxide)
2. Anaerobic (without oxygen):
   $C_6H_{12}O_6 = 2CH_5OH + 2CO_2$
   (one molecule of glucose gives two molecules of ethyl alcohol and two of carbon dioxide)

The processes require organic catalysts called enzymes, a catalyst being a substance which alters the speed of a chemical reaction without being destroyed by that action, i.e. the catalyst remains at the end of the chemical change. Catalysts produced by living cells are called enzymes. Enzymes are normally very specific; acting on substances of exact specification in environmental specific conditions including temperature and degree of acidity or alkalinity. Enzymes are very effective catalysts and this is thought to be a result of the fact that their molecules join their substrates at three or more points during enzymic reactions.

The metabolic process of fermentation brought about by yeast enzymes produced by yeast cells is simply represented by the second equation given above, but the complex reaction is more fully shown in the metabolic pathways diagram shown on the front and back end papers of this book. (*Note*, the diagram also indicates how the metabolism may proceed to the production of acetic acid.) The reason the yeast cells organise and allow these processes to take place is to provide energy for the cell to maintain and continue its vital living processes. Many other metabolic processes take place allowing the cells to obtain basic material with which to grow and propagate. For this purpose, not only sugars but other substances, often in only trace quantities, will be required. Not all sugars will follow the metabolic pathway shown in the diagram. Some molecules will fall by the wayside and, with the multitude of other minor metabolic processes, create the vast number of trace substances found in yeast cells and the alcoholic beverages which they produce. Intermediate substances of the metabolic pathway may be acted upon by different enzymes, and thus a breakaway metabolic path with a different end-product is formed. For instance, acetaldehyde with toxic propensities can be found in wine in trace quantities.

The aerobic metabolic pathway releases considerable energy, while the anaerobic fermentation produces less than one-tenth of this energy. The end-product (alcohol) of the latter is still rich in captive energy—hence alcohol can be ignited to give light and heat. Yeast in aerobic activity rapidly multiply but no alcohol is produced. An anaerobic fermentation produces alcohol but little reproduction. Both processes produce carbon dioxide gas which, being heavier than air, will form a layer over a fermenting vat. A *must* or grape juice fresh from the press has been well aerated during its handling. Therefore, aerobic activity takes place since oxygen is readily available. The yeast cells rapidly reproduce, producing also water and carbon dioxide. The carbon dioxide forms a layer over the vat which prevents more oxygen (from the air) from reaching the yeast. When the remaining oxygen in the *must* is all used, anaerobic conditions take over and an alcoholic fermentation now takes place.

A single enzyme molecule could effect this reaction in the largest vat of *must*, but it would take a very long time during which the *must* would be vulnerable to attack by other organisms of infinite type and species, all eager to further their 'life' processes. Also, enzymes are easily prevented from their catalyst function by other marauding chemical reactions. Thus, it is necessary to have a good supply of enzyme producers in the fermenting vat.

Fermentation will end when the environment in which the enzyme can act as catalyst no longer exists. This will happen naturally, for example,

(i) when all the sugar has been used (when wine, for example, will have been fermented to a state of dryness: *sec*);

(ii) when the alcoholic content reaches a concentration (about 16° G.L.) which the yeast cannot tolerate; and because of

(iii) a drop in temperature (sometimes in spring in northern climates the rise in temperature may produce a further slight fermentation—of particular importance in the manufacture of Champagne).

Fermentation can also be stopped by the artificial poisioning of the enzymes by adding sulphur dioxide to the fermentation or by heating (pasteurising) the fermenting liquid (heating to 60° C. for thirty minutes would be sufficient). The sulphiting is essential for the preservation of light wines such as those produced in Germany, and is also a method of preserving some residual sugar if a sweet wine is required. Pasteurising kills the yeast and any other similar organisms present, but the process has its drawbacks.

How do the yeasts come in contact with the *must*? The bloom on the grape—that dull greyish coating on the grape skin—is composed of many micro-organisms, the majority of them yeasts. The pressing process will wash sufficient off to initiate the fermentation. With the production of red wines, the grape skins are included in the vat, so no problem arises. Modern methods of vinification often include a light dosage of sulphur dioxide to a fresh grape *must*. This has the effect of preventing or retarding the action of the micro-organisms present. Fortunately the wine yeasts have a greater tolerance to sulphur dioxide than most other micro-organisms, so a light sulphiting gives the yeast cells a flying start over the other organisms. The dosage also enables the vineyard proprietor to add his own selected wine yeast.

MALTING

The enzymes produced by yeasts are capable of fermenting simple specific sugars, but they cannot work on the starches which are the growing-foods of barley. The germinating barley grain, however, produces an enzyme which can break down the starch food and energy store for the growing embryo barley plant. This enzyme, called diastase (or by its new name β-amylase), acts on the starch to produce a disaccharide—maltose. Maltose can be acted upon by the enzymes produced by yeast cells. The kilning process applied to the germinating barley by the gentle and careful application of mild heat kills the germinating grain but leaves most of the enzymes and resultant maltose intact. The malting process calls for considerable skill. Enzyme production is required, but the germinating process must be halted before the embryo plant uses up the starch for its own generation. Dry barley malt may be stored and is a convenient form in which to be transported.

The best brewing process involves the grinding of the malt to grist and admixture with water in a mash tun. This allows the enzymes to continue their work and starch materials from other sources may be added to the mash tun in order to provide more maltose. The resultant sweet wort drawn from the mash tun is boiled in a copper; the wort is sterilised and all enzyme action ceases. When the wort is cool and in a fermenting vat, yeast is added, and the yeast enzymes start their work.

An extra enzyme process must take place. Maltose is a disaccharide, the molecule of which is split by an enzyme produced by yeast called maltase to give two molecules of glucose. The metabolic processes take over on the lines of the diagram given on the end papers at the front and back of the book.

Of course, metabolic pathways were unknown to the ancients and unexplored by our grandfathers. The human pathway was pointed by accident, observation, trial and error, luck and experience. Perhaps it was a primrose path through mankind's vale of tears. If so, these were by-lanes, stimulating thought, leading eventually to the scientists' laboratories; which is well and good provided that the scientists remember that, like the ancients and our grandfathers, men sometimes want to get inebriated—if it is the right stuff.

GLOSSARY OF TERMS

Abbocato	Italian for 'soft caressing'. Associated with sweet wines.
Abfullüng	Bottling.
Acerbe	Immature acid wine.
Acid	Imparts lasting qualities, ADDS bouquet and flavour. Too much acid makes wine sharp or sour. Too little makes wine flat.
Adegas	Portuguese warehouse for storing wine.
Age	Refers to the maturing of wine.
Agrafe	Iron clasp which holds down the first cork on a Champagne bottle.
Aigre	Sour wine. *Vinaigre*—Vinegar.
Ainé	Senior partner.
Albariza	Chalky soil found in the best sherry country of Spain.
Alcohol (ethyl)	C_2H_5OH, obtained by the action of yeast on sugar during fermentation. Its strength can be further increased by distillation.
Alembic	A Still.
Aligoté	Big yielding white grapevine in Burgundy.
Amer	Bitters.
Amer picon	Bitter-tasting French apéritif.
Anada	Vintage wine in Spain.
Appellation Contrôlée	French law which guarantees the origin of the wine named on the label. Also called *Appellation d'Origine*.
Âpré	Harsh.
Aqua Vita *Eau-de-vie* *Uisge beatha*	Water of life or spirit.
Arenas	Sandy soil in Southern Spain.
Argol	Tartaric deposit thrown as wine matures in cask.

Arrope	Boiling down of wine to sweeten and add colour to sherries.
Asciato	Italian for dry wine.
Auslese	Specially selected grape bunches for making Hock and Moselle wines.
Balderdash	Mixture of drinks which are generally unrelated, e.g. wine and milk. (It is also an Irish term to describe illogical conversation.)
Barrel (wine)	Holds 26¼ gallons (119·5 litres), but it can vary.
Barrel (beer)	Holds 36 gallons (163·6 litres).
Barros	Clay soil in southern Spain.
Baumé hydrometer	Instrument used for measuring sugar content in wines and spirits.
Beer	Fermentation of barley, malt and hops.
Beerenauslese	Individually selected ripe grapes for making Hocks and Moselles.
Beeswing	Floating sediment that has not settled with the crust in Vintage Port.
Bianco *Blanco*	} White
Black velvet or Bismark	A mixture of equal quantities of chilled Champagne and Guinness.
Bin	Slot for holding a bottle of wine in a cellar.
Bock	Beer tankard made of glass which holds about ½ pint (285 cm³). Used in France for drinking draught beer.
Bocksbeutel (*Boxbeutel*)	Attractively shaped bottle for holding the Steinwein of Franconia. Now used extensively in Portugal.
Bodega	Spanish cellar, warehouse or bar.
Body	Description of strength and fullness in wine.
Bois	Wood—*Gout de Bois*—woody taste.
Boude	Bung.
Bonded	Wines and spirits are bonded and kept in a warehouse under Government supervision until the Customs and Excise duties are paid by the purchaser.
Bota	Spanish for Butt or Cask. Holds 108 gallons (490 litres).
Bottle	Standard size holds 75 cl.
Bottle sickness	Happens to newly bottled wine. Disappears after some months.

Bottoms	Lees or dregs left after racking or decanting. In a 36 gallon (163·6 litre) barrel of beer, the natural sediment—yeast and hop débris—amounts to about 1 gallon (4·5 litres).
Bouche	Mouth.
Bouchonné	Cork.
Gout de Bouchon	Corky tasting wine.
Bouquet	Aroma, smell or nose of wine.
Brandewijn *Branntwein*	} Burnt wine—Brandy.
Breed	Name used to describe fine quality wine.
Brut or *Nature*	Driest Champagne—generally no sweetness added.
Butt	Cask holding 108 gallons (490 litres).
Cabinett or *Kabinett*	To describe wine good enough for the German vineyard proprietor's own cellar.
Capataz	Head cellarman of a Spanish cellar.
Capiteux	Heady wine, high in alcohol.
Cask	Wood container for wines, beers, spirits.
Cave *Cava*	} Cellar.
Caviste	Cellar worker.
Cellar	Below ground storage area.
Cep	Vine stock.
Cépage	Vine variety.
Chai	Above ground storage area.
Chambrer	To bring wines (usually red) to room temperature.
Chaptalisation	Addition of sugar to grape must to secure higher alcoholic content. Amount is strictly controlled by law.
Charnu	A full bodied wine.
Château	Castle—also means a wine from a particular vineyard.
Château Bottled	*Mise en bouteille au château.* Signifies that the wine has been bottled at the château, which in itself is a guarantee of quality.
Claret	Englishman's name for the red wines of Bordeaux. Comes from the French *clairet* meaning clear, bright, light.
Climat	Vineyard.
Clos	A walled vineyard, especially in Burgundy.
Cobblers	American drink for warm weather. Made from wine or spirits, fresh fruit and ice shavings.

Collage	Clearing wine of its sediment.
Copita	Spanish sherry glass.
Cork	Usually made from the bark of Spanish or Portuguese oak (Quercus suber).
Corky	When a wine has been diseased by a faulty cork.
Cortado	A sherry, between an amontillado and oloroso.
Corsé	Full bodied.
Côtes	Vineyards located on hills.
Coupage	Vatting or blending of wine.
Crémant	Creaming, slightly effervescent.
Criadera	Nursery for young sherries.
Cru	Growth, also wines of a similar standard.
Crust	Deposit which has gathered especially in bottles of vintage port.
Cuit or *Cotto*	'Cooked' wine.
Cups	Long mixed drinks usually made in glass jugs.
Cuve	Vat.
Cuvée	Blend of wines.
Dame—Jeanne or *Demijohn*	A wide-waisted covered glass wicker jar which holds 13·5-45·5 litres. Used for storing Madeira.
Decanter	Glass container of different shapes and often highly ornamented.
Decanting	The transference of the liquid from bottle to decanter.
Dégorgement	Release of sediment especially in Champagne bottles.
Demi-sec	Half dry, fairly sweet.
Depôt	Sediment.
Diastase	The enzyme complex which causes the starch in malted barley to be converted into invert sugar.
Distillation	The application of heat which extracts alcohol from fermented liquids.
Domaine	Privately owned vineyard in Burgundy.
Dosage or *Liqueur de Tirage*	Addition of sugar before bottling Champagne.
Doux	Sweet, also Dulce.
Dur	Hard.
Echt	Genuine or right.
Edel	Noble.
Edelfäule	Overripe almost rotten grapes. 'Noble Rot'.
Edelgewächs	Best vintages.

Égrappoir	Machine used to de-stalk grapes before pressing.
Eiswein (G.)	Ripe grapes which have become iced or frozen while on the vine. Seldom occurs but makes delicious wine.
Elixirs	Liqueurs made from the finest distillates.
Esters	Combination of acids and alcohol which gives wine its bouquet.
Estufa	Hot chambers where young madeiras undergo heating or baking.
Extra sec	Less dry than *Brut*.
Faible	Thin wine.
Fass No. or *Fuder No.*	Cask number.
Faul	German for mouldy or foul.
Fein	Fine, *Feinste*—Finest.
Feints	The last from a spirit pot still. The first are Foreshots. The in-between is called 'the heart'.
Fermentation	Action of yeast on sugar which converts the latter into roughly equal parts of alcohol and carbon dioxide.
Fiasco	Wicker-wrapped bottle used for Chianti and some other Italian wines.
Filtering	Making wine bright.
Fine	Brandy of no great distinction.
Fine Champagne	Finest brandy.
Fine Maison	Brandy of the House or Restaurant.
Fining	Clearing wine in cask or tank. Isinglass, whites of egg, gelatine and some clays are used for the purpose.
Fino	Driest sherry.
Flaschenschild	Label.
Flor	Flower—yeast growth on some sherries maturing in cask in Spain.
Fort	Strong.
Fortified	Strength added by addition of grape spirit.
Foudre	Huge casks for storing wine.
Franc	Clean-tasting.
Frappé	Iced.
Friche	Fresh.
Fruité	Fruity.
Fuder	German cask.
Fumet	Definite bouquet.

Fürst	Prince.
Fusel Oil	Alcohol (not Ethyl) found in spirits.
Gallon	4 quarts, 8 pints, 4·54 litres, 1·2 (American gallons).
Garrafa	Decanter.
Gay-Lussac	French scale for measuring alcoholic strengths. ABR. G.L.
Généreux	Generous wine—in alcohol. A fortified sweet wine.
Geropiga	Natural port or special liquid made to sweeten other Portuguese wines.
Gewachs	Vineyard of.
Glühwein	Mulled wine, spiced and sweetened.
Goldbeerenauslese	Individual bunches picked of fully ripened grapes
Goût	Taste.
Goût Américain	Fairly sweet.
Goût Anglais	Dry.
Goût d'Évent	Flat.
Goût Française	Sweet.
Goût de Moisi	Musty.
Goût de Paille	Straw.
Goût de Piqué	Going towards vinegar.
Goût de Taille	Uncouth, made from final pressing of grapes.
Goût de Terroir	Earthy.
Growth	Can mean a vineyard.
Heads	First spirit to emerge during distillation.
Hectare	2·47 acres.
Hectolitre	Liquid measure equalling 22 gallons.
Hock	Rhine wines. Abbreviation of Hochheim.
Hogshead	Cask of different sizes.
Hors d'Age	Should it appear on a brandy bottle it means beyond recorded age.
Hydrometer	An instrument to record the density of alcohol in a wine or spirit.
Impériale	Large bottle. Holds between 6 and 9 bottles. Claret is sometimes matured in them.
Isinglass	Fish gelatine often made from the bladder of the sturgeon, used for fining.
Jahrgang	Vintage, year.
Jarra	Jar of varying sizes.
Jeroboam	4 bottles, a champagne bottle.

Jigger	1½ oz. measure (42·6 cc.).
Jeropiga	Boiled-down grape juice, used in Portugal to sweeten wines.
Keg	Cask.
Keller	German for cellar.
Kellerabfülling or *Kellerabzug*	Estate bottled.
Lagar	Trough for pressing grapes in Spain and Portugal.
Lage	Site.
Lagered	Storing of beer during which time it is fined and carbonated.
Lees	Sediment.
Léger	Light wine.
Levante	Hot winds in the sherry district of Spain.
Limousin	Special oak for maturing cognac.
Liqueur d'Expédition	The sugar and old wine added after the disgorging to Champagne.
Liquoreux	Heavy sweet wine.
Lodge	Where port and madeiras are stored.
Maderization	Caused by too much oxygen during fermentation or maturation. It turns white wines brown in colour and flat to taste.
Maestro Vino	Master wine used for adding colour to Málaga wine.
Malt	Grain which has germinated.
Marc	Brandy from the 3rd or 4th pressing of the grapes.
Mash	Mixture of ground malted barley or other cereal and water.
Mesa	Table wine.
Méthode Champenoise	2nd fermentation in bottle. Champagne Method.
Méthode Cuve Close	Making sparkling wine by tank method.
Mildew	A vine disease which occurs mostly in damp weather.
Millésime	Vintage date in France.
Mistelle	*Must* which has had its fermentation stopped by the addition of brandy at a very early stage.
Morgen	A German acre of land.
Mou vin	Lifeless wine.

Mouillé	Watered.
Moût	Unfermented grape juice.
Mousseux	Sparkling.
Muffa Nobile	Noble Rot.
Mûr	Ripe.
Mut	Balanced.
Must, most, mosto	Unfermented grape juice.
Natur, natuerwein	A wine with no sugar added, a natural wine.
Nero	Black or deep red wine.
Nerveux	A strong, full-bodied wine.
Nicolauswein	Wine made from grape gathered on St. Nicholas Day—6 December.
Nip	Very small bottles of spirits or champagne (split).
Nu	Bare. Cost of wine without its overheads (cask, bottles, etc.).
Nube	Cloudiness.
Obscuration	Amount of false reading on an hydrometer caused by impurities—mainly sugar—in the alcohol.
Œechsle	Is a standard which determines the specific gravity of a given *must*. It will show the number of grammes by which one volume of *must* is heavier than an equal volume of water, the sugar content being in the region of 25 per cent. of this measurement. So, 100 litres of *must* with a reading of 100° Œechsle will contain some 25 kilogrammes of sugar.
Oeil de Perdrix	Tawny pink wine, colour of 'Patridge eye'.
Oenology	Study of wine from a scientific point of view.
Offener Wein	Wine sold by the glass.
Oidium	Fungus disease on vines.
Oloroso	Heavy golden sherries which are dry in their natural state.
Ordinaire	Wine for everyday use, usually cheap.
Originalabfullüng	German equivalent to Estate Bottling or *Mise au Château*.
Palma	Classification of young fino sherries.
Parfume	Fragrance of perfume in wine.
Passe-Tous-Grains	Burgundy blend of $\frac{1}{3}$ *pinot noir* to $\frac{2}{3}$ *gamay* grapes.
Pasteur, Louis	French scientist renowned for his work on fermentation and pasteurisation.

Pastis	French name for aniseed-flavoured apéritifs.
Patent Still	Patented by Irishman Aenaes Coffey in 1832. A continuous still.
Paxarette	A sweetening wine made from the P.X. grapes. Sometimes used to age whisky in America.
Pedro Ximénez (P.X.)	Grapes in the sherry country of Spain.
Pelure d'Oignon	Colour of onion skin. Red wines which gradually take on this colour due to their great age.
Perlwein	Effervescent wine.
Pétillant	Semi-sparkling or creaming wine.
Petit	Small.
Phylloxera vastatrix	Vine louse from America which devastated European vineyards in the 1870's.
Pièce	Hogshead—225 litres.
Pint	Liquid measure of 20 oz. (568·2 cm³).
Pipe	Usually applies to a cask of port holding about 115 gallons (522·5 litres).
Piqué	Pricked.
Piquant	Sharp-tasting wine.
Pisador	Person who treads grapes in sherry region.
Plastering	Addition of gypsum (calcium sulphate) to grapes when they are being pressed.
Plat	Flat or dull wine.
Portes greffes	American vine stocks resistant to *Phylloxera* on which European stock is now grafted as a remedy against the pest.
Pourriture Noble	Noble Rot—grapes left on vine until they become like raisins similar to *Edelfaule* in Germany.
Précoce	A wine which has come forward too early—a precocious wine.
Pressoir	Maturing wine press.
Proof	Method of measuring alcoholic strength of a liquid.
Punt	The dip in the bottom of a bottle for extra strength.
Pupître	A wooden frame for holding champagne bottles during the *Remuage* process.
Puttony	Hungarian bucket for gathering grapes in the Tokay district. Holds about 13·5 kilos.
Quartaut	Barrel holding about 56 litres.
Queue	Burgundy cask holding 2 hogsheads.
Quinta	Portuguese Estate or vineyard.

Race	Breed.
Racking	Changing wine from one cask to another, leaving the sediment behind in the old.
Raki	Balkan countries' name for a spirit flavoured with liquorice and aniseed.
Raya	System for classifying sherry.
Rectify	To change a natural spirit in some way, either by redistilling or adding colour and flavourings.
Refreshing	Adding younger wine to older.
Rein	Pure.
Remuage	The guiding of sediment down to the neck of the bottle. Associated with the production of champagne.
Robe	French for colour of wine.
Roundeur, Rund	Round.
Rosé	Pink wine.
Rotwein	Red wine.
Ruby	Young, deep-red port.
Saccharometer	An instrument for measuring sugar content in *must* or wine.
Sacramental wine	Altar wine for the Eucharist. May be red or white and must be the natural grape wine.
Sack	Anglification of Spanish Seco, a dry fortified still wine.
Saké	Beer made from rice.
Sancocho	Boiling *must* down to $\frac{1}{3}$ of its volume. This is used to sweeten and colour sherries.
Scantling	Wooden beams to support casks in cellars.
Schloss	German for castle.
Schlossabzug	Estate bottled.
Schnapps	German, Dutch name for spirit.
Schneewein or *Eiswein* (G.)	Snow wine.
Schorle-Morle	Mixture of wine and aerated mineral water.
Sec, secco	Dry.
Sediment	Deposit in wines as they age.
Sekt	German sparkling wine.
Sève	Flavour and body of wine which augurs for it lasting well.
Sykes hydrometer	The hydrometer for measuring alcoholic strength, named after the man who invented it.

Solera	System for blending and maturing sherries to give a consistent standard.
Soutirage	Name in Champagne for racking.
Soyeux	Smooth, silky.
Spitzengewächs	Best German growths.
Spitzenweins	Best wines.
Spritzig	Slightly effervescent wine.
Spumante	Italian for sparkling.
Staatsweingut	Vineyard owned by the State.
Still	An apparatus either of the 'pot' or 'patent' variety where fermented wash or wine is distilled into a spirit.
Still wine	Non-sparkling wine.
Stück cask	Measure in Rhineland holding 1 200 litres.
Tannin	Astringent acid in wine found in stalks, pips and skins of grapes.
Tappit-hen	Scotch bottle which holds 3 imperial quarts which is equivalent to $4\frac{1}{2}$ reputed quarts.
Tent	Spanish for sweet wine.
Tête de Cuvée	Best growth, best wines from any vineyard.
Tinaja	Large earthenware jar.
Tintourier	Grapes for colouring.
Tirage	Bottling.
Tonelero	Cooper.
Traube	Grape.
Traubensaft	Grape juice, *must*.
Trocken	Dry.
Ullage	Wine lost through evaporation or leakage. Describes also the air space in cask above fluid.
Usé	Wine past its best.
Vat	Large casks for blending and maturing wines and spirits.
Velouté	Velvety.
Vendange	Vintage. Harvesting of grapes.
Vendangeur	Vintage worker.
Venencia	Silver cup attached to a long whale-bone handle for sampling sherries from cask.
Verbessert	Sugaring of wine in a poor year to increase alcoholic content.
Vert	Green, young wine.

Viejo	Old.
Vigne	Vine.
Vigneron	Wine maker.
Vignoble, vinedo	Vineyard.
Vin, vinho, vino, Wein	Wine.
Vin de garde	Wine for laying down.
Vin de Goutte	Poor-quality wine from last pressing of grapes.
Vin de Messe	Altar wine.
Vin de Paille	Straw wine. Grapes have been allowed to dry out on straw.
Vin de Pays	Small local wine.
Vin de Doux	Sweet wine.
Vine	Plant on which grapes grow.
Vintage	Gathering of grapes.
Vintage wine.	Wine of one year.
Viticulture	Culture of the vine.
Vitis	Vine genus.
Wachstum	Growth.
Wash	Fermented liquor before it goes for distillation.
Wassail	From the Anglo-Saxon *Weshal* to mean 'Be of good health'.
Weeping	Leaking cork.
Weingut	Vineyard.
Weisswein	White wine.
Wine	Fermented juice of freshly gathered grapes.
Woody	Wine with the smell of cork.
Würzig	Spicy.
Yeast	Uni-cellular fungi found on skins of grapes which during fermentation act on the natural grape sugar to convert it into alcohol and carbon dioxide.
Yeso	Calcium sulphate (gypsum) which is sprinkled on grapes during pressing to slow down fermentation and add acidity.
Zapatos de pisar	Special boots used for treading grapes in the Sherry district.

APPENDIX

BOTTLE SIZES (Capacity)

	Metric Centilitres	British Fluid ounces
Alsace (Flute)	72	25
Anjou	75	26
Bordeaux	75	26
Bordeaux Magnum	150	53
Burgundy	75 or 80	26
Rhine & Moselle	70	24
Port ⎫ Sherry ⎬ Madeira ⎭	75·75	30
Brandy	70	24
Whisky	75	26

CASK SIZES (Capacity)

Wine	Cask	Metric litres	British Imperial Gallons
Alsace	Aume	114	25·1
Anjou	Piece	220	28·4
Bordeaux	Barrique	225	49·5
Burgundy	Piece	228	50·1
Rhine & Moselle	Doppelohm	300	66
Port]	Pipe	522·5	115
Sherry	Butt	490·7	108
Madeira	Pipe	418	92
Brandy	Puncheon	545·2	120
Whisky	Butt	491	108

CAPACITY AND VOLUME

Metric	British
1 litre	1·760 pints
1 hectolitre	22 gallons
28·4 cm³ (millilitres)	1 fluid ounce
0·142 litre	1 gill
0·568 litre	1 pint (20 fluid ounces)
1·136 litre	1 quart

Vendange

LENGTH

Metric		British
1 centimetre	=	2/5 inch
1 metre	=	3·28 feet
1 kilometre	=	0·621 mile

AREA

1 hectare 10,000 m²	=	2·47 acres

WEIGHT

Metric		British
1 gramme	=	0·035 ounce
1 kilogramme	=	2·205 pounds
1 tonne (1000 kg)	=	0·98 tons

BIBLIOGRAPHY

A Word Book of Wine (Walter James, London 1959)
Booth's Handbook of Cocktails and Mixed Drinks (J. Doxat London 1966)
Champagne: The Wine the land and the people (Patrick Forbes, London 1967)
Encyclopaedia of Wines and Spirits (A. Lichine, London 1967)
Grossman's Guide to Wines, Spirits and Beers (New York 1964)
Guide to Drinks (U.K.G.B., London 1965)
Guidance in the Technique of Tasting (J. M. Broadbent, London 1963)
Liqueurs (Peter A. Hallgarten London 1967)
Port (Rupert Croft-Cooke, London 1957)
Rhineland Wineland (S. F. Hallgarten, London 1951)
Sherry (Rupert Croft-Cooke, London 1955)
The Wines of Bordeaux (E. Penning-Rowsell, London 1969)
The Wines of Burgundy (H. W. Yoxall, London 1968)
The Compact Wine Guide (Luke Bayard, London 1969)
The Kindred Spirit (Lord Kinross, London 1959)
The Wines and Vineyards of France (Louis Jacquelin and René Poulain translated by T. A. Layton, London 1962)
Wines and Spirits (L. W. Marrison 1962)
Wine (Hugh Johnson, London 1966)
Wines of the World (Edited by André L. Simon)

INDEX

Index

Index

Index